Reader Series
in Library and Information Science

Published *Readers* in the series are:

Reader in Library Administration. 1969.
Paul Wasserman and Mary Lee Bundy.

Reader in Research Methods for Librarianship. 1970.
Mary Lee Bundy and Paul Wasserman.

Reader in the Academic Library. 1970.
Michael M. Reynolds

Reader in Library Services and the Computer. 1971.
Louis Kaplan.

Reader in
Library Services
and the Computer

edited by

Louis Kaplan

1971

NCR **MICROCARD® EDITIONS**
901 TWENTY-SIXTH STREET, N.W., WASHINGTON, D. C. 20037, 202/333-6393
INDUSTRIAL PRODUCTS DIVISION, THE NATIONAL CASH REGISTER COMPANY

Printed in the United States of America.
Published by Microcard Editions,
901 26th Street, N. W., Washington, D. C. 20037,
a part of the Industrial Products Division,
The National Cash Register Company

Foreword

Unlike many other academic disciplines, librarianship has not yet begun to exploit the contributions of the several disciplines toward the study of its own issues. Yet the literature abounds with material germane to its concerns. Too frequently the task of identifying, correlating, and bringing together material from innumerable sources is burdensome, time consuming or simply impossible. For a field whose stock in trade is organizing knowledge, it is clear that the job of synthesizing the most essential contributions from the elusive sources in which they are contained is overdue. This then is the rationale for the series, *Readers in Library and Information Science.*

The *Readers in Library and Information Science* will include books concerned with various broad aspects of the field's interests. Each volume will be prepared by a recognized student of the topic covered, and the content will embrace material from the many different sources from the traditional literature of librarianship as well as from outside the field in which the most salient contributions have appeared. The objectives of the series will be to bring together in convenient form the key elements required for a current and comprehensive view of the subject matter. In this way it is hoped that the core of knowledge, essential as the intellectual basis for study and understanding, will be drawn into focus and thereby contribute to the furtherance of professional education and professional practice in the field.

Paul Wasserman
Series Editor

Contents

Introduction

I
THE CHALLENGE

Technology and Libraries—*National Advisory Commission on Libraries*   5
Automation and the Princeton University Library—Part II of the Annual
   Report of the Librarian—*Princeton University Library*   11
A Proposal for the Development of an Integrated, Computer-Based
   Bibliographical Data System—*Herman H. Fussler*   20

II
VARIETIES OF RESPONSE

Technology and Libraries: A Survey of Current Applications and Trends—
   Information Systems Technology Staff, System Development Corporation 25
Automation in the Harvard College Library—*Richard De Gennaro*   40
An Integrated Computer-Based Bibliographic Data System for a Large
   University Library: Problems and Progress at the University of
   Chicago—*Charles T. Payne*   51
Library Automation at UCLA—*Anthony Hall*   55
Bibliographic Automation of Large Library Operations Using a Time-Sharing
   System—Project BALLOTS—*Allen Barnet Veaner*   61
Automation Activities in Library of Congress—*Library of Congress*   65

III
THEORY OF MANAGEMENT

The Development and Administration of Automated Systems in Academic
   Libraries—*Richard De Gennaro*   69

IV
NEW SERVICES

Position Paper on Extra-Library Information Services—*DeWitt O. Mylatt
   and Donald A. Barclay*   81
The Library and the Technical Information Center—*J. McGowan*   89
CAS Computer-Based Information Services—*W. C. Davenport*   94
Computer-Based Selective Dissemination of Information (SDI) Service for
   Faculty Using Library of Congress Machine—Readable Catalog (MARC)
   Records—*William Joseph Studer*   101
Information Network Prospects in the United States—*Joseph Becker*   108
M.I.T.'s Plans for Project Intrex—Information Transfer Experiments—
   Carl F. J. Overhage   115

V
CATALOGS AND THE COMPUTER

The Computerized Catalog: Possible, Feasible, Desirable?—*Wesley Simonton*   125
An Analysis of Cost Factors in Maintaining and Updating Card Catalogs—
  J. L. Dolby and V. J. Forsyth   131

VI
COPYRIGHT

Information Storage and Retrieval by Computer—an Emerging Problem for the
  Law of Copyright—*Steven Allan, et al.*   149

VII
INFORMATION RETRIEVAL TESTING

Information Retrieval from the Management Point of View—*Louis Kaplan*   171
Automatic Text Analysis—*G. Salton*   175
The Testing of Index Language Devices—*Cyril W. Cleverdon and J. Mills*   189
Evaluation of the MEDLARS Demand Search Service—*F. W. Lancaster*   206
Selected Results from an Inquiry into Testing of Information Retrieval
  Systems—*Tefko Saracevic*   218

ADDITIONAL READINGS   238

Introduction

In the winter of 1968/69 I conducted a seminar in which were enrolled four students working towards the Ph.D. in the library school at the University of Wisconsin. The common topic was the computerized library seen from the administrative and management point of view. Except for a brief consideration of the physical features of computers and a visit to the campus Computer Center, the technical side concerned us only indirectly.

We were mainly concerned with questions such as these: what demands are being made of librarians, and to what extent are librarians responding to these new demands for service; in the age of the computer, what new services are feasible; how does a library staff organize itself in order to enter upon computerization; what problems are associated with computerization, such as, copyright and the making of book catalogs?

When I learned from Mr. Albert Diaz of NCR/Microcard Editions that he was the publisher of a series of reprints in the general area of information science, I suggested that the insights I had gained in the aforementioned seminar would make it possible for me to offer him a selection of materials on the subject of library services in the age of the computer. A meeting with Mr. Diaz and Dr. Paul Wasserman, general editor of the series, resulted in the decision to move ahead.

The selections are intended mainly for students in library schools, and for librarians in the field who have not yet made themselves conversant with the literature of computer-based operations. This is not a book, to state the proposition in the negative, for those who wish to read on the theoretical aspects of computers.

The selections are brought together in seven sections. The first, the *Challenge*, includes material on what is expected of librarians in the age of the computer; as is explained by Herman Fussler in the third selection, these expectations cannot be met except with computer-based operations.

The second section, *Varieties of Response*, does not by any means exhaust developments in American libraries. It does, I believe, contain representative descriptions of some of the best work being accomplished. An introduction to these selections will be found in the editorial comment immediately preceding this section.

The third section, *Theory of Management*, contains an outstanding article by Richard DeGennaro of Harvard. The particular contributions made in this article are described in the editorial comment immediately preceding this third section.

New Services, the fourth section, required a considerable degree of selection among a wealth of material, and is indicative of the wide variety of services which libraries are beginning to offer in the age of the computer. The considerable range of such services is exhaustively indicated in the first selection of this section, while those that follow describe specific services now being offered, or services in the planning stage.

The material in the fifth section, *Catalogs and the Computer*, is on a subject that has elicited considerable discussion. The two articles selected are on two aspects of the subject, namely, filing problems, and comparative costs.

The sixth section, *Copyright*, contains an article from the legal point of view. The more traditional library view of copyright has been ably represented by Verner Clapp in an article cited in the section on additional readings.

The seventh section, *Information Retrieval Testing*, is a subject which has excited the attention of but few librarians, yet its influence on subject indexing could in time prove considerable. My reading here has been extensive as the result of having conducted a

1

seminar on the topic within the Wisconsin library school. So important is the literature that I believe that no fewer than five articles ought to be included in order to do my part in awakening librarians to the subject.

On the work done at Cranfield, Cleverdon is a natural choice because he has been the senior worker at that location. A one-time collaborator of his, Lancaster, was an ideal choice to evaluate MEDLARS. I am grateful to Tefko Saracevic for letting me have his summary article on the work done at Case Western Reserve. On automatic indexing, Salton is the obvious choice. My only problem with Salton was to find that one of his articles just right for this book. The one chosen seems to me to be a good example of exposition of a technical subject for general readers. Finally, I have overcome a certain amount of diffidence by including my own article on the subject, for the reason that the management point of view is rarely considered, and because it serves as a summary and introduction to the more complicated articles on information retrieval testing.

And now for a frank word to my readers. Do not ask whether certain pieces were omitted because of my failure to gain permission from editors or author. I can assure you, for better or worse, I was able to include every article which I felt ought to be included.

L. K.

I
THE CHALLENGE

In the summer of 1945 there appeared a now famous article in the *Atlantic Monthly* by Vannevar Bush. At the time, librarians reading that article little realized it contained for them a challenge which two decades later would be unmistakable and unavoidable. Bush's argument was this: "The summation of human experience is being expanded at a prodigious rate, and the means we use for threading through the consequent maze to the momentarily important item is the same as was used in the days of the square-rigged ships."

Bush had a good deal to say too about technological advances which he felt reasonably sure would make possible a much greater miniaturization of microfilm, thus granting to scholars the possession at their fingertips of a great body of information.

Bush, a scientist, typically had less patience with library classification than do humanists. The problem, he wrote, was the artificiality of classification systems (scientists are still working on that one). The solution was for each scientist to do his own indexing, using a system which associated various subjects. Reading of his solution, one thinks immediately of coordinate indexing.

Since 1945, with a growing awareness of the possibilities of the computer and of microforms, critics of the conventional library have grown more numerous, and sometimes more reckless. The temptation to beat the conventional library about the ears is strong enough, and to a degree warranted; when it helps obtain a research or developmental grant, the urge sometimes becomes irresistible.

In any event, aside from the time required to improve services, most librarians would agree with one critic who makes these points: on the physical side, a remedy must be sought to the frightening expansion of library buildings. Intellectually, the conventional library is not distinguished for its retrieval efficiency. Operationally, the price of labor continues to drive up the cost of processing, which with other factors has caused a greater rise in the cost of operation than the cost of other services and goods in the marketplace.

Library users, says one critic, are "irked." When single copies circulate, others must wait. And materials are obtained, if at all, only after maddening delays. So disenchanted have readers become, especially the natural scientists, they have sought out with considerable success in some instances substitutes for the conventional library. One factor in this flight is the failure of the conventional library to deal adequately with technical reports, government documents and patents. The inadequacies of the indexing (retrieval) system is still another contributing factor. Among these scientists the idea grew that a new kind of information specialist would be needed to replace the conventional librarian.

This, briefly, and too simply related, is the challenge. Unfortunately, as is pointed out by the authors of the first selection in this anthology, the remedy to library users is not met simply by subjecting library processes such as acquisitions, cataloging and circulation to computer controls. If librarians continue merely to extrapolate current trends, "there will probably be no net gain in service" and "even some deterioration of service is likely to occur because of the vast increases in published materials that must be dealt with." What is required, according to the argument of this essay, is a whole new concept of a national information network, or at the least a national effort to identify and act upon high-impact projects such as an expanded, computer-based union catalog.

Mr. Dix's statement (the second in this section) is interesting precisely because it is written by a humanist. Much less sure of the remedies, and obviously trying to avoid large scale local commitments that might not pan out, Mr. Dix is nevertheless fully aware of the challenge. "The application," he writes, "of the high-speed digital computer to information storage will beyond any doubt produce a major revolution in libraries."

Though unable because he is a humanist to accept the primacy of disjointed data, as against "consecutive text," Mr. Dix recognizes that great changes are coming. New indexing efforts are to be entered upon, conversion of catalog data to machine readable form is inevitable, and greater use of microforms is predicted.

Mr. Fussler, author of the third selection, is a professional librarian by training and experience, with special competence in the area of natural science. Acting on the challenge of the computer comes more readily to him than it might to others. On the other hand, Mr. Fussler refuses to go beyond what he deems is his immediate responsibility. Wary of national network schemes and advanced information retrieval projects, Mr. Fussler claims that "the needs of readers for improved intellectual and physical access appear to be well in excess of the current library response capabilities." As a first order of business, Mr. Fussler wishes to put his own house in order. If I may be permitted to say it for him in my own way, he believes that a house that is not wired to receive electricity will profit little from the existence of a national grid. In any event, the national grid will take much longer, so that there is time locally to develop the necessary bibliographical controls and to establish a firm machine-readable record. Large scale conversion of records, like the national network, will need to wait. Without these developments locally, there will be no "truly effective development and utilization of future national or regional information system designs and networks."

Technology and Libraries

National Advisory Commission on Libraries

INTRODUCTION AND SUMMARY

Introduction

The basic objective of this report was to assist the National Advisory Commission on Libraries—and, through it, other interested audiences—in examining the applicability of technology to libraries, possible library systems of the future, and problems of effecting a transition between the present and the future. In accordance with this basic purpose, the project team endeavored to present as objective and balanced a review of technology as possible, without either overemphasizing or minimizing its achievements or potential. The analyses and conclusions contributed notably to the deliberations of the Commission, which judged this report to be one of the most valuable of its studies. For this reason, the entire text appears here in somewhat revised and updated form.

The major types of libraries of concern here are public libraries, libraries in educational institutions, and special libraries. For purposes of this report, state libraries are treated together with public libraries, rather than as a special category. Some attention is also given to selected librarylike information facilities. The technology domain is considered to cover both equipment and techniques that presently have some impact on library systems.

Statements and predictions in this report are based on findings reported in the literature, on interviews, or on System Development Corporation (SDC) staff studies. References are given wherever possible. A special word regarding statistics is necessary. It is acknowledged that statistics concerning libraries are not wholly satisfactory. Nevertheless, there is some agreement among librarians that the statistics are *relatively* accurate. The reader is cautioned to interpret any statistics offered in this report in their relative, not absolute, sense.

Some aspects of libraries and technology are given less attention than others in this report because they are the subject of other, more complete and detailed reports commissioned by the National Advisory Commission on Libraries. An effort was made to exchange outlines, drafts, and ideas with other study groups to minimize both omissions and unnecessary duplication.

This report consists of six sections and includes an analysis of present and projected library service requirements, a survey of potentially applicable technology, a description of current applications and trends in the use of technology, a prediction of future directions in library operations and services (including a discussion of the problem of planning for transition from the present to the future), and recommendations for a program of action. The following summary of major findings and recommendations of this study group highlights the contest presented in the subsequent sections 2 through 5.

Summary

Present and Projected Library Requirements

The purpose and general character of library services have not changed greatly over the past forty years. What have changed for most libraries are the range and volume of demand and use. The rapid and pervasive growth of specialization in new subject matters, together with an increasingly large and literate user population, has placed severe burdens on libraries of all kinds.

If the nation's libraries are to keep pace with the growing pressures of literature expansion and service requirements, the libraries will need to accelerate and expand some of the programs for library improvement that some of them have already undertaken; and if the libraries are to do *more* than keep pace—i.e., to provide better and broader service than they now do—a much more aggressive and integrated approach to improvement will be needed. To bring about a nationwide improvement in libraries, it will be necessary to think in terms of more interdependent modes of operation. It will also be necessary to take better advantage of the developing technology.

SOURCE: Reprinted from *Libraries at Large,* edited by Douglas M. Knight and E. Shepley Nourse, (Bowker, 1969), pp. 282-88, by permission of the publisher. Copyright 1969 by the R. R. Bowker Co.

Technology Related to the Library

The domain of technology applicable to the library encompasses such areas as data processing by computers; procedural technologies such as document storage and retrieval, automated indexing and classification, machine translation, automated abstracting, and automated question answering systems; and a variety of related equipment and materials technologies, including microform techniques, reprography, computer-assisted publication techniques, and materials handling and storage devices and procedures.

Computer technology has the greatest *potential* impact for library operations. Computer equipment is currently available in a number of configurations spanning a purchase range from $6,000 to $10 million. Although not adequate to meet all of the processing needs of very large libraries, it is quite adequate for a wider range of individual library automation tasks. Barriers that stand in the way of library applications include cost, lack of adequate library-oriented computer programs and associated procedural methodology, too little computer memory capacity, and limitations in the input and output equipment.

The next five to ten years are likely to see at least a tenfold reduction in computer-system costs for a given level of performance, while computer speed and storage capabilities will increase several-fold. These changes will accelerate the library use of computers both for housekeeping tasks and for assistance to bibliographical tasks.

How much and what kind of computer capability libraries *should* have is impossible to determine now. Two quite different computer-support concepts present themselves: (1) a large number of geographically remote consoles, connected by data-transmission lines to very large, powerful, time-shared computers; and (2) individual use of separate computers of the smaller and less expensive kind now beginning to appear. Both concepts will probably be adopted: time-sharing by the smaller libraries and private computers by the larger, more affluent libraries.

As for procedural technology, a number of applications of computers to processing textual material offer promise to library operations. Many operating systems in business, industry, and the military currently store and retrieve data from files. These operations are similar, in some respects, to those required for the storage and retrieval of bibliographical information, and some of the techniques developed for data-retrieval work are applicable to types of library data that can be highly structured and formated. Automatic analysis of nonformated full-text materials is a more complex task, and accordingly, progress in fully automated retrieval of textual content lags behind that in formated data-handling systems.

Fully satisfactory programs for automatic indexing or subject-heading assignment are not yet available; still, some current systems provide a high degree of automation of other retrieval functions. One system permits users to pose requests directly to the computer system and to receive computer assistance in identifying document representations meeting prescribed criteria. Such systems are not yet within the economic range for use by library patrons but could be used to provide assistance to library personnel. With decreasing computer costs, more ready-made programs, and better-trained library staff, such services can eventually be extended directly to library users, particularly in special or experimental libraries.

Fully automated indexing, classification, abstracting, machine translation, and question-answering must still be considered to be in the research or development stage. However, substantial assistance to library processes is likely to come, in the very near future, from concepts of operation in which the machine serves as an aid to, not a replacement for, the librarian or information specialist. Computer-aided instruction is likely to play an important role in training library personnel for work in computer-based systems and in helping patrons learn to use such systems.

The third area of technology related to libraries encompasses related equipment and materials technologies. Microforms—previously valued for reasons of space-saving and materials preservation—are also used increasingly as a medium of communication. Inexpensive microform readers are currently available. During the next five to ten years we may expect the establishment of large-sized microfiche collections and significant improvements in microform technology, including stable color microfilm, sophisticated microform-handling equipment, direct information transfer between microimage and computer subsystems, and ultramicroform technology. The current trends of lowering costs and increasing quality will continue for copying, offset printing, and the printing and reading of fiche.

The advent of photocomposition—computer-controlled preparation of reproduction masters with electro-optical techniques—is very important because it provides libraries with the option to abandon card catalogs in favor of book-form catalogs, up-to-data versions of which could be printed in multiple copies to be available in several locations in the library. The availability of library materials—either text or catalog-type information—in machine-readable form will provide an opportunity to explore other computer applications economically.

Printed materials will be the primary carriers to be dealt with for some years, and few libraries will be able to use electronic means exclusively to manage their information. Texts will have to be stored and handled by humans, aided in some instances by mechanical devices. There are some promising materials-handling devices—conveyors, tubes, containers, lifters, stackers—some of which can be useful in future systems where materials-handling is largely computer-controlled. Most of these devices appear too expensive at present for widespread use.

Transmission of materials is becoming increasingly important to libraries, particularly in relation to possible network operations. Of the several means for the transmission of materials, mail is currently still the most practical. Efforts are under way to create working systems that employ advanced communications technology to support retrieval of material from a central store and its transmission to different places. Both the accuracy and the data-transmission rates of various kinds of telecommunications equipment can be expected to increase in the near future. It is not yet clear whether there will be sufficient equipment compatibility to serve the purposes of highly integrated library networks.

Current Applications and Trends

A number of libraries, primarily the larger academic libraries and special libraries, have begun to use data-processing equipment in their operations. All of the major library functions (acquisitions, cataloging, circulation control, serials management, reference work, etc.) are drawing attention in this connection. The emphasis is primarily on functions related to technical processes and circulation control, rather than reference services.

Certain aspects of the acquisitions process lend themselves particularly well to data processing, and some groups of libraries have even been exploring the idea of cooperative or centralized processing for some aspects of the acquisitions process.

The most popular application of technology in the cataloging process has been to reproduce catalog cards. Book catalogs, frequently used many years ago but abandoned in favor of card catalogs, are returning to favor with the help of the computer and computer-controlled typesetting procedures. In cataloging, as well as in acquisitions, the combination of interlibrary cooperation and new technology offers great potential for the reduction of costs and wasteful duplication of effort. The Library of Congress MARC Project, which is a prototype of a national network for the distribution of machine-readable catalog data, provides an example of this potential.

Data-processing technology is being used for a variety of tasks associated with circulation control, and a few institutions are beginning to work toward the development of on-line operations that will tie a circulation-control system directly into a computer at all times. Such a system will bring libraries a step closer to still another feasible approach, that of operating circulation-control systems on a network basis within a region.

A number of projects are under way to use data processing for serials records control. Few institutions, however, have operational systems, and those that exist do not perform all the necessary functions of serials management. The project at the Library of Congress to determine what elements of information should be put into machine-readable records for serial titles can provide a valuable framework on which individual libraries can build and through which they may eventually participate in regional or national serials projects.

In comparison with other library operations, the reference function shows very little in the way of applications of technology for most libraries. Very few libraries have automated their information- and document-retrieval functions. There are a few primitive automated-data-retrieval systems, but they are nearly all in information centers, not in libraries.

Technologies other than data processing are being put to use in libraries. Microforms are being used increasingly, but their vast potential still seems to be untapped. Materials-handling equipment, specialized communications equipment, storage equipment, etc., have all found some use in libraries, but such use has largely involved the *adaptation* of equipment and procedures developed for other purposes, rather than those especially tailored to meet library needs.

Many libraries have looked to technology to reduce costs or to hold them constant. Cost-consciousness sometimes has not been extended to consider the effect of changes on the users of libraries: some ostensible cost reductions may "cost" the users more than they save in time, effort, or even money.

Technology offers an opportunity to provide access to and services for nonmonographic materials of all kinds as good as those that have been furnished for printed monographs. There are also indications that use of technology may allow new services to develop in libraries to serve certain user groups better. Technology may also provide a means of improving the organization and management of libraries.

At present only about 3 percent of the approximately 24,000 libraries in the United States are using data-processing equipment. One can foresee that in the future many more libraries will seek to use such equipment, especially computers. Much of the effort is likely to be focused on particular problems in particular libraries. Much more co-ordination would be desirable to channel these disparate efforts into a national effort that would bring all aspects of our technology to bear on the problems of library operations.

Future Directions in Library Operations and Service

There are two different approaches toward prediction of the nature of the library of the future. One approach stresses the continuation of extrapolation of current trends. The other approach stresses what it is theoretically possible to achieve. Both approaches are useful: the first is useful in short-range planning because it takes adequate account of the problems of transition; the other takes note of distant goals, which helps to broaden the horizons of one's thinking.

An extrapolative view, which assumes no major acceleration of effort, sees the large majority of libraries operating much as they do today over the next ten years. In spite of continuing improvements undertaken by libraries, there will probably not be any *net* gain in service for the majority of individual libraries. Indeed, some deterioration of service is likely to occur because of the vast increases in published materials that must be dealt with. Large categories of nonbook materials will continue to be neglected to a large extent. Without some form of accelerated planning and support the majority of libraries are not likely to be able to participate in or benefit from emerging network-arrangements.

A conditional view of library activities, which assumes major acceleration of effort over the next ten years, sees libraries becoming elements of one or more integrated networks. Through connection with a network, libraries could provide their staff personnel with better tools, with relief from some processing chores better handled through the network, and with network-supported facilities for handling reference problems. The library's users could also be provided with much more in the way of materials and services, such as outright distribution of certain kinds of materials replacing loans. The availability of nonbook materials could be increased in libraries of all kinds and sizes across the nation.

There are a number of problems of transition from the present to the future that are not entirely technological in nature. Libraries, already facing serious staff shortages, may find it very difficult to obtain staff with the broad training and experience necessary in both the requirements of library operations and those of technology. Too, library users will need better training in exploiting available library services and facilities. Here, technology itself offers some promise of providing useful tools.

Standards of operation, as well as standards necessary for the compatibility of bibliographical data, are still lacking in the library world. As new data files are created and old files are converted, this problem will become more serious. The several possible approaches to standardization need active consideration if the many separate and independent library organizations are to achieve adequate cooperation and communication using the newer technologies.

A Program of Action

Several approaches offer themselves for the improvement of the nation's libraries. One is to depend on the mechanisms already being used to improve library operations and service, without attempting to accelerate the rate of improvement. This approach requires no drastic change in present activities, concepts of service, funding, or patterns of involvement of the Federal Government. On the other hand, most libraries would almost certainly continue to lose ground through this approach in the face of increasing processing loads and demands for service.

A second approach would be to plan and

attempt to develop a nationwide, highly integrated library system. Such an approach would permit certain kinds of systemwide operations that are not likely to evolve otherwise. It would also reduce duplication of effort by many individual libraries. On the other hand, this approach has some very stringent requirements—e.g., common, agreed-upon goals and strong top management— that might be difficult to meet at this point in time.

The third approach, which this report recommends, focuses on more limited goals and subsystems or networks, and attempts to identify and support *selected* high-impact projects. This approach recognizes the operational independence of most of the nation's libraries, while at the same time taking advantage of their willingness to participate in interdependencies that offer mutual benefits. This approach also has the advantage of not precluding the undertaking of other projects and programs.

Some high-impact projects could and should be aimed at the development of model subsystems that could later be incorporated into a more fully integrated nationwide system. Five such projects are recommended for consideration; undertaken together, these projects could lead to operational systems in from two to four years.

1. A Prototype of Regional Libraries.
2. An Expanded Computer-based *National Union Catalog.*
3. A National Bibliography.
4. A National Referral and Loan Network.
5. A National Library Storage and Microform Depository System.

Although these high-impact projects are dependent on technology, and although they involve subsystems that will eventually be important in extensive, technology-dependent national networks, they do not contribute directly to the exploitation of technology by individual libraries. It is recommended, therefore, that concurrent with the operations-oriented projects a comprehensive program of technology-oriented library research, development, and education and training be undertaken. It should encompass hardware specification and development, procedural (software) specification and development, direct supporting research, and education and training. Also recommended for consideration as part of this program is the establishment of a test bed for handling new forms of nonbook materials.

Before such activities can or should be undertaken, several things must be done. These are offered as the primary recommendations of this report:

1. The basic approach of using high-impact projects, together with supporting research, development, and education and training, should be examined and, if possible endorsed as the means by which library improvement will be sought during the next five to ten years.
2. The particular high-impact projects and research and development requirements outlined in this report should be examined by the Commission and by other interested members of the library and information science community, in the light of other issues, requirements, and constraints, to determine what priorities these and other possible projects should be assigned at this time.
3. For those projects selected for implementation, arrangements should be made to develop more detailed objectives, together with preliminary cost appraisals and implementation schedules.
4. For those projects selected for implementation, arrangements should be made to identify all potential sources of support and, at the appropriate time, to obtain the funds necessary to carry out the projects and programs selected.
5. Responsibility for carrying out the activities indicated or implicit in the foregoing recommendations should be placed at a high administrative level in an existing or new agency of the Federal Government or in a public-private body created for this purpose.

The last recommendation is of particular importance. The need for assessment and planning for libraries does not diminish or disappear because the National Advisory Commission on Libraries has presented its Report. To ensure that effective planning and implementation continue, a permanent body is needed that can be responsible for: (1) keeping informed on the existing and prospective state of library service and operations, (2) planning for improved library service at both national and local levels, (3) developing legislative proposals, (4) coordinating various projects affecting library service, and (5) planning and coordinating financial support, from both the public and private sectors.

Of the several possibilities that suggest themselves for such a permanent body, the most attractive one involves extension of the life of the former National Advisory Commission. This would help to ensure continuity of thinking and planning and would take advantage of the interest expertise, communication, and working arrangements developed by the Commission. The permanent Commission would need to be supported by a highly capable, full-time technical staff, some of whose members might be drawn from the Government or private sector for extended periods of time. This of course is quite similar to the first recommendation in the Commission's Report, the establishment of a National Commission on Libraries and Information Science as a continuing Federal planning agency.

Whatever the planning mechanism actually adopted, it is critically important not to lose momentum. A sizable and indeterminate time gap between the Commission's work and the development and implementation of an action program could itself foster a paralysis of planning on the part of libraries and might lead to yet other status surveys covering much the same ground as the present Commission has covered. Technology and the needs of library service are certainly changing, but the changes are not so rapid or erratic that they should encourage a succession of independent assessments. The need for library improvement is clear, and so is the potential contribution of advanced technology. Aggressive, concerted, and timely action should be taken now to effect a nationwide improvement of our libraries.

PRESENT AND PROJECTED LIBRARY REQUIREMENTS

Kinds of Requirements

It is widely accepted that people have needs for library services; i.e., access to books, serials, re-ports, and other library materials, and/or the information contained in them. Satisfying those needs imposes requirements for the design, construction, operation, and evolution of library systems. Requirements, in system-design terminology, are formal statements describing functions that need to be performed to allow a specific set of objectives to be met.

There are several categories of library users, whose needs differ greatly from one to another. These needs, in turn, imply several kinds of requirements for different kinds of library services. From the perspective of a given library serving a given public, it is useful to distinguish three related types of requirements: (1) requirements for direct service to users; (2) internal operational requirements, essential for rendering direct service in a library; (3) external operational requirements; i.e., requirements for interfacing with external systems of libraries and other information-handling organizations.

In the United States, the purpose and character of library services have not greatly changed over the past forty years. What have changed for most libraries are the range and volume of demand and use, including the demand for faster and more accurate response.

Some of these needs cannot be met easily, if at all, by improvements in internal operating techniques. Rather, they require consideration of new and more complex forms of interlibrary dependency. Thus, increasing attention is now being paid to the external operational requirements of libraries. For a given library these requirements may involve a series of dependencies on the existence of several different kinds of networks; e.g., of libraries, publishers, and communications.

Automation and the Princeton University Library—Part II of the Annual Report of the Librarian

Princeton University Library

INTRODUCTION

The application of the high-speed digital computer to information storage and retrieval will beyond any doubt produce a major revolution in libraries, just as it is doing in other fields. The shape of the new library world which will emerge from the computer revolution and other relevant forms of technological innovation is now dimly apparent, although the details are not clear. It is time for the Princeton University Library to formulate its policies and its tactics in order to take full advantage of the new technology as various elements of it become available for useful application, and we shall avoid a considerable amount of confusion and waste motion if this academic community understands these policies and approves of them. Therefore, I propose to devote my annual report this year to a review of the current possibilities and a statement of the tentative policies which might be adopted. These policies must be tentative, for this is a fluid and fast-moving field, but they may form for the present the basis of the Library's program in this area.

It might be useful, in this discussion, to set aside for the moment the concept of the library as a collection of books and to think of it instead as one part of the process of information transfer, as one segment of the conveyor belt which moves the product of intellectual activity, whether a poem or the specifications for a housing development, from the mind of the creator to the mind of a receiver. The simplest form of this process—and one which is still of substantial importance, even at the scholarly level,—is direct, face-to-face, oral communication. The effectiveness of this process can of course be multiplied by technical means, the village gossip becoming Walter Cronkite.

Yet for many purposes oral transmission is an awkward process. What is required is a process by which the newly-created concept or formulation can be recorded and preserved intact, held in suspension indefinitely until it is needed by someone else. Man has solved this problem by inventing writing, by which the product of some intellectual activity can be recorded in a single manuscript, then either transmitted to someone else or stored for future transmission. The invention of printing made it possible to produce these records more efficiently and economically in multiple copies. Libraries came into being as devices to collect, organize, and hold these recorded products of the creator until needed by the consumer, millponds to store the water until it is released selectively through the sluice-gate. Now, with the growth of technology, questions have been raised as to whether the physical book, as we know it, and, as a consequence, the library as we know it are not obsolete instruments for this purpose.

THE STORAGE OF THE INTELLECTUAL CONTENT OF BOOKS

As the total amount of intellectual activity to be recorded and stored has increased, the size of the millpond has grown until it threatens to become an ocean. For example, Professor Derek J. de Solla Price, Yale historian of science, has calculated that 80% to 90% of all scientists who ever lived are now alive—and presumably producing scientific literature. This growth is not new, but has developed since the beginning at a remarkably consistent exponential rate. "It seems beyond doubt that the literature in any normal, growing field of science increases exponentially, with a doubling in an interval ranging from about ten to about fifteen years." (*Science Since Babylon*, New Haven, 1962, p. 102). As a consequence university libraries, which must preserve for use an essential portion of this growing literature from the universe of knowledge, find themselves constantly pressed for space. Merely to provide space to shelve the books, buildings are being expanded and new buildings are being constructed all over the country.

Those responsible for the financial management of libraries keep looking hopefully to the new technology for help. A brief and necessarily

SOURCE: Reprinted from the Annual Report of the Librarian for the Year Ending June 30, 1966, revised version, pp. 7-28, by permission of William S. Dix, University Librarian.

somewhat superficial review of the prospects may be useful.

The Computer

In what part of this process can the digital computer improve efficiency or lower costs? It has two relevant characteristics:

1. It has a good memory. It is possible to translate the works of Shakespeare into machine language, store them in a computer, and print them out when required, retranslated into natural language. But while the computer has a retentive memory, it is not a large one at present. The figures are a bit slippery, for one can gain in storage capacity by sacrificing some speed, but it has been estimated by competent authorities that by 1985 it will probably be possible to store in a fast, random-access digital memory the equivalent of about 1,000 200-page books. The maximum size of the largest fast, random-access memory could continue to double every two years, and thus it might be possible to store in this way the contents of about one million volumes by 1996. Thus now and for the next few years at least, the technology and the economics of the matter do not suggest that the computer could replace the printed book as a device for storing the total amount of information contained in even a modest library.

2. It can calculate rapidly. While its memory is still relatively small, the computer has the capability of extremely rapid manipulation of the data which it stores. Thus, for example, it can perform complex mathematical operations or it can seek out from its stored data all the units of information which possess some common characteristic—but only of course if the data have been properly organized as they are fed into the computer and if detailed instructions or programs are prepared to instruct the computer in what is required of it.

Combining these two capabilities, memory (relatively small) and manipulation (relatively rapid), one can see immediately that the computer provides a probably useful substitute for certain kinds of books, those which contain large amounts of data, essentially numerical, which are stored for the purpose of being retrieved selectively when needed and perhaps manipulated in some way in the process. Thus, a 1-in-1,000 sample of the population returns of the 1960 U.S. Census is available in machine-readable form from the Bureau of the Census. Other kinds of raw data, such as election returns, can be stored in the computer and manipulated with ease. The Inter-University Consortium for Political Research, of which Princeton is a member, is forming a pool of data of this sort which will be available to members in machine-readable form. For specific and limited purposes such as this, information can be transferred and used effectively without the use of a book at all. The possible area of applicability is sufficiently large to cause some book publishers concern. Herbert S. Bailey, Jr., Director of the Princeton University Press, has published some interesting speculations on this subject in an article in the *Saturday Review of Literature* for June 11, 1966, "Book Publishing and the New Technologies."

But the principal purpose for which most people use most books is a different one: the desire to read a sequence of words or symbols just as they were set down by the author, whether the sequence of words is a work of the creative imagination such as a poem or a new derivation in mathematics, an interpretation of historical events such as a study of the economic causes of a war or an analysis of primitive tribal marriage customs, or a document itself such as a political propaganda pamphlet. Of course, some users of libraries on some occasions are seeking facts or information in a narrow sense, where the sequence of words used to convey the information is of no consequence, such as tabular data. In these situations the computer may already offer an acceptable storage device for intellectual content, but these situations seem to me to represent a minority of book-reader relationships. I am aware that in taking this point of view I differ from some of the premises of such eminent thinkers on the subject as J. C. R. Licklider, who in directing an extensive study for the Council on Library Resources of the "concepts and problems of man's interaction with the body of recorded knowledge," excluded "consecutive reading" as "the modal application in the domain of our study." (See J. C. R. Licklider, *Libraries of the Future*, Cambridge: The M. I. T. Press, 1965.) I still believe that consecutive reading is a major and indispensable part of transferring the product of the human intellect. I furthermore believe that the continuation of civilization is in some measure dependent upon the preservation of the sentence as a unit of communication. But Mr. Licklider was trained as a scientist and I as an English teacher, and we are perhaps at this point simply looking in different directions.

It will be some time before the computer can store and transmit the intellectual content of books as efficiently and as economically for most purposes as the book as we know it. In other words, viewed simply as a potential solution to the serious problem of finding space for the enormous number of books now required to record existing and constantly increasing knowledge, the computer seems to offer no prospect of solving the problem in viable economic terms during the lifetime of library buildings now being constructed. No institution whose life depends upon immediate access to a large general research library—e.g., no university—can count upon the computer alone as a substitute for enlarged buildings to house its growing collections, at least until the present generation of new buildings becomes obsolete.

Microphotography

Microphotography seems at this time to offer a more promising method of storing the intellectual content of books when for space or other reasons some more efficient substitute for the conventional book is desirable. For many years libraries have been using microforms to store and make available certain kinds of material: extremely bulky material (newspapers); material known to disintegrate in a relatively short time (newspapers again); material not readily available in its original form (foreign official archives or excessively rare books); etc. They will obviously continue to expand their use of microforms whenever they serve the needs of scholars and students by increasing the locally-held resources of libraries or when the economic advantages through the saving of space become inescapable. The conversion locally of full-size originals to microform solely for space-saving is not now economically advantageous, and it seems likely that the increased use of microform must depend upon the constantly increasing availability of material produced centrally and in multiple copies by groups of libraries, by commercial microform publishers, and by government agencies.

Higher reduction ratios, up to and beyond one hundred diameters, should be available soon and will have an obvious impact. I have recently held in my hand a single sheet of film about the size of a playing card which contains the entire Bible. Both technological and economic barriers are being overcome. Reader-printers with which one can read microform and produce on demand full-size reproductions of selected images are broadening the utility of this medium for users. For a good many years various devices for locating and displaying automatically individual items from a microform store have been under development and actual production. For various reasons none has yet had wide library use.

Just how far this sort of thing will go in replacing in libraries the printed book in its original form remains to be seen. Leaving aside the legitimate function of at least large research libraries to preserve at least some books as originally printed, some kinds of scholarship cannot be done without access to the originals. As for the rest, learning can hardly flourish if the transfer of knowledge or the contact between "book" and reader does not take place above a certain minimum level of convenience and a certain minimum level of economic viability. These minimum levels in the production and use of microforms are gradually being reduced.

For the individual library the tactics of dealing with microreproduction seem fairly obvious. It will acquire material in this form as it can afford it and when it best meets the needs of its patrons, hopefully avoiding the temptation of acquiring enormous masses of seldom-used material just because it is available; there will still remain situations in which it is cheaper and more effective for a scholar to spend a summer in London working in the Public Record Office than it is to photocopy massive archives. The individual library will continue to collaborate with other libraries in the microcopying and often the joint ownership of microcopies of material appropriate to this treatment, such as newspaper files. It will continue to work with other libraries in bringing microforms under full central bibliographic control. But it will of necessity continue indefinitely to acquire most of its "information" in conventional book and journal form.

Facsimile Transmission

Facsimile transmission is another area of advancing technology of obvious significance to libraries. If one could obtain with sufficient speed and at low enough cost a copy of a book from another library, it might not be necessary to hold that book locally. There are now available commercially devices which can transmit text over ordinary long-distance telephone circuits with greater simplicity of operation. But the machine cost seems to be about thirty cents a page and the actual transmission time about six minutes a page. Thus a single use of a 200 page book seems to cost about $60.00 and to require 20 hours in transmission—plus the cost of a long-distance line for 20 hours, plus the cost of converting a bound volume into single-sheet photocopies, which the transmitter can accept, plus the wages of an operator. Other devices are much faster but require the use of special cables between stations. Note that facsimile transmission does not solve the space problem if the copy thus received is retained by the library. The economic factor to be considered is the cost of transmission for each use *versus* the cost of storage locally.

There seems to be nothing for libraries to do in this area but encourage the improvement of the technology, planning in the meantime for national networks which text transmission may make possible and participating in pilot experimental projects as they become feasible. The further development of communications satellites is obviously highly relevant, either for direct transmission or, as has been suggested, to release the existing network of surface TV transmission cables for library use.

THE LIBRARY OF THE FUTURE

It is difficult to resist the temptation to speculate, as many have done, about the library of the future, combining these three technological elements of computer storage, microreduction, and remote transmission to develop a national or regional research library system which would place in the hands of every reader the text he wants, instantly and at bearable cost. It is quite clear that revolutionary changes in the storage, handling, and even publication of texts are on the way. The task of the individual library in the meantime is to make sure that the specialists in information theory and technology and the hardware manufacturers are fully aware of library needs and applications, to add a realistic library point of view to governmental and private planning for national and other information systems, to maintain sufficient awareness of this rapidly changing field to participate whenever it seems useful in experimental applications, and of course to avoid heavy investment in new materials or procedures which the coming revolution will make obsolete. I am convinced that both conventional books in large numbers and the buildings required to house and use them will be necessary for at least another generation. The growing financial burden of books and buildings may be eased somewhat by

imaginative cooperation and utilization of improving technology, but for a long while it will continue to grow inexorably in any university where the hope or the reality of true excellence is a central principle.

This discussion thus far has been limited to the intellectual content of the library and methods of storing and transferring this content. This is an area in which expectation has perhaps been higher than performance and in which there has therefore been more than a little loose talk. Generally imaginative and well-informed people have sometimes pressed librarians to automate in areas where neither the systems theory nor the equipment are yet available. This pressure can lead to mistaken adventures in automation which can be costly both in money and library service.

I am not suggesting that research and experiment in these matters is not a legitimate activity for institutions, organizations, and individuals with the competence and the facilities to undertake them. Indeed, only by such research can the new science be developed and only by experiments can its technology be made available for application by libraries in improving their services and their role in information transfer. I am saying simply that there is no reason why each library should conduct independently the basic research and development work necessary to automate its procedures.

BIBLIOGRAPHIC CONTROL

Although automation of the intellectual content of general reserach libraries seems not to be feasible yet, there are areas of vital concern to libraries in which the new technology is ready or nearly ready for library application. The image of the library as a millpond, storing recorded knowledge until it is needed, may serve us again, if only to point up a significant difference. The sluice gates which release the stored water to turn the millwheel are not required to be selective. Any water will do, so long as there is enough of it. The user of the library, unlike the millwheel, is selective; he requires not unselected water but specific bits of information of knowledge from the store. It is a prime function of the library not only to maintain the reservoir but also to assist the user in a variety of ways to draw from it selectively just what he needs. As the size of the millpond has increased to oceanic proportions, the ability to organize the pool and to retrieve from it selectively what one wants has become progressively more difficult and more important.

Two elements of this selective use should be discusses, the first briefly, the second in a little more detail, for it is the area where the computer seems to have a direct and important library application.

Abstracting and Indexing

One often reads now of the "information explosion," and it seems to be true that recorded information, still largely in the form of conventional books and journals, is coming in such a flood that most scholars have difficulty in sorting it out, either to "keep up with their fields" or to get at specific and relevant information when they need it. To assist them, a staggering number of abstracting and indexing journals and services have been developed during the past half century. To their production new information theory and computer technology are being applied, but the product still reaches individual libraries and scholars almost entirely in conventional form. That is, a complex and highly automated process is now used by the National Library of Medicine to produce the major guide to medical literature known as *Index Medicus*, but the product used by most medical researchers is still a column of print down which the user runs his eye in search of the subject which interests him and the bibliographic references under that subject.

Now, however, machine-readable tapes containing this information are beginning to be distributed to regional centers, and the scholar may ask the computer to search out for him the references he seeks or to distribute to him automatically information about new literature on specific subjects previously selected by him. It is obvious that the availability of this sort of data in machine-readable form will increase and that the individual library will supply a computer-based service of this sort in many fields to its users when it becomes available at a cost that is feasible.

The creation of machine-readable abstracts and indexes to any large body of literature presents formidable problems which obviously must be solved at the national or international level, by those national libraries which serve as surrogates for many other local libraries or by national learned or professional societies such as the American Chemical Society. It would be folly for a single university library to attempt to develop independently with its own funds any broad abstracting service, thus duplicating work done elsewhere. Once the computer-based record is available from a central source, its use by a local library presents no serious technical problems, only a cost problem. The role of the individual university library, then, is only to encourage the development of central sources and to prepare itself to use these resources, when they are available at justifiable cost, just as it now uses the comparable but less refined conventional printed resources which are produced centrally and to which it now subscribes.

The Catalogue

A second type of bibliographic control must be established in each library. The dictionary catalogue on cards has become in this century the customary device for exercising this control over the books and journals in a library. It usually provides a description of each bibliographic unit, sufficiently full to distinguish it from all other units; an author entry, either personal or corporate, by which the cards can be arranged in alphabetical order; a classification number by which each book is assigned a relative position, according to its subject, in the total spectrum of human knowledge and by which the book itself may be located on the shelves of the library; and a very few subject headings, key words which identify in general terms what the book is about, which appear at the top of duplicate cards so that they may be filed in the same or a separate alphabet. Without this card catalogue or something like it all but the smallest libraries would be chaotic.

The development and maintenance of this catalogue is obviously a complex and costly business, now requiring the expenditure on the average of approximately one-sixth of the annual budget of each university library.

The substitution of a computer memory for this card catalogue as a central store of bibliographic information now seems to be the most promising application of the computer to library procedures. In other words, the information now contained on the catalogue card can be translated into machine language and stored in a large computer. The user of the library can get at the information stored in the computer by means of a computer print-out in book form or in card form, but while this procedure presents some technical internal advantages, it would hardly justify the major costs of conversion.

When terminal equipment becomes available—and much research and development remains to be done—the user may be able to carry on a "dialogue" directly with the computer through a "console." He should be able to present his question directly to the computer memory: "What books does the library have on this subject?", "Where is this book?", etc. The computer answer can be presented on something like a television screen, and the inquirer can communicate further with a light-pencil, as the dialogue becomes more specific. The computer can print out a bibliography or detailed references upon request. The number and location of consoles need be limited only by cost. Consoles could be located in branch libraries or even in individual faculty offices or student rooms.

The use of the computer should make it possible to tag each bibliographic entry with a much more refined system of descriptors or subject headings, and the information contained in abstracts and indexes may eventually be incorporated into the computer store, thus taking the user far more directly and deeply into the content of books and journals than libraries have hitherto been able to do. The Project INTREX Planning Conference, conducted in 1965 by M. I. T., went on to speculate about the "on-line intellectual community," in which not only these sorts of information would be stored in the central computer but also work-in-progress, such as laboratory notes, individual reactions of scholars, and the whole intellectual dialogue of a university community might be recorded and conducted.

Now even if one stops where this whole program seems to him to approach the realm of fantasy, it is an expensive process. Aside from the cost of equipment, the cost of translating each of the more than two million main entries in the Princeton University Library's catalogue into machine language is formidable. The development of character-recognition equipment to do this automatically would help, but equipment is not yet available which would read even the variety of Roman alphabets represented, much less Cyrillic, Arabic, Chinese, etc., etc. Even if these entries were converted, the cost of writing the complex programs required to instruct the computer would be substantial.

The Systems Approach

If one approaches the problem from a total systems point of view, the cost appears more nearly justifiable. It seems possible to have the computer play a major role in the entire process of adding a book to the collections, from the moment a decision is made to acquire the book until the book is on the shelf and the bibliographic record fully available in the on-line computer store. From the beginning of the process with the search to make sure that the book is not already in the library, a record can be fed into the computer and, taking advantage of the efficiency of the computer in accepting additions and revisions, this record can be perfected progressively. During this process the computer can prepare the order for the dealer, check on outstanding orders, keep the rather complex financial records, accumulate and organize the various elements of descriptive and subject cataloguing and classification, prepare book labels and book cards, and produce various cards and lists as required, such as selective lists of new acquisitions. This enumeration is by no means complete.

The computer cannot perform the intellectual operations of cataloguing. It can, however, do a great many file-keeping and clerical operations for which it is increasingly difficult in all libraries to find competent personnel. It can do some of these internal library operations better than they are now being done. No one seems prepared at this time to say with certainty that the computer will perform these operations more inexpensively than they are now being done.

It should be emphasized at this point that no large university library has a computer-based system of the sort which I have sketchily outlined now in full operation. Various elements of it are being tried on an experimental basis in individual libraries, including Princeton. A distinguished committee of information storage and retrieval experts has studied the bibliographic operations of the Library of Congress and reported that it would be feasible to convert them to automated methods over a period of ten years at a conversion cost of $50 to $70 million. The Library of Congress is now proceeding rather cautiously with further studies looking toward this automation. The University of Chicago Library has planned a system of the sort which I have outlined to handle current acquisitions, and it received in July a grant of $118,000 from the National Science Foundation to begin this development in the first year of the program, estimated to require three years.

It now seems reasonably clear that this is the objective toward which the Princeton University Library should move as it enters this new era of automated libraries: the conversion of its present manual systems to an integrated, computer-based, bibliographical data system.

Serial Record Control

Another aspect of internal library operations which is related to the system which I have described but which is separate is serial record control, the tedious process of checking in current serials, claiming missing issues promptly, the checking and paying of bills for subscriptions, and controlling of the binding process. These operations seem susceptible to computer control, but no library has yet installed a successful system for handling a current serial list as large as the more than 19,000 which Princeton receives.

Major work on such a system should probably await further experience and particularly the development of the larger bibliographical data system, with which it should be integrated. A book-form catalogue of Princeton's current serial holdings would be useful, particularly in branch libraries. It could be produced and periodically updated by already-available computer methods and should probably be undertaken soon.

Circulation System

Several computer-based circulation systems, for controlling the loan of books, are in operation in other libraries. They eliminate the tedious manual filing of book cards required by our present system, they speed up the return of books to the shelves, and they offer the promise of providing with relative ease a detailed analytic record of the use of books which would be a useful management tool in a number of ways, including the identification of titles which should be duplicated because of heavy use. Yet these systems, if they are to be fully effective and at the same time to offer to the borrower the same very simple and quick charging operation as our present system, require the provision of a machine-readable book card for each volume in the collections, a quite expensive operation. Since this card can probably be provided at less cost as a by-product of the large processing system discussed first, the development of a computer-based circulation system should probably be deferred until the larger system is under way.

TACTICAL CONSIDERATIONS

How do we get there? Several considerations suggest themselves as prerequisites to any tactical decisions.

1. The necessary equipment and procedures cannot be simply bought off the shelf. A great deal of research and development still remains to be done before a system of this sort can be put together.

2. This research and development work cannot be done adequately by members of a library staff at the same time that they are carrying on daily library operations. Computer science and technology and information storage and retrieval have become highly specialized fields of expertise. Basic research of this sort in a university is usually carried on by members of the faculty or research staff as a normal professional activity, using the library as a laboratory for experimental or pilot operations. As an alternative, specialists of this sort may be added to the library staff, but they will probably prefer a home in a faculty department which has a continuing program of teaching and research in this area. In any event, a systems specialist will have to be added to the library staff to work with members of the regular staff, however sophisticated, in the actual installation and operation of the new system.

3. While there are on the Princeton faculty men of national eminence in the computer and data storage and retrieval fields, there is no departmental or inter-departmental program directed specifically toward general library applications, as there is at certain other institutions such as M. I. T., Johns Hopkins, and the University of Chicago.

4. There is personal satisfaction and perhaps some institutional glory to be attained by a library which pioneers in this new field, but there are also dangers. The daily conventional routines of acquisitions and cataloguing must be maintained until the moment of conversion lest regular service deteriorate seriously. Premature and fragmentary conversion or the almost inevitable dead ends of experimental programs may seriously disrupt normal operations.

5. Increasingly, no library can stand alone, and whatever system is developed must be compatible with developing hardware programs, and other large systems. If this principle is not observed carefully, the total investment in conversion may be lost as reconversion becomes necessary. As an earlier parallel it might be noted that the Princeton University Library became committed a half century ago to a classification system which became unique as the Library of Congress system

became almost standard for university libraries. It becomes increasingly clear that we shall have to extricate ourselves from this position at considerable cost or continue in still more wasteful isolation.

6. This isolation is wasteful because it does not permit us to take full advantage of elements of the cataloguing operation which are now increasingly being done centrally. Under a computerized system there will be still greater economy and efficiency in being able to use the product of centralized, machine-readable cataloguing copy, not to mention the advantages of full participation in the national research library network which will almost certainly evolve.

This major point may require further elaboration and illustration. Fully aware that it should be possible for a book to be catalogued once and once only and for other libraries acquiring the same title simply to use the original cataloguing and avoid wasteful duplication, librarians have for more than one hundred years been trying to work out a national system which would achieve this result. The achieving of such a system has turned out to be surprisingly difficult, and last year Princeton, for example, still had to do original cataloguing for 62% of the books it added. It was able to get cataloguing copy for 38% of its new acquisitions through the program begun in 1901 by which the Library of Congress sells to other libraries for the cost of printing and distribution copies of the cards prepared for its own acquisitions. Because of its unique classification system Princeton still had to add its own classification to most of this copy.

In May of this year Congress began funding a program proposed by the Association of Research Libraries and incorporated in the Higher Education Act of 1965. Under this program the Federal Government assumes for the first time, in the national interest, responsibility for the cataloguing through the Library of Congress of all books of research interest published anywhere in the world and making this cataloguing copy available to other libraries. Rapid progress is being made toward the implementation of this decision, but the program being developed by LC will hardly approach full operation for about three years.

Distribution at present is through the conventional means of catalogue cards and proof sheets, but it has from the beginning been envisioned that as soon as it is feasible this copy will be made available in machine-readable form so that it may be fed automatically into local systems of the sort I have described. As an experiment the Library of Congress will begin distributing in September to a dozen libraries machine-readable copy for a portion of the current cataloguing.

These developments apply only to current output, but it seems inevitable that a way will be found to convert cataloguing copy for the older LC collections or the still larger retrospective National Union Catalogue into machine-readable form.

Thus it seems inescapable that whatever automated system Princeton develops must be compatible with the system adopted by the Library of Congress. This is essential so that we may take full advantage of LC's current cataloguing output in machine-readable form and hopefully be able to obtain copy in this form for converting the bibliographic record of our existing two million volumes to automated form and thus avoid the major cost of local conversion. It might be possible at the same time to convert the Princeton classification system at minimum cost to the LC system.

7. Some systems experts believe that conversion of any operation to automation can be done most effectively on a total basis, rather than by attempting to adapt an existing system to automation. If this principle is sound, it seems to follow that the Princeton University Library should at the proper time abandon its present manual systems and adopt at one time a totally new, tested, integrated, computer-based bibliographic data system which is completely compatible with the Library of Congress and other emerging systems.

8. These considerations suggest that the Princeton University Library should not now make any major commitment to independent research and systems development but at the proper time ally itself through financial support with another library of the same general size and type which is already developing the sort of system which I have described with a view to adopting the entire system when it has been perfected and tested. Some adaptation will of course be necessary, but a system being developed in "modules," such as the one at the University of Chicago, should be adaptable with relative ease.

9. When this arrangement is made, the Princeton University Library should probably add to its own staff a systems expert who might spend approximately half of his time at the other

university assisting in the development of the system and the other half at Princeton preparing our staff and systems for conversion.

10. There is no clear agreement yet as to whether an automated library system of this sort will require its own independent computer or whether it can utilize a large central university computer on a shared-time basis. These alternatives should therefore be borne in mind by those concerned with the development of space in the Firestone Library and those concerned with the planning of Computer Center resources for the entire University. Hardware compatibility with the other allied university would of course be essential in any arrangement of the sort I have suggested.

RECOMMENDATIONS AS TO POLICY AND TACTICS

I recommend therefore:

1. That this report and the course of action which it proposes be studied and after appropriate discussion and revision be approved as broad policy by the President, the Trustees Library Committee, and the Faculty Library Committee.

2. That the Princeton University Library make no major effort for the present to adopt a system for the computer-based storage of the intellectual content of the Library.

3. That the Library begin when it seems feasible the orderly and prudent conversion of its bibliographic controls to a computer-based system.

4. That toward this end an attempt be made to establish a working relationship with another library or other libraries already engaged in developing such a system, contributing financially toward the development of that library's system with a view to adopting essentially the same system at Princeton after it has been tested.

5. That when this arrangement is made, a systems expert be added to the staff of the Princeton University Library to help develop the system of the associated library and to prepare for its initiation later at Princeton.

6. That other key members of the staff of the Princeton University Library be encouraged to increase their knowledge of automated systems through visiting other installations, attending short courses and institutes, etc.

7. That the President appoint a special committee of faculty members with special competence and interest in information theory and computer science to advise the Librarian on the development of the Library's program of automation.

A Proposal for the Development of an Integrated, Computer-Based Bibliographical Data System

by Herman H. Fussler

This proposal is closely related to several basic contemporary aspects of the handling of recorded information for educational and research purposes:

University libraries play a critically important role in making information available to a large constituency whose efficient access to information is of vital importance to the nation. However, the needs of readers for improved intellectual and physical access appear to be well in excess of the current library response capabilities. Present systems are slow, costly, difficult to use, and frustrating in other ways, despite the massive service and acquisition loads that are now carried by libraries. For a number of reasons, large basic improvements in the speed, assurance, ease, and basic efficiency of the access to locally-held recorded information seems unlikely to result from simple extensions in the quantity of available manpower, better training of staff, more space, and other similar adjustments in existing patterns of service and organization. While many basic improvements in the quality and ease of access to recorded information will be dependent upon national bibliographical and other developments beyond the control of the individual university, improved speed, ease, and efficiency in the local levels of both physical and intellectual access are also of critical importance to the strength of a large portion of the nation's educational and research processes. Furthermore, such local improvements will be a prior requirement if there is to be a truly effective development and utilization of future national or regional information system designs and networks.

There are at least two other fundamental aspects of the internal operations of libraries and their services to readers, to which this proposal is also related. First, an extremely high proportion of all the internal processing and other operations of libraries are based upon access to catalog data and related data files that describe and analyze the contents of the bibliographical units held by the library, or that contain other records of the current status or use of these resources. Data from these basic files are searched, compared, extended, extracted, deleted, rearranged, matched with data from other files, or otherwise manipulated, for an extremely large portion of all the end purposes connected with library operations and reader access to information. Such record generation and manipulation, in consequence, also accounts for a very significant proportion of all library operating costs. Secondly, many, though not all, of the routines or operating decisions associated with the use of these basic data files are highly formalized, and do not require interpretative or qualitative intellectual judgments, i.e., they tend to be "yes" or "no" actions, depending upon the internal data.

The two basic situations described above lead strongly to the conclusion that a computer-based system for the integrated handling of many of these record-related operations should not only be feasible, but should, under the right circumstances, be much more efficient in performance, and, ultimately, lower in unit costs, than traditional systems largely based upon manual routines of file searching, transcribing, retranscribing, and otherwise using, maintaining or manipulating the basic data files.

DESCRIPTION OF THE PROPOSAL

Objectives.

The general objectives of the proposed system can be summarized as follows:

1. To improve substantially the response time of libraries in almost all of their routines in order to provide readers with very much faster, more current, and more accurate access to library resources.
2. To extend the scope and quality of library

SOURCE: Reprinted from a proposal by the University of Chicago Library to the National Science Foundation (1965?), pp. 2-3, 6-11, by permission of Herman H. Fussler, Director.

services to readers, at small incremental costs, through such services as the ability to generate current acquisition lists, tailored for different groups of users; the ability to meet current-awareness interests; the capability of handling fast recall and notification procedures; the ability to generate specialized bibliographies; the ability to handle reserve books in more expeditious ways, etc.

3. To assemble library performance data. Such data are extremely difficult, costly, and in many cases, virtually impossible to collect with existing manual systems. Yet the effective modification of operating systems and the construction of valid theoretical models of library or other information systems are critically dependent upon access to basic data on library performance and users' requirements. With a computer-based system it will be possible to obtain at modest incremental costs, extremely current data on patterns of resource use, book availability, duration of use of various types of material, dealer performance, and a variety of other operating data of critical value in reshaping operating policies and resource development and access patterns.

4. To stabilize, and hopefully reduce, the unit costs of many library routines that, under traditional manual procedures, tend to rise with labor costs, and, beyond certain capacity levels, to increase in unit costs with increases in loads.

5. To provide basic library record systems that will be capable of relatively easier change and alteration to meet changing needs or concepts in the intellectual organization or content-analysis of library resources, in the location of books and other materials within the system, in discard operations, and other rapidly changing requirements of user-oriented systems.

6. To provide data systems that will easily be capable of handling existing levels of bibliographical analysis and descriptions, and yet be adaptable to more sophisticated levels of analysis of content or more detailed bibliographical descriptions, or unconventional search techniques, than are now possible with card catalogs and other manual systems. The proposal envisages a three-year investigation of bibliographically-related search strategies and techniques and file-organization problems for which adequate solutions have yet to be developed.

7. To provide systems that can take full advantage of machine-readable bibliographical data generated by the other agencies such as the AEC, NASA, the National Library of Medicine, the Library of Congress, etc.

8. To provide systems, in both hardware and software, that are capable, at reasonable cost, of adjusting to long-term growth and the very sharp changes in loads that characterize library operations. A part of the stress in conventional library operations is the result of both growth and extreme variations in loads. It is easier and more economical to design computer systems to give full service at maximum loads than to design manual systems for such responses, and to expand the capacity of computer systems to meet growth as required.

Basic constraints on the system design include: (1) The hardware, software, and system design package, once its feasibility has been demonstrated in an operational situation, must be economically feasible for a typical large university to utilize within "normal" budget limitations. (2) The system design and programming should be adaptable to the evolution of a variety of improved consoles and other terminal equipment. (3) All basic operating data shall be available in speed and in form at levels at least equal to those common to manual systems. For example, manual circulation systems in theory can provide information on the location of material within a few minutes of a transaction; in comparison, batch computer processing may not be capable of providing locational information for some hours after a transaction.

Description.

More specifically, it is proposed to design, develop, test, and evaluate in operation an integrated information processing system which will unify all elements of information about each bibliographical item added to the library into a computer-accessible record, reducing or eliminating repetitious copying, the need for many existing auxiliary files, and much of the presently required manual file maintenance. An element of information, once entered, need not be re-entered and can be used with other elements of information or files to produce, on demand and at the time and place most useful for the overall system, the various outputs required to meet readers' needs or processing functions. The input of general processing data will start as of July 1, 1966, or before, and will include all 1966 imprints received before this time. Modular programs will be developed to give access to these basic data and to modify them, as may be appropriate, for as many library operational routines as the computer technology, the operational requirements of the library, the needs of the readers, and the economics of the system will permit. Remote terminal computer input/output capability is planned with both real time querying and response and batch print-out capability depending upon the varying requirements of readers and particular routines. A system has been planned that will offer a wide variety of access modes, print-out capabilities, and, at rather low cost, characterfont flexibility, including Cyrillic and other non-Roman alphabets.

It is intended to use this highly integrated system, ultimately, to handle readers' requests for material or catalog searches, and to provide almost instant information on availability and location; to prepare specialized bibliographies, or to supply current awareness references; to handle want lists, recall, or holds for readers. It will be used to speed up almost all processing operations by handling such routines as searches prior to ordering; to prepare book and serial purchase orders, catalog cards ready for filing, selective book catalogs where indicated, manual and machine-readable circulation cards, accessions lists, bindery tickets, call number labels, book pockets; to handle book fund accounting, dealer claims, etc.; to generate performance data on book use, book availability, dealer performance, staff processing performance, and other operational matters.

Initially, existing levels of bibliographical analysis and description will be used for the basic machine readable record, but when the system becomes fully operational it will be possible to extend the depth of subject analysis to cover classes of material now excluded from conventional catalog controls, and to make other changes

or extensions in the level or character of bibliographical description and control.[1]

Readers can initially be helped most if the "internal" services of libraries are fast and efficient. Without such improvements the development of more sophisticated access devices will be of only limited utility because it will prove difficult and slow to get the necessary material into a library and from a library into the hands of a reader. Therefore, the initial emphasis will be given to the development of a fully integrated system of book processing and book circulation. Future attention will be given to certain aspects of serial processing and recording and to the operational potential of the system for current awareness dissemination, possible direct reader inquiries by console, and related aspects of access to resources.

The proposed system is a logical extension of certain other mechanized or computer-based systems for handling library-related bibliographical data essentially in (1) the extent to which all current[2] basic bibliographical data will be held in a random-access computer store in a form suitable for an extremely wide variety of end purposes, thus eliminating repetitive manual generation of records for different files which must be independently maintained, searched, etc.; (2) the degree to which the system will integrate a wide variety of library operational, processing and reader needs; (3) the capability for multiple station, remote terminal querying; (4) the capability for modifying, deleting, updating, and otherwise changing the basic data store; (5) the capability for real time responses with the objective of much more rapid information on document status or availability; (6) the application of such a data processing system to a large general research library; and (7) the degree to which the system should be capable of utilizing machine readable data from other sources, such as the Library of Congress, the National Library of Medicine, etc. In utilizing such data, it is important to note that universities may have information requirements quite different in scale or character from those of national libraries.

FOOTNOTES

[1] An investigation being carried out by Don R. Swanson, of the University of Chicago Graduate Library School, is concerned with the intellectual aspects of catalog use and content. We would expect that any changes in the content of bibliographic format or level of analysis deriving from this kind of study could be implemented at some future time in an operational system such as we propose to develop.

[2] The input of retrospective data will be deferred until the system has been thoroughly tested and the input costs can be fully justified.

II
VARIETIES OF RESPONSE

Descriptions of non-integrated computer-based library operations are naturally enough abundant in a profession which for years has not been bashful about telling "how we do it good in Podunk." A number of these are quite useful, but in this section I have brought to bear on the subject only those materials that indicate an awareness of an integrated, systematic approach to computer operations. By integrated and systematic, I mean an approach to computerization which does more than concern itself with a single, isolated library function such as circulation, or a serials holdings list.

In the first article in this section the staff of the System Development Corporation report on a survey of data processing equipment conducted in 1966 by Creative Research Services. Unfortunately, no attempt was made in this survey to distinguish between computers and other mechanized equipment. On the other hand, even as conducted the survey is revealing if one accepts the belief (widely held) that a library accustomed to unit cards and other data processing equipment will move more readily into computer controlled operations. I agree fully with this, especially after having visited the University of Maryland where the move towards computer controls is being taken in stride largely because of their experience with unit card equipment.

The survey referred to is interesting on several counts. First, only 638 libraries were actually using data processing equipment. Second, the urge to do something about serials is evident; however, the term "serials control" is not clear in that lists of holdings are quite a different matter from serials accounting. The latter has been a thorny problem for several who have wrestled with it.

It is no surprise that circulation is of major interest, and it has been quite interesting to note that some academic libraries have bypassed unit card equipment, making the leap from an old fashioned two card book operation to one based on a computer.

Public libraries with a large number of branches have a large stake in book catalogs, as is evident from the survey. Most KWIK indexes, however, are to be found in special libraries.

The main point to notice with regard to developments at the Library of Congress is that several major projects are of the high-impact variety called for in the very first selection in this anthology. These are the MARC II project, the National Serials Data Program, and even more recently, the study of conversion priorities compiled by Henriette Avram of the LC staff.

Of the four remaining examples, each gives us a different approach to computerization. UCLA is remarkable for its Center for Information Services, its Institute for Library Research, the Medlars Search Station, and for its management of one of the ERIC libraries. Furthermore, UCLA is working on a wide variety of "in-house" processes such as circulation, serials accounting, serials listing, card production and book catalogs. One of its "showcase" projects, visited by many librarians, has been the evolutionary development from an outmoded two-card procedure in circulation, to unit card equipment and then on to plans for a computer-based operation. Here again can be seen the truth of the statement that unit cards are a broad bridge to computer operations.

Harvard is mainly of interest in that it chose to eschew the "whole hog" approach. Harvard believes a more cautious attack is in order, fearing the leap into the world of on-line, third generation computers. In addition to its work with circulation, acquisitions, serials control and the production of cards, Harvard came to the conclusion, since its old sheet shelf list was unmanageable, to begin its gradual conversion to machine readable data. As a result, Harvard has begun to print out sections of its shelf list, and these have proven useful as a reference tool not only in Cambridge but in other libraries.

Finally, we come to Chicago and Stanford, which with MIT (see the article by Overhage in Section IV), are exploring the farthest frontiers of computerization in academic libraries. Both are working towards an integrated on-line system in which strict controls will be maintained on materials from the moment an order is placed, through accessioning, and then on to the circulation function. Controls such as these are notably lacking in present day libraries.

Stanford is attempting more than "in-house" controls; it seeks through a series of terminals in branch libraries to bring to users direct access to records of holdings, purchases and circulation. Even private files are planned to become part of the total campus network. Here we have what is probably the boldest scheme of operation within an academic library.

Technology and Libraries: A Survey of Current Applications and Trends

Information Systems Technology Staff,

System Development Corporation

INTRODUCTION

According to a recent survey, 1130 of the approximately 24,000 libraries in the United States either have, or plan to have within two years, some aspect of their operations performed by data processing equipment.[1] Of this number, only 638 actually have some operational mechanized process; the others only had plans for mechanization. The majority of the 1130 were libraries having over 50,000 volumes.

Figure 1, based on figures from the survey, gives some rough indications of how data processing is being applied. All of the major library functions are drawing attention, although the emphasis is primarily on functions related to technical processes requirements. For libraries that are currently using data processing equipment, the function that has received the most attention (209 libraries) is probably that of serials management. The accounting function of the acquisitions process is also very popular, and logically so, since libraries are typically part of larger organizations whose functions in the accounting area may have been automated for some time. For other acquisitions functions, such as the production of purchase orders and accessions lists, the majority of libraries presently using data processing equipment for these functions use electric accounting machinery, rather than electronic computers.

Circulation control is also a popular mechanized function, and 165 institutions are using data processing equipment for circulation control. Data processing equipment is also being used for the reference function, i.e., document retrieval; this was found in 131 installations, 76 of which were special libraries in industrial organizations. No public libraries, and only 18 colleges and universities, were undertaking this type of activity.

The following sections briefly describe major operations within libraries and review current applications of technology to these operations.

Since specific procedures vary widely, even within libraries of the same size and type, the operational procedures described must be understood to be *typical* ones.

Professional librarians and others who are already familiar with library operations may wish to skip the "Description" section for each function and read only the "Applications of Technology" sections.

FIGURE 1. Number of Libraries in the U.S. Using Some Form of Data Processing Equipment, as of October 1966 (Selected Functions)

Function	Total
Acquisitions Functions*	
Acquisitions	102
Accessions lists	170
Accounting	235**
Cataloging Functions	
Catalog cards	101
Book-form catalogs	125
KWIC indexes	135
Circulation Control	165
Serials Control	209
Union Lists	133
Reference Functions	131

*It is not possible to add sub-groups together, since some libraries are represented in each, e.g., a library may produce all three: catalog cards, book catalogs, and KWIC indexes.

**An unknown number of libraries have payroll operations included in this function.

ACQUISITIONS FUNCTION

Description

A logical starting point in discussing library operations is that of acquisitions, since materials

SOURCE: Reprinted from the staff report to the National Commission on Libraries entitled, *Technology and Libraries.* 1967. pp. 39-64, by permission of System Development Corporation.

must be selected and acquired before they can be used. The book trade is very specialized, and typical library practice is to carry out the purchasing functions within a specialized library department, rather than to use a purchasing department of the parent organization.

Contemporary U. S. publications from the larger trade and textbook publishers can be obtained anywhere in the country with a minimum of difficulty. The only problems likely to be encountered by a library dealing solely with such materials lie within the strictly clerical operations of handling the paperwork involved in the ordering process, and service from some publishers is likely to be slow. Sometimes legal requirements of the parent organization add to the delay.

Research libraries, academic libraries, and some public and special libraries purchase materials in foreign languages, and/or printed in every country of the world.

The acquisitions process is complicated by the fact that not all countries have a well-established book trade. For this reason, the Library of Congress, under recent legislation expanding the importation of foreign materials into the country, has found it necessary to establish and man field stations in certain countries.

Some libraries have additional problems with out-of-print materials—items that are rare, old, fragile, etc., and in exotic languages. Libraries are forced frequently to deal with particular vendors whose special requirements require some kind of special paperwork, or prepayment, which, under the rules of the particular library, may be very difficult to make and cause a great deal of extra effort. All of these factors have a bearing on the way that technology and automation may or may not be applicable.

Other types of acquisitions present special problems. For example, some libraries receive Federal, state, or local government publications automatically as designated depositories, while some acquire foreign government documents or the voluminous publications of the United Nations and its agencies. Depository libraries must claim materials that are due them, but are not received, for one reason or another, and must maintain records, even though there is no financial matter at stake.

Despite recent improvements in the distribution of government documents, there are still large numbers of documents produced by various Federal agencies that do not find their way into the normal distribution channels through the U. S.

Government Printing Office. For many of these documents it is not possible to achieve regular distribution and receipt by a particular library. Thus, a great deal of effort must be expended to discover and acquire such materials.

The acquisitions department also handles non-book materials, for example, maps, phonograph records, tapes, slides, motion pictures, and microform versions of various standard publications. These all have special problems of acquisition.

A specialized aspect of acquisitions is the gift and exchange operations carried on by many libraries. Many gifts come to the libraries in poor physical condition and without a listing of the items included. To check such materials in order to determine which items to retain is very time-consuming and unless the gift is a particularly valuable one, it is probably more costly to the library, in the long run, to accept such materials than it would be to buy the relatively few items that it really wants.

The most critical problem connected with receiving large gift collections without a catalog is that the library must invest the time to produce a catalog of the collection if it wishes to derive any benefit from the gift. This is both a clerical and a professional operation, and is discussed in more detail under "Cataloging Functions."

Exchange is perhaps more perculiar to academic or certain governmental libraries than it is to most public or special libraries. Agreements for the exchange of materials free of charge conserve the book funds of the institution and, more importantly, they are the only way that some materials can be obtained *at all* from some foreign countries. For example, several U. S. academic institutions have been able to establish exchange agreements with academic institutions in Red China, and are thus able to acquire materials that cannot be easily obtained in any other manner. The same is true for the Soviet Union and certain other nations. Such agreements, however, require diplomacy on the part of the exchange librarian, and maintenance of accurate and timely records of the exchanges, even though the volume of material received by exchange is generally small. There are a few libraries in the country (such as the Library of Congress) that have a very large exchange program.

Certain libraries also use "blanket orders," a scheme for ordering, on approval, all materials published on a particular subject. Where the volume of materials received is large, these agreements with book vendors or publishers may involve considerable record keeping, as well as very complicated financial arrangements with accounting departments; but the resulting speed of delivery and ease of selection are worth the additional paperwork, if any.

The final area of acquisitions to be discussed here is that of *continuations*, which can be defined as all materials outside of the one-time orders that bring in a complete item. They include serials, series, terminal sets, works issued in fascicules, anything issued in some numbered or ordered sequence, and other "extended procurement." Regularity of issue is not a factor.

Serials are a form of continuation that are issued more or less periodically without a definite cutoff date. This contrasts with monographic series, which have no definite ending point, but which do have a predictable end (e.g., the collected works of a given author, now deceased).

Serials have a unique aspect that causes them to be handled, in most libraries, as a separate operation. For a given serial title, an order once placed will result in the receipt of issues of that serial for years into the future, for most serials are published with the expectation that they will continue indefinitely.

The operational problem with continuations of any sort is not so much the placing of the original order but the maintenance of the records necessary to keep track of the continuing delivery of the items. Such continuations may extend over many years and over the employment period of several individuals. Serials are discussed in more detail in the section "Serials Management Functions."

A useful starting point for describing the operation of a typical acquisitions section is the one at which requests are received. The library first searches to see whether the material is already owned by the library, has been ordered, or is being processed in the cataloging section. After this preliminary check is made, if the library decides to order the material, enough additional information about the item to establish a correct entry is sought, and an order is prepared and sent to a vendor or to the publisher. A record is kept of this order, notices are sent to any interested parties or departments, and a particular departmental book fund may be charged. When the item is received, copies of the order are pulled from the outstanding order file and other files, and the book then moves into the cataloging process. Part of the acquisitions function may be the ordering of Library of Congress cards. Sometimes that function is carried out by the cataloging section. They receive a copy of the purchase order and, in turn, send a card order to the Library of Congress or to some other card service.

Applications of Technology

Certain aspects of the acquisitions process lend themselves particularly well to automation or to the use of other forms of technology. For example, the production of orders to vendors is very similar to the production of orders in any purchasing activity, and computers can do this very readily. The maintenance of purchasing records and the charging of funds against particular budgets are other activities that have been successfully mechanized in the business world and that are being mechanized in some libraries.

There were 102 libraries actually using some form of data processing in their acquisitions process, as of October 1966. A recent survey reported that 419 institutions had *plans* for use of data processing in acquisitions, and that of these 419, 139 planned to begin such use by the end of 1968. These projects in acquisitions are endeavoring to do one or more of the following: (1) order library materials; (2) maintain financial records; (3) collect and record statistics on the order process; and (4) print lists in various arrangements of materials in process.

Financial reports may be arranged in a variety of ways, for example, on the basis of materials ordered, by fund, by subject categories that are not represented by funds, by accumulation of items ordered from particular vendors, by standing orders, etc. It is sometimes useful to know how many items have been ordered from particular vendors over a period of time, the amounts spent with these vendors, the discounts received, how rapidly particular vendors have responded to orders over a period of time, total number of orders placed within a particular calendar period, etc.

Lists of materials in process are useful for a number of purposes, especially when items on order can be entered and located in a variety of ways. The typical method in the past has been to enter under a selected entry in an order file with no cross-references. This makes it exceedingly difficult, if one does not have precise information, to discover materials actually on order. Using lists that can be arranged in various manners, on-order and in-process materials can be controlled throughout the time from receipt of request within the division, mailing of the order to a vendor, receipt of the order, and cataloging, to the time they are ready for use.

While there are some automated acquisitions systems operating, we know of none that includes *all* of the possible products or operations listed above. A few institutions have either planned or are implementing systems that are as "complete" in concept as one could currently hope for.

Aside from the use of data processing equipment, and in some cases the use of related accounting machinery or bookkeeping machines, libraries have done little experimentation with available technologies. Very few libraries utilize materials-handling equipment, such as dumbwaiters, conveyor belts, etc., in the acquisitions area. Some libraries have experimented with communications devices such as Deskfax, direct photocopying devices such as the Photoclerk, edge-notched cards, and automatic typewriters. In general, though the area of materials-handling and the use of photography in processing have not been given as much attention as "automation." While photography may not hold as much long-range potential, either for the reduction of costs or improvement of output, it is an area that is not receiving the research and development attention it deserves.

Since the acquisitions procedure seems to be so similar in libraries of comparable size and type, a number of cooperative projects have been started to develop processing centers for groups of libraries. Such cooperative processing centers have been in operation for some time in northern California, Alabama, Michigan, Ohio, North Carolina, and Indiana; and centers are being studied in Colorado, New York State, Ohio, and other places. These centers will perform all the typical functions—preparation of orders, selection of vendors, checking-in of materials, cataloging, etc., and finally delivering the items, ready for the shelf, to the participating libraries. It is apparent, of course, that such centers can operate in the same (manual) way that most library acquisitions departments have operated for many years. Yet, the use of data processing equipment makes the cooperative processing center a much more attractive proposition.

The potential savings of cooperative or centralized processing centers have not always been realized. For example, a recent study of a centralized processing center in Illinois showed that although personnel were relieved of the processing task and work-space pressure was relieved in some of the participating libraries, the actual cost of processing through the center was, for some of the participants, greater than costs of doing the work themselves.

Reported costs of existing cooperative centers vary widely. The reported costs are difficult to compare with previous costs, since almost no one has obtained cost figures during a previous *operational* period and then studied the same operation after the processing center has been established. In addition, the services provided may differ from one center to another. For example, some centers use very simplified cataloging, whereas the center in Illinois mentioned above used a cataloging code that resulted in better quality but more expensive cataloging than had previously been the case in the individual libraries.

The Association of Research Libraries has been studying the possibilities of cooperation for many years. Under their Farmington Plan, individual institutions undertake the purchase of foreign publications from a certain area or on a certain topic, and then serve as a national center for such materials, thus relieving other institutions from purchasing in that particular field. Recent activity at the Library of Congress under Title II of the Higher Education Act has also served to further the cause of cooperative purchasing and processing. These cooperative activities could be the beginnings of true networks.

It is difficult to predict with accuracy the extent to which the trend toward centralized and cooperative processing can be carried. The cooperative processing center or the centralized purchasing center tends to limit free enterprise within the book trade. It is conceivable that a cooperative or centralized purchasing activity could be large enough to dispense with the services of booksellers at the retail level or even the wholesale level, and deal directly with publishers in all cases. If extended over a large enough geographical area, this could adversely affect the fortunes of a number of booksellers. Also, there are numerous legal barriers in the way of widespread cooperative purchasing and processing, if the members are located in different political jurisdictions (i.e., different counties, states, or countries) or if some members are publicly supported and others are privately supported.

CATALOGING FUNCTIONS

Description

Libraries have developed highly complex systems to categorize the materials they acquire to make them accessible to the library's clientele on the basis of subject matter, author, and title of the work. In the "cataloging and classification" process, numerous categorizing schemes are used, the most widely used being the Dewey Decimal Classification and the Library of Congress Classification systems. Alphabetically arranged subject headings are also used, as well as the occasionally used newer techniques such as descriptors, keyword-in-context, etc.

The amount of effort expended in the description of the item varies from library to library; some libraries expend a great deal of effort on a precise physical description of library materials, as well as on their subject categorization. Apart from the physical description of the item, there is the matter of assigning an "entry" to the material. Because of the nature of the so-called "dictionary catalog" (on small cards), the concept of *main entry* has been important in cataloging work. Selecting the main entry, putting it into proper form, and selecting appropriate subject headings and classification numbers or coordinate indexing terms are time-consuming tasks.

In most libraries, the descriptive cataloging and the subject classification are done by the same people; in others this work is separated; in still others, catalog sections are operated in conjunction with the acquisitions activities. In many libraries, the catalogers use Library of Congress printed catalogs for guidance, but they also maintain their own "authority" files, which give proper forms of names, series titles that are used or not used in that particular library's catalogs, proper forms of subject headings, etc. Libraries typically maintain special catalogs known as "shelf lists," which are maintained in the same order as the books are shelved within the library. It is an inventory record primarily, but can sometimes be used as a "classed catalog," since the file is usually organized by the classification scheme in use in the library.

The end result of operations in a cataloging section is a series of codes assigned to a given item, and a description of the item. Together these constitute the cataloging entry for that item. Typical library practice in the past has consisted of making catalog records on $7\frac{1}{2} \times 12\frac{1}{2}$ cm. cards. Printed cards may be purchased from other organizations, e.g., the H. W. Wilson Co. or the Library of Congress, or produced at the local library.

A particularly nagging problem for many libraries is that of "arrearage," which is the general term given to the large quantities of uncataloged materials so frequently found in catalog departments. Libraries often acquire large collections in one transaction, completely overloading the catalogers. More and more libraries have these unprocessed backlogs, for they are reluctant to pass up any chance to acquire materials that may, later, be unavailable or available only at greatly increased prices.

Applications of Technology

The most popular application of technology to the cataloging process has been to reproduce catalog cards. Although the cost of purchasing cards from the Library of Congress is relatively low, some libraries prefer to produce all of their own cards using copy provided by the Library of Congress proofsheets (proof copy of new catalog cards) or Library of Congress printed catalogs. These libraries are sometimes able to reduce the costs below that of cards obtained from the Library of Congress. Techniques sometimes involve photocopying, but a few libraries rekeyboard the item on paper tape for production of the necessary cards by automatic typewriter or computer. "Book catalogs" are catalogs in the form of a book (or codex) rather than individual cards. This form of catalog, frequently used many years ago but abandoned in favor of the card catalog, is returning to favor. With the new technology, some of the disadvantages of the early book catalogs are no longer serious. The major objection to book catalogs of the past was that the cost of keeping them up to date was prohibitive. With present-day equipment, especially computer-controlled typesetting or computer printing in upper and lower case letters, the cost of reprinting catalogs on a regular basis has become much more competitive with the cost of maintaining large, complex card catalogs. A further advantage of the printed book catalog is that it can be produced in multiple copies for use at a large number of service points, including distant ones.

A few libraries are now producing catalogs by computer in a book form, with holdings arranged by author, title, and subject. These are produced on a regular basis and updated as necessary.[2] Some libraries are producing (or planning) cumulative monthly lists of currently cataloged items, authority lists of subject headings, and lists of currently cataloged items arranged by the special interests of the library or its clientele. In addition, some projects are seeking to gather by-product statistics for library administration, e.g., work-performance records by cataloger.

The combination of interlibrary cooperation and new technology offers great potential for the reduction of costs and wasteful duplication of effort in cataloging. There are already a number of smaller cooperative processing centers that combine acquisition and cataloging functions, presumably with economic advantage to the participating libraries. The Library of Congress also continues to play an increasingly important role in cataloging. Because LC catalogs a significant percentage of books acquired by libraries in the United States, it has been—on economic considerations alone—an effective agency for the reduction of cataloging effort by a large number of libraries in the country. In fiscal 1966, over 72 million cards were distributed by its Card Division. With its expanded role in procuring materials abroad and cataloging them more promptly, even greater savings are possible. The MARC Project, which is a prototype of a national network for the distribution of machine-readable catalog data, has great potential in this respect.

There are other aspects of the cataloging process that could benefit either by centralization or mechanization. A cooperative, centralized operation could consolidate "authority files" or even "official catalogs," and the consolidated authority file could become a part of a union catalog for the participating libraries.

Aspects of technology other than data processing are also beginning to contribute to the cataloging process. There has been some interest in camera equipment that a cataloger could use to copy data from available LC printed catalogs or other national bibliographic records. Only recently has a camera been introduced (by the Polaroid Company) that was especially intended for use by catalogers. Whether it is satisfactory is not yet known.[3] Materials-handling equipment also has potential, although this area has not been exploited to any large extent. A few libraries have installed large rotary shelves to offer better access to large reference sets, such as the Library of Congress printed catalogs. Some forms of compact storage have also been developed, but relatively little study has been made of possible improvements in materials handling to support the cataloging process.

Some equipment has been developed to aid in the placement of call numbers, letters, and numbers on book spines. This is a relatively unglamorous part of processing, but one that is necessary in every library. The tool developed for this purpose by the American Library Association's Library Technology Program (LTP) works reasonably well, and saves some amount of time and money, but it will not work with the most modern typewriters.

A few libraries have considered certain aspects of purchasing, receiving, and cataloging as a single process, and are attempting to establish systems that capture the bibliographic information concerning each item ordered, at the time it is ordered. This abolishes the need for re-keyboarding time and time again, throughout the entire system. This is a promising approach, especially for handling currently published material, for which full identifying information is available. If consideration is limited to contemporary publication in English, by far the bulk of the acquisitions in libraries of the United States, there is no question that this goal can be achieved. If there were library networks, interconnected by communication links, keyboarding could be further reduced by storing the bibliographic information for each item in a machine-readable store. Any other library could then call out the complete record from the store by inputting only a small portion, sufficient to identify the entry. It might be possible to use only the Library of Congress catalog card number to retrieve the complete bibliographic record.

There are at least two current attempts to implement some of these ideas. The MARC Project has already been mentioned. Another major effort is in New York State, where a network is being planned for a medical library system. It is anticipated that there will be a centralized technical processes center for the entire New York State University system, with communication lines linking all of the libraries.

In the near future, the use of computers to produce book catalogs will undoubtedly become more widespread, particularly with the advent of devices that can transform computer output directly onto film. The Chemical Abstracts Service, which is preparing to print *Chemical Abstracts* entirely from computer output in a few years, has a device that will take computer output (using a character set of 1452 separate characters) and place it on film, from which it can then be made into an offset printing plate. The same process could be used to produce library catalogs, either union or individual. In addition, microfilmed catalogs produced in this fashion could readily be copied and distributed in cartridge form, so that libraries could have union catalogs for their patrons at many points at a relatively low cost.

Communications technology could also be important in relation to uses of the catalog. One idea, which few libraries seem to have considered, is to establish direct communication from the public catalog area to the catalog department, to help reference personnel or patrons obtain assistance in the use of the catalog. Communications technology may also prove very useful in relation to storage facilities. There have been some efforts to establish such facilities for a group of libraries in an area of low real-estate cost. The use of "slow-scan" TV to send tables of contents, etc., to distant patrons over ordinary telephone lines, apparently not yet studied, is worth investigating.

The problems of arrearage might be eased by better exploitation of data processing technology and, possibly, materials handling technology. Various schemes have been devised by some large academic libraries to produce brief descriptions of these materials and then to store them away. None seem to have followed the lead of some special libraries, which have used data processing to produce permuted indexes to their arrearages. The use of compact shelving of various types might enable libraries to handle their arrearages more effectively. Most libraries have not planned for such shelving, however, and its installation and use may be considered too expensive.

CIRCULATION FUNCTIONS

Description

Most libraries employ some kind of circulation control system to keep track of the materials borrowed from the library. Such systems vary from the very simple to the extremely complex, in accordance with the type and importance of information needed. In England, some libraries give their patrons a number of tokens, which are exchanged, one by one, for books that they take from the library. When a book is returned, the patron receives a token back, but no *record* whatsoever is kept to show what book the patron has or who has what book. The only apparent use of the tokens is to restrict the number of materials that a patron can have out from the Library at one time. Libraries in the United States usually want much more information and control.

It is in the area of circulation that we find perhaps the greatest operational differences among the three general types of libraries identified earlier. Although most public libraries do seem to have some sort of limit on the number of books that patrons may take out at one time, they *generally* attempt to maintain controls only with re-

spect to the date of return. Thus, there is usually no way to discover what materials are out to what particular borrower. Some academic libraries have special circulation problems, in that they have special collections of materials that are loaned for very short periods of time. These items may carry rather high fines for even short periods of overdue use, and record keeping is a large operational problem for these libraries. Academic libraries, in general, feel it necessary to be able to determine who has a particular item when it is out and to control the length of time materials are out. Special libraries generally try to keep some sort of inventory of materials out to each borrower but they tend to be especially liberal regarding their loan periods. Some special libraries also need to maintain control of security classified documents, not a typical problem in either academic or public libraries. For such documents, the concept of "accountability" is paramount.

Another, rather specialized, aspect of circulation control involves nonbook materials, which have their own unique problems. For example, the circulation of motion picture film involves not only circulation control, but "booking in advance." This requires specialized records, as well as efficient routing and distribution. Other materials loaned by libraries also have specialized requirements. Phonograph records and audio tapes, for example, require special handling not typically afforded book material. Circulation of periodicals for limited periods and their inspection after each use present additional problems that seemingly demand human attention and have relatively little potential for mechanization. However, technology might have some answers if the proper efforts were made to discover them.

In recent years, circulation control has received much attention, no doubt because many libraries have acute problems in this area.[4] Academic libraries, especially, have had their circulation systems very much in the public eye. Some have had operating problems that cause long queues to build up at chargeout points. (Waits of up to an hour for service are reported in the literature.) Such conditions cause considerable dissatisfaction among the patrons. Thus, a number of them have selected circulation control as a first step toward automation.[5]

Applications of Technology

According to the Creative Research Service Survey, about 165 libraries are now using data processing technology to support the circulation control function. Current projects in this area seek to do the following: produce lists of materials actually in use and identify their location; produce lists of materials in use by individual borrower; produce overdue notices automatically; collect circulation statistics by borrower category, subject category, or any other particular category of interest to the library. Subfunctions of some of the foregoing processes are those of producing lists of materials having one or more requests outstanding ("holds and recalls"), so that management action could be taken; producing cumulative records of the use of particular items, with automatic notification of materials used so frequently that they are likely to need rebinding; and producing annual listings of materials out on long-term loans to certain categories of borrowers.

Some public libraries have had very comprehensive circulation control systems for years. Perhaps the most outstanding is the Montclair (New Jersey) Public Library, which uses custom-built IBM equipment to keep track of the records by item, by borrower, and by due date. Only recently has comparable equipment become generally available. A few academic libraries now have systems that permit an inventory of materials out to a particular borrower. Others can run an inventory for *all* materials out on long-term loans, but cannot answer directly the question, "What materials are loaned to the borrower, Mr. Jones?" All of the operating automatic or semiautomatic systems work on a "batch" basis.[6] The concept of batch processing implies that data are fed to the computer all at one time, rather than being fed to it from time to time, "on line." A few institutions are beginning to work towards the development of actual on-line operations that will tie a circulation control system directly into a computer at all times. None of these is yet operational.

Using data collection equipment tied directly into a computer, libraries could handle one- or two-hour loans; this would demand considerable random-access memory, but the value of the use statistics that could not be gathered any other way might well justify the added cost. Within libraries of a size large enough to have branch operations, a limited network arrangement could be useful for circulation control. All the branches could participate in the one common system by the use of remote data collection devices, thus placing in one central computer record the total circulation file. This would enable librarians to ascertain the current availability of particular

titles within the system, much as the airlines check for available seats. Public librarians have not felt that this was a necessary part of their service in the past, but they might well do so if the system permitted it.

Circulation control could also be operated on a network basis within a region, it would seem, quite efficiently. Many libraries banded together could afford equipment that no individual library, or even several libraries, could afford. This might allow effective on-line operations at a reasonable cost. Efforts along these lines will undoubtedly begin to take place; there is already some research under way along these lines by private organizations.

The concept of cost/effectiveness has usually been absent from the discussion of circulation control systems, especially in connection with existing manual systems. Cost/effectiveness is not the same as cost, a distinction often ignored. An all-too-common approach to circulation control considers only the lowest possible cost of the operation to the library. The idea that circulation statistics can also provide important management information over a period of time seems not to have taken hold yet, for few public libraries have sought to devise circulation systems that would enable them to collect such management data at a reasonable cost. Future efforts undoubtedly will begin to see more attention paid to this. Cost to the user is also a topic which is beginning to attract attention.

After materials are used, they must be reshelved or replaced by the circulation section. Technology has had as little effect in this operation as it has had in the similar operation of "paging" books in libraries that do not allow their patrons access into the stacks.[7] While some use has been made of pneumatic tubes to transmit call slips and even books, these are point-to-point operations, and materials must be taken off shelves and replaced by hand.

Some interesting suggestions for materials handling have been made, for example, that the principle of the linotype could be used to position, deliver, and replace a book in a particular place within a collection. Following this suggestion, a staff member of the Council on Library Resources has outlined a system using plastic boxes to contain and transport books in and out of the stacks. It appears that no one in the library world—even including the Council itself—has taken such suggestions seriously enough to initiate experimental work.

Remington-Rand has recently announced a system which is, in effect, an automatic stack and is intended primarily for automatic handling for storage and retrieval of materials kept in file folders. The manufacturer claims that the system will handle materials in codex form. The economics for library operations of this system are unknown, since only a prototype of the equipment exists at the present time.

REFERENCE AND REFERRAL FUNCTIONS

Description

Reference and referral is another aspect of the public service side of all libraries. It includes helping the patrons find and identify materials of interest, making requests to other libraries, if necessary, and helping patrons in the use of reference tools. Reference work also includes the production of specialized bibliographies. Public libraries also have a "reader's advisory" function. This is generally not considered important or necessary in special libraries or academic institutions, where the patrons are students, faculty, or research personnel.

Part of the help given patrons involves interpretation of the library's catalog. Thus, card catalogs are typically placed in a public area where they are handy to the reference and circulation sections, even though this may make them very unhandy for personnel in the technical processes area. In some libraries greater use of library catalogs or library reference materials is made by the staff of the library itself rather than by patrons. However, the library's orientation toward service to its patrons usually dictates a location convenient for their use.

Some part of the public services section of the library, usually the reference department, will handle requests to other libraries for materials the library does not have. In the area of interlibrary loans, library cooperation has been truly remarkable. All libraries, public and private, can obtain interlibrary loans, not only throughout the United States but overseas. Some of the larger libraries have used communication devices such as the teletype to handle their interlibrary loan requests. The Library of Congress with its National Union Catalog[8] serves as a focal point for the activity in this country, although certain academic libraries may have local cooperative agreements within a region, and therefore make their requests within that local group before using the Library of Congress resources. For these reference and referral functions of interlibrary loans, union catalogs are almost indispensable. Without them, interlibrary loan activity would require circularizing a large number of libraries until one located a particular library that had the desired material.

Reference work frequently involves making copies of library materials for patrons. Sometimes these are copies of tables from reference works that cannot be removed from the library. Since circulation of periodicals is frequently restricted, there is also heavy traffic in photocopies of articles. There is also frequent demand for microform materials, especially the widely used roll microfilm in 35mm format.

Applications of Technology

Very little in the way of technology, with the exception of communication devices, can presently be found in most reference departments. A very few libraries have automated their information and document retrieval functions. In general, these systems work as follows. A variety of guides or indexes to document holdings is available, from which users select key words, subject headings, uniterms, etc., as search keys. The search produces lists of document numbers, sometimes including abstracts of materials matching the subject criteria input.

There are also some primitive automated *data* retrieval functions along the same lines, generally using some type of subject categorization for the construction of search requests. Most data retrieval systems can do only such simple things as producing a series of sentences that contain some prescribed or desired words, or a listing of physical data that meet certain criteria. Most of the automated data retrieval systems are in information centers; almost no *libraries* have automated data retrieval functions.

Project Intrex at MIT combines some aspects of document and data retrieval within a library function. Intrex (information transfer experiments) is a program of research experimentation directed toward the functional design of new library services that might become operational at MIT and elsewhere by 1970. The research program is addressed mainly to the broad problem of *acces—* in particular, access to bibliographic material, documents, and data banks. The four areas of activity encompassed by the core program of Project Intrex are: an augmented catalog (computer stored), full-text access at stations that are remote from the store, fact retrieval, and network integration.

Some current mechanization projects have implications for reference. For example, where libraries have mechanized their catalog records, using computers either to print cards or to produce book-form catalogs, there is also the inherent capability to produce specialized listings of materials in a particular area. The computer can be used to retrieve references and tailor a bibliography specifically to the needs of the patron, with limits, for example, on date of publication, language of materials, and subject headings.

Some communication devices have been used in libraries for some time. The Electrowriter and other similar systems have been used to transmit handwritten requests from one point in a library to another, or from a branch library to another element of the system. Several recent projects, have explored the use of telefacsimile processes to transmit needed materials from one library to another. While the promise is great, so is the cost. Here again, libraries are making use of equipment and technology developed for other uses and not especially suited to library problems. For example, the typical facsimile process is not usable with bound materials, except through the use of the television camera. With the typical commercial television equipment and common carrier transmission systems, the cost for transmitting even a few pages is very great. No work has been done, so far as we are able to determine, with "slow-scan" TV processes[9] for library purposes. Lecture demonstrations have been held at several places in the country where materials used by the lecturer at the transmitting end were displayed on a screen at the receiving end. Such equipment is said to work over voicegrade lines and does not involve too great a transmission time. On the other hand, it produces only a display, not hard copy, at the receiving end.

Typical library equipment for using microforms is far from satisfactory for long-duration usage. For some reason, existing optical technology has not been exploited to the fullest. Microfilm equipment manufacturers seem to think that microfilm readers and other types of microform readers must *always* be "portable," and librarians have, apparently, accepted this position. Yet, such machines are usually placed in a particular location, used there, and rarely taken from that location, and could just as well be built-in. This would ease the normal restrictions on size and would allow the optical designer additional freedom to use long focal lengths to improve display on the screen. Existing standard optical techniques could be used to build a high-quality reader that would be comfortable for a patron to use over a long period of time, in a reasonably well-lighted area.

Such equipment has not been built because the development cost seemed prohibitive without a guaranteed market. Not enough librarians have been actively concerned with utilization of microforms to demand the better products that could be made, and no efforts seem to be under way to improve the situation. Yet microforms will need to be used more extensively in libraries in the future. Large numbers of books printed over the past century are deteriorating, and some of these undoubtedly will be preserved *only* in microform. Most libraries that want them will be able to afford them only in microform. The possibility of large library collections (e.g., one million volumes) solely in microform is also very much on the horizon. The increasing amount of material available in microforms will undoubtedly help to accelerate efforts to improve the handling, storage, and use of microforms.

Some effort is being made to bring techniques of automated "information retrieval" to reference work. A few libraries are already contemplating the use of computer equipment to make their catalog records available on-line, and are also considering placing computer display consoles in locations for use by patrons. Reference librarians may well be "tied into" the circuit so that, if the patron's own searching of the library catalog is unsuccessful, he can call a reference librarian, who can interact with the patron and the computer to assist. Before this is an everyday occurrence, a great deal of experimentation must be carried on to determine what kind of retrieval system is required for such interaction, and what kind of preparation and training are required of both the librarian and the patron.

The development and use of statistics regarding reference service has always been a shaky affair in libraries, largely because reference activity is very complex and because the personnel involved with reference functions have not had adequate time to record all of the daily transactions. This area will undoubtedly receive attention in the future, as computers are called upon to interact with librarians and patrons. Such devices could allow the easy compilation of management information forms that could be very useful for library administration. For example, the use of statistics rapidly gathered from interlibrary loans and arranged for easy interpretation could enable the library administration to improve the library's collection systematically. Most libraries try to do this now, but without appropriate tools, it often must remain a pious hope rather than an actuality.

SERIALS MANAGEMENT FUNCTION

Description

Serials were described earlier, in the section on Acquisition, as one form of continuations. It is difficult to say what constitutes a serial in a given library; most libraries have their own definitions that they follow. For purposes of discussion, we will consider as serials anything listed in *New Serial Titles* or the *Union List of Serials*.

Because they appear in such a wide variety of forms, and because of the difficulty of maintaining records concerning them, serials have frequently been handled by a completely separate operating division within libraries, especially in libraries of medium to large size. Smaller libraries do not usually have the wide variety of serials that the larger public, academic, and special libraries have.

Although the more esoteric, foreign language, scholarly journals cause great difficulties in handling serials records, it is the sheer volume of details necessary in maintaining serials that is the primary source of trouble. Also, serials have an additional problem that only infrequently is important in dealing with monographic works, namely binding. Periodicals have many separate, discrete parts that must be gathered together and placed in some sort of hard cover for preservation. Most libraries either replace their unbound journals with microforms or bind them, which adds an additional aspect of record keeping. Records must be kept of what is at the bindery; separate records are needed of what is bound and what is not, because these materials may be shelved in separate locations.

Large libraries with many branches have a tremendous record-keeping problem, since they try to record the exact items housed in any particular location. If an attempt is made to centralize such records manually, it can only be done economically in one place. Thus, branch locations may not have ready information on what materials may be in other branch locations.

An especially time- and manpower-consuming function is the claiming of serials which do not arrive on time, or at all. In order to carry on claiming, up-to-date information on serial receipts is necessary, because some serials, if not claimed promptly, will be out-of-print and unavailable. Claiming can be seen to be especially demanding of diligence and accurate records.

Union lists are another especially important aspect of serials management, since no library in the country has all of the journals ever published, even those of the United States. Every year, literally thousands of new journals—scientific, technical, and others throughout the world—are "born," and thousands "die," seemingly with a gradual net gain of live titles.

Applications of Technology

There is an unknown but sizable number of projects under way to convert serials records and record keeping to machine-readable forms so that they may be produced in a much more timely fashion. Some of the work on book catalogs has promise for serials management. For example, book catalogs, extended to include periodical and serial holdings and reproduced in multiple copies, have been successful in alleviating the problem of providing ready information to branch libraries on serials holdings. Once there has been a sizable conversion of serials information to machine-readable form, it should be considerably easier to create and maintain union lists of serials. The monumental compilation of the third edition of the *Union List of Serials of Libraries in the United States and Canada* is a case in point: This final edition took literally decades to complete.[10] If all the records had been machine readable and computer programs had been available to manipulate them, new editions could have been produced on a yearly basis.

Communication devices and data processing equipment offer tremendous potential for tying together the holdings of one library with that of another, within regions, and nationally. With the addition of the capability of transmitting facsimile copy through communication links, it becomes possible to consider centralizing, on a regional or even national scale, serial holdings of lesser-used materials. There have been efforts along these lines—without advanced technology—by libraries in the past, a prime example being that of the Center for Research Libraries, located in Chicago.

The question of cost/effectiveness becomes important in such considerations, and at the present, providing copies of journal articles for distant patrons is probably better carried out by common reproduction equipment and the U.S. mail, than by costly telefacsimile processes. Initial efforts are already under way, in certain regions of the country, to produce union lists of serial holdings for certain organizations having numerous branches,[11] and such efforts will undoubtedly accelerate in the near future. A most encouraging development is the recent beginning of a project at the Library of Congress to determine precisely what elements of information should be put into a machine-readable record for a serial title. This is the groundwork on which a national serial data project can be built, and that hopefully will be undertaken at the Library of Congress in the near future. Both this effort, and the recent known desire of the EDUCOM Network Task Force to convert the *Union List of Serials* to machine-readable form deserve greater support than they now have, since they offer tremendous potential for all libraries, not only in the United States, but worldwide.

The semivoluntary efforts of the American Society for Testing Materials (ASTM) to establish a uniform code for serial titles were noteworthy; ASTM offered to assign a standard code ("CODEN") to any serial title submitted to them in any field of knowledge. The Franklin Institute of Philadelphia has recently assumed responsibility for the CODEN effort. Standardization efforts of this kind, which help to establish codes for use in computer-based files, ought to have greater national and international support.

Despite several years of effort in the automation of serials records, relatively few institutions have operational systems, and those that exist do not perform all the necessary functions of serials management. Current projects undertake to produce the following types of records and control information: lists of currently received materials; cumulative lists of holdings, that is, materials actually in the library; claim reports for issues that have not been received by a prescribed time; production of tags for bindery use; orders for new subscriptions and a renewal of the entire subscription list; financial records showing categories of expenditures by funds, by subject, by language, etc.; lists of materials not owned by the library that are needed to fill in gaps in holdings. Current efforts are aimed at producing all of the items above, but no one system does. Very few institutions have attempted to integrate work in this area with automation in other aspects of their operations.

SPECIAL COLLECTIONS AND MATERIALS

Description

Libraries handle a wide variety of materials, in addition to books and magazines. Some libraries include the functions of museums, with collections of manuscripts, letters, art objects, etc., all of which demand special treatment.[12] Some materials are given to libraries with restrictions on their use that the library must observe. Frequently, the physical items are more important than their intellectual contents, e.g., rare books, manuscripts, etc.

Some special collections are easier to categorize for subject use than book materials. For example, maps almost always refer to some geographic area that can be identified, if necessary, by precise coordinates of latitude and longitude. Art and architecture slides always refer to either a geographic location or a physical object. Although such materials may have a subject orientation that must be identified, subject use is much more limited than it is for book materials. The same is true for phonograph records.

Special collections usually impose special storage requirements upon libraries. Both manuscripts and some kinds of books must be kept under controlled environmental conditions or they will disintegrate. (Even ordinary books are not particularly long lived but they are usually more easily replaced.) Other materials do not necessarily need a special environment, but must be protected from public access because of their rarity or fragility.

Applications of Technology

A great deal of specialized equipment is needed for the use of materials such as phonograph records, slides, and maps. Libraries typically use whatever equipment is commercially available, both for display and for storage. Better equipment than is currently available undoubtedly could be developed specifically for libraries.

A number of fairly new academic institutions, e.g., Oral Roberts University, in Oklahoma, and Oakland Community College, in Michigan, are attempting to develop learning centers built around highly sophisticated and complex audiovisual equipment that has been especially designed to handle film strips, language tapes, video tapes, programmed lesson materials, etc. These institutions feel that if the library is to remain a significant part of the academic enterprise, it must involve itself in handling these materials and in processing traditional library materials into new forms that coordinate better with the audiovisual approach. There is some indication that there may be more interest by libraries in the use of these special forms of materials and equipment. This appears to be necessary to avoid competition between "media" personnel and librarians on the campus.

Libraries that handle special collections as their prime function are few in number, considering the total number of libraries in the country, and some persons have wondered whether such libraries need be considered in relation to the "national" problem. There are, in fact, some profitable lines of action that could be taken, with better application of technology, to improve the use of some of the special collections. For example, union catalogs have been produced for certain forms of rare materials, such as manuscript collections. It is now well within the state of the art to develop a truly comprehensive union catalog or national inventory of rare materials. Such a catalog would be widely useful and its maintenance relatively simple, since, compared with regular library collections, the growth of these special collections is not very rapid.

IMPLICATIONS FOR FUTURE APPLICATIONS OF TECHNOLOGY

It seems clear, from the foregoing examination of current applications of technology to libraries, that more and more libraries will soon be seeking to use data processing equipment to support various aspects of their operations. Some will do so in the hope of saving money; others may do so primarily to improve their operations and service. The latter is probably a more realistic goal. Use of data processing has not saved money for many libraries yet. However, it has enabled them to improve operations that they considered critical, to stabilize the number of employees and sometimes to maintain certain operations which were ready to break down under continued manual operations and increasing workload. Machines may help to alleviate the recognized shortage of manpower in libraries long before recruiting and educational programs are able to meet the challenge. Too, despite some conspicuous fail-

ures, there is sufficient evidence to indicate that use of machines can improve service to library users in ways which additional manpower cannot. Judging by the CRS survey cited earlier, many near-future applications of technology to libraries are likely to be largely on a "hit-or-miss" basis, with each library focusing on its most pressing current problem. This is an understandable tendency; yet the greatest potentials of technology may have to do with functions or services that are *not* currently being performed by most libraries. For example, most libraries have tended to be concerned much more with the monograph than with any other physical carrier of information or data, in spite of the fact that the number of monographs published each year is relatively small compared to other printed materials: periodical issues, report literature, government publications, etc. Although numerous local and regional union catalogs of monographs exist, and there is even a National Union Catalog, there are *no* union catalogs available for such materials as documents from the United States Government Printing Office. Use of existing technology could greatly enhance access to such documents. If the depository list of the Superintendent of Documents were to be published, using computer-controlled typesetting, as part of the *Monthly Catalog* issued by the Government Printing Office, depository libraries would no longer need to maintain their own catalogs (which consist largely of simple inventory files, rather than full-fledged catalogs, as are available for monographs). Technology could also improve access to other kinds of non-monographic materials.

Technology can also be exploited for the extension of typical library activities to serve certain user groups better. For example, Project Intrex at MIT is examining (among other things) the expansion of the descriptive and subject cataloging of library materials, so that catalog data available to potential users will include evaluations as well as strict descriptive indications. Undoubtedly, other efforts will be undertaken to expand existing library operations into new areas that have not been feasible in the past because of limitations in the equipment and methods available. This raises the question: Is it not possible that entirely new areas of service could be identified with subsequent creation of appropriate techniques and equipment? Without question, libraries of all types, as they are now constituted, are exceedingly valuable to our society. But how much more valuable could they be if their *role* were seriously examined, with a particular view to the development of new concepts of services such as continuing education?

Another aspect of libraries that one may not immediately associate with technology is their organizational structure. This structure has traditionally included operational and service functions, but might not the current and new technology of the near future offer the possibility of changing the entire organizational concepts of libraries? Do they need to continue operating in the traditional manner, with the traditional departments? Several libraries undertaking automation programs have found that existing divisions could be efficiently combined into larger operating units when data processing equipment was put to work. If this aspect of library operation and management were given the attention it deserves and made the focus of design studies, could not significant improvements be expected in the *total* library system?

Just as computer technology provides the opportunity for individual libraries to think in terms of larger units of operation, so, too, does it provide the opportunity for groups of libraries to work together in ways that would be difficult, if not impossible, without the use of advanced technology. Although most of the current library automation efforts are oriented to the individual library, the time would appear to be ripe for many of these disparate efforts to be channeled into a better-focused national effort that would seek to bring all aspects of our technology—not just the techniques of data processing—to bear on the problems of library operations.

In this vein, a recent reviewer of library automation efforts has written in the 1967 *Annual Review of Information Science and Technology*:

"In the past, much of the automation literature has consisted of reports of individual and quite isolated projects. This was perhaps necessarily so because the vision to see the relationship between the new technology and bibliographic processes was limited to a few individuals who often seemed to be 'marching to the tune of a different drummer'. This may be the classic pattern of technological advance, but this reviewer believes that to continue to regard automation as the plaything of an avant garde elite is dangerous. We have reached the point where further achievements will depend on the ability of a lot of us—librarians, computer specialists, system analysts, and information entrepreneurs of various ilk—to march, at least occasionally, in step."

In her survey of recent progress this reviewer gave primary attention to literature that described cooperative movements or literature that presented an honest attempt to discuss, not so much an individual project, but the principles and concepts involved. She summarized things this way:

"To this reviewer the single most important facet of the literature of 1966 is that it clearly reveals that there is a vast and growing number of marchers, that national and international ventures are being planned and some are even under way, that there is an ongoing search for a *modus vivendi* between the library world and that of the specialized information center, and that at least minimum standards for machine-processable data are almost upon us."

It would appear that both the full exploitation of technology and the library needs of society will demand a reorientation of libraries from individual, isolated, operating units into a cohesive national (or even international) structure capable of offering a given level of information service at any point in the nation.

FOOTNOTES

[1] While there is some question whether the figures reported in the survey are entirely accurate, there can be little doubt that only a small percentage of the libraries in the country are actually using or working toward data processing technology.

[2] One of the unresolved problems connected with the computer production of book catalogs is the filing sequence of entries within a particular catalog. Existing filing rules demand a high level of human intelligence for their accomplishment. The rules must be modified to some extent in order that a computer can follow them. There is not yet unanimous agreement within the library community just what modifications should be made.

[3] Other efforts have recently been announced for development of a "Bibliographer's Camera." The Council on Library Resources is sponsoring this work.

[4] A number of studies have been made of circulation control systems within recent years, under the sponsorship of the Library Technology Project of the American Library Association. While these studies have been, in general, carefully planned and have produced some useful results, there has not been complete agreement on the validity of the techniques used in the studies or their results. The benefits of management information have been completely overlooked as a desirable by-product of a circulation system, and are not even considered in the assessment of costs. At the present time, the effort seems to be to use data collection equipment solely for the purpose of solving operational problems.

[5]A case in point is Johns Hopkins University, which has devised what seems to be a fairly expensive system of circulation control, the design criteria for which had as a prime requisite the ease and speed of moving through the circulation control point from the *patron's* viewpoint.

[6]There are a fair number of systems, more or less similar in operation, that use data collection equipment: for example, at University of Southern Illinois, University of Missouri, Washington University, Santa Clara Public Library, etc.

[7]At the Technological University Library in Delft, Holland, a special telephone system is used to transmit the stack location of the desired item to a "page" in the proper area of the stacks. The page picks up the book (or responds that the book is not there) and places it on a specially designed spiral chute, which delivers the book to a pickup point.

[8]The National Union Catalog at the Library of Congress was established with the aim of recording locations throughout the country of primarily scholarly material.

[9]Some studies have been made with closed-circuit TV, but these were made some years ago prior to the advent of the slow-scan process. For ordinary TV use the costs are now too great because of bandwidth requirements.

[10]The exact number of years involved is a matter of definition and is the subject of controversy.

[11]For example, State University of New York with its 58 branches.

[12]To group these functions under the term "museum" does not imply that they are not used by scholars.

Automation in the Harvard College Library

by Richard De Gennaro

This article will begin by outlining the basic approach that has been followed in introducing computer and other machine systems into the Harvard College Library and by explaining why this approach was adopted. It will then describe the specific projects that have been undertaken since 1963 in the Widener Library, with some indication of their present status and their prospects. A third section will attempt to view in perspective what has been accomplished thus far, pointing out both the immediate and practical gains that have been realized and the more general, long-term benefits that can be anticipated. Against this background, the concluding portions of the article will briefly consider the outlook for future developments in automation at the national level and will suggest how these developments can be expected to affect the Harvard Library.

This is an account of automation in the Harvard College Library, not the Harvard University Library as a whole. The Countway Library of Medicine (then the Library of the Harvard Schools of Medicine and Public Health) entered the field two years before Widener in a pioneering cooperative project with the medical libraries at Yale and Columbia; it continues to develop systems for its own use and, as the Regional Medical Library of New England, is a major participant in projects sponsored by the National Library of Medicine. An excellent list of serial holdings has been developed by Baker Library at the Harvard Business School, which also entered the automation field before Widener. These efforts deserve separate treatment and they are not directly related to developments in College Library; consequently it has seemed desirable to confine this article to the series of projects based in Widener.

THE HARVARD APPROACH TO AUTOMATION

The Harvard University Library consists of nearly one hundred separate units with approximately 8,000,000 volumes and an annual budget of more than $8,000,000. The Library adds some 200,000 volumes each year, and approximately half of its holdings are in languages other than English. It has a staff of more than 600, of whom 200 are professional librarians with language, subject, or other special qualifications. The staff has had a long history and tradition of providing excellent library service to the Harvard community.

Widener Library is the central unit of the library system. It has nearly 2,500,000 volumes in the Widener building, with another 500,000 in two storage areas outside. It acquires some 50,000 new volumes each year. Because of its age and other special circumstances, it developed its own cataloguing, subject headings, and classification systems either previous to, or concurrently with, the Library of Congress, whose systems are becoming the national standard. In a library as old, as large, and as complex as Harvard's, the problems of automation must necessarily be approached with a mixture of conservatism and boldness.

The Library has much to conserve, including outstanding collections of books and journals in many areas, and a first-class bibliographical apparatus that has been built up carefully and at great expense during the last century. The Harvard Library must build on its strength and make the past investment continue to pay dividends at an increasing rate in the future.

It now operates successfully on traditional lines, and it expects to become a successful automated library in the future; but the transition to this future library must be made without disrupting the organization and crippling current services to users. The established systems cannot be abandoned until new ones have demonstrated their superiority. On the other hand, a bold approach is also needed to counteract the natural tendency of an institution such as this to resist change. There is no question that profound changes in the Library must be made during the next decade if it is to continue to fulfill its traditional mission and to respond to the new and increasing demands that

SOURCE: Reprinted from the *Harvard Library Bulletin,* 16: 217-236 (July, 1968), by permission of the publisher. Copyright 1968 by Harvard University.

will be placed on it in the future. Library automation is not a luxury to be indulged in for the sake of glamour; it is essential for the survival of the Library as a vital force in the University. The term "automation" in this context is not limited to computers but also comprehends the rapidly developing field of reprography (the aggregate of processes and methods used for copying documents) for it is the combination of these two technologies that will effect the coming revolution in libraries and information handling.

Most of the tools and concepts currently in use in academic libraries, including the card catalogue, the standardized 7.5 by 12.5 cm. cards prepared and distributed by the Library of Congress, subject headings, and classification systems, were developed and introduced in the second half of the nineteenth century. Since then, many great libraries have been doubling in size every twenty years, and the only response that has been possible to increasing growth and workloads has been to add manpower and build more space to house the books, staff, and catalogues.

Using traditional methods, libraries apparently cannot respond to the demands of modern scholarship unless they continue to grow at this geometric rate, yet it is obvious that this course would soon call for buildings and for costs of impossible dimensions. New techniques and concepts are needed, and a period of innovation in libraries was begun during the present decade with the development of new technology in reprography and computer-based systems. Much of the new technology is not yet reliable and inexpensive enough to be introduced into library operations, but some of it is. Developments in computer technology occur so rapidly, moreover, that it seemed essential at Harvard to prepare for fundamental changes as soon as possible by introducing as much of the new technology as could be used. In this way the Library could take advantage of early systems to improve its services and, more important, could become capable of developing and adopting more sophisticated systems as technological advances made them practicable.

Three basic approaches to automation in the Harvard College Library were considered. The first, which can be characterized as a cautious "wait for developments" approach, can be supported on the grounds that computer-based library systems are still in the developmental stage, that they are still of dubious value from an economic standpoint, and that it is wasteful and unnecessary for every library to undertake the costly and difficult work of development. In effect, this approach would leave automation to others. It was rejected on two counts. It seemed unworthy of an outstanding library, and it assumed, mistakenly, that Harvard could afford to wait for the situation to shake down and stabilize (which may never happen) before beginning to benefit from machine systems.

The second can be characterized as a direct approach to a total or integrated system. Here the premise is that, since a library's operations are all interrelated and interconnected, the logical procedure is to design a total system from the start to include all machinable operations in order to make the most efficient and economical use of the computer. This approach is reasonable and other libraries are attempting it.[1] It was rejected by Harvard, however, because of the size and complexity of the library and because neither the state of library automation nor the state of computer technology seemed to be sufficiently advanced to justify the risks that would be involved. It has been said facetiously that the total system concept would be right for Harvard if we could get God to design it.

The third approach can be characterized as an evolutionary approach leading eventually to an integrated system. It takes a long-range and conservative view of the problem of automating a large and complex library. The ultimate goal is the same as with the total systems approach, but the method of reaching it is more cautious and pragmatic. This is the approach that Harvard chose. It sees the introduction of automated systems into the Library as progressing in stages, each building on its predecessors. Harvard is still in the first stage of this approach—a stage in which, using its own staff to operate the equipment that is available, the Library undertakes a series of projects for designing and utilizing basic systems to do particular jobs. The immediate aim is to raise the level of each "housekeeping" operation, such as circulation, shelflist maintenance, book ordering and accounting, catalogue input, etc., from its manual stage to a relatively simple and economical machine system.[2]

During this first stage, which started in 1963 with the design and implementation of the Widener circulation system, the Library has recruited and trained a competent staff and has created a Data Processing and Photographic Services Department with a regular budget, equipment, and space in which to work. In short, it has been acquiring essential experience and building a capability to do the more sophisticated systems work that will be required in the next stages of development.

An attempt will now be made to describe the various specific projects that have been undertaken to date. Each is interesting in itself, and each needs to be understood if the total effort is to be seen in the perspective of future developments at both the local and the national level.

THE DEVELOPMENT OF SPECIFIC PROJECTS

Circulation System

The College Library's introduction to data processing equipment and techniques came with the design and installation of a punched card circulation system in July 1963. The old manual system could no longer cope with the steadily increasing load that had been placed upon it in the previous decade. The staff had been augmented to a point of diminishing returns and it was obvious that the Library needed a new system with greatly increased capacity and accuracy. A few other large academic libraries had already successfully introduced data processing techniques in this area, but no system then in operation exactly suited Widener's needs.

Foster M. Palmer, then Associate Librarian for Reference and Circulation, investigated the possibilities, and within a few months designed and installed a circulation system based on punched cards and electric accounting machines.[3] Several refinements and improvements were made, certain operations were computerized during the first year of operation, and a major improvement—conversion of the circulation file (currently on IBM cards) to a daily computer printout—is now under development.

The punched-card circulation system accomplished several things: it substantially improved the accuracy and reliability of the circulation records, it provided a system capable of handling a greatly increased circulation load at a stable cost, and, perhaps the most important of all, its outstanding success proved the value of data-processing techniques in the Library and gave the staff the experience and confidence to proceed with development of applications in other areas.

Current Journals in the Sciences

In the spring of 1964 the Library undertook a modest project to create a ready-reference tool which would list in a single alphabet the journals currently received in seven departmental science libraries. The Library's data processing unit, under the supervision of an assistant director, then consisted of a single intern, Mrs. Susan K. Martin, who gathered, coded, and keypunched more than 3,000 entries for journal titles from seven libraries. After she had also written the necessary programs for the IBM 1401, the first edition of the list was issued in one hundred copies in January 1965.[4] A third enlarged edition is now in preparation. This list is primarily for use within the University, but a few copies have been made available for outside distribution.

Current Journals is looked upon as a useful interim reference list and will probably be continued in its present form and scope until it can be replaced by a more comprehensive and versatile union list of serials produced by more advanced techniques with a considerably greater expenditure of effort and resources.

The IBM-Sponsored Education Program and Systems Study

In June 1964 the IBM Corporation embarked on a study with the assistance of the Library staff to determine how computer technology might be used to assist in performing certain "housekeeping" operations. In addition to this systems study, IBM sponsored a week-long orientation program in Cambridge during September for twenty-five senior members of the University Library staff. This educational program was extremely effective in creating an understanding of computers and an interest in the role that they may eventually have in the Library.

The IBM systems study concentrated on four principal areas: circulation, acquisitions, serials control, and cataloguing; it concluded with a recommendation that the Library embark on a major automation program. The proposal was set aside by the Library administration in consultation with representatives of the Harvard Computing Center because it was overly ambitious and prohibitively expensive. However, the IBM study and proposal produced valuable indirect results by stimulating key members of the Library staff to consider various alternative approaches to the problem of introducing computer systems into the Library and to make certain basic decisions. In the first place it was decided that, given the lack of experience and the primitive state of the library automation art at the time, it would be unwise to attempt a "total systems" approach—particularly in an institution as old, large, and complex as the Harvard Library. It was also decided that concentration of initial efforts on the simpler applications would be desirable in order to provide experience and that special attention to problem areas in the Library's operation ought to bring to light opportunities for projects that would produce a significant return on the investment. Obviously the staff was not sufficiently large or experienced to undertake work on more than one or two areas in the initial stage. The prevailing view was that preference should be given to a bibliographical project which would have direct value for the Library's readers as well as the staff. Since there was general agreement that automation efforts in university libraries ought not to assume the characteristics of a moon race, it seemed preferable to avoid duplication of the efforts and resources that were being invested by several other libraries in certain areas such as serials control.

1. *Catalogue-card production.* This is an area of fundamental importance in the long run because computerization would create cataloguing copy in machine-readable form which could then be used in a variety of important ways, particularly in book catalogues. Reproduction of cards, however, was not a problem at Harvard, and the Library was reluctant to undertake the input of catalogue data into computers before the Library of Congress and the research library community as a whole had been heard from on standardized formats, etc. In addition, the Harvard Medical Library was involved in this area with Yale and Columbia, so it seemed wise to wait and learn from their experience.

2. *Serials control.* This was—and continues to be—a problem for the Library, but it appeared to involve such complex systems and conversion problems that it was not well suited for an initial project with relatively inexperienced and limited staff. Moreover, as has been noted already, several other libraries with less complex records were working on this problem and again it seemed wise to wait and benefit by their experience.

3. *Acquisitions ordering and accounting.* This was a serious problem area in 1964, and it seemed to be a function which could be computerized by the staff then available. While other libraries had tackled this problem, it seemed unlikely that their efforts would be of much value in Harvard's particular situation. This, therefore, was assigned a high priority.

4. *Circulation control.* This did not present problems in 1964. As reported above, the Library had already installed an economical and efficient punched card circulation system, and it seemed best to let this activity alone for a few years.

5. *Shelflists.* Since the Widener Library had continued to use the old sheaf shelflists that were started in the nineteenth century, shelflist maintenance was a very severe problem. There seemed to be no question about the desirability or the technical feasibility of converting the sheaf shelflist to machine-readable form and replacing the manuscript volumes with computer printouts. This would be a complex but manageable systems problem, and the staff had or could acquire the competence to do the job. The real difficulty was to convert more than 1,600,000 shelflist entries (mostly handwritten and in many languages) to machine-readable form. It appeared, however, that conversion would cost much more than it was worth if a shelflist produced and maintained by the computer continued to serve the same limited functions that it had always served in the past, i.e. use in the assignment of book numbers and occasional consultation by library staff and readers.

Thus, after a thorough review of the five potentially interesting areas, it seemed that the best prospect for application of computer techniques in the Harvard Library would be in the acquisitions ordering and accounting functions, and there was some reluctance to make this the initial effort because its impact would be felt only indirectly by the library's users. A second and more imaginative review of the shelflist problem was then made, and the idea developed that, with the aid of the computer, the traditional shelflist might be transformed into a kind of classified catalogue with alphabetical and chronological indexes, which would be useful to readers and staff alike. The paragraphs that follow will briefly describe this idea and explain how the initial pilot project developed into a major program of shelflist conversion and publication. Something will also be said of this program's potential for further developments.

The Shelflist Conversion and Publication Project

A library's shelflist is a record of the books arranged in the order in which they appear on the shelves. Since book collections in most American libraries are arranged according to logical and detailed subject classification schemes in order to facilitate browsing and retrieval (rather than by size or order of accession), it follows that the shelflist should have great potential value to readers if it can be expanded and made available to them in some convenient form. A conventional shelflist differs from a classified catalogue in two principal respects: it records each book only once, no matter how many subjects the book covers, and it lacks author and title indexes. The Widener shelflist conversion and publication project has been an attempt, with the aid of computer technology, to develop the conventional shelflist into a new kind of classified catalogue of the Library's collections for the use of scholars, and at the same time to facilitate the task of maintaining the official copy of the shelflist for the use of the Library staff.

Shelflists have traditionally served two main purposes: as an inventory record of the books in a library and as an indispensable tool for assigning new numbers to books that are added to the collection. For most libraries the maintenance of a shelflist is a fairly routine process and involves merely filing one copy of each main-entry card into the card shelflist in call-number order. However, the Widener Library shelflist (with the exception of a few recently created classes) is handwritten in loose-leaf volumes rather than on cards and is therefore a difficult record to use and maintain. This was the standard form for a shelflist in the nineteenth century when Harvard Library's shelflist was started. Conversion of the shelflist to card form had been considered and rejected several times in the past on the grounds that cost of conversion would not be worth the advantages to be gained, and these advantages were always thought of in terms of the traditional uses of the shelflist.

As has been explained more fully elsewhere,[5] in September 1964 when the IBM proposal was under review, it was realized that conversion of the Widener manuscript sheaf shelflists to machine-readable from could do much more than improve the official copy for internal use; it could enable the Library to publish an expanded version for public use. Computer technology had made it possible to reconsider the question of converting the shelflist, because significant additional uses could be made of the information once it was in machinable form.

The plan envisaged a class-by-class conversion of the shelflist and creation for each class of a computer printout to replace the existing official copy. In addition, a four-part catalogue of each class would be produced and published as part of a series. The first part would contain a copy of the classification schedule which would serve as a table of contents or key to the second part. The second part would be a listing of the titles in the class in call-number (i.e. classification) sequence with subclass headings interspersed at appropriate places in the lists. These two parts together would serve as a kind of classified catalogue or browsing guide to the books in the particular subject area covered by the classification schedule. Part three would be an alphabetical listing by author (by title, in the case of anonymous works) and would be obtained by a programmed computer sort of the original entries. This third part would provide an additional approach to the class and would serve as a brief finding list for books in the subject area. By using this list the reader would avoid some of the inconvenience of consulting a 6,000,000-card catalogue to find the call numbers of books in a specific field. The fourth part would list the entries (excluding periodicals and serials) chronologically by date of publication. This chronological list would obviously be of some value as a reference tool, and could also yield information about the quantity and rate of publication in a field and help to determine patterns of development as well as strengths and weaknesses in the collection.

Before converting the estimated 1,600,000 entries in the shelflist, it was necessary to undertake a small pilot project to determine the feasibility and cost of shelflist conversion and to gauge the usefulness of the new alphabetical and chronological arrangements. Historical works on the Crusades have been placed in a special classification in Widener, and this small segment of the shelflist, containing 1,200 entries, was selected as the pilot project to test formats and provide experience, because it was the smallest meaningful class in the Widener stacks and yet contained an excellent representation of the handwriting, language, and conversion problems that would be encountered in the larger classes.

In the pilot project and in the initial phases a decision was made to accept the standard upper-case computer print. This reduced the time and cost of keypunching and the writing and testing of programs, and, while less attractive and less legible than would have been preferred, upper case was believed to be adequate for shelflist requirements. Keypunching proved to be less difficult than had been anticipated, however, and in June 1966 the input requirements were changed to include upper and lower case and diacritical marks. Unfortunately, the available computer print chain, though it can print upper and lower case characters, does not have the diacritical marks.[6] This defect will be remedied in the future either by acquiring an expanded print chain or by using a photocomposition process for the production of printer's copy.

Two versions of the classification schedule were made. For the pilot project the existing form of the schedule was edited, typed, and reproduced by offset to serve as the table of contents to the list. (This process was later computerized.) In addition, each heading in the schedule, together with its corresponding call number, was keypunched on cards which were then merged by machine with the main deck of cards containing the shelflist entries. Finally, all cards were converted to magnetic tape, which is used for sorting and printing and serves as the master record.

The programming for the pilot project and subsequent upper-case work was done in Autocoder by Forest M. Palmer,[7] Associate University Librarian. The family of programs for upper and lower case work was written by Mrs. Susan K. Martin and Charles W. Husbands, systems librarians. A canned sort program (IBSYS) is used to obtain the alphabetical and chronological lists on the IBM 7094 computer; the rest of the processing is done on an IBM 1401 computer in Widener.

The pilot project, which was completed by January 1965, proved that conversion could be done at an acceptable cost. In order to test formats, printing costs, and the reaction of users, a paper-cover edition of the four-part Crusades shelflist was produced by offset in January and distributed to professors and librarians both in Cambridge and elsewhere. This first shelflist was received with considerable interest and enthusiasm and it was decided to continue conversion operations and to publish the completed classes in a numbered series entitled the *Widener Library Shelflist*. Arrangements were made with the Harvard University Press to handle the sale and distribution of the volumes.

To date twenty volumes have been published and several others are in preparation.[8] The volumes are priced to cover some computer costs and all costs of printing and distribution, but the Library is absorbing all conversion and editorial expenses as part of its regular budget. At the present time, six keypunchers or paper-tape typists, an editor, and a systems librarian are working full-time on shelflist conversion. Sales and subscriptions for the series (largely to libraries both domestic and foreign) have reached a level that provides a secure financial base for the venture, and continuation of the series seems to be assured.

Shelflist conversion at its present level has become an established activity and thus far more than 300,000 entries, nearly 20 per cent of the total, have been converted. As the number of titles in the machine system grows to a critical size, the Library will have a data bank large enough to make possible meaningful experiments in manipulating the data in various ways and for various purposes. Each entry has its basic elements tagged and has been assigned a language code, a volume count, and a serial or monograph code. Some possible future uses for this data bank that suggest themselves are production of book cards for a circulation system, production of classified accessions lists, and the creation of new finding lists based on combinations of language, date, and place of publication. The merging of several related classes into a single list has already been accomplished with excellent results. The production of updated editions for internal use and, whenever it seems desirable, for publication is a simple matter. One line of development which is particularly interesting is the possibility of turning the Library's shelflist into a true classified catalogue by assigning as many base classification numbers to current books as their subject content would require. One number would indicate the physical location of the book and the others would merely indicate facets of content. A single book could then appear several times and in various classes. With slight modifications the existing system can accommodate this innovation. Another interesting potential development is the attempt of the Institute for Latin American Studies at the University of London to use the Latin American shelflist tapes as the basis for building a union list in machine-readable form of Latin American holdings in British libraries.

As it now stands, the Widener shelflist program, like many other present library computer systems, is regarded as an interim system designed to extract the maximum return from a simple existing bibliographical record of the contents of the Library. It is expected that in time the system will become obsolete and the imperfect shelflist entries will be superseded by standard bibliographical records in the emerging Library of Congress MARC II format about which more will be said later. The expectation is that a central bibliographical agency will convert and distribute these entries. It seems reasonable to suppose, however, that this conversion effort is still some years in the future and that, in the meantime, Harvard will have realized a satisfactory return on its investment in converting an abbreviated bibliographical record.

As an important by-product, the Widener shelflist project has provided a firm foundation upon which to build other library automation projects. It provided the initial justification for having the Harvard Computing Center locate one of its IBM 1401 systems in the Widener building. It also helped justify the creation of a Data Processing Department with a regular budget, an experienced staff, input equipment, and a sizable block of space in which to work. The existence of this staff, equipment, and organization have made it possible for the Library to take on new projects in a routine manner. The shelflist project also provided incentive and the means for embarking on an important program for rehabilitating the basic tools that are used by the Catalogue Department, such as the classification schedules and the cumulative supplement to the subject-headings list, both of which are being converted to machine-readable form and produced in multiple copies for internal use. These and other projects will be briefly described in the following paragraphs.

Classification Schedules and Subject-Headings List

The book and journal collections in Widener are classified according to a unique scheme which was developed and is maintained by the staff of the Catalogue Department. In 1965 the class schedules for the scheme existed in only two typewritten copies which had a large accumulation of corrections and additions and were badly in need of revision. Since clean and correct copies of the schedules were wanted in connection with shelflist publication, a major program was undertaken in 1966 to revise and edit the schedules and to use computer technique to facilitate the process. The schedules are converted into machine-readable form and a computer program[9] is used to facilitate editing and to format and print them for in-

ternal use as well as for publication in the shelflist volumes.

The *List of Subject Headings Used in the Public Catalogue* was in a state similar to the classification schedules. It is a system unique to Harvard (but following closely that of the Library of Congress); the last typescript edition had been completed in 1931 and numerous additions and changes had been made. A new edition in multiple copies was badly needed and work on this, which began in January 1964, was completed in July. All headings in the list were typed on tabulating cards, one line per card, and the cards were then photographed by a high-speed automatic (Listomatic) camera to produce masters for printing a limited edition for internal use.[10]

The Listomatic process was selected because upper and lower case typography with diacritical marks was essential, and in 1964 the available computer print-chains at Harvard were limited to the standard 48 character upper case font. The plan also called for maintaining the list by issuing periodic cumulative supplements by Listomatic, but this was discontinued because the supplements were too small for efficient production by this high-volume-oriented process. When an upper and lower case computer print-chain became available in 1966, a system for producing the supplement to the list was designed and a program was written for printing the supplements in an efficient two-column format. Conversion of data for the supplement to machine-readable form and production by this method on a quarterly basis have become routine. The same system can be used to format and print the basic list when it becomes sufficiently out-of-date to warrant a new edition.

Acquisitions Ordering and Accounting

The old manual system of ordering and accounting for books had been put under considerable strain in recent years because of the increasing volume of work and because of the necessity for obtaining greater fiscal control over the Library's limited book funds. The system was geared to an earlier period when the rate of acquisitions was somewhat lower and funds were sufficient to cover normal demands upon them. By 1966, with needs in many subjects exceeding the available resources, it was clear that the loose existing system was no longer adequate and a new approach was needed. The experience of several other academic libraries with computer-based systems indicated that mechanization was both technically and economically feasible and would produce the kind of stringent control over outstanding orders and book-fund accounts that was required. In the spring of 1966, Colin McKirdy, a librarian experienced in computer-based acquisitions systems, joined the staff and was assigned the task of designing a computer-aided ordering and accounting system for Widener. Since an IMB 1401 computer was to be installed in the Library before the end of the year, it was decided the system around that machine. Certain limitations of this computer, which has only 8,000 positions of core storage and no random access (disc) capability, and a limited budget for computer time dictated that the initial system should be as simple and economical as possible.

The system was put into effect in September 1967 with a minimum of change-over problems and has proved to be as valuable as was anticipated; refinements are being added in the light of this experience. The new system provides more rapid, more comprehensive, and more accurate information on the status of accounts and funds than had been available, and eliminates a good deal of drudgery, such as the manual conversion of foreign currencies. The next step will probably be expansion of the system to include periodical subscription data.

Participation in the MARC Experiment

All of the projects previously described were local developments without direct relationship to activities on a national level. This was necessarily the case because, until late in 1966 when the Library of Congress launched the MARC experiment,[11] there had been no significant program linking research libraries in a common effort to solve library automation problems. The advent of the MARC experiment marked the beginning of a line of development which will eventually culminate in a network linking the nation's research libraries in a communications system based on computers and reprography.

One prerequisite to a network of this kind is the development of a standardized format for recording bibliographical data in machine-readable form. The Machine Readable Catalog experiment (MARC) was an effort by the Library of Congress to take the first step in designing and testing such a format. The first version of the format, known as MARC I, was a system for tagging and identifying the many elements in a catalogue entry so that they could be manipulated by machines in various ways and for various purposes. The Library of Congress undertook to convert its catalogue data for current English-language books into machine form in the standard format and to distribute magnetic tapes containing this data to sixteen participating libraries on a weekly basis. The experiment ran for a year and Harvard was one of the participants. The basic goal was to discover and investigate the problems involved in distributing and using catalogue data in this form; as a result, there is now a foundation upon which to build an improved standard format and distributing system. The experimental system has been continued and is evolving into an operational one; during July 1968, using magnetic tape, the Library of Congress will begin to distribute much of its catalogue data in an improved format (MARC II) on a regular subscription basis.

Harvard made a substantial contribution to this common effort and gained considerable experience in manipulating tape files of complex data. Since this was an experimental project, the Library made no attempt to integrate the MARC data into its routine cataloguing operations, but rather limited itself to studying the promptness of receipt of the data and to writing programs for retrieving entries for books in particular subject areas and for creating name and title indexes to the tapes.[12]

The MARC experiment as conceived by the Library of Congress was limited to a one-way flow of catalogue data, from the Library of Congress to the sixteen participants; however, since the network that can be expected to evolve from MARC will evidently require two-way exchange of data, the Harvard Library applied to the National Science Foundation for a grant to enable it to supplement its participation in the MARC project by experiments with input and transmission of data.[13] Funds from this grant, which was approved in December 1966, were to be used to pay for adapting the systems design and programming developed at the Library of Congress and for using the same equipment (a Dura Mach-10 paper-tape typewriter) and similar editing and production methods to put into machine-readable form data produced by Harvard cataloguing. Thus Harvard would be able to put samples of its original cataloguing on magnetic tapes and send them to the Library of Congress in order to study the problems involved in making the MARC concept a two-way exchange. In a secondary but related experiment, the Library also proposed to use the same equipment in comparing the efficiency and cost of paper-tape input with the IBM 029 Keypunch which was being used for the shelflist conversion project. The latter study was completed on schedule but the former—adaptation of the MARC input system—was considerably delayed when the MARC I format was superseded by MARC II. This made it necessary for the Library of Congress to redesign its input system, a task which is still in progress at this writing.

BENEFITS OF WORK TO DATE

The Library's work in automation has produced some results of immediate practical value; it has also prepared the Library to undertake further work from which it should benefit greatly in the long run. It has already provided more efficient circulation and acquisitions systems, and has renovated basic records, including the subject-headings list, classification schedules, and the official copy of the shelflist. Useful bibliographical tools such as the published volumes of shelflists and the list of current journals in the sciences have also been produced. Even so, these products of work to date are less significant than the foundation for future advances that has been provided by the development of a general approach to library automation in the Harvard context, the building of a capable and experienced professional and clerical staff, the procurement of various pieces of electronic data-processing equipment including card-handling machines, keypunches, paper-tape typewriters, and an IBM 1401 computer system, as well as the fitting out of an adequate space in an already overcrowded building for this staff and equipment. Moreover, all these elements were welded into an effective organizational structure with a regular annual budget when a combined Data Processing and Photographic Services Department was created in 1966. In short, the projects described above have served as the vehicle for building a capability to undertake increasingly complex automation activities in the coming years.

The merging of the Photographic Services unit with Data Processing may at first glance seem somewhat premature, but this is a natural and logical relationship and one which will have increasingly important implications as both technologies develop concurrently and become increasingly interdependent in the future. One initial result of this merger has been the utilization of experience gained in shelflist publication and distribution to create book catalogues by photo-graphing cards in languages which cannot yet readily be processed by computers. *The Catalogue of Hebrew Books in the Harvard University Library* in six volumes is currently in preparation, and production of a catalogue of Arabic books in four volumes will be undertaken shortly. Other projects drawing upon this experience with photographic technology and data processing are under consideration.

FUTURE DEVELOPMENTS

The development of a MARC II input system for current cataloguing at Harvard is the Library's most important project and deserves the highest priority for the immediate future, because this is the foundation upon which future automation of the bibliographic apparatus will be built. The acceptance of the MARC II format as the standardized communications format for bibliographical data marks the beginning of a new era in library automation. This has international as well as national implications.[14] In the pre-MARC II period, every system was unique; all the programming and most of the systems work had to be done locally. In the post-MARC II period, libraries will begin to benefit from systems and programs that will be developed by the Library of Congress and elsewhere, because they will be designed around the standard format. The effect will be to accelerate and facilitate library automation. An input system for current cataloguing will be the first package available, and this will be followed by programs to sort and manipulate the data in various ways. The task of the Harvard Library will be to adapt these sub-systems and programs to its own particular operating environment in order to develop the capability for inputting local cataloguing data in the standard format. It will also have to develop an efficient means of altering, adding to, and making effective use of the catalogue data on tapes that will be supplied by the Library of Congress on a regular basis beginning in July 1968.

Work on the MARC II format has been brought to a point where this format can be used for monograph entries, but a considerable amount of development remains to be done before it can be used to describe serial entries with their detailed holdings statements. This work is actively in progress as part of the recently organized National Serials Data Program sponsored jointly by the Library of Congress, the National Library of

Medicine, and the National Agricultural Library.[15] A standard serials format within the MARC II framework is expected to emerge within a year, and work will then proceed on a national serials inventory in machine-readable form. This is a program which will have a significant influence on the direction and rate of library automation in all libraries, including Harvard. To adopt fully the MARC II system and its serial variant in the Harvard context will be a formidable task; but the potential return will make it well worth the investment of time and energy that will be required over the next several years. Once this central and basic module of the bibliographical system has been designed and put into operation, the present acquisitions, circulation, and shelflisting modules can be redesigned to make them all mesh into a single integrated system.

Ultimately the entire retrospective bibliographical record will have to be converted to machine-readable form in these standard formats before a truly integrated bibliographical system can be implemented in large research libraries. For each library to undertake to convert its own catalogues would be prohibitively expensive, and it seems reasonable to assume that procedures will be developed and financial resources provided for organizing this conversion at a national bibliographical center with a central data bank that each library can use to recreate its own catalogues in machine-readable form.[16]

Developments in the field of library automation since 1960 have been extremely rapid and somewhat chaotic, with an orientation toward purely local systems. With the advent of the MARC experiment two years ago and other developments on a national level, the orientation is beginning to shift toward national or standard systems, and some trends and guidelines are beginning to emerge. Though it is still too early for a library such as Harvard to attempt to lay down a rigid plan and timetable for the development of a master integrated system, Harvard has been able to adopt a general approach toward automation. That approach can be characterized as evolutionary or pragmatic, and this paper has attempted to describe it. Harvard is building a flexible capability for developing increasingly complex systems and for contributing to and capitalizing on developments on a national and even international level while continuing to get the maximum practical benefits from its locally oriented systems.

FOOTNOTES

[1] The libraries of the University of Chicago, Washington State University, and Stanford University are notable examples.

[2] The various approaches to library automation are discussed at greater length in Richard De Gennaro, "The Development and Administration of Automated Systems in Academic Libraries," *Journal of Library Automation*, I (Spring 1968) [in press].

[3] Foster M. Palmer, *Punched Card Circulation System for Widener Library–Harvard University* (Cambridge, Harvard University Library, 1965). 29 l. A gift from Alexander M. White, '25, helped to defray expenses of installing the new system.

[4] Harvard University Library, *Current Journals in the Sciences* (Cambridge, 1965). 90 p.

[5] Richard De Gennaro, "A Computer Produced Shelflist," *College and Research Libraries*, XXVI (July 1965), 311–315, 353.

[6] Harvard University Library, Data Processing and Photographic Services Department, *Input Procedures for Widener Library Shelflist Conversion; Classification Schedule Conversion; Subject Heading List and Supplement* (January 1968). 24 l.

[7] For a technical description of the project in its early stages, see Foster M. Palmer, "Conversion of Existing Records in Large Libraries, with Special Reference to the Widener Library Shelflist," pp. 57–80 in *The Brasenose Conference on the Automation of Libraries, Proceedings of the Anglo-American Conference on the Mechanization of Libraries held at Oxford . . . 30 June-3 July 1966* (London & Chicago, Mansell, 1967.)

[8] Published classes include: *Crusaders; Africa; Twentieth Century Russian Literature; Russian History Since 1917; Latin America; Bibliography; Reference Collections; American History; China, Japan and Korea; Periodical Classes; Education; Literature; Southern Asia;* and *Canadian History and Literature.* In preparation are: *Latin American Literature; Economics;* and *Slavic History and Literatures.*

[9] The initial computer program was written by Foster M. Palmer and a later expanded version was written by Charles W. Husbands.

[10] Harvard College Library, *List of Subject Headings used in the Public Catalogue* (Cambridge, Harvard University Library, 1964). 817 p.

[11] Henriette D. Avram and Barbara Markuson, "Library Automation and Project MARC," pp. 97–127, in *The Brasenose Conference . . .* (see note 7).

[12] Cf. the summary by the officer of the Library chiefly responsible for Harvard relations with the project: Foster M. Palmer, *Harvard University Library Participation in the MARC Project* (February 1, 1968). 18 l. and Appendix, 200 p.

[13] *Implementing the MARC Project Input System for Current Cataloguing in the Harvard University Library, A Proposal Submitted to the National Science Foundation, Office of Scientific Information Services*, Richard De Gennaro, Principal Investigator (November 2, 1966), 9 l.

[14] The *British National Bibliography* has adopted a MARC II compatible format as a standard and is developing a computerized bibliographical input and distribution system for British publications coordinated with that of the Library of Congress.

[15] Elaine W. Woods, *National Serials Data Program (Phase 1), A Working Paper* (Washington, Library of Congress, August 1967). 12 l.

[16] One possible method has been suggested by Richard De Gennaro, "A Strategy for the Conversion of Research Library Catalogs to Machine Readable Form," *College and Research Libraries*, XXVIII (July 1967), 253–257.

An Integrated Computer-Based Bibliographic Data System for a Large University Library: Problems and Progress at the University of Chicago

by Charles T. Payne

The University of Chicago Library is working on a project for the development of an integrated, computer-based, bibliographical data system for a large university library. This project title is awkward, but it is descriptive, and it stresses some important features of the project: (1) a third generation computer with random-access disk files and remote terminal access capability is being used to implement a real-time library data processing system; (2) the library system design is based on the operational requirements of a large university library and does not attempt to solve the problems of other types of libraries nor those of national systems; (3) the system is highly integrated in that all processing data for the technical processing operations (acquisitions, cataloging, binding, etc.), as well as bibliographic descriptive data, are handled in a single system; and (4) the title emphasizes, we hope, that this work is developmental and experimental.

The long range goals of this project are those of a totally automated library system and thus can now be defined only in general terms. Enormous problems will have to be faced before any sort of total library system can be achieved, including problems such as file conversion, massive file organization and management, and related searching techniques. Even in the early stages of development, where the system design has been defined in detail, much original development work had to be done in implementing and, at times, in nudging forward the state of the art of computer applications. Nothing in our development to date has shown our approach to library automation to be invalid. It will be some time, however, before we have proceeded far enough and have had sufficient operating experience to make meaningful evaluations of costs, benefits, and performance.

A number of factors have helped shape the project design and development. Among the most important is Herman Fussler, the Director of the University of Chicago Library, who has long been an advocate of the application of machine technologies to solve library problems and who has expended a great deal of effort on the problems of how libraries, both locally and at national levels, can best take advantage of the emerging computer technology. His influence has been important in the development of this project both in long-range planning and in handling of immediate realities. A second factor is the situation at Chicago which demands consideration of both the immediate problems of a badly overcrowded Harper Library and the expectation of vastly different operational conditions in the projected new Joseph Regenstein Library. This situation has affected both the project schedules and the system design. The third major factor influencing the project development was the emergence of a third generation computer with its enormous potential for library systems development. This came during our planning phase, and we made the decision to by-pass punched card and batch processing development and move directly to an on-line operation. The project has cut its teeth on-line, so to speak, and it has been a learning experience. Another and most important factor in the development of this project has been the generous cooperation of the National Science Foundation in providing a substantial portion of the funding. Progress on the project would have been much slower without this aid.

It is good to have long-range plans, even if ill-defined, but in the real world of system design and implementation one must proceed in well-ordered stages and must work within the confines of the possible, or almost possible, and make use of on-the-shelf equipment. The first stage in the

SOURCE: Reprinted from the *Proceedings of the 1967 Clinic on Library Applications on Data Processing* (Graduate School of Library Science, University of Illinois, 1968) pp. 29-40, by permission of the publisher. Copyright 1968 by the University of Illinois Board of Trustees.

project was called the Book Processing System. The remainder of this paper will be a description of the Book Processing System, its implementation, problems, and present state, followed by a discussion of the implications of on-line technology.

In library technical processing operations almost all work can be described in terms of data handling, including those intellectual operations in book selection and in cataloging. The over-all design feature of the Book Processing System is to incorporate all data relating to an item being processed into a single machine record. This includes the bibliographical descriptions, the various processing information such as dealer, fund, bindery, etc., and other operational data such as time in cataloging, cataloger's identification, etc. All production output is generated from the machine records, including orders, claims, cancellation or confirmation notices, fund accounting and invoice processing reports, catalog cards, bindery tickets, book pocket and spine labels, distribution lists, processing file lists, operational statistics, etc.

The potential savings by elimination of repetitious copying, sorting and file maintenance are substantial. In addition, from a given point, the library is creating machine readable records for all materials processed. This seems to solve the problem of machine readable records for future material. If only someone would now solve the problem of the past—the problem of conversion of retrospective records.

In order to handle all of the different data by machine it is necessary to identify and define each element of information that goes into a record. These elements of data are identified by tagging codes. The data elements (with few exceptions) and therefore the item records, are variable in length. Basically, our tagging codes are three-digit numbers which define the various elements of information, e.g., 010 item number, 035 dealer, 520 title, etc. In addition, certain tagging codes initiate actions within the computer system at the time of input. Other codes can change the status of a record within the file. Still others affect or direct output processing and formatting. Every tagging code has a definition that includes input requirements, data content and form, and (if any) resulting processing operations. A numerical code scheme for machine identification of data elements was adopted early in the development of this project. Tagging codes had been used elsewhere for handling bibliographical data and no obviously superior scheme was readily apparent.

Counts of the total number of possible elements in bibliographic and processing quickly led to use of a 3-digit number. The provided enough code positions so that the various types of entries were assigned individual codes. The output format, therefore, can be defined by the tagging code and no references need to be made elsewhere to determine this. It was possible to build in relationships between the various types of entries.

Over one hundred specific tagging codes were assigned, about two-thirds of which cover bibliographic description. The various elements that make up the complete record can be input at different times. The first input creates the record in the machine file. In operation, the elements of data are input at the time of generation in the library, e.g., at the time of ordering and receiving material, or when it is cataloged. We also have editing routines for correcting or altering previously input data.

The computer used for implementation of this system is an IBM 360 model 30 computer. This is a small computer and it has a modest core size of 32 K bytes. The computer and peripheral equipment are housed across campus from the Library and its use and costs are shared with other groups. Simultaneous, shared use of the computer has been worked out for applications of both the Library and the Maniac III experimental computer project of the Institute for Computer Research. This is not, however, a large scale, time-shared operation in the true sense.

Connected to the computer are two disk drives with about 14.5 million character on-line storage capacity. The Library has two IBM 1050 terminals. These are connected by telephone line to the computer. Each 1050 unit consists of a typewriter keyboard and printer, paper-tape reader and punch, and an auxiliary printer. The printing elements are the easily interchangeable "golf ball" type, similar to the Selectric typewriter, and offer the potential of providing libraries with a very large character set capability, at a relatively modest cost. It will take some sales potential, however, to persuade the manufacturer to develop the character set potential.

The type of terminal described above is known as a slow speed terminal. The maximum line transmission rate is about fifteen characters per second—much slower than a high speed line printer. We are using the 1050 for printing catalog cards at the present time. The printing speed is slow, but this is not a disaster in terms of computer time when operating in a shared, or multi-programming mode.

It takes the computer the same amount of time to format a card for output whether for a high or slow speed printer, and it is free to do other work while printout is going on.

We do not see the 1050 as a permanent solution for the bulk of production printout. We will probably continue to use these or similar terminals for input, for production printout needed in the library on a tight schedule, such as orders, foreign alphabet printout material, for worksheet printout, etc. For the bulk of catalog card printout, a high speed line printer with the universal character set may be used if it becomes available. Various reported developments in non-impact printers sound very interesting and may be a future possibility. In any case, efforts have been made to keep the machine records independent of the means of input or of output. The stored machine records are coded in 360 internal code. The records as such are not formatted for output, but are merely strings of tagged data. The machine record does not look like a catalog card. This data handling system should be versatile enough to allow for any future developments in input-output equipment.

So far discussion of the Book Processing System has concerned data handling—the item record and its elements—and equipment; this was preliminary to talking about programming. In any computer processing, there are two aspects of the programming to consider—the system software, or computer operating system programs, and the applications programs. In the normal course of batch processing, the computer system software can be pretty much ignored. The programmer adapts to the existing operating systems and languages in the development of his programs. Further, most university computation centers have developed large, established sets of system software that will cover almost any need.

It is when the basic operating software for a computer system does not exist that it becomes most noticeable. Our early experience on the 360/30 was with an "undebugged" basic operating system—data file management programs that no one could make work, autotest programs for "debugging" that were themselves "undebugged," and a complete absence of teleprocessing control programs. In effect, although we have called Book Processing implementation our first phase, our actual first phase was to develop an operating computer system.

The situation is vastly improved now. New and improved software packages have been released by the manufacturer. It is not even absolutely necessary to program in assembly language anymore. But the basic lessons are still there: (1) the software must perform the function required; (2) it must be thoroughly tested; and (3) in any on-line operation it must be resident in core at all times. This latter can become a critical factor in simultaneous shared use of the computer where core size is small.

The applications programs for an on-line operation must be available when called. This means that the applications programs must be resident in core or be available in on-line, random access storage. It quickly became apparent that all of the Book Processing applications programs could not be held in core. In fact, as it worked out, not even the entire set of programs for certain single operations (i.e., catalog card format) could be held at one time and, therefore, program overlays have since been used.

For the input phase the system will:

(a) call in the proper programs on command from the library terminals,

(b) set the conditions to accept data from the library,

(c) check each incoming record against the file to see if it is a new record or update of existing record and call in this indicated data file management program,

(d) scan the input for logical errors,

(e) edit out unwanted blanks, carriage returns, line feeds, tabs, etc.,

(f) convert codes BCD to hexadecimal,

(g) scan for output distribution requests,

(h) create entry in key table for requested output,

(i) enter data into the file, and

(j) perform necessary editing.

These programs are operational and will handle input of all record elements that have been defined so far. We also have operational a major off-line set of programs that construct output stacks working from the input key table. The stack table programs work now for catalog cards only.

From the initial input for distribution, the input phase programs create a key table. The off-line stack program sorts these by type of output (now catalog cards only). From the key table and from the data files, these programs create entries in the stack tables for every card wanted. The new stack entries are merged with previous entries remaining from incomplete output printing. These stacks are sorted by location, by type of array, and by entry (or call number).

The catalog card output phase is a set of programs for on-line production output and is also operational and in use. This is a complex set of programs, but very quickly explained. It does the following:

(a) accepts command from the library terminal and calls in programs,
  (b) selects stack tables for requested locations,
  (c) selects card for output,
  (d) formats call numbers and saves,
  (e) formats text (lines and words) and saves,
  (f) formats card, and
  (g) prints out.

All but the print-out takes but a fraction of a second and then the computer waits to do the next card. In simultaneous operation with Maniac applications, it works for them during this period. This output gives cards for each requested location in filing array. Work is in progress on programs to include charge card, pocket label, and order printing production.

Two additional useful programs are in operation. One prints, on demand, the exact form of the machine record for any item, the only change being translation of machine code to output printing characters. The other program gives counts of the card stacks and is used to schedule output printing. The next major applications programming effort will go into fund bookkeeping, invoice handling, and other acquisitions processing.

The procedures described above are still a long way from a total functioning library system. Much work that had not been tried before has been performed, however, and some things are beginning to be known about this mode of operations. A year ago no one knew about some of the things which now appear obvious. We can see many implications of on-line processing. Some, in conclusion, are discussed below:

(1) System development will become open-ended; the almost unlimited opportunity for change and improvement is irresistible. There is no point where you can say that this is as far as you want to go.

(2) This means that the library systems development staff, the computer systems staff, and the programming staff will become a permanent part of the library and will not be just a temporary bother.

(3) The combination of high core requirements and low computer utilization indicates that future economies will be in the large, university-wide, time-shared computer rather than the computer dedicated to library use alone.

(4) On-line library operations will, of necessity, be simultaneous shared computer operations, even on a dedicated machine. By the time one implements systems for technical processing, with heavy input/output requirements, plus circulation, with immediate response needs, the library will be time-sharing with itself.

(5) In discussions of on-line operation, one frequently hears mentioned the prospect, usually imminent, of putting a terminal on every cataloger's desk or in faculty offices, or scattered around elsewhere. Our experience is that lines are expensive, the terminal equipment is expensive, and the transmission control unit at the computer end is expensive. Rather than spread terminals around we have tried to effect maximum line utilization for terminals we have. The economics on this should improve, but until they do, it seems likely that most on-line terminals will be stationed in data processing rooms and at specific heavy-load work counters.

(6) The library needs staff members trained both in library operations and in computer science. It has been our experience that computer people will underestimate the library requirements by at least an order of magnitude even when the requirements are documented. The library needs a voice that can talk to the computer policy committee and look after the long-range interests of the library. The library should participate in the planning of computer facilities and see that its future plans and requirements are taken into consideration.

Library Automation at UCLA

by *Anthony Hall*

The UCLA Library has been engaged for the past six years in an active program of study and development of automated systems for library operations. Thus, the Library has been involved in automated developments almost from the beginning of the current wide-spread interest and has maintained a position of leadership among other large research libraries.

At present there are more than twenty-four staff members, including professional librarians, computer programmers, and technical support people, engaged full-time in the development of automated systems in the UCLA Library. This figure does not include the time spent by library administrative personnel and others who devote considerable portions of their time to automation work in addition to their regular line responsibilities.

Developments in library automation have progressed at an ever-increasing rate over the past few years but have been hampered to some extent, particularly in large institutions, by lack of research support funds. This situation began undergoing a dramatic change, with funding last year of a major feasibility study to be conducted at the Library of Congress to determine the uses to which automation may be utilized in the national library for internal processing and for interaction with other research libraries. The first development of this program, code named Project MARC (Machine-Readable Catalog Copy), which has been initiated with the installation of a computer in the Library of Congress, involves the distribution, by the Library of Congress, of computer tapes containing machine-readable cataloging copy. These tapes are being distributed to a small group of libraries on a test basis over a one year period. Following this trial period, the Library of Congress anticipates transmission of the data directly from its computer center to the participating libraries by means of data transmission terminals. The UCLA Library is one of the ten research library participants in this important project.

Two additional developments which are of primary importance to systems work in large research libraries have recently taken place. The first is the awarding of a grant by the National Science Foundation to the University of California Institute of Library Research, to develop a Center for Information Services within the UCLA Library System. Work has commenced on the first phase of this five-year project which will be carried forward jointly by the Institute of Library Research and the UCLA Library.

The second development involves a National Science Foundation grant to the Chicago University Library, which has recently acquired an IBM System/360 computer system, to develop and implement an integrated computer-based data system for library processing operations.

These two programs are completely complementary in fully covering the scope of automation in large research libraries, the Chicago study dealing with internal operating procedures, and the UCLA study covering the retrieval of information for public service and for operational purposes.

AUTOMATION ACTIVITIES AT UCLA

Center for Information Services

The Center for Information Services program involves the development of specifications for computer programs, equipment, and procedures for a library-centered agency which will collect data from a variety of existing automated retrieval systems and will process the data in such a fashion as to make it easily accessible to researchers and other patrons.

The range of information to be covered by this center will be extremely wide since data from a great many disciplines is rapidly becoming available in machine-readable form. Automated retrieval systems in special subject areas such as those being produced by the National Library of Medicine, Chemical Abstracts, NASA, and the Library of Congress; and data-banks of computer stored information containing laboratory results, census information and urban planning data exist in great variety, in terms of coverage, content, depth of indexing, equipment and soft-ware requirements, etc. The Center for Information Ser-

SOURCE: Reprinted from a manuscript copy issued by the Library of the University of California, Los Angeles, 1967, 10p., by permission of Paul Miles, Assistant University Librarian.

vices program aims to coordinate processing so as to standardize the researcher's approach to these systems and thereby make the largest possible amount of data conveniently accessible to him. The Center for Information Services will be the first center of its kind offering access to automated data in a width of scope never before possible.

The Center, which will contain a library computer system, specially trained personnel, and storage facilities for approximately 2,000 reels of data processing tape, is scheduled to become operational in 1969 and will at that time be available to graduate students, faculty and researchers who will have access to the central store of automated data by means of remote terminals located at service points within the University Research Library, in the major branch libraries, and elsewhere on campus. The terminals will be connected to the University Research Library computer system which will in turn be connected to more powerful research computing equipment in the University Computing Facility.

MARC Project

The Library of Congress' MARC Project, mentioned above, requires the active involvement of the UCLA Library in determining the most efficient ways in which machine-readable bibliographic data may be used. This program has met with tremendous enthusiasm to the extent that a large number of libraries have asked to be allowed to participate on a secondary-user basis. As a primary participant, UCLA receives Library of Congress computer tapes weekly, distributes tapes to secondary users, will conduct use and cost studies, and will develop additional programs for manipulation of this data. We plan to conduct local tests involving manipulation of this data "on-line" in anticipation and support of the Library of Congress' suggestion that the data may be available on a direct transmission basis in about a year's time.

The MARC Project offers the possibility of great advances both in terms of potential access to the Library of Congress catalogs by researchers at UCLA and as a means of speeding up the processing of books within the library, thereby providing faster availability to the public.

MEDLARS Search Station

The National Library of Medicine's Medical Literature Analysis and Retrieval System (MEDLARS), which commenced operation in 1963, is perhaps the most advanced of the larger informa-

tion systems now in operation. At the National Library of Medicine, individual articles in several thousand biomedical journals are being analyzed by indexers, and the information entered into computer storage. This data is then presented in periodically issued indexes and is cumulated on tapes which can be searched for the retrieval of information in specific areas. The tape citation file now contains over 450,000 entries and is growing at the rate of some 14,000 per month. Under contract with the National Library of Medicine, the UCLA Library has established a MEDLARS Pilot Demonstration Station within the Biomedical Library where demand searches are currently being carried out, and has participated with the Health Sciences Computing Facility in the reprogramming of MEDLARS tapes for greater machine utilization.

Brain Information Service

The UCLA Biomedical Library is also participating with the National Institute for Neurological Diseases and Blindness in the development of the Brain Information Service, an automated documentation center specifically concerned with the basic neurological sciences. At present a store of citations including data from the MEDLARS files is being compiled on magnetic tape. In the summer of 1967, a study concerning the feasibility of on-line processing utilizing terminals connected to the Health Sciences Computer Facility is scheduled to commence. The Brain Information Service is one of a number of documentation centers which will form a network designed to support research in selected areas of medicine of particular concern to the NINDB.

Clearinghouse for Junior College Information

The UCLA Education and Psychology Library is cooperating with the School of Education in the development of a documentation and retrieval center for junior college information. This clearinghouse is one of twelve centers established through the Educational Research Information Center (ERIC) of the U. S. Office of Education, and will serve as an area of experimentation with the institute of Library Research.

As mentioned earlier, the MARC, MEDLARS, BIS and ERIC systems represent systems which may be incorporated in the Library Center for Information Services at the appropriate time.

The preceding descriptions have dealt with systems which involve library automation in the area of information retrieval and which act to improve library reference service through automation. The MARC project also presents specific advantages in internal library processing, and at this point we will shift emphasis to this aspect of library automation.

The use of computers for financial and inventory records in business is well established. There are massive records of these types in library operations including cycles of requisition, purchase order, payment, accounting, processing and circulation control. Some of these records are very similar to those in business, although, in most instances, the fact that substantial bibliographical and other non-numerical data are inter-related with numerical data means that an adequate system for handling library records is much more complex. Typical business inventories, for example, tend to involve multiple copies of a relatively small range of identical items. Library records, on the other hand, tend to involve single items only, with wide ranges of record complexity, in extremely large numbers. As a rule, the larger the library, the more voluminous will be its files and the greater the complexity of its records.

Analysis of a large research library as a total operating system is a task of such magnitude that it can only be accomplished through the expenditure of very large sums of money. Library budgets until recently have not included funds for research, so that efforts in improving procedures by means of automation have been limited to a few operations within the whole system, usually those which were experiencing difficulty in operating efficiently. Although this approach has much to offer in terms of expediency, it does present difficulties in establishing efficient relations between the various operations where a total-system specification does not exist.

Fortunately, we can now look to the Institute of Library Research and the Library of Congress and Chicago University Library studies to provide a total systems approach to library processing. However, experience has shown that in the case of libraries, few automated systems are directly transferrable because of considerable differences in library systems in terms of such factors as policies, functions, and service patterns as well as significant variations in the equipment which is locally available for data processing. Therefore, we anticipate the use of programs developed by similar institutions as extremely valuable aids, in the development of programs specifically for UCLA Library

operations, rather than as packaged systems which can be applied without modifications. Furthermore, while these larger studies are being developed, we are currently seeking to initiate more efficient operations, improve problem areas, and educate the library staff in the uses of automation.

CURRENT PROJECTS

Current projects in the automation of library processes at UCLA are as follows:

Development of an automated circulation control system in the University Research Library: This system, which is the most advanced now in operation in any research library of comparable size, utilizes IBM data collection terminals and a variety of unit record equipment. Machine-readable book cards, and transaction cards or user identification badges, are inserted into the data collection terminals which produce a punched-card record of the transaction. The terminals are fully compatible with computer operations and it is our intent to install an on-line circulation control system throughout the library system (University Research Library and branch libraries) following the anticipated installation of a computer system in the University Research Library in 1970.

Discussions are continuing on the issuance of campus identification badges which will serve as machine-readable library user badges for all students, faculty and other university personnel. Machine-readable book cards for the circulation system are now being produced as part of the regular cataloging procedure. Book cards for other libraries in the system are soon to be produced in anticipation of the eventual on-line circulation control system.

Development of an automated serials control system in the Biomedical Library: This system, which is now operating on an experimental basis, utilizes a computer for bibliographic control of approximately 12,000 active and inactive serials in the Biomedical Library collection. At present the system is producing check-in cards, bindery notification cards and daily acquisitions lists for about 75 per cent of the titles currently being received. In addition, a complete serials holdings list is generated monthly, and special subject lists of serials titles are being produced on demand. The system was designed with the intent that it be capable of being expanded to cover the total UCLA Library holdings of approximately 40,000 serials records.

Automation of the central serials department fiscal files: The first, report generation, phase of this project will be completed shortly. This will provide much needed fiscal control data which is presently not available. The second phase of this program will aim at the automatic maintenance of this important central file. Development of the automated fiscal file will provide the balance of the record provided for in the aforementioned bibliographic system, thus providing the potential for a complete and unified automated serials control system.

Development of a computer-produced union list of serials (titles and locations) for the UCLA Library System: This will provide valuable control and public service data which is presently not available because of the volume and diversity of files, decentralization of holdings and service, lack of clerical personnel, etc. Again, this interim system will contribute to the overall serials control program in that it will provide input to the total system serials bibliographic file. Publication of this list is tentatively expected in the Fall of 1968.

Automatic production of catalog cards and book catalogs: Using a DURA automatic typewriter, studies are being conducted to determine the feasibility of producing catalog card sets with this equipment. This program will relate directly to the Library of Congress Project MARC described earlier. Very shortly we will investigate the possibility of computer-produced catalog cards using the MARC tapes and input from our own catalog department using the automatic typewriter.

Both the MARC computer tapes and the coded paper tape produced by the automatic typewriters offer potential data for computer-produced book catalogs, acquisitions lists, special bibliographies, etc. Studies to determine the feasibility of producing computerized book catalogs for the UCLA College Library and the Education and Psychology Library are to be initiated soon.

Automation of administrative files: This program has commenced with the conversion of library personnel files to machine-readable form. Since it was felt that the upper-lower case format would be desirable, the data was coded in this form and can be reproduced as desired utilizing the library's special character print chain which is installed in University Computer Facility equipment. A feasibility study is being initiated to determine areas of concentration in and scheduling for the automation of administrative files and procedures.

Automation of technical processing in-process file: A program is being developed to provide for a computer maintained in-process for books being passed through technical processing operations in the Engineering and Mathematical Sciences Library. This program will provide for more complete information and more varied approaches than can usually be provided for in technical processing files. As with the Biomedical serials project, it will provide a pilot project for a possible automated total system in-process operation.

FUTURE DEVELOPMENTS

The projects listed above are all currently in progress. During the period between now and 1969, we anticipate further development as follows:

Circulation Control: Prior to 1970, a computer program will be written for an on-line circulation control system utilizing existing IBM data-collection terminals and an IBM System/360 Library computer system. Beginning with the University Research Library, the College Library and the Education and Psychology Library, most if not all of the remaining branch libraries will be brought into the system progressively as additional terminals are acquired.

Advantages to be gained by this system will be the centralization of records and elimination of a variety of circulation files; at charging points, automatic checking of borrower badges and immediate notification concerning any which may have been invalidated; immediate updating of circulation records and capability for interrogation thereof; at discharging points, immediate notification of hold requests and print-out of hold data for insertion in books; automatic preparation of overdue notices, fine notifications, lists of charges by various groups of borrowers, and lists of reserve books; scheduling of staff for various operations; and preparation of reports dealing with statistical data, budget information and patterns of circulation.

Serials Control: The current projects listed above indicate our progression toward development of an automated central serials control file containing both bibliographical and fiscal data. This development will continue through 1969 toward the eventual development of an on-line control system which we feel is required for efficient control of a collection as large and as widely dispersed as that which exists in the UCLA Library System. Equipment available in the Library in 1970 will make possible the development of an on-line system probably using display terminals at locations where serials are received. Check-in data will be keyed into the terminals as issues are received, thereby updating the central computer file. Benefits will include elimination of many complex manual files; instant input and inquiry capabilities for improved processing and reference operations; automatic preparation of orders, bindery slips, claim notices, fiscal reports and listings by a variety of approaches; automatic encumbering of funds; and production of statistical analyses and other administrative information.

Production of Catalog Cards and Book Catalogs:
The card catalog (central public catalog or the shelf list) is the bibliographic key to the holdings of the library. Development of a total system for the library requires that this file be automated and, together with technical processing files, be made available to processing and service points on a direct-access basis. The size of the UCLA catalog prohibits immediate conversion of the entire file to machine readable form. However, in connection with the Library of Congress MARC Program, we will move toward that eventuality. By 1970 we anticipate computer production of catalog card sets, book cards, book labels, acquisition lists, special bibliographies and book catalogs for significant portions of the collection. We have every reason to believe that automated Library of Congress cataloging data will be available to us on a direct access basis. Planned installation of display terminals in the various library catalog departments will enable cataloging staff to view Library of Congress data; reformat and supplement it, as required for our purposes, directly on the terminals; and automatically enter it into the computer store. Prior to this development, we will investigate the feasibility of entering original cataloging copy, produced locally, into computer storage utilizing the same coding procedure and equipment as that now being used by the Library of Congress. The computer which is to be installed in the University Research Library will be almost identical to the system recently installed at the Library of Congress. Electronic handling of cataloging data will offer tremendous savings in the elimination of present procedures which require continual re-typing, proofreading, revising and filing of a variety of records containing basically the same information. Machine-readable records offer the potential for a computer-produced University of California Union Catalog and a variety of special listings and bibliographies which are now economically unfeasible.

Technical Processing In-Process Files: An Engineering and Mathematical Sciences Library pilot project will provide data concerning the feasibility of an off-line control system for books-in-process. As with serials, it is felt that a total control system for the volume of material passing through all of the library's processing departments will probably have to take the form of an on-line system if it is to offer substantial advantages over existing systems. If this proves to be the case, development of the on-line system will proceed through 1970. There are however, several operations within the over-all technical processing system which may lend themselves to improvements through off-line automation. In the near future we plan to investigate the feasibility of automating the desiderata file, containing material which has been found to be currently out-of-print, and the file containing titles available for exchange with other libraries. Automated procedures should facilitate the frequent review and revision required for efficient maintenance of these files.

A second study for potential automation involves the bindery in-process file which records the progress of books and serials through the binding cycle. Possible benefits resulting from automation would include the automatic preparation of bindery slips for serials as the appropriate number of unbound issues are received; improved file maintenance; automatic charging and discharging of books taken from the circulation collection to be bound; and easily-provided statistical reports dealing with bindery performance.

The on-line general in-process file mentioned above will permit the staff to quickly locate a given book as it passes through the various processing operations in the acquisitions, cataloging, marking and circulation units. Quick and accurate location of individual titles is essential in efficient acquisitions[2] systems in order that unwanted duplication will not occur. At present, manual searching involves long and tedious procedures. Each department needs to know with great accuracy specifically which books are being processed at a given time, both for process control and for public service requirements. Because of these needs, the processing departments maintain a great variety of files, again containing essentially the same data in slightly different form. The on-line central file will eliminate the need for these multitudinous sub-files.

In the automated system, we will provide for advantages such as immediate inquiry and search capabilities; automatic preparation of purchase orders and claims for items not received; automatic encumbrance of funds; periodic preparation of budget statements; computer-produced listings of new books received and automatic preparation of statistical analyses and management data such as special reports on dealer performance and price trends.

The catalog department will be able to use the on-line system to provide a centralized locating device for books assigned to various catalogers, and as a means of displaying the bibliographic data established by the acquisitions unit, thus providing a potential base for the development of the final catalog data. As described earlier, formatting and alterations in the record can be accomplished directly on the display terminals in the catalog department.

Administrative Operations: Finally, we look to continuing automation of library administrative operations to provide, in addition to advantages mentioned above, more efficient control of personnel and office records, supply and equipment funds, and inventory and space assignments; improved budget forecasting information particularly in terms of performance budgeting; and preparation of management information reports involving various areas of concern such as salary and wage trends, changing service patterns and book storage requirements, which will enable the administration very early to become aware of changing aspects within and outside of the system which may effect its performance, and to take appropriate action, possibly based on a test of the proposed changes utilizing a computer-simulated library system.

In our opinion, the specialized nature of library computer programs, the extremely large files involved, the complexity of the records and particularly the special handling problems for the great variety of data to be processed indicate that a computer system should be located in the library and should be administered and operated by library personnel. Accordingly, plans for Unit 11 of the University Research Library now include specific space assignments for an IBM System/360 computer system and auxiliary equipment as well as for systems personnel and a Center for Information Services tape processing and storage area.

The computer system will be used in connection with the Center for Information Services program for presentation of data from the various retrieval systems, on display terminals located throughout the Library system. Tapes will be mounted by Center for Information Services personnel on a scheduled basis. Programs requiring processing on more powerful equipment will be handled through direct coupling with University Computing Facility equipment.

A second function of the library computer will be the processing of library research and development projects such as the proposed on-line serials and acquisition control programs. Library research projects are presently being conducted at The University Computing Facility where equipment and software are oriented toward scientific rather than bibliographic work. Despite excellent cooperation and assistance on the part of the University Computing Facility staff, the normal scheduling of operations and the limitations placed upon the use of the equipment for processing scientific programs, impose severe restrictions upon the efficient processing of Library bibliographic work. The library computer system will be organized specifically for bibliographic data processing and will be capable of efficiently handling the major portion of library research and development programs. Projects requiring more powerful equipment will be run utilizing the connection with the University Computing Facility for processing, and the library facility for input and output.

The third function of the library computer system will be the processing of regular library production work as the various projects described above become operational. As these modules are established on a regularly operating basis and are related to each other, the ultimate goal of a total system for the library will be achieved. Activities occurring in any unit of the Library System will automatically be reflected in the integrated system. Direct connection with data processing facilities at the Library of Congress and other large research libraries will provide a wealth of bibliographic data on an on-line basis. This data, combined with on-line access to centralized in-process and processed data for monographs and serials in the UCLA system, will allow the elimination of a multitude of redundant files in a variety of locations. These capabilities will provide for increased operating efficiency and for the development of new areas of library service.

Bibliographic Automation of Large Library Operations Using a Time-Sharing System— Project BALLOTS

by Allen Barnet Veaner

PROBLEM AND OBJECTIVES

Statement of the Problem

The research library problem has two major components: internal technical processing and user communication. Inundated with a greatly enlarged influx of new materials in various media, the research library's inadequacy in processing new acquisitions for the user is manifest. Solution of this first problem will enable the library to prepare itself for solving the second problem, which calls for transforming the library into a new kind of institution characterized by a two-way communication facility. Provision for effective user feedback will enable the library to work more harmoniously with the user and much more efficiently for him.

The university library exists to communicate bibliographic information and full text to its community of users. As a storage depot, the university library is reasonably efficient, but in relation to the user it is not a sufficiently active instrument; the user is forced to initiate virtually all the action necessary to acquire the information he needs. Behind the alphabetico-logical complexity of the library's chief communication instrument—the card catalog—lies the assumption that the user will energetically seek to master its organization. Unfortunately, this assumption is not true. Comprehension of such a complex instrument is the result of many years of experience, and a brief encounter with library files is often frustrating and stifles further contact. Despite this, the myth still flourishes that the scholar will or should discipline himself to master this tool. We believe that the time has arrived to improve the tool significantly.

Each generation of technological progress exhibits a pattern of time convergence: the interval between generations grows shorter and shorter. In the face of spectacular achievements in space and computer technology, the university research library almost appears as the dinosaur of the modern educational facility: sluggish in response to new user demands, seemingly inflexible in behavior, inextricably tied to the past. It is this very contrast which explains how the modern user's attitudes differ so strongly from those of a generation or two ago. Today's user is no longer content to patiently dig in the labyrinthine maze of bibliographic tools, or conform his thinking to formalized bibliographic rules, or wait long periods to get his research and teaching materials. More often than not he does without and remains frustrated, or goes elsewhere.

Impatience is not the only impediment to effective utilization of library resources. The modern scholar is an interdisciplinary man, who seeks to synthesize new ideas by welding together concepts from a variety of areas. Yet the traditional organization of bibliographic tools, services, indexing and classification schemes, tending as they do to compartmentalize knowledge into static, artificial categories, represent for many researchers the very opposite of their requirements. Hence, in the face of dynamically changing concepts and ideas, the scholar may actually be unable to communicate his inquiry in a manner that is acceptable to the library's tools. In short, the bibliographic instruments which should be the researcher's keys to his source data, are inert. Additionally, catalogs, circulation files and serials records are spatially dispersed, and if users with diverse, overlapping interests are to be served effectively, the inevitable result is replication of records and record maintenance. The most effective researchers are those who enjoy excellent informal, personal contacts with their colleagues (the familiar "invisible college"); it would be highly desirable to provide users with a new kind of instrument, one that provides two-way communication, and which to a certain extent resembles an intelligent, responsive colleague. The development of a sort of "intelligent

SOURCE: Reprinted from a proposal by Stanford University to the Office of Education (1967?), p. 1-6, by permission of David C. Weber, Director, Stanford University Libraries. The Principal Investigator on this project is Allen B. Veaner.

colleague" with whom the researcher can carry out interactive dialogue is an ultimate aim of this project.

Specifically, the problems of disseminating bibliographic data to the academic and research community center about the following factors: the publication explosion, the inability of manual systems to respond rapidly to complex technical processing requirements, slow and ponderous responsiveness in an environment which has grown accustomed to speed, inefficient—and in some instances non-existent—methods of communicating with the user, rapidly rising unit processing costs, and distressingly increasing clerical staff turnover. For instance, although the technical processing staff at Stanford has expanded in proportion to the rate of acquisition increase, the time and effort required to process materials has remained relatively static, and unacceptably meager resources can be devoted to improving services to users. Other major research libraries face similar problems.

Statement of Objectives

Stanford University proposes to continue development of an integrated computer-based, technical processing system having substantially the same detailed objectives outlined in the original proposal. The BALLOTS effort is now, however, within the context of an overall objective broadened considerably in the past eighteen months. Close collaboration between this project and the Stanford Physics Information Retrieval System (SPIRES) enables the Library to formulate as its long range goal the provision and management of a unified, campus wide information system servicing a variety of published machine readable files, as well as private files maintained by the individual user. The Provost and the Director of Libraries have endorsed this reformulation of the library mission within the University.

Meanwhile, those goals specific to the library remain valid and will receive the project's full and complete attention. As detailed in the initial proposal, they are as follows:

(a) Technical processing (procurement, cataloging, finishing and circulation)

1. Provide central bibliographic control over each item being acquired, from the moment a request has been entered, until the corresponding physical item has been acquired and readied for use, regardless of which Stanford library originates the request, where the item

is to be housed, or the method of procurement. This control is to comprehend all items purchased or accepted by gift or exchange, and information concerning materials in process is to be accessible as needed. (Fulfillment of this objective will allow all Stanford libraries to consult with each other concerning book purchase action or plans, and thus spend available book funds more wisely.)

2. Provide rapid local access to Library of Congress MARC data.

3. Eliminate the duplication of bibliographic work now occurring when autonomous libraries outside the Main Library system buy a book already ordered or held by the University, and vice versa.

4. Minimize repeated hand transcription or retyping of data and messages, a task that is particularly onerous in the procurement of out-of-print books but is also burdensome in the book finishing (shelf-preparation) operation.

5. Eliminate most manual filing operations.

6. Drastically reduce errors associated with filing, typing and hand transcription.

7. Speed the flow of physical materials through processing—e.g. through automatic printing, much more rapid file consultation, and simplified record-changing for books that are lost or transferred or replaced by variant editions.

8. Simplify and routinize claiming of missing issues of periodicals.

9. Simplify "check in" of continuation issues by eliminating the need to search for a formal entry.

10. Enable the library to schedule more systematically the binding of periodicals and other serials.

11. Provide all staff selecting books for purchase with unified information on continuation issues not held, for easier filling of lacunae.

12. Prepare to share machine-readable serial information records with neighboring institutions or national research institutions, when possible.

13. Maintain more up-to-date physical control over the collection, so that when a book is requested the Library can accurately report its location, if it is not on the shelf.

(b) User Communications

1. Provide library users with a direct means of communicating with the library, regarding holdings, purchasing, and circulation.

2. Facilitate communication between the Library's book selection personnel (curators, librarians, etc.) and the Library's clientele by providing selectors with a remotely accessible central bibliographic record which indicates the status of any item being added to the collections.

3. Enable users to inquire directly concerning the circulation status of volumes for which there exists a machine readable cataloging record. (There already exists a complete machine-readable catalog for everything in the Meyer Undergraduate Library).

4. Enable user of main catalog to initiate purchase suggestion as byproduct of inquiry which indicates that the Library lacked the requested title.

(c) Management

1. Free supervisory personnel from routine repetitive tasks for work requiring human judgment; specifically, lighten the supervisor's training load for clerical help.

2. Provide authorized persons with immediate budgetary, current expense and commitment information on book funds and other library funds.

3. Prepare regular analyses of book fund expenditures by library unit, broad subject category, country, or region of origin, language, or vendor.

4. Present accurate statistical data in a form immediately useful to management, e.g. graphs and tables of production quantities, lost or misplaced books, hourly payroll expenditures.

5. Unify and simplify the financial records required to maintain continuations and serials without interruption and to process invoices.

6. Generate data to establish usage patterns to determine borrower preferences, optimum shelving locations, policies for discard or storage, need for ordering of added copies, and need for concentration of acquisition in certain subject areas.

DESCRIPTION OF ACTIVITIES

What is to be Done?

An automated technical processing facility combining acquisition and cataloging is to be activated. This facility was designed during the first phase of Project BALLOTS and several successful feasibility demonstrations have been conducted with on-line typewriter terminals. The Library now intends to move ahead with the visual displays already proposed, and begin implementing the design. MARC tapes furnished by the Library of Congress will be converted into machine searchable records and stored on direct access devices. MARC records will form the first part of the automated technical processing system's data base. A second data base, the In-Process File, will be created from selected MARC data and originally keyboarded data to constitute the master record for material being obtained for the Library. Once material has entered the Library and its data certified, another record, the Library Holdings File, will be created. This third data base will be the beginning of a machine readable equivalent of the card catalog.

All three files will be searchable from direct access devices by terminals. Multiple search points will substantially improve inquiry facility for library materials; access will be provided by Library of Congress card numbers, personal authors, corporate authors, title words, conference or meetings, subjects, key words, and dates. Coordinate searching, using any of the above search approaches combined with each other using the logical operators (like AND, OR, NOT) will free the searcher from the rigid, limited search patterns which now characterize bibliographic inquiry.

The In-Process File data will be used for generating all acquisition outputs, i.e., purchase orders, claims, cancellations, notices for the National Program for Acquisition and Cataloging (NPAC), reports to management, statistics, want lists, and notifications to the faculty. This variety of output now requires multiple keyboarding of data, much of it identical. Hence, the automated system, with its single keyboarding requirement, will produce substantial saving of clerical manpower. For current materials, pending search requests will be run against incoming MARC records to eliminate the drudgery of iterative manual searching of Library of Congress records. Duplicate bookkeeping operations will be eliminated. Decentralization of searching will save many wasted footsteps and man-hours. Beginning with the Physics Library, terminals will be installed also in a number of department libraries including Communication, Computer Science, and Law. Also to be included in the initial implementation will be selected acquisition processing for the Law Library. Because law literature and research are branching widely into the social sciences, it is considered essential for librarians in the School of Law and the School of Humanities and Sciences to have ready access to a combined In Process File.

A generalized, file building facility already exists which allows any campus user to build and query a "private file" for his own use at his own or someone else's terminal. Messages may be composed at any terminal, stored in the 360/67, and forwarded to oneself or another user for later querying. It is expected that this message switching, or "store and forward" facility, will provide an attractive means of communicating to faculty and branch libraries notifications of received and processed books. Eventually, notification messages can be regularly matched to a user's "profile" or preference; any user already having a terminal could avail himself of this service at very modest cost, and the plethora of notification slips now distributed could be replaced with a more efficient, customized way of communicating bibliographic notices.

For the circulation function and the technical processing of government documents and serials, system requirements will be established during the second grant period. A circulation system will be designed and implemented. The Meyer Undergraduate Library with its complete, machine-readable bibliographic record, constitutes the ideal test environment for the circulation system. Work on the design of a serials control system will be carefully coordinated with the Library of Congress' National Serials Data Program.

Automation Activities in the Library of Congress

Library of Congress

MARC

Work continued on MARC II, the new format developed for the communication of machine-readable bibliographic information. At the Midwinter Conference of the American Library Association, the format was adopted as a standard by the three divisions most directly affected (ISAD, RSD, and RTSD). As reported, the other two national libraries, NAL and NLM, have also adopted the format for use in their systems. The UK/MARC System, under the direction of the British National Bibliography, will use MARC II in an experimental project in England later this year. A report on MARC II was issued in May, describing the new format in terms familiar to both librarians and computer specialists.

This publication, entitled *The MARC II Format: A Communications Format for Bibliographic Data* (167 p.), is for sale by the Superintendent of Documents, Government Printing Office, for $1.50 a copy.

Computer programs to implement the new format are being written and tested at LC. The developmental period extended beyond the anticipated time and, under a revised schedule, the distribution of tapes under the MARC Pilot Project will be continued until June 30. The changeover to MARC II will take place during July. In August a test tape containing a limited number of records will be issued. In October the Library will begin distribution on a subscription basis of tapes containing catalog records for all current English-language monographs. They may be obtained from the Card Division at an annual cost of $600. Eventually the MARC Distribution Service will be expanded to include other languages and forms of material. The subscription price will be subject to change as the Library gains experience.

The final report on the MARC Pilot Project is in press and will be issued in the early fall. In addition to an account of the Library's experiences during the project, the report includes an appendix reproducing reports made by the MARC participants. A summary of the report is being distributed with this report to ARL and it is also available at the LC booth in the exhibit area.

Central Bibliographic System

Task III—a description of the bibliographic function in system terms—of the work on the Central Bibliographic System was completed on schedule. The final report in four volumes has been delivered to the Library and is being reviewed.

Some of the major features of the recommended system are that it provides for the continuous maintenance and updating of the Library's central files of bibliographic information (the "official catalog," including authority data, the shelflist, acquisition files, shared cataloging files, the serial record, process files, binding files, loan and circulation files, etc.) and allows simultaneous access by staff members throughout the Library to data in all of these files. The recommended system eliminates the need for maintaining manual printing files by automatically selecting, formatting, and composing material for book catalogs. A novel and important feature of the system is that it would be possible to monitor the movement of material by the immediate recording of withdrawals from stacks, returns to issue desks, arrivals of books on decks, and the passage of in-process material between work stations. This would permit staff and users to ascertain rapidly and accurately the status and location of material.

The projected system would accommodate itself to the expanding shared cataloging as well as the other overseas acquisition programs of the Library. The Task III report shows such a system to be technically feasible with equipment that is available on the market. A response time of 5 seconds for real-time queries is shown to be achievable under the projected 1972 load conditions.

With regard to implementation, a modular approach has been decided upon. Specifications for terminal devices will soon be developed as will a study to see if current optical character recognition (OCR) technology offers a feasible method for file conversion.

SOURCE: Reprinted from the *Minutes* of the Association of Research Libraries, June 22, 1968, Appendix M, pp. 95-98, by permission of the Association.

Serials Data Program

The first phase of the development of the National Serials Data Program, being undertaken in cooperation with NAL and NLM, is scheduled to be completed by September 30, 1968. By that date, a content format for serials that is comprehensive, economically feasible, and satisfies user requirements will have been formulated.

The development of a preliminary, but comprehensive list of data elements (Task A) has been completed. It was this list that formed the basis of the user survey (Task B), which has also been completed.

The user survey was conducted for the Library by Nelson Associates, Inc. Its objectives were to elicit responses from potential users of the program as to the desired outputs and services of a national serials system, to obtain comments and suggestions as to the inclusion of certain items in the program, and to give potential users a voice in the development of the program.

A final report on the user survey was submitted by Nelson Associates on May 31, 1968. Altogether 168 persons from 40 institutions were asked to respond to approximately 375 questions and also to comment freely on any specific or general aspects of the program. This report is extremely detailed in its analysis and will supply valuable information to the designers of the serials format.

Work on Task C—analysis and pre-design—is nearing completion. Data elements needed for local control of the national program have been collected and functional flowcharts of the serials operations of the Library have been prepared. Intensive analysis is being done on the data elements, such as indicating alternative ways of representation and identifying problem areas that must be resolved before any decisions on the format can be made. Work has begun on constructing a cost-benefit study to evaluate the expense and difficulty of having a specific data element in the system against the value of having it there.

The development of a universal numbering scheme for serials, a priority item according to the user survey, is being undertaken in cooperation with the Z-39 Committee of the United States of America Standards Institute.

Subject Headings on Computer Tape

As reported previously, the magnetic tapes used to print the seventh edition of the *Subject Head-*ings Used in the Dictionary Catalogs of the Library of Congress* at the Government Printing Office have been converted to conform with the MARC II format structure. The tapes are available from the Card Division for $75 and a detailed explanation of the format will be included with the sale of the tapes. Mail orders must be paid for in advance and cannot be charged to Card Division accounts.

The Information Systems Office has extended the subject headings project to include an in-depth study which will detail the requirements of a subject headings processing system. This system will provide a method of maintaining and updating the machine-readable subject headings tape so as to produce cumulative supplements. The system will also provide a method of converting this tape to a format compatible with GPO requirements for the printing of future editions of the list of subject headings.

LOCATE

As reported previously, the Library of Congress Automation Techniques Exchange (LOCATE) was established in the Information Systems Office to collect and disseminate information about automation programs for libraries. For the present, reference service to other libraries will be limited generally to citations of materials already available at the exchange, but LC plans to expand the activities later to include more services to other institutions.

LOCATE has provided LC with information about existing and proposed automation projects useful in the MARC Pilot Project and will continue to do so in connection with the Library's system development study, both of which affect other libraries. It also is helpful to foreign visitors planning itineraries including library automation projects in specific geographical areas. The LOCATE files are set up by State, within a State by city, and within a city by institution. In addition, a subject file contains material on general automation systems.

When the files are sufficiently developed and organized, LOCATE will give three types of service: (1) reference—preparation of bibliographies and listings of reports, articles, etc.; (2) referral—assistance in response to specific inquiries; and (3) access to the file material.

III

THEORY OF MANAGEMENT

In an article by I. A. Warheit (*Journal of Library Automation,* volume 3, March 1970) the point is made that librarians are only beginning to study computerization from the viewpoint of a unified system. Most computer projects, it is true, have been largely devoted to single functions, such as a serials holding list, or the processing of some function within acquisitions, with little regard to future developments.

In the article by De Gennaro which follows, the logic of developing a unified system is recognized, but the wisdom of moving directly from a manual system to a unified, on-line system is questioned. De Gennaro argues that a library staff needs first to be organized to gain experience with off-line controls. Furthermore, the great expense involved in developing a unified on-line system must be kept in mind.

Many persons have thought of an evolutionary development as consisting of moving from one library process to another (for example, from acquisitions, to circulation, to cataloging) until the whole of the task is completed. De Gennaro, however, provides a quite different insight; to him, the evolutionary process consists of moving from the manual stage to increasingly complex operations in successive stages. In the first stage, using standard, tested equipment, the library organizes its computer development on the existing manual procedures. In the second stage, librarians begin to incorporate significant developments in equipment and software, thus moving towards a unified on-line system. Thus, librarians will be moving from one mechanical system to another, instead of from a manual system to a greatly complicated mechanical system for which they lack the necessary experience.

De Gennaro argues that in the first stage the systems organization should be led by library trained persons who have gained experience with computer projects. The number of computer projects led by librarians certainly bears out his judgment.

But the second stage, says De Gennaro, may require outside consultants, and in this connection he develops a very interesting analogy. As in the planning of a library building, the consultant recommends an architect and a firm to carry out the construction. Working with a program furnished by the library staff, the consultants complete the design details, and then oversee the work of the firm employed to carry out the assignment. Once the assignment is completed to the satisfaction of the consultant and the librarians, it is assumed that the library staff by this time is competent to manage the system designed for it.

As is true of most writers, De Gennaro recommends a systems staff that is not tied to any single department of the library. The chief of this service would presumably report to the chief librarian, would have his own budget, and concern himself chiefly with designing improvements. In automation, a system is never a final product.

The importance of De Gennaro's article has been widely recognized, and it is likely to have considerable influence.

The Development and Administration of Automated Systems in Academic Libraries

by Richard De Gennaro

The first part of this paper considers three general approaches to the development of an automation program in a large research library. The library may decide simply to wait for developments; it may attempt to develop a total or integrated system from the start; or it may adopt an evolutionary approach leading to an integrated system. Outside consultants, it is suggested, will become increasingly important. The second part of the paper deals with important elements in any program regardless of the approach. These include the building of a capability to do automation work, staffing, equipment, organizational structure, selection of projects, and costs.

Since most computer-based systems in academic libraries at the present time are in the developmental or early operational stages when improvements and modifications are frequent, it is difficult to make a meaningful separation between the developmental function and the administrative or management function. Development, administration, and operations are all bound up together and are in most cases carried on by the same staff. This situation will change in time, but it seems safe to assume that automated library systems will continue to be characterized by instability and change for the next several years. In any case, this paper will not attempt to distinguish between developmental and administrative functions but will instead discuss in an informal and nontechnical way some of the factors to be considered by librarians and administrators when their thoughts turn, as they inevitably must, to introducing computer systems into their libraries or to expanding existing machine operations.

Alternative approaches to library automation will be explored first. There will follow a discussion of some of the important elements that go into a successful program, such as building a capability, a staff, and an organization. The selection of specific projects and the matter of costs will also be covered briefly.

APPROACHES TO LIBRARY AUTOMATION

Devising a plan for automating a library is not entirely unlike formulating a program for a new library building. While there are general types of building best suited to the requirements of different types of library, each library is unique in some respects, and requires a building which is especially designed for its own particular needs and situation. As there are no canned library building programs, so there are no canned library automation programs, at least not at this stage of development; therefore the first task of a library administration is to formulate an approach to automation based on a realistic assessment of the institution's needs and resources.

Certain newly-founded university libraries such as Florida Atlantic, which have small book collections and little existing bibliographical apparatus, have taken the seemingly logical course of attempting to design and install integrated computer-based systems for all library operations. Certain special libraries with limited collections and a flexible bibliographical apparatus are also following this course. Project INTREX at M.I.T. is setting up an experimental library operation parallel to the traditional one, with the hope that the former will eventually transform or even supersede the latter. Several older university libraries, including Chicago, Washington State, and Stanford, are attempting to design total systems based on on-line technology and to implement these systems in modules. Many other university libraries (British Columbia, Harvard, and Yale to name only a few) approach automation in an evolutionary way and are designing separate, but related, batch-processing systems for various housekeeping functions such as circulation, ordering and accounting, catalog input, and card production. Still other libraries (Princeton is a notable example) expect to take little or no action until national standardized bibliographical formats have been promulgated, and some order or pattern has begun to emerge from the experimental work that is in progress. Only time will tell which of these courses will be most fruitful. Meanwhile the library administrator must decide what approach to take; and the approach to automation, like that to a building program, must be based on local requirements and available resources (1,2).

For the sake of this discussion the major principal approaches will be considered under three headings: 1) the wait-for-developments approach, 2) the direct approach to a total system, and 3) the evolutionary approach to a total system. The use of outside consultants will also be discussed.

The Wait-For-Developments Approach

This approach is based on the premise that practically all computer-based library systems are in an experimental or research-and-development stage with questionable economic justification, and that it is unnecessary and uneconomical for every library to undertake difficult and costly development work. The advocates of this approach suggest that library automation should not be a moon race and say that it makes sense to wait until the pioneers have developed some standardized, workable, and economical systems which can be installed and operated in other libraries at a reasonable cost.

For many libraries, particularly the smaller ones, this is a reasonable position to take for the next few years. It is a cautious approach which minimizes costs and risks. For the larger libraries, however, it overlooks the fact that soon, in order to cope with increasing workloads, they will have to develop the capability to select, adapt, implement, operate, and maintain systems that were developed elsewhere. The development of this capability will take time and will be made more difficult by the absence of any prior interest and activity in automation within the adapting institution. The costs will be postponed and perhaps reduced because the late-starters will be able to telescope much of the process, like countries which had their industrial revolution late. However, it will take some courage and political astuteness for a library administrator to hold firmly to this position in the face of the pressures to automate that are coming

from all quarters, both inside and outside the institution (3).

A major error in the wait-for-developments approach is the assumption that a time will come when the library automation situation will have shaken down and stabilized so that one can move into the field confidently. This probably will not happen for many years, if it happens at all, for with each new development there is another more promising one just over the horizon. How long does one wait for the perfect system to be developed so that it can be easily "plugged in," and how does one recognize that system when one sees it? There is real danger of being left behind in this position, and a large library may then find it difficult indeed to catch up.

The Direct Approach To A Total System

This approach to library automation is based on the premise that, since a library is a total operating unit and all its varied operations are interrelated and interconnected, the logic of the situation demands that it be looked upon as a whole by the systems designers and that a single integrated or total system be designed to include all machinable operations in the library. Such a system would make the most efficient and economical use of the capabilities of the computer. This does not require that the entire system be designed and implemented at the same time, but permits treating each task as one of a series of modules, each of which can be implemented separately, though designed as part of a whole. Several large libraries have chosen this method and, while a good deal of progress is being made, these efforts are still in the early development stage. The University of Chicago system is the most advanced (4).

Unlike the evolutionary approach, which assumes that much can be done with local funds, home-grown staff, batch processing and even second generation computers, the total systems approach must be based on sophisticated on-line as well as batch-processing equipment. This equipment is expensive; it is also complex, requiring a trained and experienced staff of systems people and expert programmers to design, implement, and operate it effectively. Since the development costs involved in this approach are considerable, exceeding the available resources of even the larger libraries, those libraries that are attempting this method have sought and received sizable financial backing from the granting agencies.

The total systems approach has logic in its favor:

it focuses on the right goal and the goal will ultimately be attainable. The chief difficulty, however, is one of timing. The designers of these systems are trying to telescope the development process by skipping an intermediate stage in which the many old manual systems would have been converted to simple batch-processing or off-line computer systems and the experience and knowledge thus acquired utilized in taking the design one step further into a sophisticated, total system using both on-line and batch-processing techniques. The problem is that we neither fully understand the present manual systems nor the implications of the new advanced ones. We are pushing forward the frontiers of both library automation and computer technology. It may well be that the gamble will pay off, but it is extremely doubtful that the first models of a total library system will be economically and technically viable. The best that can be hoped for is that they will work well enough to serve as prototypes for later models.

While bold attempts to make a total system will unquestionably advance the cause of library automation in general, the pioneering libraries may very well suffer serious setbacks in the process, and the prudent administrator should carefully weigh the risks and the gains of this approach for his own particular library.

The Evolutionary Approach To A Total System

This approach consists basically of taking a long-range, conservative view of the problem of automating a large, complex library. The ultimate goal is the same as that of the total systems approach described in the preceding section, but the method of reaching it is different. In the total systems approach, objectives are defined, missions for reaching those objectives are designed, and the missions are computerized, usually in a series of modules. In the evolutionary approach, the library moves from traditional manual systems to increasingly complex machine systems in successive stages to achieve a total system with the least expenditure of effort and money and with the least disruption of current operations and services (5).

In the first stage the library undertakes to design and implement a series of basic systems to computerize various procedures using its own staff and available equipment. This is something of a bootstrap operation, the basic idea of which is to raise the level of operation—circulation, acquisitions, catalog input, etc.— from existing manual systems to simple and economical machine systems until major portions of the conventional systems have been computerized.

In the process of doing this, the library will have built up a trained staff, a data processing department or unit with a regular budget, some equipment, and a space in which to work: in short, an in-house capability to carry on complex systems work. During this first stage the library will have been working with tried and tested equipment and software packages—probably of the second generation variety—and meanwhile, third generation computers with on-line and time-sharing software are being debugged and made ready for use in actual operating situations.

At some point the library itself, computer hardware and software, and the state of the library automation art will all have advanced to a point where it will be feasible to undertake the task of redesigning the simple stage-one systems into a new integrated stage-two system which builds upon the designs and operating experience obtained with the earlier systems. These stage-one systems will have been, for the most part, mechanized versions of the old manual systems; but the stage-two systems, since they are a step removed from the manual ones, can be designed to incorporate significant departures from the old way of doing things and take advantage of the capabilities of the advanced equipment and software that will be used. The design, programming, and implementation of these stage-two systems will be facilitated by the fact that the library is going from one logical machine system to another, rather than from primitive unformalized manual systems to highly complex machine systems in one step.

Because existing manual systems in libraries produce no hard statistical data about the nature and number of transactions handled, stage-one machine systems have had to be designed without benefit of this essential data. However, even the simplest machine systems can be made to produce a wide variety of statistical data which can be used to great advantage by the designers of stage-two systems. The participation of non-library-oriented computer people in stage-two design will also be facilitated by the fact that they will be dealing with formalized machine systems and records in machine readable form with which they can easily cope.

While the old stage one of library automation was one in which librarians almost exclusively did the design and programming, it is doubtful that stage-two systems can or should be done without the active aid of computer specialists. In stage one it was easier for librarians to learn computing and to do the job themselves than it was to teach computer people about the old manual systems and the job to be done to convert them. This may no longer be the case in dealing with redesign of old machine systems into very complex systems to run on third or fourth generation equipment in an on-line, time-sharing environment. There is now a generation of experienced computer-oriented librarians capable of specifying the job to be done and knowledgeable enough to judge the quality of the work that has been done by the experts. There is no reason why a team of librarians and computer experts should not be able to work effectively together to design and implement future library systems. As traditional library systems are replaced by machine systems, the specialized knowledge of them becomes superfluous, and it was this type of knowledge that used to distinguish the librarian from the computer expert.

Just as there is a growing corps of librarians specializing in computer work, so there is a growing corps of computer people specializing in library work. It is with these two groups working together as a team that the hope of the future lies. The question of who is to do library automation—librarians or computer experts—is no longer meaningful; library automation will be done by persons who are knowledgeable about it and who are deeply committed to it as a specialty; whether they have approached it through a background of librarianship or technology will be of little consequence. Experience has shown that computer people who have made a full-time commitment to the field of library automation have done some of the best work to date.

Stage-two, or advanced integrated library systems, may be built by a team of library and computer people of various types working as staff members of the library, as has been suggested in the preceding discussion, but this approach also has its weaknesses. For example, let us assume that a large library has finally brought itself through stage one and is now planning to enter the second stage. It may have acquired a good deal of the capability to do advanced work, but its staff may be too small and too inexperienced in certain aspects of the work to undertake the major task of planning, designing, and implementing a new integrated system. Additional expert help may be needed, but only on a temporary basis during the planning and design stages. Such people will be hard to find, and also hard to hire within some library salary structures. They will be difficult to absorb into the library's existing staff, administrative, and physical framework. They may also be difficult to separate from the staff when they are no longer needed.

USE OF OUTSIDE CONSULTANTS

There are alternative approaches to creating advanced automated systems. The discussion that follows will deal with one of the most obvious: to contract much of the work out to private research and development firms specializing in library systems.

What comes to mind here is an analogy with the employment of specialized talents of architects, engineers, and construction companies in planning and building very large, complex and costly library buildings, which are then turned over to librarians to operate. When a decision has been made to build a new building, the university architect is not called in to do the job, nor is an architect added to the library staff, nor are librarians on the staff trained to become architects and engineers qualified to design and supervise the construction of the building. Most libraries have on their staffs one or two librarians who are experienced and knowledgeable enough to determine the over-all requirements of the new building, and together they develop a building program which outlines the general concept of the building and specifies various requirements. A qualified professional architect is commissioned to translate the program into preliminary drawings, and there follows a continuing dialogue between the architect and the librarians which eventually produces acceptable working drawings of a building based on the original program. For tasks outside his area of competence, the architect in turn engages the services of various specialists, such as structural and heating and ventilating engineers.

Both the architect and the owners can also call on library consultants for help and advice if needed. The architect participates in the selection of a construction company to do the actual building and is responsible for supervising the work and making sure that the building is constructed according to plans and contracts. Upon completion, the building is turned over to the owners, and the librarians move in and operate it and see to its maintenance. In time, various changes and additions will have to be made. Minor ones can be made by the regular buildings staff of the institution, but major ones will probably be made with the advice and assistance of the original architect or some other.

In the analogous situation, the library would have its own experienced systems unit or group capable of formulating a concept and drawing up a written program specifying the goals and requirements of the automated system. A qualified "architect" for the system would be engaged in the form of a small firm of systems consultants specializing or experienced in library systems work. Their task, like the architect's, would be to turn the general program into a detailed system design with the full aid and participation of the local library systems group. This group would be experienced and competent enough to make sure that the consultants really understood the program and were working in harmony with it. After an acceptable design had emerged from this dialogue, the consultant would be asked to help select a systems development firm which would play a role similar to that of the construction company in the analog: to complete the very detailed design work and to do the programming and debugging and implementation of the system. The consultant would oversee this work, just as the architect oversees the construction of a building. The local library group will have actively participated in the development and implementation of the system and would thus be competent to accept, operate, maintain and improve it.

Success or failure in this approach to advanced library automation will depend to a large extent on the competence of the "architect" or consultant who is engaged. Until recently this was not a very promising route to take for several reasons. There were no firms or consultants with the requisite knowledge and experience in library systems, and the state of the library automation art was confused and lacking in clear trends or direction. It was generally felt that batch-processing systems on second and even third generation computing equipment could and should be designed and installed by local staff in order to give them necessary experience and to avoid the failures that could come from systems designed outside the library.

Library automation has evolved to a point where there is a real need for advanced library systems competence that can be called upon in the way that has been suggested, and individuals and firms will appear to satisfy that need. It is very likely, however, that the knowledge and the experience that is now being obtained in on-line systems by pioneering libraries such as the University of Chi-

cago, Washington State University and Stanford University, will have to be assimilated before we can expect competent consultants to emerge.

The chief difficulty with the architect-and-building analog is that while the process of designing and constructing library buildings is widely understood, there being hundreds of examples of library buildings which can be observed and studied as precedents, the total on-line library system has yet to be designed and tested. There are no precedents and no examples; we are in the position of asking the "architect" to design a prototype system, and therein lies the risk. After this task has been done several times, librarians can begin to shop around for experienced and competent "architects" and successful operating systems which can be adapted to their needs. The key problem here, as always in library automation, is one of correct timing: to embark on a line of development only when the state of the art is sufficiently advanced and the time is ripe for a particular new development.

BUILDING THE CAPABILITY FOR AUTOMATION

Regardless of the approach that is selected, there are certain prerequisites to a successful automation effort, and these can be grouped under the rubric of "building the capability." To build this capability requires time and money. It consists of a staff, equipment, space, an organization with a regular budget, and a certain amount of know-how which is generally obtained by doing a series of projects.

Success depends to a large extent on how well these resources are utilized, i.e. on the overall strategy and the nature and timing of the various moves that are made. Much has already been said about building the capability in the discussion on the approaches to automation, and what follows is an expansion of some points that have been made and a recapitulation of others.

Staff

Since nothing gets done without people, it follows that assembling, training, and holding a competent staff is the most important single element in a library's automation effort. The number of trained and experienced library systems people is still extremely small in relation to the ever-growing need and demand. To attract an experienced computer librarian and even to hold an inexperienced one with good potential, libraries will have to pay more than they pay members of the staff with comparable experience in other lines of library work. This is simply the law of supply and demand at work. To attract people from the computer field will by the same token require even higher salaries. In addition, library systems staff, because of the rate of development of the field and the way in which new information is communicated, will have to be given more time and funds for training courses and for travel and attendance at conferences than has been the case for other library staff.

The question of who will do library automation—librarians or computer experts—has already been touched upon in another context, but it is worth emphasizing the point that there is no unequivocal answer. There are many librarians who have acquired the necessary computer expertise and many computer people who have acquired the necessary knowledge of library functions. The real key to the problem is to get people who are totally committed to library automation whatever their background. Computer people on temporary loan from a computing center may be poor risks, since their professional commitment is to the computer world rather than that of the library. They are paid and promoted by the computing center and their primary loyalty is necessarily to that employer. Computer people, like the rest of us, give their best to tasks which they find interesting and challenging, and by and large, they tend to look upon the computerization of library housekeeping tasks as trivial and unworthy of their efforts.

On the other hand, a first-rate computer person who has elected to specialize in library automation and who has accepted a position on a library staff may be a good risk, because he will quickly take on many of the characteristics of a librarian yet without becoming burdened by the full weight of the conventional wisdom that librarians are condemned to carry. The ideal situation is to have a staff large enough to include a mixture of both types, so that each will profit by the special knowledge and experience of the other.

To bring in computer experts inexperienced in library matters to automate a large and complex library without the active participation of the library's own systems people is to invite almost certain failure. Outsiders, no matter how competent, tend to underestimate the magnitude and complexity of library operations; this is true not only of computing center people but also of independent research and development firms.

A library automation group can include several different types of persons with very different kinds and levels of qualifications. The project director or administrative head should preferably be an imaginative and experienced librarian who has acquired experience with electronic data processing equipment and techniques, and an over-all view of the general state of the library automation art, including its potential and direction of development.

There are various levels of library systems analysts and programmers, and the number and type needed will depend on the approach and the stage of a particular library's automation effort. The critical factor is not numbers but quality. There are many cases where one or two inspired and energetic systems people have far surpassed the efforts of much larger groups in both quality and quantity of work. Some of the most effective library automation work has been done by the people who combine the abilities of the systems analyst with those of the expert programmer and are capable of doing a complete project themselves. A library that has one or two really gifted systems people of this type and permits them to work at their maximum is well on the way to a successful automation effort.

As a library begins to move into development of on-line systems, it will need specialist programmers in addition to the systems analysts described above. These programmers need not be, and probably will not be, librarians. Other members of the team, again depending on the projects, will be librarians who are at home in the computer environment but who will be doing the more traditional types of work, such as tagging and editing machine catalog records.

In any consideration of library automation staff, it would be a mistake to underestimate the importance of the role of keypunchers, paper tape typists, and other machine operators; it is essential that these staff members be conscientious and motivated persons. There are responsible for the quality and quantity of the input, and therefore of the output, and they can frequently do much to make or break a system. A good deal of discussion and experimentation has gone into the question of the relative efficiency of various keyboarding devices for library input, but little consideration is given to the human operators of the equipment. Experience shows that there can be large variations in the speed and accuracy of different persons doing the same type of work on the same machine.

Equipment

One of the lessons of library automation learned during the last few years is that a library cannot risk putting its critical computer-based systems onto equipment over which it has no control. This does not necessarily mean that it needs its own in-house computer. However, if it plans to rely on equipment under the administrative control of others, such as the computer center or the administrative data processing unit, it must get firm and binding commitments for time, and must have a voice in the type and configuration of equipment to be made available. The importance of this point may be overlooked during an initial development period, when the library's need for time is minimal and flexible; it becomes extremely critical when systems such as acquisitions and circulation become totally dependent on computers.

People at university computing centers are generally oriented toward scientific and research users and in a tight situation will give the library's needs second priority; those in administrative data processing, because they are operations oriented, tend to have a somewhat better appreciation of the library's requirements. In any case, a library needs more than the expressed sympathy and goodwill of those who control the computing equipment—it needs firm commitments.

For all but the largest libraries, the economics of present-day computer applications in libraries make it virtually impossible to justify an in-house machine of the capacity libraries will need, dedicated solely or largely to library uses. Even the larger libraries will find it extremely difficult to justify a high-discount second generation machine or a small third generation machine during the period when their systems are being developed and implemented a step or a module at a time. Eventually, library use may increase to a point where the in-house machine will pay for itself, but during the interim period the situation will be uneconomical unless other users can be found to share the cost. In the immediate future, most libraries will have to depend on equipment located in computing or data processing centers. The recent experience of the University of Chicago Library, which is pioneering on-line systems, suggests that this situation is inevitable, given the high core requirements and low computer usage of library systems. Experience at the University of Missouri (6), suggests that the future will see several libraries grouping to share a machine dedicated to library use;

this may well be preferable to having to share with research and scientific users elsewhere within the university. A clear trend is not yet evident, but it seems reasonable to suppose that in the next few years sharing of one kind or another will be more common than having machines wholly assigned to a single library; and that local situations will dictate a variety of arrangements.

While it is clear that the future of library automation lies in third-generation computers, much of their promise is as yet unfulfilled, and it would be premature at this point to write off some of the old, reliable, second-generation batch-processing machines. The IBM 1401, for example, is extremely well suited for many library uses, particularly printing and formatting, and it is a machine easily mastered by the uninitiated. This old workhorse will be with us for several more years before it is retired to Majorca along with obsolete Paris taxis.

Organization

When automation activity in a library has progressed to a point where the systems group consists of several permanent professionals and several clericals, it may be advisable to make a permanent place for the group in the library's regular organizational structure. The best arrangement might be to form a separate unit or department on an equal footing with the traditional departments such as Acquisitions, Cataloging, and Public Services. This Systems Department would have a two-fold function: it would develop new systems and operate implemented systems; and it would bring together for maximum economy and efficiency most of the library's data processing equipment and systems staff. It will require adequate space of its own and —above all—a regular budget, so that permanent and long-term programs can be developed and sustained on something other than an *ad hoc* basis.

There are other advantages to having an established systems department or unit. It gives a sense of identity and esprit to the staff; and it enables them to work more effectively with other departments and to be accepted by them as a permanent fact of life in the library, thereby diminishing resistance to automation. Let there be no mistake about it—the systems group will be a permanent and growing part of the library staff, because there is no such thing as a finished, stable system. (There is a saying in the computer field which goes "If it works, it's obsolete.")

The systems unit should be kept flexible and creative. It should not be allowed to become totally preoccupied with routine operations and submerged in its day-to-day workload, as is too frequently the case with the traditional departments, which consequently lose their capacity to see their operations clearly and to innovate. Part of the systems effort must be devoted to operational systems, but another part should be devoted to the formulation and development of new projects. The creative staff should not be wasted running routine operations.

There has never been any tradition for research and development work in libraries—they were considered exclusively service and operational institutions. The advent of the new technology is forcing a change in this traditional attitude in some of the larger and more innovative libraries which are doing some research and a good deal of development. It is worth noting that a concomitant of research and development is a certain amount of risk but that, while there is no such thing as change without risk, standing pat is also a gamble. Not every idea will succeed and we must learn to accept failures, but the experiments must be conducted so as to minimize the effect of failure on actual library operations.

Automated systems are never finished—they are open-ended. They are always being changed, enlarged, and improved; and program and system maintenance will consequently be a permanent activity. This is one of the chief reasons why the equipment and the systems group should be concentrated in a separate department. The contrary case, namely dispersion of the operational aspects among the departments responsible for the work, may be feasible in the future as library automation becomes more sophisticated and peripheral equipment becomes less expensive, but the odds at this time appear to favor greater centralization.

The Harvard University Library has created, with good results, a new major department along the lines suggested above, except that it also includes the photo-reproduction services. The combination of data processing and reprography in a single department is a natural and logical relationship and one which will have increasingly important implications as both technologies develop concurrently and with increasing interdependence in the future. Even at the present time, there is sufficient relationship between them so that the marriage is fruitful and in no way premature. While computers have had most of the glamour, photographic technology in general, and particularly the

advent of the quick-copying machine, during the last seven years has so far had a more profound and widespread impact on library resources and services to readers than the entire field of computers and data processing. Within the next several years, computer and reprographic technology will be so closely intertwined in libraries as to be inseparable. It would be a mistake to sell reprography short in the coming revolution.

PROJECT SELECTION

No academic library should embark on any type of automation program without first acquiring a basic knowledge of the projects and plans of the Library of Congress, the National Library of Medicine, the National Library of Agriculture, and certain of their joint activities, such as the National Serials Data Program.

As libraries with no previous experience with data processing systems move into the field of automation, they frequently select some relatively simple and productive projects to give experience to the systems staff and confidence in machine techniques to the rest of the library staff. Precise selection will depend on the local situation, but projects such as the production of lists of current journals (not serials check-in), lists of reserve books, lists of subject headings, circulation, and even acquisitions ordering and accounting systems are considered to be the safest and the most productive type of initial projects. Since failures in the initial stage will have serious psychological effects on the library administration and entire staff, it is best to begin with modest projects. Until recently it was fashionable to tackle the problem of automating the serials check-in system as a first project on the grounds that this was one of the most important, troublesome, and repetitive library operations and was therefore the best area in which to begin computerization. Fortunately, a more realistic view of the serials problem has begun to prevail—that serial receipts is an extremely complex and irregular library operation and one which will probably require some on-line updating capabilities, and complex file organization and maintenance programs. In any case, it is decidedly not an area for beginners.

A major objection to all of the projects mentioned is that they do not directly involve the catalog, which is at the heart of library automation. Now that the MARC II format has been developed by the Library of Congress and is being widely accepted as the standardized bibliographical and communications format, the most logical initial automation effort for many libraries will be to adapt to their own environments the input system for current cataloging which is now being developed by the Library of Congress. The logic of beginning an integrated system with the development of an input sub-system for current cataloging has always been compelling for this author—far more compelling than beginning in the ordering process, as so many advocate. The catalog is the central record, and the conversion of this record into machinable form is the heart of the matter of library automation. It seems self-evident that systems design should begin here with the basic bibliographical entry upon which the entire system is built. Having designed this central module, one can then turn to the acquisitions process and design this module around the central one. Circulation is a similar secondary problem. In other words, systems design should begin at the point where the permanent bibliographical record enters the system and not where the first tentative special-purpose record is created. Unfortunately, until the advent of the standardized MARC II format, it was not feasible, except in an experimental way, for libraries to begin with the catalog record, simply because the state of the art was not far enough advanced.

The development and acceptance of the MARC II format in 1967 marks the end of one era in library automation and the beginning of another. In the pre-MARC II period every system was unique; all the programming and most of the systems work had to be done by a library's own staff. In the post-MARC II period we will begin to benefit from systems and programs that will be developed at the Library of Congress and elsewhere, because they will be designed around the standard format and for at least one standard computer. As a result of this, automation in libraries will be greatly accelerated and will become far more widespread in the next few years (7).

An input system for current cataloging in the MARC II format will be among the first packages available. It will be followed shortly by programs designed to sort and manipulate the data in various ways. A library will require a considerable amount of expertise on the part of its staff to adapt these procedures and programs to its own uses (we are not yet at the point of "plugging-in" systems), but the effort will be considerably reduced and the risks of going down blind alleys with homemade approaches and systems will be nearly eliminated

for those libraries that are willing to adopt this strategy.

The development and operation of a local MARC II input system with an efficient alteration and addition capability will be a prerequisite for any library that expects to learn to make effective use of the magnetic tapes containing the Library of Congress's current catalog data in the MARC II format, which will be available as a regular subscription in July, 1968. In addition to providing the experience essential for dealing with the Library of Congress MARC data, a local input system will enable the library to enter its own data both into the local systems and into the national systems which will begin to emerge in the near future.

Since the design of the MARC II format is also hospitable to other kinds of library data, such as subject-headings lists and classification schedules, the experience gained with it in an input system will be transferable to other library automation projects.

COSTS

The price of doing original development work in the library automation field comes extremely high —so high that in most cases such work cannot be undertaken without substantial assistance from outside sources. Even when grants are available, the institution has to contribute a considerable portion of the total cost of any development effort, and this cost is not a matter of money alone; it requires the commitment of the library's limited human resources. In the earlier days of library automation attention was focused on the high cost of hardware, computer and peripheral equipment. The cost of software, the systems work and programming, tended to be underestimated. Experience has shown, however, that software costs are as high as hardware costs or even higher.

The development of new systems, i.e., those without precedents, is the most costly kind of library automation, and most libraries will have to select carefully the areas in which to do their original work. For those libraries that are content to adopt existing systems, the costs of the systems effort, while still high, are considerably less and the risks are also reduced. These costs, however, will probably have to be borne entirely by the institution, as it is unlikely that outside funding can be obtained for this type of work.

The justification of computer-based library systems on the basis of the costs alone will continue to be difficult because machine systems not only replace manual systems but generally do more and different things, and it is extremely difficult to compare them with the old manual systems, which frequently did not adequately do the job they were supposed to do and for which operating costs often were unknown. Generally speaking, and in the short run at least, computer-based systems will not save money for an institution if all development and implementation costs are included. They will provide better and more dependable records and systems, which are essential to enable libraries simply to cope with increased intake and workloads, but they will cost at least as much as the inadequate and frequently unexpansible manual systems they replace. The picture may change in the long run, but even then it seems more reasonable to expect that automation, in addition to profoundly changing the way in which the library budget is spent, will increase the total cost of providing library service. However, that service will be at a much higher level than the service bought by today's library budget. Certain jobs will be eliminated, but others will be created to provide new services and services in greater depth; as a library becomes increasingly successful and responsive, more and more will be demanded of it.

CONCLUSION

The purpose of this paper has been to stress the importance of good strategy, correct timing, and intelligent systems staff as the essential ingredients for a successful automation program. It has also tried to make clear that no canned formulas for automating an academic library are waiting to be discovered and applied to any particular library. Each library is going to have to decide for itself which approach or strategy seems best suited to its own particular needs and situation. On the other hand, a good deal of experience with the development and administration of library systems has been acquired over the last few years and some of it may very well be useful to those who are about to take the plunge for the first time. This paper was written with the intention of passing along, for what they are worth, one man's ideas, opinions, and impressions based on an imperfect knowledge of the state of the library automation art and a modest amount of first-hand experience in library systems development and administration.

REFERENCES

1. Wasserman, Paul: *The Librarian and the Machine* (Detroit: Gale, 1965). A thoughtful and thorough review of the state of the art of library automation, with some discussion of the various approaches to automation. Essential reading for library administrators.
2. Cox, N. S. M.; Dews, J. D.; Dolby, J. L.: *The Computer and the Library* (Newcastle upon Tyne: University of Newcastle upon Tyne, 1966). American edition published by Archon Books, Hamden, Conn. Extremely clear, well-written and essential book for anyone with an interest in library automation.
3. Dix, William S.: *Annual Report of the Librarian for the Year Ending June 30, 1966* (Princeton: Princeton University Library, 1966). One of the best policy statements on library automation; a comprehensive review of the subject in the Princeton context, with particular emphasis on the "wait-for-developments" approach.
4. Fussler, Herman H.; Payne, Charles T.: *Annual Report 1966/67 to the National Science Foundation from the University of Chicago Library; Development of an integrated, Computer-Based, Bibliographical Data System for a Large University Library* (Chicago: University of Chicago Library, 1967). Appended to the report is a paper given May 1, 1967, at the Clinic on Library Application of Data Processing conducted by the Graduate School of Library Science, University of Illinois. Mr. Payne is the author, and the paper is entitled "An Integrated Computer-Based Bibliographic Data System for a large University Library: Progress and Problems at the University of Chicago."
5. Kilgour, Frederick G.: "Comprehensive Modern Library Systems," in The Brasenose Conference on the Automation of Libraries, *Proceedings.* (London: Mansell, 1967), 46-56. An example of the evolutionary approach as employed at the Yale University Library.
6. Parker, Ralph H.: "Not a Shared System: an Account of a Computer Operation Designed Specifically and Solely for Library Use at the University of Missouri," *Library Journal,* 92 (Nov. 1, 1967), 3967-3970.
7. *Annual Review of Information Science and Technology* (New York: Interscience Publishers), 1 (1966)-. A useful tool for surveying the current state of the library automation art and for obtaining citations to current publications and reports is a chapter on automation in libraries which appears in each volume.

IV
NEW SERVICES

Admirably suited to the purposes of this anthology is the survey by Myatt, made for the National Commission on Libraries. Myatt and his co-workers have identified a large number of "extra-library" services, but whether the definition they provide is successful for the purpose of distinguishing between the conventional library and the "extra-library" is questionable. In any event what is abundantly clear is that in the realm of servicing documents (especially nonbook documents), and in the analysis of information, the traditional library functions minimally at best.

From the management point of view, given the will, and the financial means, traditional libraries can provide these extra-library services. To a limited extent, this is already taking place. On the other hand, as Myatt rightly points out, there is no reason to regard the two kinds of libraries as competitive. Certainly Myatt is right in suggesting that librarians acquaint themselves with these "extra" services and make use of them, even to the point of establishing terminal connections.

McGowan's article fits in well with Myatt's, providing a specific example of an "extra-library" service, the "technical information" center. McGowan's center is a natural extension of a conventional library, one giving more intensive and better informed reference service by virtue of its reliance upon subject specialists.

Perhaps the best way to grasp Becker's network concept, is to distinguish between the levels of information transmitted. It must be admitted that there is a considerable difference between a network established to facilitate inter-library loans, and a network used to transmit the superior kind of reference service described by McGowan. Some networks are "single-directed," such as the Chemical Abstract services described by Davenport; by this, I mean that the information flows from the single service center to its many subscribers. Quite a different network is achieved when a large number of institutions (such as Becker describes as belonging to EDUCOM) begin reciprocally to exchange data and other information.

The essay on Selective Dissemination of Information (SDI) by Studer is taken from the first chapter of his Ph.D. dissertation on this subject. Studer's account makes the point that a "current awareness" service is a shotgun affair compared to the specific requirements of profiles established for a selective dissemination operation. Though most SDI projects concern themselves with the natural sciences, the idea is spreading. Thus, Pandex, a commercial venture, has entered the social sciences, while in political science, information on foreign political parties is made available through Northwestern University.

No anthology dealing with new library services could ignore Project Intrex, and no more authoritative source than Carl Overhage, could be found to describe it. Much of Intrex has been concerned with the experimental development of hardware, but among its other features, more understandable to librarians, is the "augmented catalog." Into this catalog, Intrex would enter much more information about authors than is traditional; thus, material from indexes, chapter headings and tables of contents would be supplied.

With respect to access via terminals (such as the cathode ray tube), Intrex envisions much more input than the bibliographic entries projected at Stanford. The ideal is to provide data in a format peculiarly useful to the individual needs of the users. Nor would Intrex stop at the borders of the M.I.T. campus, offering as it would, its services as part of a national network. It is most difficult for an outsider to judge how much of this is purely visionary, and as might be expected, critics of the priorities assigned by the Intrex staff are not lacking. Even so, librarianship cannot escape the influence of this interesting experiment. In this context I believe it is correct to refer to the Stanford developments as operational minded, compared to those at M.I.T. which are experimental minded.

Position Paper on Extra-Library Information Services

by DeWitt O. Myatt and Donald A. Barclay

EXTRA-LIBRARY INFORMATION SERVICES

Introduction

Over the past quarter century there has been a significant change in the relative position of the home, the office, the school and the library as sources of information. In the past the school and the traditional library far exceeded the home and office as places for acquiring information. Today this gap between the school and library on the one hand, and the home and office on the other has diminished. As sources of information the home and office have risen dramatically in relation to the other two, even though all four of them have increased significantly as sources for acquiring information.

Along with these changes in our information environment is the change of emphasis in the kind of information people seek today. Because of the rapidity of change and the pace of current events, people are faced with the difficult problem of keeping abreast of these changes, especially when these changes are related to one's own profession or vocation. Thus a special demand has been created for almost instantaneous information about a new hypothesis, a discovery, a scientific or technological breakthrough, a medical advance, or any other kind of finding. The media too have changed. The most prominent ones employed today to convey new information are newspapers, journals, reports, television, and convention papers.

In combination, the changes in the information environment, the demand for current information, and the media by which that information is distributed have created a number of pressing problems for our libraries. Helping the library establishment find solutions to the problems created by these changes are the extra-library information services that have developed in and out of government over the past several decades.

Many new library-like information services have been devised to cope with these changes. Today there are at least three basic types of extra-library information services attempting to store and retrieve information and facilitate its transfer. The first type is the document-handling service which attempts to facilitate the flow of report literature of all kinds. The Defense Documentation Center and the Clearinghouse for Federal Scientific and Technical Information are two prominent examples of this type. The second type of service is the data-handling center which attempts to provide greater access to and use of data of all kinds. Several well-known examples are the National Space Science Data Center, the National Oceanographic Data Center, and the Bureau of the Census. Information analysis centers, which have as their expressed purpose the synthesizing of information within a particular discipline or among related disciplines, make up the third type of extra-library information service. The Nuclear Safety Information Center, the Battelle-Defender Information Analysis Center, and the Nondestructive Testing Information Analysis Center are examples of this type. Although extra-library information services vary in structure and function and often perform the functions of more than one of these basic types, it is useful to categorize them in this manner for discussion purposes.

In dealing with extra-library information services this paper will confine itself to those types of efforts that have as a common denominator with libraries the storing and retrieving of information for public and governmental use. Excluded for this reason are the mass media such as radio, television, and newspapers, and such arrangements as command and control systems and corporate management information systems.

THE RISE OF EXTRA-LIBRARY INFORMATION SERVICES

A number of reasons can be given for the rise of extra-library information services. The first and most popular one is that these services have devel-

SOURCE: Reprinted from a report made to the National Advisory Commission on Libraries, 1967, pp. 1-17.

oped as a response to the tremendous increase in the number of documents being published. To control the information explosion it became necessary, therefore, to establish a number of information storage and retrieval centers and to develop new techniques to cope with the flood of printed material.

The inadequacy of libraries to meet new information demands is a second reason given for the emergence of extra-library information services. However, to blame the traditional libraries for not recognizing the need for innovation and for new services, and further for not taking steps to alleviate the situation by experimenting and adopting new methods of information transfer, is rather short-sighted. The information explosion did not occur in the number of books being published but in the proliferation of other forms of documents. When these other forms began to create storage and retrieval problems, information systems came into being. For the most part, these problems arose initially outside the normal purview of the traditional library.

More important than the information explosion or the lack of initiative on the part of libraries as reasons for the development of extra-library information services are the social changes that have taken place in our society. Already mentioned is the change in our information environment and the kinds of information people are seeking. Tied closely to these changes is the attitude with which we view information. The dictum "You can't get today's job with yesterday's skills," illustrates the fact that life is now considered a continual learning process. Today information is regarded as a vitally important commodity but one that has the tendency to become obsolete over a short period of time. Rapid change produces the obsolescence and the necessity of having quicker access to a store of up-to-date information. A person cannot act responsibly as a citizen or keep abreast of his profession without continually keeping up with the changes taking place. It is not the library that fails in this respect but the medium of the book that is at fault. The book's ability to convey knowledge of broad and permanent value cannot be challenged; it can only be questioned as a means for conveying up-to-date information. The report literature and the various types of information services serve this purpose in a much more adequate way.

Technology is another important explanation for the development of information systems. It first provided the means to publish economically a wide assortment of documents in paper-bound form. The proliferation and use of this form of literature resulted in many problems for libraries but it answered, at the same time, the need for a rapid means of communicating information. Libraries were ill-equipped to handle this wide variety of documents. The lifespan of these documents was short and therefore created archival problems that were extremely difficult to manage within the library. At the same time, the immediate utility of these documents had widespread importance, creating and intensifying the problems of dissemination for libraries. To seize, retrieve, and disseminate these kinds of documents it became obvious to many people that new methods were required to handle them.

Technology not only made possible numerous types of documents, but it also provided the means which greatly assisted in their control. The computer was first applied to the development and maintenance of indexes of documents, allowing for greater depth of indexing and more comprehensive retrieval of information locked in documents. The use of the computer in this manner is still quite new, but there seems to be little doubt that it will one day replace the card catalog as we know it today.

Although slow in being applied to indexing, the use of the computer has not stopped at this point in the information transfer process. Like the book, the computer is becoming a medium of information transfer itself. In the United States there are over 200 well-established data-handling centers and perhaps a greater number of management information systems. In these centers the computer provides storage of and access to recorded, but in many cases unpublished, information. Although management information systems are restricted in their use by their corporate settings, data systems are accessible to many people who desire the information and have a legitimate need for it. The development of management information systems and data-handling systems can be attributed to the very existence of the computer and, comcomitantly, the desire to develop better and more efficient means of handling information.

The reasons given here for the rapid development of the various extra-library systems now in operation outside of the formal library network constitute only those reasons considered to be of major significance.

CHARACTERISTICS OF EXTRA-LIBRARY INFORMATION SERVICES

From the foregoing synopsis of the types of extra-library information systems and reasons for their development, several broad generalizations can be made about their characteristics. Although many of their functions are similar to those of traditional libraries, the services provided by extra-library information systems differ in many respects.

In the main, extra-library information services place greater emphasis on information than on documents. Although documents comprise a major part of their store and are the major source of their information, extra-library information services attempt to index to a much greater depth the information contained in the documents. To achieve this end practically all information systems have adopted open-ended classifications schemes in order to avoid the restraints imposed by the hierarchical schemes of the Dewey Decimal and Library of Congress systems. The newer schemes permit more intensive indexing of the information and more comprehensive retrieval of information contained in documents.

Extra-library information services are more active disseminators of information. They work toward getting the information into the hands of those who can use it. Document-handling systems such as Defense Documentation Center, the Clearinghouse for Federal Scientific and Technical Information, and the NASA system send to their users on a regular and frequent basis a bibliographic listing that includes abstracts of their new acquisitions. Other systems have alerting techniques such as Selective Dissemination of Information (SDI) to keep their customers informed of articles and reports of interest to them. The underlying commitment of these systems is to get the information into use by making their customers aware of its existence.

Another distinguishing characteristic of extra-library information services is that their collections maintain file integrity. They achieve this by selling (or giving) to their customers copies of the documents in either hardcopy or microform. This practice is in marked contrast to that of libraries which lend their materials and require that they be returned.

Such a procedure eliminates the problems of follow-up for the return of documents and prevents the slow erosion of a library's collection due to loss of or failure to return documents. An important added advantage of allowing the user to keep the materials sent to him is that it tends to develop specialized collections in his private files.

For extra-library information services, the book is a minor rather than a major medium of information transfer. Information systems deal primarily with technical reports, journals, symposium and convention papers, maps, drawings, and other types of printed material which can be easily duplicated for dissemination. The volume of these kinds of documents is probably as great as, if not greater than, the volume of published books. To effectively accommodate this mass of printed material in its diversity of forms, extra-library information systems had to be developed to store and retrieve it if these kinds of documents were to be made accessible to the public.

The use of these forms indicates the kind of information they convey. The specific attribute of the information is currency or up-to-dateness and extra-library information services concentrate on making available to their customers information that has this quality. Consequently, the life span of active usage for this up-to-date information is relatively short and therefore its high usage rate drops off drastically after several months or years. At this point extra-library information systems establish criteria by which the information that has a low usage rate or has lost its current value can be purged from the active files and placed in an inactive archival file. Extra-library services assume as one of their main responsibilities the job of collecting and maintaining this kind of information. This responsibility denotes one of their their chief characteristics.

It follows then that extra-library information services emphasize the organization of information for current and specialized usages rather than stressing long-term future utility of the information. The indexing and classification schemes employed by these services reflect this emphasis. The use of subject-matter specialists for indexing purposes adds greater weight to this emphasis and also greater competence in the center's area of specialization. It has almost become standard practice for extra-library information services to employ subject-matter specialists and then train them in the field of information science.

The way in which extra-library information services are structured and the nature of the information they contain dictate and are dictated by the type of clientele they service. In general, the users have immediate and pragmatic applications for the information they require. The customers who use these services therefore have a vital interest in state-of-the-art reports, progress reports, and position papers; facts of all kinds, such as chemical compounds and their properties, number of voters or welfare recipients, etc.; and figures or statistics of all kinds, such as building starts, opinion polls, etc.

It must be emphasized that all of these characteristics are of a general nature and therefore it is difficult to apply all of them to any one extra-library information service. Nor are they completely exclusive vis-à-vis libraries. There is one characteristic, however, that is almost universally true of extra-library information systems—one that points out in a very forceful way the characteristics already mentioned. To extra-library information services the reading room is not an essential part of their operation. Its de-emphasis makes obvious the type of services extra-library information systems render and how they must operate. It points out the different way in which a book is regarded in contrast to a paper-bound document and it also indicates the different way in which they are treated.

SERVICES OFFERED TO USERS OF EXTRA-LIBRARY INFORMATION SERVICES

Probably the most important service that extra-library information services offer the user is access to information unavailable in libraries. An excellent example of such a service is the Science Information Exchange (see Exhibit J). At present there is no other organization which offers such comprehensive coverage of research in progress. All of the document-handling centers in the Federal Government also constitute a reservoir of information unavailable in libraries. By concentrating on a specific subject area, extra-library information services become the most comprehensive source for specialized information. This is the case for such information services as the Mechanical Properties Data Center.

A second service or advantage offered the user of extra-library information services is convenience. A person using these services does not have to leave his office either to order or pick-up the materials he desires. These steps are accomplished by mail or telephone and, in some cases, electronically through a computer console and a display screen. Many of these services provide their customers with an index to new materials received by the center. This index, consisting of abstracts of documents, simultaneously provides the user with a permanent record of the documents available to him from the center, a handy catalog for selecting and ordering documents, and a means of keeping abreast of current research. The Technical Abstracts Bulletin from the Defense Documentation Center is a good example of such a service. Selective Dissemination of Information (SDI) is another well-known technique providing the user a convenient means of keeping abreast of the papers in his field. Through these techniques, extra-library information services extend their services to the offices of their customers.

Manipulation of information is a distinct and work-saving advantage certain information services offer their customers. Since these services store their information on computer tape, the answer to a query can be tailored to meet the parameters set forth by the individual. This kind of manipulation is done on a regular basis by the Science Information Exchange. Other information systems providing this service are the individual systems belonging to the Council for Social Science Data Archives. The Bureau of the Census will also offer this kind of service as part of the 1970 Census. A few examples of requests requiring computer manipulation may help to illustrate the point. If a person wanted the opinions expressed about a particular subject by individuals living within a specified area during a certain period, he could get this information from the data centers which store the computerized results of the Harris or Gallup polls. If one wanted to know the number of patients treated in U.S. hospitals for a particular disease in five western states and the types of treatment given, he could obtain this information form the Commission on Professional and Hospital Activities, sponsored by the American College of Physicians and the American Hospital Association. In these instances the original information is coded and stored on computer tape. The computer then manipulates the information to fit the specified parameters of the requestor such as the number of states, the type of disease, etc. Because these services are now relatively expensive, they are not in widespread use. However, they should become in the next few years an important additional resource for research work, since they provide a means to find and use information and to derive new data from previously unrelated sources.

The ability of extra-library information services to provide the most current information available is one of their important qualities. As was discussed in the previous section, these extra-library services achieve this by storing, retrieving and disseminating the latest documents that contain up-to-date information considered valuable to their clientele. Moreover, they concentrate on keeping the time between submission of a report and its entry into the system as short as possible. Generally, it takes from four to six weeks for most of the Federal Government document-handling systems to accomplish this step. In contrast, it takes a much longer period of time for a book to be published and reach the shelves of libraries. These efforts by extra-library information systems are slowly gaining the confidence of the public as the best sources for current information, while, at the same time, clarifying the distinct advantage of the traditional library as the best source for information of long-term or permanent value.

Like the library establishment, extra-library information services have large general collections covering a variety of subjects (e.g., the Clearinghouse for Federal Scientific and Technical Information, the National Referral Center and the Science Information Exchange) and also many specialized services covering comprehensively a small subject area of interest. These specialized extra-library information services may, in some cases, differ in name only from special libraries, but where they incorporate many of the characteristics of extra-library information services, they must be considered as belonging to that category. The benefits offered users of these specialized extra-library information services parallel those of the special library but with the added advantages of those services mentioned above.

LIBRARIES AND EXTRA-LIBRARY INFORMATION SERVICES

A Reassessment of the Division

The term extra-library creates a dichotomy which in many ways is unfortunate. It places in juxtaposition to the traditional library all of the other information sources. On the one side is the library establishment composed of the Library of Congress and all of the other research, special, university, public, industrial, and government libraries; on the other side are the document-handling systems, referral centers, clearinghouses, data systems and information analysis centers.

This dichotomy is particularly unfortunate to the degree that it suggests that libraries and extra-library information services are in competition with each other or that extra-library information services are in some way a threat to the continued existence and growth of traditional libraries. Moreover, the dichotomy clouds the fact that libraries and extra-library services are, in all likelihood, more complimentary than competitive. It is probably much more practical to view extra-library information services as services that complement those of traditional libraries.

The dichotomy is unfortunate in a more fundamental sense. Because there is no clear-cut basis for distinction, the foundation upon which the division rests is practically non-existent. Moreover, the dichotomy tends to obscure the primary difference between the two media now in use for transferring information.

The context in which to clarify these ambiguities has as its basis the two media employed today to transfer information. The first medium used for this purpose is the printed page; the second is the electronics medium. Of primary concern here are the organizations that have the basic function of storing or archiving of information in anticipation of later use, regardless of the transfer medium they employ. Within this context, those systems that handle information stored in documents are libraries and many of the systems (specifically document-handling systems and indexing and abstracting services) now considered to be in the extra-library information service category. For these systems, the printed page constitutes the means by which information is transferred from the generator to the reader. The goal of these organizations, therefore, is to facilitate this process of transfer.

The information systems that are attempting to develop and use the electronics medium to achieve the same goal are principally data-handling centers, management information systems and teaching machines. One might argue that even these systems have as their product a computer printout which is, for all practical purposes, a document. One might also argue that their input is derived from documents. But in the majority of cases the output of these systems is unique and tailor-made for the requesters. The output or answer could just as easily have been received on a display screen. The receipt of the information would depend on the length of the answer and the use the requester wanted to make of it.

As for the input, an increasing number of systems are getting their information directly from the source rather than waiting for the information to be published, then using the published document as the source of input. This shows that such a step can be bypassed although the information may eventually appear in published form.

Recognition of these two modes of transferring information establishes a clear-cut distinction between libraries and extra-library information services.

The Computer and the Transfer of Information

In the majority of cases today where the computer is being applied to the information transfer process, it is being used to enhance the storage and transfer of documents. The use of the computer permits greater flexibility and depth of indexing of documents. Computers also enhance the flow of documents when they are applied to the housekeeping functions of libraries. Using computers in this way tends to make documents a more viable medium of information transfer. But according to Marshall McLuhan, when a new medium comes into being we initially attempt to make it increase the utility of the old medium it is offsetting. The application of computers to libraries would tend to substantiate this view. Undoubtedly, such efforts are enhancing the utility of all kinds of printed materials and therefore should be encouraged.

But the question remains as to the position of the computer as a medium of information transfer in its own right. How should the computer be used? If it is in fact a new medium of information transfer, what are the consequences in relation to our libraries? A look at how the computer is being applied to the information transfer process outside of the library should help to provide at least some partial answers to these questions.

Today, there are over 40,000 computer installations in the United States, each one processing millions of bits of information. More specifically, there are over two hundred data centers, covering practically every discipline, which are storing and retrieving information electronically. This number does not include the hundreds of corporate management information systems or the one thousand commercial data processing service centers throughout the United States. All of these activities are capturing to a greater degree the computer's real potential in the field of information processing and transfer. When the practice of sitting down before a computer console, interrogating the system, and receiving an answer on a display screen becomes a more widespread prac-

tice, the computer will no doubt be considered at that time a medium of information transfer in its own right.

In a broad sense what we are witnessing today is the first step leading toward the development of such a system. The first step in this process is logically the collection of data in computerized form. The number of data centers collecting information and storing it on computer tape has grown from two or three in 1950 to over 200 today. The Chemical Information System, National Oceanographic Data Center, National Standard Reference Data Program, National Earth Science Data Center, National Water Data Program, the Cancer Chemotherapy Data Center, and the member organizations of the Council for Social Science Data Archives are some of the more obvious efforts in which the computer is being employed as an electronic medium of storage, retrieval and dissemination.

These efforts derive their data from many sources but the literature is still their main source. When viewed as the first step in creating an electronic information system the process is naturally one of converting the old records into the new computerized form. This, of course, is a massive job and one that will take a considerable amount of time and manpower.

It should be made clear that only certain types of information are amenable to this process. The kinds of information that are most suitable are facts and statistics of all kinds. The computer has already been shown to be a more flexible means of storing and retrieving this kind of information than is the printed page. Conceptual information, on the other hand, is better suited to the document as a means for storage and dissemination. Dr. Harold Lasswell of Yale University, in an article in the *Saturday Review* stated that "The computer revolution has suddenly removed age-old limitations on the processing of information, including the linkage of data with competing theories of explanation."[1] This statement goes a long way in explaining why people in many fields of interest are converting existing data into computerized form. And it explains why there is so much interest in gathering new data for computer processing.

What are the consequences of such developments for our libraries? There are two rather immediate ones although they are not as yet large enough to be measured. These consequences, however, will become more obvious as electronic information systems develop stronger bases and therefore become more broadly useful. First, people will use these data systems to get specific information rather than turn to the library for reference material. For example, a social scientist can receive today an up-to-date biographical sketch of an east European leader from the Archive on Political Elites in Eastern Europe at the University of Pittsburgh, thereby saving himself the trouble of gathering together a sketch of his own from library materials. Other examples can be given using other fields where data systems already exist such as law enforcement, history (old voting and census records), and engineering. If library users place less reliance on handbooks and contemporary reference documents containing a high degree of factual information and greater reliance on data centers containing the same information in a more up-to-date and comprehensive form, it will certainly relieve libraries of the time-consuming task of answering specific questions requiring factual answers.

The second consequence has to do with the acquisition of data by these centers. Some data, primarily in the scientific and technological fields, are being transmitted directly to the data centers for storage and retrieval. Sending one's initial findings directly to a data center cuts down, at least to some degree, the reporting of such information in a printed form, to the degree this occurs, the document-handling burden of libraries is lessened.

WHAT EXTRA-LIBRARY INFORMATION SERVICES OFFER LIBRARIES

This paper endeavors to clarify the role of extra-library information services for the National Advisory Commission on Libraries; first in the context of the assignment and second, in the context developed in the preceding two sections. In considering what extra-library information services offer to the library, each context will be dealt with separately, starting with the generally accepted one provided for this assignment. Libraries might profit most from the experience document-handling systems have had in automating various functions of their operation. Bibliographic control is well established in libraries, and document-handling systems have not added appreciably to this function. However, where they have added a new aspect in bibliographic control (e.g. greater flexibility) it would appear wise for libraries to consider its inclusion into their system.

Extra-library information services have placed considerable emphasis on the problem of subject-matter control, as reflected in the development and use of open-ended classification schemes, greater depth of subject indexing, and the use of subject-matter specialists. It would appear that many of these developments could be superimposed on the existing structure of library classification and indexing schemes as libraries begin to automate their present practices.

Extra-library information systems offer a growing number of back-up resources to which librarians can turn to get information for their customers. Special librarians, for the most part, are aware of and use the extra-library information systems within their own specialty. But in those areas where librarians lack familiarity with extra-library information services, greater reliance on the National Referral Center, Science Information Exchange and other like services could measurably enhance their effectiveness in relation to their customers. An awareness of the numerous information systems available can be of great help to users, to libraries, and also to extra-library information services. It would help the extra-library information services to know more about the size and type of clientele they wish to serve. More importantly, it would help to develop a more viable and close-knit network between libraries and the extra-library services.

What do extra-library information services utilizing the electronic medium of information transfer offer the traditional library? The long run implications for the library are impossible to foresee. In the immediate future, however, there are several. First, electronic information transfer services will help to clarify the kinds of information best suited for each medium. This process of clarification will help the libraries in their selection of new materials. Documents containing unevaluated data or data that has been entered into a data center could receive a lower order of priority. This kind of policy would be especially applicable if the library had a rapid means of access to the data centers.

Second, traditional libraries should consider the prospects of placing within their establishment terminal equipment connected to data centers. By adding terminal equipment, libraries could offer their customers a new and rapid service unavailable to most people today. So situated, the library would continue to perform its historic role as an institution providing access to the total resources of human knowledge.

RECOMMENDATIONS

1. *It is recommended that libraries and extra-library information services be considered as integral parts of the total information transfer process.*

Extra-library information services should be included in any discussion or deliberation concerning the present status of American libraries. Omission would only lead to greater division between libraries and extra-library services. Recommendations of the Commission should help to draw these two branches together into a close-knit working relationship. This could be done in the allocation of funds, in the establishment of standards, or even in the development of library statistics.

2. *It is recommended that the professional library associations develop an easy and efficient method to keep librarians informed of existing and new extra-library information services.*

Like the inter-library loan system, extra-library information services should be regarded as back-up resources for the librarian. An easily up-dated reference tool could initially serve this purpose. With such a tool librarians could familiarize themselves in the use of these extra-library services. Using these services librarians could develop better working arrangements with them, gain better knowledge of the breadth and depth of the subject area they cover and learn in greater detail the types of services they offer. This knowledge could then be passed on to the library's users.

3. *It is recommended that the professional library associations investigate the possibilities of acquiring terminal equipment connected to one or more of the extra-library information services.*

Such a step could first be done on an experimental basis with those extra-library services that have a high degree of automation. University and special libraries are excellent candidates for terminal equipment tied to systems that cover scientific subjects or certain areas in the social sciences. Municipal libraries could investigate the possibilities of having a terminal connected to their city's urban data center. Information concerning such possibilities should be developed by either the library associations or through Federal Government agencies.

4. *It is recommended that a study be conducted to ascertain the feasibility of applying to libraries the indexing concepts and automated file search methods now used in extra-library document-handling systems.*

To date, the application of computers in library operations has differed significantly from their application in extra-library document-handling systems. This difference is largely attributable to the manner in which indexes to the document collection are constructed, maintained, and searched.

Library indexing assigns documents to a predetermined position in a classification scheme. The resulting index codes are difficult to process by computer; it is especially difficult to up-date such indexes. Automated up-dating and searching of indexes is facilitated by serially assigned accession numbers and concept coordination search procedures such as are currently used in extra-library document-handling systems. The potential utility of these methods should be studied and tested. Study should include consideration of hybrid configurations embodying the coordinated search capability, yet retaining the shelving convention of current library operations.

FOOTNOTES

[1] Lasswell, Harold D. "Do We Need Social Observatories?", *Saturday Review*, August 5, 1967, pp. 49-52

The Library and the Technical Information Center

by J. McGowan

The technical information center has emerged as one of the mechanisms that deal with scientific and technical literature. Although there has been a great deal of interest in technical information centers during the last few years, the concept is not an entirely new one. The origins of the technical information center can be traced back to library services, and many of the techniques that are currently used in such centers have been developed by professional librarians.

The John Crerar Library in Chicago long ago recognized the need for a specialized type of library service, and as early as 1946 organized a department called the Research Information Service which offered industry various kinds of information services. There are at the present time several centers patterned after the John Crerar Library. The Franklin Institute Library, The Engineering Societies Library, and the Library of Congress are some of the organizations which offer various information and bibliographical services.

For the purpose of this presentation, the technical information center that will be discussed is defined as:

1. A department which is a unit of a library with responsibility to library management.
2. A department which charges a fee for its services that covers the full cost of the operation.
3. A department which relies on the library collections to provide information services for an external user group upon request.

In this context, the technical information center emerges as a library oriented function conceived to utilize and exploit the printed resources of an organized and established collection. It employs the services of subject specialists who are familiar with the literature in their respective fields. The product of such an activity is bibliographical.

There are certain precedent conditions that must be met before a library can establish such a center:

1. It must have a large and comprehensive collection.
2. It must have a reputation of service to the industrial and scientific community.
3. It must be located in an area that contains a large number of industrial and research facilities.

Within the library organization, the technical information center is identified most closely with the reference services. Its objectives are similar, and its methodology and techniques are similar. Many regard certain technical information center functions as an extremely high order of reference service. The organization of the information center, however, is not patterned on the library reference department. It bears no resemblance and is not in any way comparable. The technical information center operates as a self-contained unit that derives its complete support from fees. As such, it must be concerned with the optimum allocation of personnel, resources, and equipment to produce information services that will derive income to cover the full cost of the operation. This cost includes not only the salaries, but also space, heat, light, various services, and an allocation charge for the use of the library materials. Personnel working in the center charge time against specific work orders, and are never utilized in library tasks. The center is regarded as an income-producing facility at all times, and operates very much like any business activity. Its income and expenses are carefully recorded, and monthly statements are issued for the technical information center indicating the financial status of the operation. To maintain an accurate assessment of progress and to exercise control on the center, the library and the technical information center functions are kept entirely separate. Personnel from the technical information center are not transferred to library tasks when there is no work. They automatically appear as an overhead item until they are reassigned to a job. There are cases, however, when library personnel are transferred to the center. Under such circumstances, the person's time is charged against the account of the center. This practice is

SOURCE: Reprinted from *Technical Information Center Administration,* edited by A. W. Elias (Spartan Books, 1965), p. 59-67, by permission of the publisher. Copyright 1965 by Spartan Books.

generally discouraged and is approved only as an emergency measure.

In planning its operation, the technical information center prepares an annual budget that includes anticipated income and a detailed breakdown of its operating expenses. This budget is adhered to as closely as possible and serves as a yardstick for management to evaluate performance. Deviations from the budget, such as using the center's personnel in library tasks, are not encouraged. The degree of cost-consciousness and the controls that are imposed are in most cases an extension of existing procedures employed in other income-generating departments of the organization, of which the library is a part. The organization's comptroller views the center no differently than any other income-producing facility, and uses the same techniques to control it. He requires that it pay all direct and overhead costs and operate in the black. Many of these allocations to overhead are judgment decisions made between library management, the technical information center, and the comptroller's office. In some cases, if the center is involved in contract work, Government auditors will participate in the decisions. There is a wide disparity in the accounting and cost control practices used by the various technical information centers. Wide differences in these practices have made comparisons of another's operations difficult.

The technical information center is in every case organized as a unit within the library organization. Its location in the structure varies, again reflecting the emphasis and importance that are placed on the activity by management and the success that the center has attained in achieving its stated objectives. In those cases where management has regarded it as an important element of its activity and the objectives of the center have been attained, the latter emerges as a full-fledged department that exerts a great deal of influence on the policies of the library. The administrative head of the center functions in a senior capacity in the library hierarchy and usually reports directly to the administrative head of the library. The technical information center management has usually had library training and is in a position to establish balanced relationships between his department and the library. In a senior capacity, he has the authority to deal directly with other units in the organization, such as the computing center, personnel department, and members of the research and development staff.

The size of the center is dictated by the volume and type of business handled, and by the efficiency of the unit. Most centers have a high product mix with a low volume for each of the services. Each request for bibliographical work is unique and there are few, if any, items which can be pulled from stock to meet the client's order. Each order has its own set of specifications requiring the use of different tools and operation times to produce the service. The basic product mix consists of the preparation of bibliographies, retrospective literature searches, selective dissemination services, translations and, in some cases, indexing and abstracting of documents. The retrospective literature searches, selective dissemination services, and translations are the basic staples of the center.

Some centers engage in abstracting and indexing activities on a continuous basis, producing specialized-subject abstract bulletins and also undertaking various types of indexing assignments on a short-term contract basis for Government and industrial clients. Because of the high product mix of the center, where each week's work differs markedly from the previous week and the volume for each is low, technical information departments are usually organized on a functional basis, where one person is assigned many different types of bibliographical work. For this reason, general-purpose bibliographical skills are most prevalent, and personnel of the center are able to handle a variety of tasks dictated by the schedule and work load. Translations do not fall into this category, although there is generally an in-house capability to deal with German and French. Other languages are usually handled by part-time consultants. One of the skills that all personnel of the center must acquire is a thorough knowledge of the collections of the library, particularly its bibliographical services and their organization. It is also advisable that the personnel have a knowledge of other libraries in the region and also know their collections to some extent. Technical information personnel are sometimes employed by the library for various reference tasks to acquire these skills before they are hired by the information center. In fact, the library may find it is hiring people for its own operation who may serve as potential candidates for future employment by the center. This is not always possible, but it affords the center the advantage of acquiring people who possess these important attributes. Because of the unique nature of many jobs, it is often necessary to rely on part-time consultants to handle highly specialized requests. Also, during peak business periods, consultants will be used. The full-time staff of the center are organized to meet a work load that is unpredictable. Requests for retrospective literature searches, translations, and so on occur at almost random intervals, and it is difficult to establish a schedule that will maximize the effective use of personnel and resources. Considerable flexibility is necessary to meet this varying work load, and for this reason many centers plan their activity around a median level.

To operate on a sound fiscal basis, it is often necessary to seek work of a continuous nature which allows planned sustained effort over a long period of time. There are indications that, without this kind of work, it would not be possible to achieve a self-supporting status. Contract-type work allows the center to continue its basic services, which are by and large of insufficient volume to support a full-time staff on a continuous basis. Some centers therefore may have Government contracts and also continue to render bibliographical services to their region. If the center becomes more directed towards contract work, its mode of operation changes and there is usually the need for supporting facilities to deal with Government agencies. Very few library organizations have these facilities at their disposal, and consequently Government-contract-type work is not a prominent feature of the technical information center.

Where the library is a part of a research and development establishment, the technical information center will have at its disposal facilities necessary to embark on this work and is usually more apt to direct itself towards this effort. In the case of The Franklin Institute, the Information Center uses the facilities of the research laboratories and relies to a large extent on the judgment and experience of its scientists and engineers. Proposal preparation may be undertaken jointly by both groups. Assistance in sales and preliminary contacts with Government agencies is often provided by laboratory personnel. Most libraries do not have this capability and will rarely enter into this type of activity in any large way.

The information services which the technical information center offers have been previously mentioned. They are the retrospective literature searches, current awareness or selective dissemination services, and translation services. As noted, some centers will engage in document indexing and abstracting assignments. This is usually done on a contract basis. This will not be discussed to any extent in this paper since it constitutes a major field in its own right. The retrospective literature search is one of the principal activities of the centers. It is basically used to investigate the published literature and to identify scientific and technical accomplishments of an earlier period. The center approaches a retrospective literature search in several ways. All requests for such work usually require that an estimate be provided. It usually requires considerable time to arrive at such an estimate and, in most cases, clients are informed that this is at best a very rough approximation of the true cost. Instead, the client may be asked to invest a few hours of time in a preliminary search to determine the extent and range of coverage needed to do an adequate job. Sometimes the client will specify the dates that he wishes covered and the publications to be searched. He will also describe as carefully as possible, usually after a considerable amount of interrogation with the technical information staff, the nature of the request in specific terms, some articles that may bear on the subject, and all facts related to the problem. It is extremely important that the technical information center person who is assigned to this job understand the problem completely. He is encouraged to discuss it with the client until he feels reasonably confident that he has all the facts at his fingertips. There are many times when this cannot be done. Clients, if they represent a large company, are usually very reluctant to divulge all the information on a company research project. At best, vagueness and generalizations are characteristic of the discourse between the client and the center. If the client has used the service over a considerable period of time, the rapport improves and many of these impediments are removed. Once the problem has been identified, the center staff analyze the type of search strategy which should be used. This step is extremely important, since on it depends success in one hour or perhaps the wasteful expenditure of time. The technical information center decides what bibliographical tools will be used to conduct the search. A bibliography, an abstracting service, indexing service, a card catalog of the library, another library in the area, an existing Government referral service, or another individual who may have the information in his possession are all considered as possible approaches. Search requests differ, and it requires a great amount of skill, judgment, and experience to select the right tools. The success of the technical information center largely depends on a variety of factors. A preliminary estimate which is based on a few hours of search time must reflect an accurate appraisal of the size of the job. The client will base his decision to undertake the work not only on the time estimate but also on an evaluation of the items which have been identified in the initial search. If these have a bearing on his problem, a full-fledged search will be authorized. This may run from a few hours to several weeks. In the latter case, the center will be in direct contact with the client, advising him of progress and supplying him with items which he can evaluate. He will be encouraged to participate in this process and add his technical judgment when needed. Photocopies of the articles may be supplied to him as they are located. The final product that he receives can take several forms. The simplest can be the photocopies of all items that are discovered. It also may be the author's abstracts from articles or it may be an abstract that appears in articles or it may be an abstract that appears in one of the bibliographical services. Rarely will the client request that the technical information center staff prepare an informative abstract for each item. It is simply too expensive. There are cases where a portion of the material may appear in a foreign language and it is necessary to translate the article or its abstract if the client is advised that it may be important. If there is an existing translation available by way of a translation pool or some other service, it will be supplied to reduce the expense. Foreign-language articles are often apt to contain data that are completely new to the client. Retrospective literature searches therefore will often focus on foreign literature to uncover new material that may not have appeared in domestic publications. A number of the references that are included in the final product usually are references to the foreign literature.

The selective dissemination service is designed to accomplish the same objectives as the retrospective literature search except that it focuses on the material that is published currently. The technical information center approaches the selective dissemination service in much the same way as it does the retrospective literature search. The staff discusses the area of technical interest that a client may wish to be kept informed in, and translates this interest into profile terms. Profile terms are words, concepts, and ideas that characterize a scientific and technical pattern. Again, it becomes important that there be clarity and precision in selecting the proper terms and that both parties fully understand each other's use and interpretation of the terms. These terms are important ele-

ments in the preparation of the selective dissemination service. The technical information center will select current journals that are most likely to contain the ideas and concepts associated with the terms and mark these off to be screened as they arrive in the library. The client will examine the list and eliminate those journals which he personally checks. If this list is sizable and there is a quantity of terms, it often becomes important, because of expense, to redefine the problem and establish narrower limits. This may be a continuous process carried out at periodic intervals as a client receives the service. The technical information center has the designated journals routed by the library to its offices; and a member of the staff scans the table of contents and title page of each journal, and checks each abstract, in an effort to identify articles which will have a bearing on the client's problem. After a number of runs, the person who undertakes this task becomes very familiar with the assignment and is usually able to handle several subject areas quite competently. Pertinent items from articles are marked for inclusion in the service. Photocopies of the articles, a list of titles, or an abstract bulletin can be supplied to the client according to his specifications at stated intervals. Usually the material which he receives is very recent and he is confident that he is up-to-date in his particular specialty.

Translations have been previously mentioned The consultants who undertake the work are selected for their technical competence and English language facility. In every case, the technical information center reviews and edits their work to insure that both conditions have been met.

In this brief review, emphasis has been placed on the operational characteristics of a library-oriented technical information center. Very little mention has been made of the larger developments that are occurring in this area and their implications for the technical information center. There are several trends which bear watching. Notable is the direct and substantial involvement on the part of the Federal Government and professional societies in the scientific and technical information field. Both groups are assuming a more direct role in the information transfer process. It is entirely likely that they will develop some type of centralized information centers in the very near future. In the case of the National Aeronautics and Space Administration, several such centers already are in operation. There is also presently in the Congress a bill (The State Technical Services Act of 1965) designed to establish technical information centers in each state. Such centers will assist local industry.

It is still too early to predict what effect if any these developments will have on the library which operates a technical information center. There is a possibility that such centers will be replaced by larger and better supported facilities. A more desirable alternative is the coupling of library technical information centers to the Government and society information systems. In such a role they can serve as regional representatives for these agencies. To qualify for this type of activity, it will be necessary for libraries to introduce new and different types of inputs into their system and to develop new skills on the part of the technical information center staff. A closer liaison between the library technical information center and the emerging government and society information activities will insure that no wide divergence occurs.

CAS Computer-Based Information Services

by W. C. Davenport

The Chemical Abstracts Service (CAS), a division of the American Chemical Society, has been providing chemical and chemical engineering information services since 1907. The problem then, as now, was that the amount of chemical literature published full-length in such "primary" sources as technical journals, patents, reports, and books was too great to be readily absorbed by individuals. In response to the problem, *Chemical Abstracts*[1] (*CA*) was introduced to provide a condensed record of chemical knowledge in the form of abstracts and indexes, a combination designed to help the individual gain access to primary literature. Today, even the condensed record is large, and its rate of growth has reached alarming proportions. As a consequence, CAS retrieval techniques are being broadened and improved.

Computer technology plays a major role in these broadened techniques, and the manner in which men and computers must interact to create effective and responsive information storage and retrieval services is the topic of this paper. The approach taken is not the computerization of a manual system, but the development of integrated information processing designed to take full advantage of the computer's speed, accuracy, and flexibility while conserving the professional intellectual effort that must be the core of any information processing system.

This paper describes the key points that characterize CAS' approach to large scale scientific-technical information systems that must handle over 100,000 documents per year. The first of these points is the "single analysis/multiple use" concept. Intellectual ability is a rare commodity and essential to an information system. Therefore, it makes sense to conserve that commodity and not use manpower to perform repetitive jobs or to waste effort analyzing information that somebody else has already analyzed. Ideally there should be only one intellectual analysis for any item of data that must be input to the system, with no other analysis required except for validation and error correction recycles.

At the same time, we also want the greatest flexibility in output. That is, we want the system to yield computer searches, manuals, "hard" documents, and increasingly more individualized services. To create this multiplicity of uses from a single analysis requires the creation of a data base, from which any number of different combinations of data can be drawn. Information added to the data base is not necessarily destined for a single specific service. It must accurately and completely cover the subject and be compatible with that already stored so that a single analysis of new information will result in a data base from which many services can be generated.

Another key concept is that computers should aid in the preparation of manual tools, such as printed abstract journals and indexes, and that computer searches should not be expected to entirely replace manual search. The computer will, instead, create new forms of manual tools and improve old forms to make them more effective.

This paper examines the above approaches and the extent of the computer involvement at CAS from three points of view: preparation of services, retrieval methods, and integration with other scientific-technical information processors.

PREPARATION OF SERVICES

CAS information services are designed both for retrieval and to help individuals keep abreast of developments concerning topics of interest: "retrospective search" and "current awareness." To provide these capabilities demands prompt accumulation and delivery of all useful news, based upon comprehensive coverage of primary literature, and in the organization, form (printed and mechanized), and degree of detail needed. Retrieval methods must provide access from many different points of view and must have built-in responsiveness to questions unforeseeable when the data is analyzed at input.

The publishing of abstract serials with indexes and the preparation of corresponding computer search files are complementary activities. Once an information processor has acquired, selected, and

SOURCE: Reprinted with permission from *Datamation* 14: 33-39 (March, 1968), published and copyrighted 1968 by F. D. Thompson Publications, Inc., 35 Mason Street, Greenwich, Conn.

prepared information for publishing, the creation of computer search files is but a modest extension. However, to exploit fully the computer's capability, computer files cannot be simply "tacked on" to the established publishing sequence. Instead, the entire publishing operation must be converted to computer processes so that operational economies can be realized and additional services can be generated at slight incremental cost: CAS has therefore adopted the data base approach: all publications and search files are entirely computer produced from the data base. (See Fig. 1.)

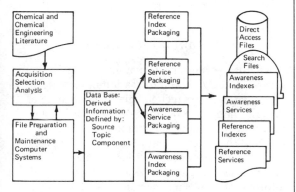

FIGURE 1. Integrated publishing and search file preparation
- ☐ Primary publications
- ☐ Manual operations
- ☐ Machine operations

The advantages of the data base-packaging approach are substantially improved currency, reduction in unit costs, new manual tools (indexes and brief "topic awareness" publications), and a computer-searchable data store. Further, the single analysis/multiple use characteristic makes effective use of the limited number of capable staff members who can be recruited for literature handling activities. The data base can also be used for future publications, such as handbooks and compendia, and can be stored in direct access units for on-demand inquiry from remote terminals.

The first phase is preparation of the base. It contains bibliographic and derived information for each document covered, identified by topic and component (for example, title, citation, author, abstract, index entries), recorded in sufficient detail for use in publications and computer search files. Computer involvement in this phase consists primarily of translating input forms (which have been designed to simplify the keyboarding task) to storage form, editing the input

for consistency and completeness, and supporting manuscript revision and correction to avoid the complete re-input of any correct data.

The second phase of the operation is packaging; this phase produces reference and awareness services, indexes, and computer search files. Reference service is the condensed record published (via computer typesetting and conventional printing) in the form of serial abstract issues and indexes. CAS prepares volume indexes every six months and collective indexes every five years. The abstracts contain enough information to answer some inquiries without reference to the primary literature; however, their primary function is as a screening device for determining whether or not the original paper is of current value. Indexes are compiled as soon as the abstract issue is composed. The computer transfers the abstract page references to the appropriate index entries, arranges the indexes, and controls typesetting to prepare master printing plates.

The awareness services are compilations of abstracts dealing with a more limited topic. They are produced by combining material selected from the *CA* issues and formatting it to highlight chemical substances and other key points. This separate publication is a small collection of topic-oriented material that might otherwise be scattered throughout a large compilation and is organized to make searching efficient. Indexes to the awareness services are prepared on a current basis and collected into volumes every six months.

As a co-product of both reference and awareness services, computer files are generated for use in searching and selective dissemination processes. The advantages of computer searching are that vast quantities of material can be scanned *and the search need not be based on either a classification system or a hierarchical index.* This latter point is particularly important in handling inquiries unforeseeable during data base preparation. Because the computer can search a large store without regard to the hierarchical arrangement, the number of access points is increased to permit effective retrieval of information not recorded at the highest index hierarchy levels. Awareness services are also important in this respect because they provide alternative (topic) organizations of the store. As a result, searches can be limited to the much smaller topic data base with which the inquiry is concerned.

Chemcial information has a characteristic not found in other scientific disciplines. This is the "language" of chemistry, which is based upon pictorial diagrams representing molecular structures, and upon complex, lengthy names that are also related to molecular structure.

Because a complex structure can be drawn with different orientations by different chemists, it is difficult for chemists always to recognize a structure. Since 1965 CAS has been operating an experiment Chemical Compound Registry System based on a computer algorithm that normalizes a keyboarded record of the elements, bonds, and attachments symbols of molecular structural diagrams that define chemical substances. The algorithm efficiently converts the record to a

unique and unambiguous form regardless of the drawing orientation or of the order in which the diagram symbols are recorded. (See Fig. 2.) Existing registry numbers are retrieved or file additions are assigned new registry numbers. These registry numbers are unique for each substance. Among the uses of the registry numbers and structural representation files are: correlating information concerning each substance despite ambiguous names and separated data sources, searching the store for specified diagram subgraph characteristics, and linking inter- and intra-disciplinary systems that are concerned with the properties of chemical substance.

REQUIRED TECHNOLOGY

Scientific-technical information processing in general, and chemical information processing in particular, requires technologies beyond state-of-the-art computer processing. As a result, implementation of data-base-oriented operations has required the development of specialized input, storage, and output capabilities. Primarily because of the complex chemical names, chemical information publishing demands the use of the Roman and Greek alphabets, upper and lower case letters, several type fonts (italics, bondface, small capital letters), and superior and inferior positions. In all, nearly 1500 symbols are used in *CA* issues. Storage problems are further complicated by the variability of the information components: for example, names of chemical substances range from two or three to several hundred characters in length. Considering the character range required, the extreme variability of the data and the fact that not all components are always present, the problem-oriented programming languages are, at best, very inefficient.

The representation problem is solved through the use of a double-byte character representation (one byte per unique character, with one additional byte to reflect the variations) in a double field arrangement that permits lexigraphical ordering unaffected by font and case. Standardization helps to reduce programming loads. The data base files are recorded in a data directed format; the same information component (field) is standardized; the same representation conventions are used in all CAS systems; and the major processing subprograms (keyboard-to-storage-form translators, edit routines, formatting routines, etc.) have been standardized.

CAS has also worked to make keyboarding more

Diagram above is a chemical structural formula. Circled numbers are references to the table below. Table represents the computer record (connection table) for the structure prior to conversion to canonical form.

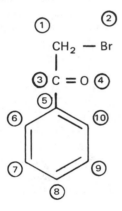

Acetophenone, 2-bromo-
C_8H_7BrO

Atom	Element	Attachment	Bond	Attachment	Bond	Attachment	Bond
1	C	2	3	1	1		
2	BR	1		1			
3	C	1	4	1	2	5	1
4	O	3		2			
5	C	6	10	1	2	3	1
6	C	7	5	2	1		
7	C	8	6	1	2		
8	C	9	7	2	1		
9	C	10	8	1	2		
10	C	9	5	1	2		

ACETOPHENONE, 2-BROMO-
C 0008H 0007BR001O 001

FIGURE 2. Computer representation of chemical structural formulas

efficient. Conventional keypunching has been phased out in favor of computer compatible magnetic-tape-generating data recorders (Mohawk Data Sciences' 1101 and 1181). Typewriter keyboards and type elements have been modified so that common symbols are directly keyboarded in lower case with flagged or programmed provision of upper-case characters. Then the upshift positions are freed for other characters such as Greek letters. The least frequently used symbols are input via three-character mnemonic codes. This approach is based on a statistical analysis where it has been found that the most common 80 characters account for 99.5% of all characters in the data base. Case, font, superior-inferior, and special symbols are accommodated by conventions using the remaining eight keyboard positions for flags. In addition, several types of keyboarding shortcuts have been developed; for example, computer programs automatically provide italicized and capitalized characters in chemical names, and the computer also expands useful abbreviations.

Computer typesetting has also been a problem. Most computer-driven printing devices offer a very limited number of characters and virtually no typeface variation. Furthermore, quality is a problem for printed publications. In 1965 CAS began using a special 120-character IBM 1403 print chain that has the full Roman alphabet in upper and lower case, 12 commonly used Greek letters, 14 special symbols, and on-line, superscript and subscript numerals

Now CAS composition is being converted to a modified IBM 2280 Film Recorder that can record all of the nearly 1500 symbols required to compose the *CA* issues. Characters are formed by program-controlled stroking of 35mm film with an electron beam. Soon, molecular structural formulas can be composed on-line with the text, eliminating the need for artwork and film-stripping, Film output is converted to offset plates for conventional printing. The quality obtained through this process is excellent (equivalent to hot type), and composition proceeds at a rate of between 1500 and 5000 characters per second, depending upon the character range used and the printing quality desired.

CURRENT STATUS

CAS is now in the midst of a step-by-step conversion of all operations to a computer basis. Our approach during this conversion has been to proceed in an orderly fashion from pilot-scale operation to full-scale production, solving problems as we went along. For example, in developing the CAS Chemical Compound Registry System, we operated on a very limited basis for six months before we began registering compounds that we encounter in indexing *CA*. Similarly, the introduction of new computer-based current awareness services has been deliberately paced: *Chemical Titles* in 1961, *Chemical-Biological Activities* in 1965, and *Polymer Science and Technology* in 1967. As a useful test of the problems to be encountered when all *CA* abstracts are computer based, we are now producing *Basic Journal Abstracts* containing the abstracts selected from 33 core journals. Each of these services has a corresponding magnetic tape search service and is available for subscription in magnetic tape form. During the next two years, we will convert *Chemical Abstracts* issues and indexes to a computer base and we will offer a new type of indexing/search service containing bibliographic identification and keyword index entries for all *CA* abstracts.

RETRIEVAL METHODS

In formation systems such as CAS operates, retrieval is the process of identifying references to documents that are likely to contain information of interest to the inquirer. As such, retrieval can take the form of an archival search, an awareness service, or selective dissemination. Any of these retrieval forms accomplish the same mission: to get the right information to the right man at the right time.

Improvements in retrieval methods, then, can be measured in increased relevancy of the information retrieval, increased timeliness in making the information available, and decreased cost in preparing the information.

In respect to printed indexes, currency and cost can both be improved through single analysis/ multiple use processing. Reducing the number of times an item must be handled reduces the time and cost required to prepare it for publication. Moreover, with a data base available from which index entries may be selected, a computer search or a magnetic tape index may precede a printed one by two or three weeks due to the savings of printing and binding time.

This must not be interpreted to mean that published indexes will be phased out in favor of computer searches. The value of indexes for manual use must be placed in proper perspective. Many information users do not have computers and many inquiries do not require the power (and expense) of computer searching. Although an over-all improvement in literature access often results from computer searching, the computer's contribution to improved manual access tools is equally significant. For example, computer generation of rotated indexes provides an increase in the useful access points available for manual use. An example is the KWIC (Key-Word-In-Context) indexes that are compiled by highlighting each non-trivial word in its preceding and following context. But although KWIC indexes have the advantage of being relatively inexpensive to prepare, the user must inquire under more than one entry; there are no "see" or "see also" cross references, and the number of index pages is greatly increased. CAS has also applied the KWIC approach to the element symbols in chemical molecular formulas to produce additional indexed access to the over-all information store without further intellectual effort. Such an index frees the user from the hierarchy used to arrange molecular formulas in a traditional molecular formula index.

As noted earlier, the primary purpose of awareness services is to deliver the information concerning a topic into a concentrated stream promptly so that a subscriber can more readily keep abreast of developments. However, related information is often appropriately included with other topics. For example, the biological effects of a given compound would be reported in *Chemical-Biological Activities* and the corresponding molecular structure is recorded in the Chemical Compound Registry. The data-base approach provides the means to interrelate these several pieces of information. Compounds discussed in *Chemical-Biological Activities* and *Polymer Science and Technology* are included in the Chemical Compound Registry System with cross-reference links established through the registry number in the awareness service and the awareness service reference in the Registry Files.

COMPUTER SEARCHING

The computer's ability to read the store of material rapidly, comparing the contents of the store with the content of an inquiry, and to select from the store those items which satisfy the inquiry, greatly exceeds manual capabilities. Although text searching does not always lend itself to exact answers, it is well to remember that where the flow or store of literature is large, comprehensive searching and scanning might not otherwise be practical. The impact of the computer text search is, simply stated, to extend man's ability to read

great amounts of information; albeit, with reduced "comprehension." As a result, computer text searching is effective and useful, even when not exact. The CAS text search systems match the inquirer's terms with terms appearing in the data base and list the bibliographic references for those information units that contain the specified terms. The search terms may be words, phrases, parts of words (prefixes, suffixes, imbedded letter sequences), author's names, journal identification, or, in fact, any stored data. The terms may be assigned numerical weights to indicate their relative importance in the search. By applying Boolean logic operaters, the searcher can construct correlative search questions requiring that several parameters be present (or absent) in a specified combination. This AND logic makes a search more restrictive. A question consisting of terms of A and B with AND logic would retrieve only references to documents that contain both terms. OR logic expands the basic search terms to include synonyms and related terms. For example, a request for references to sulfur compounds found in petroleum could be defined, in part: AND sulfur, OR sulfur, OR sulfide, OR sulphide, OR thiophene; AND petroleum, OR crude oil, OR gasoline, OR oil. A search of this type would retrieve references to documents containing any of the terms of the first group in combination with any terms in the second group. NOT logic specifies that a given term must not be present in the store being searched. The text search strategy can be very specific or quite general, as the user desires, and the search can cover the whole text of abstracts, titles, index phrases, or inverted term files.

Another CAS search system in experimental operation permits the searching of chemical structural formulas for structural subgraphs. This technique uses a comprehensive set of screens (bits indicating structural descriptors) to both provide rapid rejection of graphs and controlled degrees of question-to-file structural similarity. By including Compound Registry Numbers as parameters on a text search, it is possible to achieve correlated structural and text searching. When the entire data base is fully integrated, this correlative capability will be obtained in one run.

FUTURE CAPABILITIES

Although the current CAS search systems are serial tape-oriented processes, research in progress will result in on-line capability. Direct access storage and searching of chemical literature presents a formidable problem in the size of the store. By 1971 over 3,000,000 compounds will be in the store, abstracts will be accumulating at the rate of almost 400,000 per year, and index entries will accumulate at a rate of 3,000,000 per year. The files must be organized to obtain the best balance of storage costs and access time for a variety of access approaches and search strategies. There are suitable techniques (for example, list structuring) for direct access handling of stores limited to thousands of items. However, when the store grows to millions, these approaches become costly due to the excessive length of chains. CAS is investigating alternative approaches such as file partitioning and compact storage of efficient screens for rapidly scanning large blocks of information. It is too early to be able to determine the effectiveness of these approaches.

The packaging phase is being generalized to provide a wide range of customized services based on processing capabilities. This will make it possible to produce both standard and customized services through the application of standard processing subsystems, each controlled through parameters that specify the information sources, components, subjects, and character set options desired.

Another future capability about which we can speculate is the preparation of handbooks and compendia from the computer-based archives. Through reprocessing of the accumulated tape files, state-of-the-art compilations of abstracts and indexes can be prepared related to any topic definable in terms of the data base subjects and content. Through the combination of such periodic reviews with age-limited direct access capability, a powerful new set of tools will become available when data base archives accumulate to suitable size. Particularly attractive to the chemical community is the prospect of obtaining handbooks of molecular structures with corresponding references.

INTEGRATION WITH OTHER PROCESSORS

As information processors convert to computer-based operations, the potential for efficient information interchange increases. To exploit this, CAS and the parent American Chemical Society are experimenting to develop techniques for mechanized information interchange on a large scale.

One form of interchange is the exchange of abstracts between primary journals and secondary services. Common standards have been adopted for the ACS primary journals and *Chemical Abstracts*, permitting the use of ACS abstracts in CA with minimum additional editing. CAS/ACS cooperative experience with the *Journal of Organic Chemistry*, and the *Industrial Engineering Chemistry*, and the *Industrial Engineering Chemistry Quarterly*, has demonstrated that the approach is sound and a third journal has been added, the *Journal of Physical Chemistry*. The significance of this experiment is increased by the ACS conversion to computer-based publishing. CAS and ACS are developing a compatible set of character representation standard, file formats, and field content and identification standards that will permit direct interface via magnetic tapes produced as co-products with publications.

Another form of cooperative interchange under way is the linking of systems where there are common information requirements. Information concerning chemical substances is of concern in petroleum technology, medicine, atomic energy, food technology, agriculture and, in fact, most technological disciplines. A means of interlinking the information files is provided through the CAS Chemical Compound Registry System. For example, compound structural information of common interest to CAS, the National Library of Medicine, and the Food and Drug Administration is being routinely processed in the CAS Registry System. Structural information concerning compounds tested for usefulness in cancer research has been processed in a separate, confidential chemical structure data base under contract to the National Cancer Institute. Close coordination has been maintained between the structural handling systems of several foreign chemical companies, professional societies, and the CAS systems. Through these cooperative exchanges, the data bases of CAS and other processors are becoming compatible and directly interchangeable. Through the registry link among the various systems, it is possible to approach the store of any compatible system and to retrieve compound-oriented information from any of the other systems.

Other experiments are under way aimed at illustrating the feasibility of combining retrieval files in dissemination centers. One of these experiments, conducted by the Nottingham Research unit of the Chemical Society (London), is a selective dissemination service based upon *Chemical Titles, Chemical-Biological Activities*, and the National Library of Medicine's MEDLARS (MEDical Literature Analysis and Retrieval System) retrieval tapes. The advantage of the dissemination center approach is twofold: (a) to provide local service to organizations too small to operate large scale computer-based search systems, and (b) to combine the data bases from several disciplines into one comprehensive data base that, in total, serves the interests of participating institutions.   ■

CAS PROFILE

Chemical Abstracts Service, along with the parent American Chemical Society, is converting information systems to computer-based operations that produce a variety of literature services including reference, awareness, computer search files, and manual indexes. Material covered by CAS comes from more than 11,000 periodicals published in 54 languages, from patents issued by 25 nations, and from numerous irregular sources. All told, some 300,000 bibliographic source items are examined each year. Abstracting is provided by 3200 volunteer abstractors located throughout the world. For the past 20 years, the chemical literature has grown at the rate of 9% per year, compounded, and there is no clear indication that this rate will decrease in the near future. In 1967 the printed output of the Chemical Abstracts Service was more than 60,000 pages bearing some 570,-000,000 printed characters. **Chemical Abstracts**, the world's omnibus chemical and chemical engineering information service in the English language, carried abstracts from 258,000 papers and government reports and some 52,000 patents. By 1970, at the current rate of growth, the number of bibliographic items to be handled will grow to 360,000, and the volume of printed output will expand to some 74,000 pages, not including new services. It is expected that during the next 10 years, the number of items abstracted in **Chemical Abstracts** will exceed 3.5 million.

FOOTNOTES

[1]*Chemical Abstracts* is a weekly serial containing abstracts of selected original papers, patents, and reports of interest in chemistry. Since 1907, over 3.5 million abstracts have been prepared and published.

Computer-Based Selective Dissemination of Information (SDI) Service for Faculty Using Library of Congress Machine-Readable Catalog (MARC) Records

by William Joseph Studer

ORIGINS OF SELECTIVE DISSEMINATION OF INFORMATION

In essence the function of selective dissemination of information (SDI) is simply the dissemination of new information to individuals or groups according to their expressed interests, and as such this practice in libraries probably dates back to the very beginnings of librarianship. Like Molière's would-be gentleman who had unknowingly been speaking prose all his life, librarians through time have provided SDI service every time they have recalled a patron's interests and brought to his attention some new item of probable relevance. And even formalized versions of such service have existed from time to time.

But it should be pointed out that, although the practice of SDI is not new, its application in libraries has been generally irregular, informal, and very limited—depending variously on the memory, willingness, and free time of the librarian and contingent on the desire and ability of the patron to make his interests known.

There are a number of information dissemination services performed by various types of libraries which are often labeled as "current awareness" services. Some make use of electronic data processing (EDP) equipment in their operations, but the majority are carried out manually. In addition to SDI this current awareness category subsumes such activities as the routing of periodicals, abstract bulletins, indexes, and digests and the distribution of various types of new accessions lists. These kinds of alerting services are aimed at the broad base of a library's clientele, and as such represent the shotgun approach to information dissemination. SDI service, on the other hand, is aimed at individuals or individual groups and seeks to disseminate only that information which properly matches an explicit set of interests. Both types of service have the same goal of keeping users currently informed of new publications and are therefore sometimes erroneously considered the same; but their approaches are fundamentally different. We are concerned here only with current awareness service that is also SDI service.

When discussing the origin of the concept of selective dissemination of information, many people begin with H. P. Luhn's 1958 article in which he coined the phrase and set forth the ideas for an automated SDI service;[1] but it would be more accurate to credit the late Mr. Luhn with the innovation of using EDP equipment for SDI procedures—an innovation which became the foundation and impetus for the computer-based SDI systems that exist today. The Luhn-inspired systems represent a formalization and a large scale application of this heretofore casually performed service where computers match precise interest profiles for hundreds of users against thousands of indexed bibliographic records, providing to users on a regular basis notices for those documents that meet specified matching criteria. As in other areas of data processing and information retrieval, computerized SDI substitutes extended machine capabilities for the same functions performed in a less systematic way by human beings.

Generally speaking then, SDI service was exceptional and not highly organized until the advent of computer applications, but there is at least one notable exception. In 1939 the library of the College of Physicians and Surgeons of Columbia University inaugurated an alerting procedure which was referred to as "continuous bibliographic service."[2] This service was remarkable in its similarity to modern SDI systems, the unusual feature of course being that the operation was entirely manual. Conferences were held with users and their interests were defined and recorded. The library staff regularly scanned some 200 medical journals,

SOURCE: Reprinted with the author's permission from his doctoral thesis, Indiana University, 1968, p. 1-18 ("Background and Introduction").

as well as abstract bulletins and indexes; and citations for pertinent references were typed on 3x5 slips and sent to the users according to their specified interests. Users could request items by returning the slips to the library. At the time the article was written, 135 users were being supplied with some 16,000 citations per year. The authors felt that this type of service should be extended to all other subject areas of the university for reasons which are more pertinent today than they were in 1947:

> University librarians are increasingly conscious of the great mass of scholarly literature which pours into their libraries and is carefully cataloged, classified, and subject-headed, only to sit on the shelves untouched. It is generally recognized that one of the greatest impediments to the advancement of learning at the present time is the lack of effective means by which the findings of scholars—especially those of diverse nations and languages—can be brought to light, mobilized, and put to work. The conclusion is inescapable that the libraries of the world must in the future play a far more decisive role than at present in increasing the productivity of research. One of the major ways in which university libraries can contribute is through the establishment of a continuous bibliographic service for scholars requiring their active support.[3]

Judging from the lack of evidence in the literature, one must conclude that the response among academic or other libraries was minimal, if not totally lacking.

SDI SINCE 1959

The first automated SDI system, patterned after Luhn's design, was implemented in early 1959 at the IBM Corporation's Advanced Systems Development Division.[4] Applications of this new technique did not at first proliferate rapidly, probably because computer installations and applications were still quite limited in the late 1950's and early 1960's. By 1963 there were only some ten computer-based SDI systems in operation, and all but two of these were installed at various locations of IBM.[5] But between 1963 and early 1968, automated SDI systems have developed rapidly. The Share Research Corporation has identified 96 systems installed and 31 planned.[6] This same research firm is currently conducting an SDI systems census which will be published and updated on a continuing basis; and Mr. Terry R. Savage of the Corporation has compiled the most comprehensive bibliography to date on SDI (200 items) which will also be issued on a continuing basis.[7] Increasing interest in and the rapid growth of automated

SDI systems are further evidenced by three published survey/analysis studies undertaken during the last two years. One is a master's thesis from the University of Chicago's Graduate Library School;[8] and the other two are government research reports issuing from projects sponsored by the U. S. Army Natick Laboratories[9] and the U. S. Air Force's Office of Aerospace Research,[10] this last report presenting the preliminary findings of an uncompleted survey. In combination, these studies offer a good historical overview and state-of-the-art summary of SDI development, operations, and procedures. In recent years the topic of selective dissemination of information has also been represented at many institutes and conferences (national and international) dealing with information science. At the 1967 meeting of the American Documentation Institute (now American Society for Information Science), SDI found its way onto the formal agenda with five papers devoted to the subject.[11]

There are a number of reasons for this marked increase in interest and in the number of operational, experimental, and planned SDI systems over the past several years. The much talked about "information explosion" has proved to be not simply a cliché, but also a grim reality which has given impetus to a spreading recognition of the importance and value of information services which have the potential to present pertinent information to the right person as quickly as possible. Also to be counted as factors are a growing understanding of the computer and its capabilities and, at the same time, a steady increase in the number of computer installations and in development and applications of computer techniques for information processing. And an important stimulus is the recent availability of large, regularly incremented files of machine-readable bibliographic data from such government sources as the National Aeronautics and Space Administration, Atomic Energy Commission, Defense Documentation Center, and National Library of Medicine and from such commercial sources as Chemical Abstracts Service, Institute for Scientific Information, and PANDEX. The difficulties and costs of input preparation at the local level are often prohibitive, and local use of these centrally prepared files has provided a viable solution in many cases.

Direct SDI service to individuals or groups is also now available on a fee basis from several sources. The Institute for Scientific Information (Philadelphia, Pa.) offers Automatic Subject Citation Alert (ASCA), a weekly SDI service which monitors articles in some 1,800 scientific journals.[12] PANDEX (New York) offers a similar service covering 2,100 scientific journals, 6,000 scientific and technical books, and many technical reports and patents.[13] The SDI system of the Technical Information Dissemination Bureau of the State University of New York at Buffalo scans some 2,000 technical journals and also unclassified government research and development reports.[14] INFORM (Wisconsin Commerce Abstracts Service, University of Wisconsin, School of Business) provides a business-oriented SDI service based on articles from some 60 journals in all fields of business.[15] Some of NASA's regional dissemination centers furnish SDI service to industry from a data base of 75,000 annually processed documents.[16]

SDI'S PUBLIC–PRESENT AND FUTURE

An investigation of operating, experimental, and planned SDI systems reveals two striking aspects: (1) that, with few exceptions, this information service has been or will be established to serve various scientific and technical communities of government and industry; (2) that, given this orientation, the literature controlled by SDI systems consists predominantly of journal articles and technical reports. A notable exception to the latter is the above-mentioned PANDEX service which includes some 6,000 scientific and technical books annually. Even those who write about SDI seldom mention other potential areas of application. In the few cases where the academic science and technology communities are being served, they are usually benefiting from an outside SDI system operated by the government, industrial organizations, or commercial information services. However, this situation is hardly surprising since the vast journal and technical report literature of science and technology defies effective manual control; and government and industry, as large generators and users of this literature and as agencies having the research funds, have been at the forefront in developing means to cope effectively with the information explosion.

But computer applications to the information needs of the social sciences and humanities are on the rise, and accompanying this trend is a growing body of evidence and of suggestions that the SDI approach to literature control can usefully serve a variety of subject areas and users in the academic community, as well as elsewhere.

The Administrative Reference Library of Wayne State University (Detroit) furnishes around 100 administrators in higher education with SDI notices generated from pertinent articles in some 70 journals. The U. S. Office of Education funded this SDI experiment in 1965, but now the university finances the project.[17] In 1966 Kenneth Janda, an associate professor of political science at Northwestern University, launched an experimental SDI service for a selected group of political science faculty, using as a data base the articles in 18 relevant journals. When this service was reported in print, it was intended that an expansion of the system should follow.[18] In 1967 the engineering-science libraries of Northwestern also embarked on an experiment in SDI service to faculty using tape input provided by Chemical Abstracts Service.[19]

During the last six years several university libraries have announced plans to establish book-oriented SDI systems that would alert faculty to newly received materials in their fields of interest,[20] but unfortunately none of these plans has come to fruition—or has even reached the experimental stage. The library of the new Federal City College (Washington, D. C.) is to include among its many services a program "which will provide individual notices of new accessions of interest" to both faculty and students.[21]

The results of a 1966 survey on "the use of data processing equipment by libraries and information centers" would seem to indicate that the concept of SDI service may have infiltrated a number of academic libraries. Figures from the report show that eighteen college and university libraries are using EDP equipment in the operation of current awareness services,[22] that sixty-three have plans to establish an automated current awareness service,[23] and that forty have relevant studies under way.[24] It is impossible to tell how many of these reported services are really SDI systems (as the distinction between SDI and other current awareness services has been made). There are no pertinent references in the literature on SDI. This same survey reports that three public libraries are operating automated current awareness services, ten have plans, and six are making studies. It is doubtful that many of these represent true SDI systems. The only reference to a specific public library SDI system that has come to light relates to an ongoing experiment in Indiana,[25] which is based on an idea expounded by one of the project directors in a recent issue of *American Documentation*.[26]

The SDI technique has found its way into the discussion and recommendations of several recent studies on information transfer and networks. The

Committee on Information in the Behavioral Sciences (National Research Council) sees SDI as having a definite role to play in serving the information needs of the social sciences.[27] In a report recommending the establishment of a national library agency to serve all disciplines, the Committee on National Library/Information Systems (CONLIS) suggests that SDI service should be available.

> In addition to access to the content of all recorded information, it should also be possible to obtain current, short-term, periodic reports of information newly received.[28]

The "report of a planning conference on information transfer experiments" to be conducted at the Massachusetts Institute of Technology (Project Intrex) considers SDI in several of its sections,[29] observing in part that:

> Programs for SDI are presently operating in many libraries, mostly in industrial or government organizations; they appear to have received little attention from academic institutions. It seems particularly appropriate, therefore, that Project Intrex should undertake an experiment to determine the cost and feasibility of SDI service in a university context, and to explore the extent to which such service might be undertaken as a normal part of the library program.[30]

And in speaking of the university library and its continuing evolution, the report suggests:

> It would be extremely desirable if the library of the future could call to the attention of interested persons those documents, books, or other information sources that might be helpful to them, as these documents are published or as they are received by the library.[31]

The report of a conference on information networks conducted by the Interuniversity Communications Council (EDUCOM) also recognizes a need for SDI service:

> Current awareness service, by means of annotated acquisitions lists or selective dissemination of information (SDI), now exists in varying degrees in industry, universities, and government. Even where SDI has been offered extensively, users still find accessions lists to be of value. A network ought to offer services of both types of *(sic)* participants. Some individuals may want notification of only highly specialized materials. Others may wish to broaden their interests. The network should make both varieties of notification available under control of the user. Universities, especially, have lagged far behind in providing such services. User needs in such institutions in this respect are probably largely unrecognized.[32]

The SDI technique of information transfer in educational research was thoroughly investigated in a study performed for the U. S. Office of Education to give guidance in the development of the Educational Research Information Center (ERIC), and the conclusions strongly urge the creation of SDI systems at both the local and national levels.[33] University researchers and state education department staffs who were consulted are very much in favor of such a system.

The increasing number of SDI systems gives evidence that this automated technique has proved to be a successful means for alerting users to new literature in their fields of interest; and the foregoing presentation testifies that the practice and concept of SDI service is no longer limited to clientele and materials in its original field of science and technology although applications of SDI outside this general subject area are just beginning. We are living in an information-conscious era with a growing recognition of the information needs of many kinds of users. It would be foolhardy to speculate in numbers, but over the next decade SDI systems will likely proliferate as one part of the overall attempt to meet those needs.

ELEMENTS OF A COMPUTER-BASED SDI SYSTEM

The purpose of SDI service is to facilitate and improve the process of identifying new information by alerting users automatically to current documents in their fields of interest.[34] In attempting to accomplish this purpose, SDI systems regularly compare machine-readable files of new document descriptions with machine-readable users' interest profiles, generating for each user notices for only those documents which properly match his expressed interests. Thus the SDI system automatically selects from among the whole those items having a high probability of pertinence, while rejecting those having little or no probability of interest.

Although there are differences in approach and detail, all computer-based SDI systems work on the same basic principles and include the same basic elements:

A. Input to the System
   1. Machine-readable descriptions of documents.
   2. Machine-readable user interest profiles; and user feedback which alters interest profiles.

B. Procedures and Processes Performed
   1. Preparation of, or subscription to, machine-readable document records.

2. Initial construction and coding of interest profiles.
3. Matching of users' interests against document descriptions and selecting of records which match properly.
4. Printing and dissemination of notices to users.
5. Rating of document relevance by users and return of rating forms as feedback to the system.
6. Modification of interest profiles on the basis of feedback (which becomes input in A-2).

C. Output from the System
   1. Notices consisting of some kind of document description and accompanying rating forms.
   2. Statistics which indicate the operational characteristics of the system, e.g., number of notices sent, number judged relevant, number of items which were new, etc.

Machine-readable input generally consists of bibliographic descriptions (together with index terms and often including abstracts) of documents which form the search data base. This input is either prepared locally or obtained ready-made from a central source. User interest profiles are constructed from the same vocabulary used to index the documents and are stored on punched cards or magnetic tape. One of the various search strategies (Boolean, weighted term, etc.) effects proper comparison of document descriptors with interest profiles. Notices for properly matched documents are printed (usually by computer on two-part IBM cards) and sent to the users who rate each document's relevance on a rating form and return these evaluations as feedback to the SDI system. On the basis of this feedback, profiles are modified. Various kinds of statistics are usually generated in order to provide a basis for assessing the effectiveness of the SDI system. Most SDI installations will also provide users with copies of the documents to which they have been alerted.

THE BOOK-ORIENTED SDI EXPERIMENT— RAISON D'ETRE

The use of computers by academic libraries as a whole has been on a small scale and is still very much in the incipient or planning stages. Where computer applications are in evidence, however, they have been concerned mostly with "housekeeping" or internal control functions such as ac-

counting, acquisition, circulation and serials control, and the preparation of catalog cards, book catalogs, and accessions lists rather than being directed toward improved or extended user services. This initial concern with technical services is understandable since the repetitive routines involved are so costly on a manual basis and are such obvious candidates for automation. And to be sure, any improvement of internal management is of at least indirect benefit to users; but the typical faculty patron can see little evidence that the flurry of library automation is of significant benefit to him.

The following observation was made in a recent article on library research:

> Is it possible to use automation for increased service? Most, if not all, of the current experiments in data processing and computer application to libraries are in the area of technical services, and the use of data processing and computer equipment seems to be for the librarian's, rather than the user's benefit. . . . It is time to do some fundamental research on the development of computer applications to service, rather than limiting our vision to the field of administration and technical procedures which may ease only the librarian's task.[35]

It was in accord with this feeling that the writer undertook to make experimental use of MARC records to provide automated SDI service to faculty—a service aimed directly and exclusively at the individual user.

In early 1966 Indiana University was chosen as one of sixteen official participants in the MARC (MAchine-Readable Catalog) Pilot Project to be conducted by the Library of Congress (LC) during the latter months of 1966 and the first half of 1967—an experimental program in which LC would produce and transmit its traditional 3x5 catalog records in machine-readable form.[36] Each week the Library would send a master file magnetic tape to which had been added the catalog records for a large portion of English-language monographs processed during the previous week.

This meant that for the first time a substantial body of bibliographic records for recent books (books in the very broad sense of nonperiodical, monographic literature) in all subject fields would be available for computer manipulation; and it occurred to the writer that MARC records could provide a good data base for a book-oriented selective dissemination service to faculty.

It seemed probable that sources generally used by faculty for learning of newly published books are not as timely and inclusive as might be desired;

that the task of finding out about new books is performed irregularly and incompletely; and that the increasing rate of publication and growing inter-disciplinary bent of many faculty might be causing additional problems in identifying relevant items. With these kinds of ideas in mind, the following hypothesis was formulated with regard to providing book-oriented SDI service to faculty in the social sciences:

> That it is feasible to generate biweekly lists of notices for relevant works from the MARC file by computer-matching of faculty interests (translated into Library of Congress subject headings and classification numbers) against subject headings and classification numbers on MARC records; that these lists would provide faculty with a convenient, valuable, and extended source for learning of newly published works in their fields of interest—a source which is both broader and generally more current than the ones by which faculty are now informed of new books; and that the receipt of SDI notices would increase the amount of faculty participation in the process of recommending books for library acquisition.

The area of the social sciences was chosen because the sampling base had to be limited in some way, and the writer felt best equipped to deal with faculty interests in this general area. It is often said that current books are by and large outdated sources of information in science and technology; the journal and technical report literature is considered the primary medium for the transmission of new knowledge in these fast moving areas. Whatever the accuracy of this generalization, such is not the case with social sciences and humanities where book-type materials still constitute significant media for the transmission of new informa-

tion and ideas. And except for possible reservations about the utility of book-oriented SDI service in the broad fields of science and technology, there is no reason to assume that such an SDI system would serve the faculty in one subject area better than in another.

COMPUTER PROGRAMMING SUPPORT FOR THE SDI SYSTEM

The Aerospace Research Applications Center (ARAC) at Indiana University, an information center affiliated with the National Aeronautics and Space Administration, operates computer-based SDI and retrospective retrieval services. Having only an introductory knowledge of computer programming, the writer approached ARAC with his idea. After a discussion of the MARC Pilot Project, the MARC record format, and the requirements and purposes of the SDI experiment, the directors of ARAC expressed interest in the extension of such a service should the experiment prove successful. Thus they were willing to supply the needed programming assistance. It was concluded that an existing retrospective retrieval program could be adapted for use in matching interest profiles against MARC entries, and ARAC agreed to make the necessary modifications and to write two auxiliary programs to accomplish other requisite steps in the SDI process.

The use of computer programs which were not tailor-made meant accepting a predetermined input format and working within other limitations (which will be discussed later), but it was felt that none of these conditions would seriously affect the outcome of the experiment.

FOOTNOTES

[1] H. P. Luhn, "A Business Intelligence System," *IBM Journal of Research and Development,* II (October, 1958), 314,328.

[2] Thomas P. Fleming, Estelle Brodman, and Seymour Robb, "A Continuous Bibliographic Service in University Libraries," *College & Research Libraries,* VIII (July, 1947), 322-328.

[3] *Ibid,* p. 328.

[4] C. B. Hensley, et al, *Selective Dissemination of Information: Report on a Pilot Study, SDI-I System*, Report No. 17-039 (Yorktown Heights, N.Y.: IBM Corporation, Advanced Systems Development Division, 1961), 41 pp.

[5] C. B. Hensley, *SDI Bibliography* (Yorktown Heights, N.Y.: IBM Corporation, Advanced Systems Development Division, 1962), 9 pp.; C. B. Hensley, *Selective Dissemination of Information (SDI): State of the Art in May, 1963* (Yorktown Heights, N.Y.: IBM Corporation, Advanced Systems Development Division, 1963), 14 pp.

[6] Share Research Corporation, *SDI Systems Status* (Santa Barbara, Calif.: Share Research Corporation, 1968), 5 pp.

[7] Terry R. Savage, *SDI Bibliography-1*, SRTP-1095 (Santa Barbara, Calif.: Share Research Corporation, 1968), 26 pp.

[8] Judith Ann Holt, "Selective Dissemination of Information: a Review of the Literature and the Issues," *Library Quarterly,* XXXVII (October, 1967), 373-391.

[9] William A. Bivona and Edward J. Goldblum, *Selective Dissemination of Information: Review of Selected Systems and a Design for Army Technical Libraries.* Prepared for U.S. Army Natick Laboratories, Natick, Mass. AD636916 (Springfield, Va.: Clearinghouse for Federal Scientific and Technical Information, 1966), 110 pp.

[10] Alexander S. Hoshovsky and C.S. Downie, *Selective Dissemination of Information in Practice: Survey of Operational and Experimental SDI Systems,* OAR67-012 (Arlington, Va.: U.S. Air Force, Office of Aerospace Research, 1967), 15 pp.

[11] American Documentation Institute, *Levels of Interaction Between Man and Information; Proceedings of the American Documentation Institute Annual Meeting, New York, October 22-27, 1967* (Washington, D.C.: Thompson Book Company, 1967), pp. 284-310.

[12] See the latest brochure from the organization.

[13-15] See that latest brochure from the organization.

[16] "CAST, KASC, ARAC, and SDI, or Some New Ways to Keep Informed," *Educom: Bulletin of the Interuniversity Communications Council,* II (January, 1967), 5-8.

[17] *Ibid*, pp. 5-7.

[18] Kenneth Janda and Gary Rader, "Selective Dissemination of Information; a Progress Report from Northwestern University," *American Behavioral Scientist*, X (January, 1967), 24-29.

[19] "Northwestern Libraries Plan Info Dissemination," *Library Journal,* LXXXXII (July, 1967), 2502.

[20] Louis A. Schultheiss, Don S. Culbertson, and Edward M. Heiliger, *Advanced Data Processing in the University Library* (New York: Scarecrow Press, 1962), pp. 146-147; Edward M. Heiliger, "Florida Atlantic University: New Libraries on New Campuses," *College & Research Libraries*, XXV (May, 1964), 184; Ritvars Bregis, "The Ontario New Universities Library Project—an Automated Bibliographic Data Control System," *College & Research Libraries*, XXVI (November, 1965), 504-505.

[21] "Capital's New College Plans Unusual Library," *Library Journal*, LXXXXIII (March 15, 1968), 1090.

[22] Creative Research Services, *The Use of Data Processing Equipment by Libraries and Information Centers; a Survey Prepared for Documentation Division, Special Libraries Association and Library Technology Program, American Library Association* (New York: Creative Research Services, 1966), pp. 9, 11.

[23] *Ibid*, p. 39.

[24] *Ibid*, p. 45.

[25] "Adult Service and the Computer in Indiana," American Library Association, Adult Services Division, *Newsletter*, (Winter, 1968), 25.

[26] Charles H. Davis, "SDI: A Program for Public Libraries," *American Documentation*, XIIX (July, 1967), 139-145.

[27] National Research Council, Committee on Information in the Behavioral Sciences, *Communication Systems and Resources in the Behavioral Sciences,* Publication 1575 (Washington, D.C.: National Academy of Sciences, 1967), pp. 15, 50, 61.

[28] "A National Library Agency . . . a Proposal," *ALA Bulletin*, LXII (March, 1968), 260.

[29] Carl F. J. Overhage and R. Joyce Harman, eds., *INTREX; Report of a Planning Conference on Information Transfer Experiments, September 3, 1965* (Cambridge, Mass.: The MIT Press, 1965), pp. 49, 115-118, 238-240.

[30] *Ibid*, p. 115.

[31] *Ibid*, p. 14.

[32] George W. Brown, James G. Miller, and Thomas A. Keenan, *EDUNET; Report of the Summer Study on Information Networks Conducted by the Interuniversity Communications Council (EDUCOM)* (New York: John Wiley & Sons, Inc., 1967), p. 64.

[33] Jules Mersel, Joseph C. Donahue, and William A. Morris, *Information Transfer in Educational Research.* Submitted to the U.S. Office of Education, Contract OE-5-99-264, Final Report TR-66-15-7 (Sherman Oaks, Calif.: Informatics, Inc., 1966), various paging.

[34] The term "document" is used in the generic sense of any published material.

[35] Peter Hiatt, "The Cry for Library Research—Eloquent But Unheeded," *Wilson Library Bulletin*, XLI (May, 1967), 923.

[36] For a detailed description of all aspects of the MARC Pilot Project and the magnetic tape record format, see: U.S., Library of Congress, Information Systems Office, *A Preliminary Report on the MARC (MAchine-Readable Catalog) Pilot Project* (Washington, D.C.: Library of Congress, 1966), 101 pp. A highly condensed version of the report was published by LC's Information Systems Office in 1967: *Project MARC; an Experiment in Automating Library of Congress Catalog Data*, 16 pp.; and the director of the project discussed it thoroughly at a recent conference, for which see: Henriette D. Avram and Barbara E. Markuson, "Library Automation and Project MARC; an Experiment in the Distribution of Machine-Readable Cataloging Data," in *The Brasenose Conference on the Automation of Libraries*, edited by John Harrison and Peter Laslett (London: Mansell, 1967), pp. 97-127.

Information Network Prospects in the United States

by Joseph Becker

Unmistakable signs are pointing the way toward the creation sometime soon of a national information network in the United States. The concept of a national network implies the interconnection of existing information systems and libraries through communications. Certainly one of the great strengths of this nation is the great array of intellectual, scholarly, and research resources to be found in its libraries and information centers. Without integration and close cooperation, however, these resources will remain a series of separate, insulated institutions. But if maximum communication can be established among them, this array can be converted into a national resource of immense value to citizens throughout the country. Belief in the importance and value of information networks has been expressed at the highest levels of government during 1967/68, and if this attitude persists, the vision of a network could easily be developed into a national goal.

NATIONAL ACTIVITY

President Johnson, on two occasions in 1967, urged the integration of modern communications with library and information practices. The first speech was at the Conference on World Education in Williamsburg, Virginia, where he stated the need for providing the best library facilities in the world through exploitation of present communications technology.[1] On November 7, in Washington, D. C., when the President signed into law the Public Broadcasting Act of 1967, he remarked on the probable effects of information networks on the individual: "I think we must consider new ways to build a great network for knowledge—not just a broadcast system, but one that employs every means of sending and storing information that the individual can use." [2]

The President also appointed Eugene V. Rostow of the State Department to head a one-year commission, the President's Task Force on Communications Policy, and charged it with the responsibility of conducting a comprehensive review of United States telecommunications policy. Congress has passed a bill entitled the Higher Education Act of 1968, which includes a separate section on networks known as Title IX—Networks for Knowledge. Title IX has provisions designed to encourage and further joint programs among institutions of higher learning for the cooperative exploration of the new computer and communications technologies. Last May, in announcing the reorganization of the major health agencies, the Department of Health, Education, and Welfare stated that the National Library of Medicine would continue to serve as the Department's vital center for health communications and related scientific development.

Other national developments that are creating demands for expanded library service and for the building of information networks are the State Technical Services Act, the National Library of Medicine's program for regional medical libraries, the Regional Medical Program for Heart Disease, Cancer and Stroke, the Office of Education's support of libraries, the joint program of the Library of Congress, the National Library of Medicine, and the National Agricultural Library for development of machine-readable catalog data for monographs and serials, and the supporting programs of the National Science Foundation. During 1967, it became apparent to the National Science Foundation that the developing discipline-oriented information systems in the professional societies, the mission-oriented systems in the Federal agencies, and the private institutions and organizations with their specialized information systems would require some kind of coordination and eventual integration into a national information network.[3] These programs have not only created a new and more favorable climate for libraries and information centers but have also emphasized the critical need for communication among them.

Despite the widespread enthusiasm for networks, neither industry nor government has yet proposed a grand strategy for coordinating the diversity of

SOURCE: Reprinted from *Library Trends,* 17: 306-317 (January, 1969), by permission of the publisher. Copyright 1969 by the University of Illinois Board of Trustees.

information network schemes that are springing up independently throughout the United States. Active network programs were underway within states, regions, government, professional societies, and industry. A nationwide plan for uniting the scattered information networks is urgently needed. The Committee on Scientific and Technical Information (COSATI) of the Federal Council for Science and Technology has been trying hard to solve the network interface problems of the Federal Agencies and, in addition, established a sub-committee in 1965 to work exclusively on the development of a national system. Another committee of national scope is the Committee on Scientific and Technical Communications (SATCOM) established by the National Academy of Sciences. One of the primary functions of this group is to improve methods for promoting effective relationships between information systems and principal producers and users of scientific and technical information, and another objective is to stimulate the application of new techniques and systems for information transfer. Both COSATI and SATCOM share the belief that the earlier a basis for technical integration of networks can be established, the sooner it will become possible to incorporate these conceptions into local network planning, and the more quickly a national information network will become a reality.

Aware that a multitude of different systems were developing inside and outside the government, the National Bureau of Standards, within the past year, has initiated programs for standardizing formats for textual and numerical data exchanged through computers and communications. Also, a special Task Force was established by the White House Office of Science and Technology with the cooperation of the National Academy of Sciences for the Interchange of Scientific and Technical Information in Machine Language (ISTIM).

Although the U. S. government has been considering ways to tie together its own resources, it has not been blind to the tremendous opportunities which communications will provide for the international exchange of information. Leonard H. Marks, Director of the United States Information Agency, in an address before the National Association of Educational Broadcasters, proposed methods for implementation of a "world information grid" using satellite facilities through the INTELSAT consortium of nations.[4]

The above recounting is but a brief sketch of the very lively interest and activity prevailing within the Federal structure and the private sector in support of the information network concept. An additional network dimension exists at the state level.

Many states are readying network plans under Title III of the Library Services and Construction Act. Thus far, installation of teletype and telefacsimile networks has received the most attention but there are also signs of affiliation and amalgamation at the local level due to the availability of the MARC (MAchine Readable Catalog) computer tapes from the Library of Congress. MARC tapes are certain to have a consolidating effect on technical processing, particularly among public and school libraries.[5] The concept of a dynamic network involving all types of libraries has been advanced in Washington, New York, California and other states.

Bibliographic standardization is also being introduced abroad. The *shared cataloging* program of the Library of Congress is providing rigid specifications for the recording of bibliographic records of monographs in libraries in France, Great Britain, Denmark, Sweden, and other countries. Both MARC and the shared cataloging program constitute significant developments in the library world that will eventually facilitate network integration of bibliographic data on an international basis.

One functional group that has been active with respect to network building in the United States has been the educational community. Education's aim in this area is to improve the quality of instruction and research through exploration of the new computer and communications technologies. With the support of the U. S. Office of Education, network projects of various kinds have been initiated in many elementary and secondary school systems. In higher education a consortium was formed to further the same interest. The Interuniversity Communications Council (EDUCOM) is a voluntary consortium of educational institutions whose function is to facilitate the extraorganizational communication of a university. The concept of networking is central to the activities of EDUCOM, which, by 1968, had over ninety member institutions. An educational network among universities carries the idea of sharing to its ultimate goal; information resources available through any one member would be equal to the sum of the resources of all participating institutions.[6]

FROM COOPERATION TO COMMUNICATION

The history of information networks may be traced back to the time when librarians first recognized the benefits of interlibrary cooperation. In 1853, for example, at the Librarians' Convention in New York City, Monsieur A. Vattemare described the chronology of cooperative efforts from 1832 to that date and discussed the usefulness of international cooperation among libraries. He spoke of the desirability of having a "permanent system of bibliographic exchange between governments, a central agency on each Continent in connection with each other to negotiate these exchanges," and the value of union lists.[7] Vattemare's dream was visionary in 1853 but today his ideas can be implemented in a very practical way; some of them have already been partially realized.

Two developments are responsible for the trend toward greater interlibrary cooperation. The first stems from World War II and the increase in government-sponsored research and development in science and technology. The second is evident in the changes in American education and culture that have occurred over the past decade and which have resulted in corresponding changes in the variety and quantity of published materials. Both have a major influence on the development of special libraries and information centers. These two forces converged and combined to generate new pressures for the creation of new information services that took many different forms. The number and type of abstracting and indexing services increased, many different union lists and catalogs evolved, library acquisition and exchange programs flourished and current awareness services were started to provide greater coverage and extended refinements. Further expansion of diverse information services in this country has taken place during the past two decades. The government, for example, has established large-scale *mission-oriented* information programs at NASA, Atomic Energy Commission, and in the Department of Defense, to make the fruits of government research more widely available. In the private sector, on the other hand, the development of *discipline-oriented* information systems was emphasized. These are found in the fields of chemistry, physics, biology, geology, mathematics, and so forth, and are operated by the professional societies. Another phenomenon has been the development of specialized information or analysis centers which serve as scientific middlemen to distill, interpret, and synthesize information in direct support of the working scientist.[8] More and more, these organizations are producing machine-readable files, and efforts are underway to develop computer techniques for cross-accessing these data in order

to satisfy a variety of interdisciplinary interests. The fact that the data are machine-readable increases their usefulness, because they are susceptible both to computer processing and to communications transfer.[9]

No one library can ever hope to become self-sufficient in the face of this expanding universe of information, and it is this realization which adds impetus to the U. S. government's drive for better communications through an information network in the United States.

Through the application of the new computer and communications technologies, and with the advent of Federal, state, and local legislation and programs, there is a definite trend in the U. S. toward the establishment of regional information systems, intra-state communication networks, centralized processing centers, and so forth. Gradually, as this movement toward synthesis extends, smaller information cooperatives are likely to develop into bigger ones, and in time each will become a communications node in an increasingly encompassing network.

PROFESSIONAL MOTIVATION

Librarians are watching network developments very carefully. They are quick to grasp the meaning of interlibrary communications, and recognize the opportunity it will provide all libraries to share in the aggregate resources of the nation.[10] There are also many signs of telecommunications activity within the profession. The year 1967/68 witnessed an increase in experimentation with facsimile for interlibrary loan, a noticeable rise in the number of teletype stations in libraries, and further research into the area of remote access to time-shared computer-controlled catalogs. Interest in information networks among librarians is therefore high and is constantly gaining momentum. Three motivating forces are responsible—the first is *service*, the second *economics*, and the third *technology*.

Librarians are eager to improve their local systems and services. This aim is expressed in a series of objectives: to serve more people, to make information more uniformly available, to supplement local collections by drawing more effectively on external sources, to integrate multimedia materials into the mainstream of library activity, to individualize library service, and to change the library's image from that of a place "where the books are kept" to that of an active information center. Networks imply a degree of democratization of information, a steady increase in the ability to serve at all points of service, and cooperative sharing without constraints of time, distance, or form of data. Librarians are thus motivated to pursue the network idea because of its potential service advantages.

Economics is the second factor. Financial pressures are forcing libraries, and all information activities for that matter, to consider ways of sharing rather than duplicating materials and other resources. The publishing rate and the cost of printed materials are rising steadily, and libraries are well aware that they cannot afford the luxury of open-ended purchasing for their individual collections but are required to buy more restrictively. This means, therefore, that appropriate local collections must be built to meet immediate needs, and a mechanism, such as a network, must be devised to make readily available the resources of distant, specialized collections. Furthermore, it is costly to establish a new library for every new population center. Certainly, an expanding and shifting population requires the best library service, but the cost of proliferating comprehensive replicate collections is prohibitive. Using the distribution potential of a communications network appears to be a very attractive and realistic alternative.

The third motivating force is technology. Librarians have begun, within the past five years, to accept the premise that it is technically feasible for sound, pictures, and digital data stored at distant locations to be made available with relative ease. Computers, with their direct access capability, and communications, with their multimedia distributive capacities, can function as effective coupling devices for bringing an individual user and his sources of information closer together.[11]

WHAT IS A NETWORK?

Broadly defined, any network is an interconnection of things, systems, or organizations. Natural networks among libraries for the exchange of bibliographical information and the coordination of technical processing functions date back to the last century. The closest counterpart of a network in the library world today is interlibrary loan, which can be viewed as an organizational network. For a network to be an *information network,* more than two participants should be engaged in a common pattern of information exchange through communications for some functional purpose.

Normally, we tend to think of networks in terms of the telephone or the radio. However, these networks are primarily communication grids, whose wires and waves carry messages back and forth. Telephone and radio networks are independent of the content or purpose of the messages they carry and serve merely as arteries of communication. Where interdependence for information exists among a group of participants and there is a common function or purpose to be served, it seems logical to call such a network an information network.

Information network development is in its infancy and, as might be expected, its terminology tends to be nebulous and loose. A recent review of the 1967 literature on networks for the *Annual Review of Information Science and Technology* reported that network activities were generally identified in one of three ways.[12] Some authors refer to a network by the equipment which is used to operate it—this includes the telephone network, teletype network, and facsimile network. Some describe it by the form of data which the network carries—such as a digital network, audio network, and film network. And still others identify a network by the function it is to perform—for example, educational networks, management information networks, biomedical information networks, and financial networks.

PLANNING A NETWORK

In planning an information network, certain fundamental system design considerations should be taken into account. The first, and in this author's view the hardest to express, is *formal organization.* This assumes that a group of participants recognize the value of belonging to a common information compact and are willing to accept the responsibilities of membership. More than lip-service cooperation is required. Participants should share a sense of common purpose, of course, but even more vital is their willingness to undertake legal, fiscal, and other contractual commitments to ensure and preserve the functional integrity of the network.

Examples of commitments that network participants may be called upon to make include: provision of materials and information services to the constituency served by other parts of the network on the same basis as that provided to its own constituency; maintenance of an agreed-upon level of service in terms of dollars and people; payment of a proportionate share of the expenses incurred in network operations; an understanding not to withdraw from the network without payment of penalties; and, agreement on the responsibilities of central network authority. This list of examples is small as compared to all of the organizational factors that will surely attend information network affiliation. Nevertheless, it illustrates a few of the crucial considerations that are involved.

Adequate *provision for communication* among participants is a second prerequisite for the formation of a network. Communications are the channels or circuits that rapidly bridge and interconnect the dispersed points of a network. They may consist of telephone lines, coaxial cables, microwave stations, satellites, or some combination thereof. A communications system may be owned by a network, and if so it is called a "dedicated" system; or a user may "lease" facilities from common carriers such as the Bell System or Western Union. By and large, the commercial carriers do not lease facilities but provide a specific service, such as telephone *or* teletype *or* facsimile or television *or* data transmission, although the carrier company itself may carry these separate services on a common transmission system. Petitions have been made to the Federal Communications Commission to require the common carriers to make multi-purpose transmission capacity available in bulk to be used in a number of alternate modes under the customer's control. Various other anomalies exist in the traditional common carrier tariff schedules and these too are under study by the Commission. Lower transmission costs for information or data transfer over great distances seem imperative if information networks are to grow. Both the Bell System and Western Union are in the process of upgrading their narrow-band systems, originally designed for voice communications, to broad-band facilities capable of carrying the vast quantities of digital and analog data generated by computers, TV cameras, facsimile scanners, and other technical equipment.[13]

Not all points in an information network will require the same communications support. Communications equipment and service requirements are determined for each node in a network by calculation of the anticipated traffic volumes, measurement of the length of probable messages, and analysis of the forms and rate of data to be transmitted and received. This will usually result in the installation of different levels of equipment at various echelons of a network. Communications compatibility, on the other hand, is a firm and standard requirement for all.

A third characteristic which an information network should possess is *bi-directional operation.*

This means that information carried by the network, regardless of its form, may move in either direction. Hence each participant should be able, to some degree, to transmit as well as receive. "Conversation" between man and machines is a commonplace today for processing numerical problems through an on-line computer system. In an information network, the same interactive advantages should be forthcoming when one requests printed or graphic information at a distance. Bi-directional television is already being used by some educational institutions, and AT&T's Picture-phone may soon bring a limited degree of bi-directional television in the home and office. In an information network, provision should be made to enable users to hold two-way conversations with people, computers, or files by voice, by keyboard, or by video.

In addition to formal organization, adequate provision for communications, and bi-directional operation, another important network feature is a *directory and switching capability.* A directory look-up system in an information network may be thought of as comparable to the yellow pages of the classified telephone directory. It will enable any user of a national information network to identify the particular point in the net best able to satisfy his request. The directory does not furnish the answer to an information question but puts the user in direct touch with the best source of response. The switching station, as in the telephone system, finds the optimum communications path for sending the inquiry and receiving the reply, taking into account existing conditions of overload, emergency operation, peak use, and so forth.

CONCLUSION

Thus, it becomes clear that the development of a national information network is a complex and difficult assignment— worthy of our effort, to be sure, but not something to be worked out overnight and without a great deal of careful, deliberate planning. A nationwide network of information systems connecting local, state, regional, and national resources in the U. S. will involve highly complex system design, the utmost technical skill, and above all a sense of purpose and commitment on the part of all those concerned with the effort.

Moreover, many problems and obstacles must be overcome before such a network can be realized. We need to develop acceptable criteria for determining what is to be placed on the network, we need to clarify the rules of network participation, we need to agree on network organization and operation, we need to adopt communication standards and other common practices, we need to investigate the implications of information system integration from a social, legal, financial, and technical point of view.

What we need most of all is a workable plan, not a rigid blueprint but a flexible framework for evolutionary network development, that will guide the growth of many emerging network programs. Only with such a plan can we expect our libraries, specialized information centers, research analysis centers, and other information activities someday to mesh into a smoothly working whole.

The government can and should play a key role in preparing such a plan. It will probably continue to be one of the major influences on information network development, setting a pattern for others to follow. It may create its own information networks in specialized fields, such as medicine, or it may make funds available to the private sector in order to facilitate regional development. In any event, more and more interconnections at the local level can be expected in the years ahead. Organizational interconnections will only occur from the bottom up, but the Federal government can greatly assist this trend by providing the multipurpose arteries of communication essential to technical interconnection. Installation by the government or by the common carriers, of a nationwide broad-band electronic transfer grid for the exclusive use of the information community would have a salutary effect by setting the compatibility standards for all future network participants.

A national information network could be formed by the government as a public service, as a public utility, or as a publicly owned company through private enterprise. It is timely for the United States to consider establishing a domestic unit of some sort whose purpose it would be to furnish unity to the creation of a national information network. The unity and nationwide efficiency of the telephone and radio networks in America owes much to an early management decision to organize the program on a business basis through leasing and licensing arrangements. This proved to be the wisest and best course for the development of these networks. A similar type of management decision is needed now to point the way toward the regional organization and federated relationships which are prerequisite to the technical integration of information systems. Combined action on the part of the Congress, the Federal government, and the communications industry is the most practical way to bring this about.

In the United States, access to information is a public right. But, a rapidly increasing population and a rapidly expanding universe of information are introducing constraints and preventing the public from freely exercising this right. The object is to remove these impediments to knowledge by developing mechanisms such as networks that will facilitate the extraorganizational distribution and communication of information in all forms.

There seems little doubt that information networks will turn out to be the mechanism whereby the long-sought-after objectives of interlibrary cooperation and information sharing will be realized in the United States. The years ahead will witness considerably more experimentation in the transfer of information and data between information activities over existing dial-up commercial transmission facilities. This is certain to lead to an even greater appreciation of the benefits of an information network and of the need for its accelerated development on a national basis.

FOOTNOTES

[1] Johnson, Lyndon B. "Remarks of President Lyndon B. Johnson at the Conference on World Education, Williamsburg, Virginia, October 8, 1967," *Congressional Record,* Vol. 113, No. 162, P. H13200, October 10, 1967.

[2] Johnson, Lyndon B. "Remarks of the President at the Signing of the Public Broadcasting Act, The East Room." Office of the White House Press Secretary, November 7, 1967. (Mimeographed press release.)

[3] National Science Foundation. *Annual Report; for the Fiscal Year Ended June 30, 1967.* Washington, D. C., 1968.

[4] Marks, Leonard H. "A Blueprint for a New Schoolhouse." (United States Information Agency News Release, No. 20.) An address before the National Association of Educational Broadcasters Forty-third Convention, November 8, 1967. (Mimeographed.)

[5] Becker, Joseph, and Hayes, Robert M. "A Proposed Library Network for Washington State; Working Paper for the Washington State Library." September 1967.

[6] Interuniversity Communications Council. *EDUNET; Report of a Summer Study on Information Networks, Conducted by the Interuniversity Communications Council (EDUCOM)* (Information Science Series). Written and edited by George W. Brown, *et al.* New York, Wiley, 1967.

[7] *Proceedings of the Librarians' Convention held in New York City, September 15-17, 1853.* Cedar Rapids, Iowa, The Torch Press, 1915, p. 53.

[8] *Directory of Federally Supported Information Analysis Centers.* Sponsored by Panel No. 6, Information Analysis and Data Centers, Committee on Scientific and Technical Information, Federal Council for Science and Technology, April 1968.

[9] Henderson, Madeline M., *et al. Cooperation, Convertibility, and Compatibility among Information Systems: A Literature Review* (National Bureau of Standards, Miscellaneous Publication 276). Washington, D. C., U.S.G.P.O., 1966; and Carter, Launor F., *et al. National Document Handling Systems for Science and Technology* (Information Science Series). New York, Wiley, 1967.

[10] Becker, Joseph. "Communications Networks for Libraries," *Wilson Library Bulletin,* 41:383-387, Dec. 1966.

[11] Becker, Joseph. "Electronic Innovations in the Library," *Electronic Age*, 27:24-25, Winter 1967/68.

[12] Becker, Joseph, and Olsen, Wallace C. "Information Networks." In *Annual Review of Information Science and Technology.* Ed. by Carlos A. Cuadra. Chicago, Encyclopaedia Britannica, Vol. 3, 1968.

[13] American Library Association. *The Library and Information Networks of the Future* (RADC-TDR-62-614). Prepared for the Rome Air Development Center at Griffiss Air Force Base, New York, 1963.

M.I.T.'s Plans for Project Intrex—Information Transfer Experiments

by Carl F. J. Overhage

Project Intrex is a program of *in*formation *trans*fer *ex*periments directed toward the functional design of new library services that might become operational at the Massachusetts Institute of Technology and elsewhere by 1970. This project has been established with the twofold objective of finding long-term solutions for the operational problems of large libraries and of developing competence in the emerging field of information-transfer engineering. The project will be carried out in the School of Engineering in close concert with the M.I.T. libraries.

In the university of the future, as it is visualized at M.I.T., the library will be the central facility of an information-transfer network that will extend throughout the academic community. Students and scholars will use this network to gain access to the university's total information resources, through Touch-Tone telephones, teletypewriter keyboards, television-like displays, and quickly made copies. The users of the system will communicate with each other as well as with the library; data just obtained in the laboratory and comments made by observers will be as easily available as the texts of books in the library or documents in the departmental files. The information traffic will be controlled by means of the university's time-shared computer utility, much as today's verbal communications are handled by the campus telephone exchange. Long-distance service will connect the university's information-transfer network with sources and users elsewhere. Figure 1 presents a schematic view of this concept.

Today we do not know how to specify the exact nature and scope of future information-transfer services. We believe that their design must be derived from experimentation in a working environment of students, faculty, and research staff. A favorable situation for such experimentation exists at M.I.T. at the present time. There are library users in all academic categories who are accustomed to the experimental approach and who will cooperate in meaningful tests of new services.

In Project MAC, M.I.T. is already carrying forward a broad study of machine-aided cognition that will greatly stimulate the rise of new concepts in information transfer.

PLANNING THE PROJECT

The experimental plan for Project Intrex was formulated in August 1965 at a conference sponsored by the Independence Foundation. The membership, from both inside and outside M.I.T., was divided among librarians and documentalists, scientists and engineers, and some representatives of architecture, linguistics, mathematics, philosophy, psychology, and publishing. The report of the Intrex Planning Conference has been published.[1] The purpose of this article is to present a brief overview of the experimental program recommended by the conference. This article borrows extensively from the language of the report, and thereby attempts to capture the consensus of the participants in the conference rather than present exclusively my own viewpoint.

Three mainstreams of progress in the field of information transfer were intensively discussed: (i) The modernization of current library procedures through the application of technical advances in data processing, textual storage, and reproduction; (ii) the growth, largely under federal sponsorship, of a national network of libraries and other information centers; and (iii) the extension of the rapidly developing technology of on-line, interactive computer communities into the domains of the library and other information centers.

The university information-transfer system of the next decade will result from a confluence of these three streams. Rapid advances in information transfer by on-line computer systems will greatly extend the scope of information services in the academic community, but only if they are supported by the resources of a modernized university library and by integration with coordinated networks of local and national resources. The experi-

SOURCE: Reprinted from *Science*, 152: 1032-37 (20 May 1966), by permission of the publisher. Copyright 1966 by the American Association for the Advancement of Science.

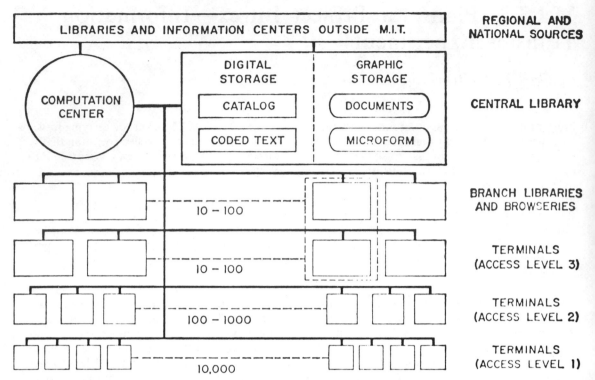

FIGURE 1. Schematic representation of an information-transfer network. Information stored in digital or in image form is accessible from terminals throughout the community. The computation center will control the flow of information in the system. The number of terminals will vary from between 10 and 100 for the best-equipped to perhaps 10,000 for the simplest.

mental program recommended by the planning conference, therefore, combines the exploitation of on-line computer technology with the modernization of some current library procedures, with emphasis on the former.

Although our discussions extended over a very large range of possible experiments, the recommended program is addressed mainly to the broad problem of *access*—in particular, access to bibliographic material, documents, and data banks. A core program dealing with this information-transfer function has been formulated, together with supporting activities and recommended extensions. Four sets of activities are proposed for this core program: augmented-catalog experiments; text-access experiments; network-integration experiments; and fact-retrieval experiments.

THE MODEL SYSTEM

To provide an environment for the performance of the Intrex experiments, the planning conference recommended the establishment of a facility called a "model library" as a place to test new ideas experimentally and to investigate competing technologies. Only by coming to grips with the real, everyday problems of setting up and running a pilot system can the project assemble the experience required to evaluate its experiments, just as it is only by serving the real needs of real users in the university community that the results of the experiments can be valuable.

The choice of the field or fields for this model has not yet been made, but it seems probable that early experiments will deal with the literature of aeronautics, astronautics, and space, and with that of materials science and engineering.

In its early stages, the model library will display, in readily attackable form, most of the basic problems of university libraries. It will therefore afford an excellent opportunity to combine the procedural background developed in the M.I.T. libraries with the capabilities of an on-line computer system for solving such problems as the selection, acquisition, and weeding of materials and the control of serial publications. But the main purpose of the model library is to serve as a medium for the activities in the core program which will now be outlined.

In an information-transfer system involving any form of storage we shall need a directory that describes the items in the store and indicates their location. In the library of today, this finding tool is the catalog. William S. Dix, the Librarian of Princeton University, has aptly called the catalog "one of the great achievements of the human intellect."[2] "Without it," he writes, "or something just as good, all but the smallest of libraries would be chaotic and useless." The catalog has become the central device that controls all operations in a large research library. Its functions and its size make it the primary target for the application of digital storage and computer control.

The advantages of the digitally encoded catalog are numerous. The user can manipulate it more easily than the conventional 3- by 5-inch cards in file drawers. Access to the catalog can be provided in many terminals at locations remote from the library. Information on each entry can be called up selectively, so that the amount of detail can be increased as the search is narrowed down. New information can be added to an entry at any time, and the old information can be deleted at will. The catalog becomes a dynamic tool which develops in response to the changing needs of library users. Many of the important features of machine-manipulated bibliographic tools have already been demonstrated in experiments at a number of libraries. A comprehensive citation index of the journal literature of physics has been provided by Kessler[3] for the time-shared computer system of Project MAC at M.I.T.

Variable depth in the catalog will permit the user to range from abbreviated entries showing only author, title, and location, through standard descriptive cataloging, to augmented catalog entries which may include references to abstracts and reviews of the item; citations of the item, and citations given in the item; the type of material, level of approach, and aim of the author; informative comments by authors, editors, librarians, and users; extracts, such as prefaces, tables of contents, and summaries; cost and source information; additional subject indexing; and records of use of the item.

Not all the information that will be found in the completed catalog will be incorporated from the first. An evolving entry is expected, with author, title, data, and location being entered early in the process and other data being added and deleted during the life of the catalog.

The augmentation of the catalog in depth would be accompanied by an augmentation in coverage, so that journal articles, reviews, technical reports, theses, pamphlets, conference proceedings, and class notes would be as comprehensively described as books are.

Operational experiments with such a catalog would seek answers, for a variety of bibliographic searches, to such questions as the following:

What simplest code will specify a document? What is the contribution of each tag? What is the most efficient search strategy? What is the best file organization?

In addition to its primary function in bibliographic search, the catalog will also have important uses in browsing experiments, in inventory control, and in recording user interaction with the information-transfer system.

TEXT ACCESS

The library user who has succeeded in identifying the documents he wishes to consult will expect a good information-transfer system to display or deliver these documents to him, with minimum delay and at a convenient location near his study or laboratory. Various techniques for providing such access are available.

The traditional library provides access by lending the original document, but that method is incompatible with the principle of guaranteed access, which should govern the information-transfer systems of the future. We must find ways of providing transient or permanent access that do not preclude the concurrent access to the same document by other users of the system.

The loan of duplicate copies, in either full size or microform, is a possible technique. Other important possibilities are visual displays on optical or electronic screens.

For permanent rather than transient access, full-size paper copies are the most obvious solution. Such copies can be made directly from the original document, or they can be derived from microform copies of the original. They can be produced at a distance by signals transmitted over electrical circuits in either analog or digital form. Permanent copies might also be supplied to users in reduced size, either on paper or on film.

The many different optical, photographic, and electronic techniques implied in this outline can be combined in different ways to provide access to text at various cost levels and with different speeds of response. The general system schematically presented in Fig. 1 shows information terminals, arranged in three access levels, that will be provided in quantities which reflect differences in cost and complexity.

The planning conference was not specific in recommending particular devices or combinations, but the nature of the recommended experiments will be clearer if some illustrative terminal equipment is mentioned here, however little it may resemble the ultimate configurations of the terminals.

In Fig. 2, the minimum equipment is shown for

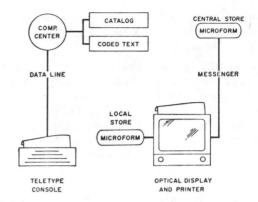

FIGURE 3. Access to text: level 2. Intermediate information terminal. A teletypewriter console with permit the user to consult the digitally encoded union catalog. A local satellite store will contain microform copies of the technical literature appropriate to the location of the terminal.

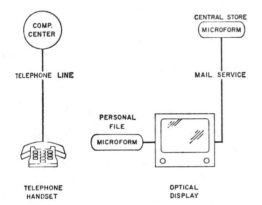

FIGURE 2. Access to text: level 1. Rudimentary information terminal for installation in every office. When interrogated by Touch-Tone dialing, the computation center will provide automatic voice replies to a limited range of directory service requests.

a rudimentary information terminal that might be provided in every office of a university. The Touch-Tone dial of the telephone handset could be used to interrogate the computation center; replies to a limited range of requests for directory service could be received as automatic voice signals. In this way, a user might ascertain, for example, the dates of the latest issues of journals available in the central library. Microform copies of documents could be delivered by mail in response to telephone requests. A microform reader in the office would be used to display material thus received, as well as information already available in a personal file.

For the more advanced resources of the next higher level, shown in Fig. 3, the user would move a short distance from his office to one of several information terminals in his department or laboratory. Here he would be able to consult the uni-

versity's union catalog by means of a teletypewriter console; the text of digitally encoded documents could also be printed out on the teletypewriter. For the field of science or technology appropriate to the location of the terminal, microform copies of documents would be available in a local satellite store; microform copies of other documents would be sent by messenger from the central library. Microform readers in the terminal would be equipped with printers so that permanent copies of selected material would be immediately available when demanded.

Figure 4 shows the comprehensive facilities that might be associated with a terminal located in the future equivalent of a branch library. For more effective dialogues with the union catalog, a television-like display with optional print-out would take the place of the teletypewriter printer. For access to full text, the local store would be supplemented with high-speed links to the central library. Television circuits, facsimile circuits, and pneumatic tubes, are shown as possible options in Fig. 4, along with messenger service. Electronic and optical display devices would be equipped with printers to make permanent copies for retention by the user.

Let me repeat that these illustrations are not intended as design recommendations. Their only purpose is to suggest the range of possibilities available with current technology. Numerous questions come to mind at once as these illustrations are examined: Will the quality of cathode-ray-tube displays be acceptable to library users? Will the members of a university community as-

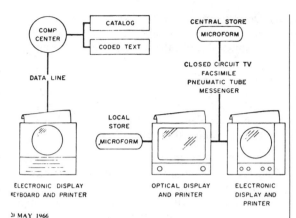

FIGURE 4. Access to text: level 3. Comprehensive information terminal. Electronic and optical displays will provide rapid access to centrally stored information in both digital and image form. Permanent copies of material desired for retention will be available on demand.

semble personal information files in microform? What is the optimum technique, in view of cost, quality, and speed of response, for the transmission of information stored in image form? How will the system handle the simultaneous display of text and high-quality continuous-tone illustrations?

These are the questions that the text-access experiment of Project Intrex is intended to answer. Many tests must be made with schemes that provide access in different forms and at different speeds, tested under realistic conditions by different users in different categories.

NETWORK INTEGRATION

My discussion so far has dealt with the information resources stored at a single university. The third experiment of the Intrex core program deals with the problems of extending the reach of the university's information-transfer system to library resources beyond its walls—to the libraries of other universities and to the great national information centers that are coming into existence. In this matter of network integration, the planning conference recommended that the initial efforts of Project Intrex be concentrated on the problem of determining what material is available at such sources. The text-access problem in the integrated network will be in many respects similar to the local problem and can be tackled as an extension

of it after some early results have been accomplished.

In seeking bibliographic access to outside resources, the user will encounter catalogs organized differently from that of his own university, even after all such catalogs have been converted to machine-readable form. This will mean that the user will not converse directly with the outside catalog. His interrogation will be restricted to his local computation center, which will respond either with catalog data on local resources or with intermediary reference services to a remote information center. The computer may assist the user in utilizing printed index-catalogs of outside sources or in formulating specifications for custom searches at remote information centers.

The planning conference suggested that this investigation first utilize the Medlars (Medical Literature Analysis and Retrieval System) bibliographic capability at the National Library of Medicine and the information system of the National Aeronautics and Space Administration. Medical literature is of increasing interest to M.I.T., and Medlars aims to cover this vast field in great depth and with fast service. The NASA system also covers a broad field of mission- and subject-related literature of exceptional interest to M.I.T. Both have the capability of computer-aided literature-search service in response to user requests, and both issue extensive bibliographies in tape and printed form. These two offer interesting contrasts in types of users, types of literature covered, and types of searches that are possible.

In addition to the use of computer-based national bibliographic services, an effort will be made to tap other research libraries, documentation centers, and information exchanges. This can be accomplished by installing teletypewriters in these facilities. Project Intrex will thus be able to explore various ways of interchanging bibliographic, indexing, and abstracting information and of overcoming divergences of format and convention that might impede cooperation.

FACT RETRIEVAL

The bibliographic organization involved in the preceding three experiments is essentially document-centered. During the expected life of Project Intrex, continued progress will be made in the rapid processing of data stored in very large files, some capability will be developed for the retrieval and assembly of facts, and many advanced systems for the automatic answering of questions will appear. It is impossible to put a precise timescale on these developments, but it is clear that research on the direct computer manipulation of facts and ideas is an important avenue toward the advanced information-transfer systems described by Licklider.[4] The planning conference recommended that some effort in pursuit of this longer-term objective be included in the core program of Project Intrex.

A first step toward automatic fact retrieval is a program to assist a user to locate in currently published handbooks the subsection containing facts he desires. An automated merged index of all the available handbooks relevant to a subfield would provide a path on which a user could traverse the bewildering forest of available reference material. Access to this automated index would be provided through consoles placed in information-transfer terminals that also contained book or microfilm copies of the reference handbooks themselves. Many users will come to the console without a clear statement of exactly what facts they are really looking for. A cleverly designed programmed interrogation should be able to extract the proper request from the user. The console will also have a key for a single command, "HELP," which will connect the user to a human reference librarian.

As the next step toward fact-retrieval systems, the contents of a particular handbook, or sections of selected handbooks, will be put into digital form for direct access and manipulation by the computer. A completely computerized data store of this kind has important advantages over a conventional printed handbook:

1) Currency: Updating and editing can be continuously, rapidly, and conveniently performed in the on-line data store.

2) Versatile organization: In an automated handbook, one can easily construct tables for new combinations of variables, different from those that were combined in the original publication. It would be possible to request, for example, a list of melting points of metals with shear strength above a certain level and density between two limits. To extract such a list from a printed handbook by conventional procedures is a slow and laborious task.

3) Computation: Whenever the facts required by a user can be computed from those in the published compendium, the desired information can be promptly generated in the computer-stored data system.

4) Output format control: With a computer-based system, one can easily present to the user a graphic plot of information usually stored in tabular form.

5) Amount of detail: Large quantities of detailed data can be included in the computerized handbook without giving rise to the cost and access problems associated with the inclusion of such material in printed publications.

If we now augment the information stored in the automatic handbook with informal experimental data, we are taking the third step in the fact-retrieval experiment. Perhaps the result might be referred to as an automated notebook. The data-bank project currently under way in the social sciences at M.I.T. in conjunction with Project MAC is an early attempt to establish such a notebook. This experimental system will include data from public-opinion polls, census data, voting data, and life-history data.

For an automated notebook to be effective, people must be able to use it without having precise knowledge of the organizational principles that determined the form of storage of any particular subject of shared data. In particular, a user must be able to have data that are organized in one way presented to him in quite another way. Thus the automated notebook will contain not only data, but programs to manipulate and reshape the data.

OTHER LIBRARY FUNCTIONS

The library is traditionally regarded as the center of the intellectual life at a university. The planning conference recognized that changes in the library system are certain to have indirect effects on other activities, some of them quite remote from the libraries themselves. As far as possible, the conference attempted to foresee the indirect implications of moving toward an on-line intellectual community, and its report includes recommendations for studies of these related problems.

For example, the planning conference discussed with considerable enthusiasm the proposition that a large body of factual information, so stored as to be open to interrogation from a variety of users with different interests and degrees of knowledge, might provide one of the most powerful teaching instruments ever conceived. It will be important for Intrex to consider as explicitly as possible what opportunities this new instrument might offer for the educational process at M.I.T.

On a less optimistic note, the possibility was considered that the proposed innovations might impede scholarship as much as they facilitated it. The leisurely perusal of a library's collection is considered by many scholars, particularly those in the humanities, to be an excellent way for students to get a feeling for the structure of a field of knowledge, and even to be an important source of serendipitous discoveries by the more advanced scholar. There is some fear that the proposed changes in library operations would necessarily preclude browsing, thus frustrating many of the library's best customers. The positive view is to try to exploit the new technology to permit a more nimble kind of browsing with greater scope than is possible in the stacks of today's libraries.

A library of the type envisioned by the planning conference can take a much more active role in providing information to its clientele than most libraries have in the past. The availability of a computer system makes it possible to keep a profile of each user's interest and to furnish documents to him even before he requests them. This kind of active library service, aimed at supporting the user's current awareness of developments in his field, is usually called selective dissemination of information (SDI). Programs for SDI are presently operating in many libraries, mostly in industrial or government organizations: they appear to have received little attention from academic institutions. It seems appropriate, therefore, that Project Intrex should explore the extent to which SDI services might be provided in a university community.

In the text-access experiments of Project Intrex, the advantages and disadvantages of producing on-demand copies of items in the library's collection will be studied. A system that operates in this manner is, in a sense, in the publishing business. For new material not yet in the collection, various kinds of limited "publication" would be possible in the information transfer network. For example, a newly created manuscript could be made available to other network users either on a selective basis or on a broadcast basis by entry in the public file. The planning conference suggested experimentation that would contribute to the wise planning of the future library's opportunities and responsibilities in this field.

Finally, the conference gave some attention to the possibility of relieving the library's problems, without diminishing its serviceability, by well-conceived rules for acquiring and weeding documents. It is widely held that the amount of good material in any scientific field at any particular time is really rather small; and one of the problems is that this high-quality signal is being drowned in a vast flood of low-quality noise. If there is any truth to this notion, Project Intrex would seem to be in an excellent position to investigate it. The augmented catalog will accumulate comments of users; citations recorded in the catalog will permit analysis of a publication's impact on subsequent authors; mechanized text access will yield data on the actual use of each item in the collection.

Other implications of the Intrex experiments were discussed, but these five—education, browsing, selective dissemination, publishing, selective retention—received the most attention at the planning conference. Although none is essential for getting the Intrex program under way, all of them are important.

RESEARCH AND DEVELOPMENT

The experimental program that has been outlined is concentrated on a few main problems that the planning conference considered both crucial and soluble. The basic policy suggested to Project Intrex with respect to supportive research and development is to undertake only those tasks that are necessary to ensure successful completion of the main experiments. Perhaps the most significant factor in the situation that Project Intrex is entering is the availability of a powerful new computer technology. The conference was distressed, however, by the primitive state of two critical items, consoles and interaction languages, and recommended that Project Intrex give attention to them.

In surveying the broad area in which Project Intrex will operate—the computer sciences, the library sciences, and parts of other disciplines ranging from psychology to electrical and mechanical engineering—the planning conference observed that there is no dearth of theory in these fields. However, there is not at present a comprehensive and basic theory of information transfer. A major intellectual challenge for Project Intrex is the development of a unifying theory that will lead to coherent design and interpretation of experiments in information-transfer systems.

The immediate effort of Project Intrex is to add details to the recommendations given in the report of the planning conference and to begin the experiments. A grant from the Carnegie Corporation is making it possible to conduct this early part of the experimental program without waiting for the more extensive funding that the complete project will require. The initial Experimental work will be performed by the Electronic Systems Laboratory of the Department of Electrical Engineering at M.I.T.

FOOTNOTES

[1] INTREX, *Report of a Planning Conference on Information Transfer Experiments,* C. F. J. Overhage and R. J. Harman, Eds. (M.I.T. Press, Cambridge, 1965).

[2] W. S. Dix, *University, A Princeton Quarterly* **26**, 3, (1965).

[3] M. M. Kessler, *Phys. Today* **18**, 28 (Mar. 1965).

[4] J. C. R. Licklider, *Libraries of the Future* (M.I.T. Press, Cambridge, 1965).

V

CATALOGS AND THE COMPUTER

We can confidently predict that the use of the computer in the cataloging process will have a significant influence upon the final cataloging product and how that product will be presented to library users. As Simonton points out, we must now once again consider whether the catalog shall be with respect to authors more than a simple finding list, as opposed to a bibliographic record in which an attempt is made to distinguish between authors and to bring all of a single author's works together in a single place in the catalog. Furthermore, many niceties of filing, which are perhaps not economical and perhaps impossible in a computer-based catalog, will need to be re-examined. Already, as a result of the computer we are witnessing a new series of studies of the catalog, as for example, the work being done by Ben-Ami Lipetz at Yale and by a research group at the University of of Chicago. Both are trying to establish how catalogs are used; at Chicago emphasis is given to the various aspects of a book that readers best remember (such as title, author, size, color).

Dolby's study of the costs of cataloging and processing in a computerized system is instructive for those who seek knowledge of how to conduct a similar local study. But in this anthology the chief concern is with services to users, and Dolby's conclusions from this point of view are these: in a situation where about 425 characters per entry are used (as against 250), and where multiple copies of a catalog are needed, the computerized procedure offers economic benefits over the manual.

From the viewpoint of the *user*, multiple copies of a catalog are indicated in any situation where the library system is decentralized because users wish to have knowledge of the total holdings of the system.

This by no means concludes the analysis. Before the decision is made to supply multiple copies to readers, the library manager must take into account the cost of the catalog processing functions, which are quite small compared to the cost of the cataloging function itself. Savings in the latter, if accomplished, therefore, will be more significant.

Furthermore, Dolby seems to be viewing the updating function only from the economic point of view. Unfortunately, no study of user time was made in a manual system, where the users need consult only a single record, compared to the computerized system in which users must consult no fewer than two records.

Thus, putting aside costs to management and looking to the problem from the user point of view, the computerized catalog brings to the reader the total record in a decentralized setting. Some users, however, are interested almost exclusively in the holdings of the largest library in the decentralized system, and these would need to consult the record of holdings in at least two places compared to the single consultation required in a manual system.

Still other factors need to be considered. Assume a manual system in which through a single consultation the reader determines whether a title has been ordered, or has been received and is being processed or has been processed and sent to the shelves. By way of contrast, assume a manual system in which the card record shows only books that have been processed and sent to the shelves. Now assume a computerized system in which the user is promised a record containing all three categories, and that in his library the manual system informs him only of the third (books ready for circulation). Obviously, in this circumstance even the user of only the main library in a decentralized system might prefer the computerized version which would require him to consult several records, namely: books ready for circulation (a minimum of two consultations); and books on order and books being processed (one consultation, but perhaps updated only once per week). Only in an on-line system, in which the increased cost in computer time is directly proportional to the number of uses, can we free the user from multiple consultations. Having gone this far, the library would surely wish to add at least two more categories to the record, that is, books charged out and books at the bindery. But the on-line system is not relevant to the Dolby's study.

The Computerized Catalog: Possible, Feasible, Desirable?[1]

by Wesley Simonton

Developments of recent years make it increasingly clear that we are at the beginning of a new era with respect to the form and method of production of library catalogs—an era in which an old product, the book catalog, has been revived as a result of new technological developments, and now challenges the card catalog as the basic device for maintaining our bibliographic records. It is not yet apparent how wide-spread or how rapid the change from the card to the book catalog may be, but because of the clear superiority of the book catalog on the points of ease of scanning and ease of reproduction of multiple copies, and because of the hope it offers of reducing or eliminating the clerical work involved in catalog preparation and maintenance, it is essential that we give careful consideration to the feasibility of a book catalog in many library situations.

Of the several possible methods for producing a book catalog, the most revolutionary one is production by a computer. The product, being basically similar to other book catalogs, is reasonably familiar to librarians; the production method as yet is not. This paper represents an attempt to relate the general parameters of computer operations to the accepted goals and procedures of our present cataloging operations, considering whether these goals and procedures can, should, or must be modified to take advantage of computer techniques and capabilities. In view of the wide range of computer capabilities and of the sizes of library catalogs, generalizations are risky, but certain basic questions may be identified.

In any consideration of the possibility of applying computer techniques to an existing operation, the first step must be a rigorous analysis of the present procedures in their totality. This step, usually done in flow chart form, is necessary because a computer cannot operate or make decisions on the basis of incomplete information, as a human being frequently can and does. This analysis often reveals illogical or inefficient steps in the present operation, as well as gaps in our knowledge of the total process. The second step involves a careful consideration of both present and future goals and products: What are we producing? Does it meet our needs? Do we want something different?

Having, then, analyzed present procedures and considered desired products, it remains to analyze the machine's capabilities and operations, to answer the questions: Can the machine do the job as it is planned? If not, are there alternative ways of achieving the desired results? Or, should the job be be replanned? (The question of relative cost is of course of basic importance, but will not be discussed directly here.)

In considering the present goals and procedures of cataloging as they are reflected in the card catalog, we may identify three broad areas of relevance to our topic:

1. Descriptive cataloging, including entry
2. Subject control, through subject headings
3. Filing

DESCRIPTIVE CATALOGING

With regard to descriptive cataloging, three goals may be discerned:

1. To provide a description of the physical object
2. To provide one or more "entries" or "access points," with a full description of the work at each point
3. To "explain" the reason for each entry, that is, to show why it has been made

The techniques for achieving these goals are essentially identified in the American Library Association *Cataloging Rules for Author and Title Entries* and in the Library of Congress *Rules for Descriptive Cataloging.*

Looking first at our techniques for description of the physical object, the objectives of descriptive cataloging are, in the familiar words of the LC *Rules* "(1) to state the significant features of an item with the purpose of distinguishing it from other items and describing its scope, contents and bibliographic relation to other items and (2) to

SOURCE: Reprinted from *Library Resources and Technical Services,* 8: 399-407 (Fall, 1964), by permission of the publisher.

present these data in an entry which can be integrated with the entries for other items in the catalog and which will respond best to the interests of most users of the catalog." To accomplish these objectives, we organize the description into three major parts:

1. The "body of the entry," consisting of the title, the subtitle, if any, the author statement (in some instances), the edition statement, if any, and the imprint
2. The "collation"
3. "Notes," used as necessary

We employ a format utilizing sentences and paragraphs, working under basic but not unanimous agreement as to what information should be placed where, and in how much detail. Application of the rules involves examination of the title-page and other parts of the item being cataloged and organizing the derived description into the parts noted above. In passing it may be noted that the tendency to place title-page information in the body of the entry persists, although such a procedure is much less mandatory than under earlier rules.

The *Rules for Entry* provide guidance in determining the various entries (other than subject headings) for a work and in selecting one of these as the so-called "main entry." In most instances, an attempt is made to select a person or a corporate body as the main entry and the person or group so selected is considered to be the "author" of the work. The main entry is frequently, though not always properly, referred to as the "most important" entry for the work. Hopefully, the rules provide sufficient guidance that the same main entry will be selected by all persons cataloging the work, so that listing in union catalogs and other single-entry bibliographic tools will be consistent, recognizing, of course, that complete unanimity for all titles cataloged is unlikely.

In applying the rules, the cataloger first considers the physical object, noting what information is given on the title-page, where it appears, and with what degree of typographic prominence. He may also take account of other information found in the work, occasionally even information found outside the work. He then applies the "logic" of the rules to determine the "main" and "added" entries to be made, seeking always to anticipate the "user's" approach and convenience as much as possible. However, the "logic" (at least the logic of "authorship" and "main entry") sometimes conflicts with the assumed, stated, or demon-

strated convenience of the user. Thus, for maps, it is frequently asserted that area or subject is a more important entry than the author entry; the recent *Standard for Descriptive Cataloging of Government Scientific and Technical Reports,* prepared by the Committee on Scientific Information of the Federal Council for Science and Technology, calls for main entry under corporate body for all reports, even if personal authors are identified; for laws, we reject the authorship principle, making entry under an arbitrary "form" heading instead of under the legislative body responsible for them. To an extent, but not completely, the "added entries" solve the problems raised in these and other situations.

Why, then, do we establish a "main entry" for each item cataloged? What are the functions of the main entry? At least five reasons or functions may be discerned. First, in most instances we feel the necessity of assigning primary responsibility to some person or corporate group, that is, of establishing the "author" of the work, on the assumption that selection for purchase or use may be influenced by this assignment of responsibility. Second, in single-entry listings, the main entry represents the only access point. Third, hopefully, we establish an "authority" for subsequent bibliographic references to the item. The fourth and fifth functions are more practical than theoretical: the main entry provides a convenient device for sub-arrangement of items under a given added entry and for locating all the entries for a given item in the catalog.

As a part of the authorship principle, the rules also provide that all of the works of a single author, either personal or corporate, shall be assembled at one point in the catalog. This collocation is achieved by adhering to the use of a single, unvarying form of the author's name, which must differ in some respect from any other similar names in the catalog.

The third goal of descriptive cataloging, explanation of the relationship of a heading to the item described, may be *explicit,* as in the case of editors, translators, and second authors, all carefully identified in the heading; it may be *implicit,* as in the case of main entry, where the format of the card identifies the entry as the author: or it may be *tacit,* that is, not shown directly and determined only by a reading of the card.

SUBJECT HEADINGS

In selecting the headings by which we provide subject access to our collections, we attempt to select a single word or phrase, usually from an "authority" or "standard" list, which encompasses the "specific" contents of the item being cataloged. The term or phrase, however, must be capable of being used for more than one item in the collection. We attempt to minimize the user's difficulties in several ways: by following the practice of specific entry consistently, by "pre-coordinating" terms to form concepts, e.g., "Classification—Music," and by a straight alphabetic filing of multi-word headings. The structure and punctuation of multi-word headings vary considerably, again in response to supposed user convenience, as we utilize adjectival phrases, inverted adjectival phrases, prepositional phrases, inverted prepositional phrases, and subdivided headings. No attempt is made to limit the length of the heading. In practice, we frequently find it necessary to use more than one heading for an item, either because it treats of more than one subject (the subjects not being subordinate to a single more generic term) or because no "existing" heading (existing, that is, in our authority list) covers the concept.

FILING

The various entries for the cataloged item are then arranged in either a single or a divided file (the latter usually in no more than two sections), with a growing tendency toward "straight alphabetic" filing arrangement insofar as possible. The "filing medium," that is, the part of the card which must be considered in filing, may consist of one, two, or three parts. In the case of main entries, the entry itself must be filed; unless it is the title of the work or represents the only entry for the "author" in the catalog, sub-arrangement by title (the second part) will be necessary. In the case of added entries, the third part may be added to the filing medium, with necessary consideration being given in some instances to the added entry, the main entry, and the title. Practice varies both between libraries and within a single library on the point of regarding the main entry in the filing of added entries; that is, filing of added entries may be either *direct to the title* or *indirect through the main entry*. Subject entries are sub-arranged either by the main entry or by the date.

COMPUTER TECHNIQUES AND CAPACITIES

A computer has been defined as "a device capable of accepting information, applying prescribed processes to the information and supplying the re-

sults of these processes."[2] For present purposes, its functions may be identified as *reading* (that is, accepting information), *computing* and *sorting* (that is, applying prescribed processes) and *printing* (that is, supplying the results). As applied to the cataloging process, we may say that the computer can

1. reproduce information with, if desired, either the addition of designated new information or the deletion of designated parts of the original information
2. sort, that is, file information at designated points
3. print the results.

How do these abilities relate to the established goals and procedures of cataloging? Our techniques have for the most part worked well in our established technology of a catalog made up of cards produced by the typewriter (or some substitute therefor), but even in the past our goals and procedures have not been accepted without question. For the most part, the implications of these questions could not be thoroughly explored because of the limitations of the existing technology. At the least, the computer provides a chance for experiments with new formats and new methods of display for our bibliographic record, and makes it necessary to reexamine our goals and procedures.

QUESTIONS REGARDING DESCRIPTIVE CATALOGING

With regard to our present procedures of descriptive cataloging, there are three basic questions. First, do we organize the information in the most effective manner? Are there situations in which material from the title-page, traditionally placed in the body of the entry, might more effectively be presented in "note" form? Second, do we need the same amount of information at each entry? Third, is the author statement as necessary as we have assumed? Further, might it be more effectively presented in note form?

QUESTIONS REGARDING ENTRY

With regard to present procedures relating to rules of entry (other than subject headings), again, three basic questions may be raised. First, is it necessary, assuming multiple entry points for a work, to establish a single entry as the "main entry"; may we not, instead, think in terms simply of "entries" rather than "main and added entries" for a work? This question relates to our conception of the basic function of the catalog—is it primarily a finding list or does it seek to go further and become, so to speak, an authority list, determining the "author" for each work listed? Second, is it necessary always to explain the reason for an entry? Undoubtedly, we must do so in cases such as editors and translators, so that we do not present a misleading entry, but can we logically explain our present practice of using the term "joint author" on only one of the two entries for a work of joint authorship? Third, is it essential to assemble at one point and identify as such the works of a single author? If no attempt were made to distinguish the various Smith's in our catalog, it would be easier to locate "Smith's *Principles of Chemistry*" than it is at present. Are there individual libraries or library situations in which the need for assembling the works of a single individual is so slight as to lead us to prefer the suggested alternative?

QUESTIONS REGARDING SUBJECT HEADINGS

With regard to subject heading practice, two basic questions may be identified. First, do we provide a sufficient number of headings for an item? (Certainly we provide far fewer on the average than are being used in indexing the technical report literature.) Second, should subject headings *describe* the contents of the item, as at present, or should they merely *indicate* the contents? That is, should we continue to use our pre-coordinated phrases as necessary, as opposed to the currently fashionable post-coordinated "descriptors" so widely used for indexing report literature? Although both of these questions are of fundamental importance in our procedures of bibliographic control, they are not as crucial to the format of the catalog as the others being discussed here and they will not be considered further.

QUESTIONS REGARDING FILING

With regard to filing techniques, three questions may be asked: First, how far can and should the practice of straight alphabetic filing be applied? Second, in sub-arranging under our present added entries, is it more useful to file by the main entry or by the title of the work? Third, in sub-arranging under a subject heading, which pattern is more useful: sub-arrangement by main entry or by date of the item?

THE COMPUTERIZED CATALOG

Figure 1 illustrates a possible new pattern for a computerized catalog, as compared with present practice. The entries on the left reflect our present practices, with full entries under the first author, the second author, and the subject entry, the latter two entries being duplicates of the first with the addition of the added entry heading. Assuming a printed catalog which stresses brief name entries for ease of scanning and arranges its subject entries in order of cataloging, on the assumption that subject entries are created for browsing, rather than locating a particular item, we might have a catalog with entries like those on the right. Here, instead of a main and an added entry for the two authors, we have simply two entries, each indicating only the entry, the title, the edition and the imprint. We have taken advantage of the computer's ability to rearrange, to add, to subtract data. We have given very brief information under the name entries, on the assumption that the user looking under a name is looking for a single work, or all of the works with which an individual is identified, and not for full bibliographic information concerning those items. We have given fuller information under the subject entries to aid the user in selecting from among the several works on this subject in our library.

The filing problem may prove to be the single element of the process which will make the application of computers to cataloging most difficult. There are two major problems here. First, a computer can handle readily only straight alphabetic filing (not to mention the difficulties introduced by punctuation). Second, the length of the filing medium creates certain practical problems. With regard to the first problem, the findings of the detailed study made of the feasibility of programming the ALA filing rules for computer filing in connection with the University of Illinois Chicago Undergraduate Division Library project on mechanization of library processes are of interest:

"1. A complex coding system must be developed so that the various data which constitute an entry can be recognized and manipulated by a computer.
2. Codes from this system must be assigned manually by a librarian and translated to a specially designed coding form before the input data for a data processing system could be created.
3. Quite large and comprehensive tables must be

Burnett, George Wesley
  Oral microbiology and infectious disease, a textbook for students and practitioners of dentistry, by George W. Burnett and Henry W. Scherp. 2d ed. Baltimore, Williams & Wilkins, 1962.
    1003 p. illus. 27 cm.

Burnett, George Wesley
  Oral microbiology and infectious disease. 2d ed. Baltimore, Williams & Wilkins, 1962.

Scherp, Henry W
Burnett, George Wesley
  Oral microbiology and infectious disease, a textbook for students and practitioners of dentistry, by George W. Burnett and Henry W. Scherp. 2d ed. Baltimore, Williams & Wilkins, 1962.
    1003 p. illus. 27 cm.

Scherp, Henry W
  Oral microbiology and infectious disease. 2d ed. Baltimore, Williams & Wilkins, 1962.

MOUTH—BACTERIOLOGY
Burnett, George Wesley
  Oral microbiology and infectious disease, a textbook for students and practitioners of dentistry, by George W. Burnett and Henry W. Scherp. 2d ed. Baltimore, Williams & Wilkins, 1962.
    1003 p. illus. 27 cm.

MOUTH—BACTERIOLOGY
  Oral microbiology and infectious disease. 2d ed. Baltimore, Williams & Wilkins, 1962.
    1003 p. illus. 27 cm.
  A textbook for students and practitioners of dentistry, by George W. Burnett and Henry W. Scherp.

FIGURE 1

developed and be accessible to the computer during the running of the program. Such tables do not now exist."[3]

In the light of these findings, the following recommendation was made: "It is felt that most nuances of library filing rules, no matter how worthy their original reason for existence, are largely lost not only upon most patrons but also upon most librarians. If library cataloging is to be economically assisted by computers and automation, the filing rules should be simplified. Ideally, the arrangement should be straight alphabetical letter by letter to the end of the word, i.e., follow a typical sort routine already available for computers."[4]

The problem of length of the filing medium may also prove a very serious one. A human being can scan as many characters as necessary to file a catalog card, and we have as yet imposed no constraints on the length of our subject headings or on our other entries. If the computer is to file as efficiently as a human being, the length of the sorting area must be as great as that of the maximum entry to be filed, which will run well over one hundred characters. Sorting of this magnitude is costly, and, as a result, some of the presently operational systems utilizing computers have employed numerical codes to represent names or subject headings, to effect more economical filing.

ADMINISTRATIVE QUESTIONS

Although the purpose of this paper has been primarily to explore the technical questions relating to a computer-produced book catalog, there are two closely related administrative considerations which should be discussed briefly. First, it is a commonplace in enlightened library theory, if not practice, at least as reflected in our literature, that work once done should not be repeated. This assertion is made most frequently with relation to bibliographic verification work in the acquisition and cataloging departments. The introduction of any sort of mechanization in the library will emphasize this position even more, since it is a basic tenet of machine operations that data be recorded only once in the total system. Strict application of of this idea to bibliographic processing would call for initiating the bibliographic record of an item when it is ordered, in as close to complete form as possible, the record to be changed or supplemented as necessary later. In the last analysis, the question arises: *Can we catalog a book when we order it?* Obviously not, in many cases. But if we are ordering from a Library of Congress proofsheet and we ordinarily follow LC practices in our cataloging, perhaps we can. The advantage of such a procedure would be that both acquisition records and catalog records might be produced from a single typing. In any case, it would seem that we may soon be able to consider a system in which we change and add to a basic record as an item moves through the processing cycle, rather than one in which we create separate, partially duplicative, records at different stages in the cycle.

The second administrative consideration relates to the psychological problems involved in changing from an essentially manual system to an essentially mechanized system, particularly on the point of the degree of technical knowledge necessary to be attained by the user of the machine. The analogy between the computer and the automobile on this point has by now become a commonplace: just as the driver of the automobile need know very little of what goes on under the hood, so the cataloger in a computerized system need know very little about why the lights are blinking. After the basic goals and decisions have been established (not that this is simple) and programs written to accomplish the goals, the original form of input to the computer may be quite similar to that used presently. Specifically, if the bibliographic information can be presented in a form similar to what Fasana has called "machine-interpretable natural format,"[5] employing various simple devices to impose precision on the data, the cataloger's worksheet may look only slightly different from that of today.

SUMMARY

A computer-produced book catalog is certainly *possible;* its format may or may not be much different from that of our present card and book catalogs, depending mostly on our own preferences in the matter. A computer-produced book catalog is *desirable* to the extent that any book catalog is desirable; if the filing problem can be solved, eliminating possible human errors in filing, it becomes even more desirable. *"Feasibility"* remains a question, at least if we include the question of cost. Book catalogs are being produced by computers today, but for the most part in relatively small, technical libraries with ready access to a computer. There is great need for experimentation, with close attention to cost, both of present and proposed methods, in a wide variety of types and sizes of libraries, before the question of feasibility can be answered. In this period of experimentation, the precepts, patterns, and products of the past must be carefully scrutinized, and only those of firmly established and continuing validity and utility permitted to influence our judgment of feasibility.

FOOTNOTES

[1] Paper presented at the program meeting of the Cataloging and Classification Section of RTSD, July 1, 1964, in St. Louis.

[2] U. S. Bureau of the Budget. *Automatic Data Processing Glossary.* 1962. p. 12.

[3] *An Investigation into the Application of Data Processing to Library Filing Rules.* A joint endeavor by the University of Illinois Library, Chicago Undergraduate Division, Navy Pier, Chicago, Illinois, and the Burroughs Corporation. 1962. p. 2.

[4] *Ibid.,* p. 3.

[5] Fasana, Paul. "Automating Cataloging Functions in Conventional Libraries." *Library Resources & Technical Services,* 7:352. Fall 1963.

An Analysis of Cost Factors in Maintaining and Updating Card Catalogs

J. L. Dolby and V. J. Forsyth:

This study enumerates and compares costs of manual and computerized catalogs. The difficulties of making comparative cost studies are examined. The report concentrates on the problems of cost element definition and on the reporting of as many comparable sources as possible. Results of cost studies are presented in the form of tables that show comparative costs of cataloging, card processing, conversion, and manual and computerized processing. There are also tables on card catalog costs. Conclusions are that the costs of manual and automated methods are essentially the same for short entries, and that there is a substantial economic advantage for automated methods in full entries.

A side benefit of the present interest in library automation is the amount of attention now being given to study of the traditional methods of librarianship. This phenomenon is hardly unique to librarianship; in almost every area of human endeavor where attempts have been made to introduce the use of computers, workers in the field have suddenly discovered that they did not understand some of their long-standing methods quite as fully as they had believed. The source of this seeming anomaly is easy to find: to program a computer, it is necessary to specify the work to be done in much greater detail than is necessary to explain the same problem to a human being, that curious human phenomenon known variously as "common sense" or "experience" making up the difference. It has not been uncommon over the past decade to hear many survivors of the "automation experience" admit that a main benefit of use of the machine was acquisition of better procedures through a more detailed understanding of the process involved.

Improved knowledge of "processes about to be automated" extends to the cost of the process as well, and with added force. In recommending the substitution of one procedure for another in a cost-conscious atmosphere, it behooves one to proffer sound financial reasons for doing so. Computers are expensive devices. They also represent expenditure of a different kind of money: capital or lease funds in place of labor expense. Thus,

although one can still hear the occasional cry that it is difficult to obtain reasonable cost data on various parts of library operations, it is becoming increasingly difficult to pick up an issue of almost any library journal that does not include at least one piece of cost information.

This paper is concerned with the cost of maintaining and updating card catalogs. As the authors have observed elsewhere (1), the cost of computing is going down at a rather spectacular rate, while the cost of labor is increasing. If this trend continues, almost every library will be forced to automate certain aspects of the catalog operation at some point in time. The cited report provided some information about the cost of computerized library catalogs. By adding a summary of the cost factors in the use of card catalogs, this article should place in slightly better perspective the more difficult problem of deciding (in the context of a particular library) when the crossover point between manual and automated methods is to be reached.

The plan of attack remains essentially the same as in the previous report: selecting from among the growing number of papers on the subject those that provide comparable sets of cost information pertinent to the various cost elements of the card catalog operation. It is appropriate, therefore, to begin this study with a brief description of the difficulties in comparing cost statistics in such a way.

SOURCE: Reprinted from the *Journal of Library Automation*, 2: 218-41 (December, 1969) by permission of the publisher. Copyright 1969 by the American Library Association.

PROBLEMS OF COMPARATIVE
COST STUDIES

Although comparative cost studies have much to recommend them, they are fraught with certain difficulties (2). In the first place, few librarians would group elementary cost operations in precisely the same way. One library may consider a particular element of cost as part of the acquisitions operation and a second as a part of the cataloging operation; a third may ignore it altogether, or include it in the burden or overhead cost. Nor is this mere capriciousness on the part of members of the library community. Library operations not only differ from one another, but they also change with time.

Consider, for example, the problem of obtaining a set of catalog cards for a particular monograph. Any or all of the following alternatives might be in use at a given library: the cards may be 1) supplied with the book as a service provided by the bookseller at some extra cost; 2) ordered from the Library of Congress; 3) provided by a centralized cataloging operation serving several libraries (as in a county or state library system); 4) prepared by catalogers working in the library; or 5) generated by computer program from standard listings (e.g., from MARC tapes).

Comparing any two of these procedures within a given library does not present any overwhelming problems, although minor questions of definition do occur (for example, how much of the cost of ordering should be allocated to the acquisitions department and how much to the cataloging department when both the book and the catalog cards are obtained simultaneously from the same source?). However, to compare costs from two different libraries, it is essential to know what proportion of each card source was used by each library. Fortunately for the purposes of this study most libraries are presently using a mix of method 2 (LC) and method 4 (own catalogers), and at least some provide sufficient information to enable determination of the appropriate mix for each. However, the problem is indicative of one essential difficulty in comparative cost analyses; and one that, although eased, would not be eliminated by having all libraries band together for adoption of a standard costing procedure.

A second difficulty arises from temporal and geographic differences in the cost of manpower. On the surface, this problem can be eliminated, or substantially reduced, by having all studies based on man-hours spent, rather than on dollars required per item, and a number of writers have suggested such a change in reporting procedure. However, the problem is not quite so simple. For example, determining the number of man-hours spent on cataloging adds cost to the study that tends to reduce the number of libraries willing to report; those that do report may or may not be a representative sample of the total.

However, there is a more basic problem. In almost all libraries the real restraint on activities is financial: there are just so many funds available for cataloging and these must be used to at least keep the backlog of uncataloged material down to the amount of space available to store it. Suppose, for instance, that the amount of material to be cataloged increases by ten percent from one year to the next and that the catalogers are fortunate enough to obtain ten percent salary increases over the same period. It is not impossible to consider that in some libraries the catalogers may be forced to "earn" this raise by absorbing at least a part of the increased load without extra help. Balancing salary increases by productivity increases is, of course, familiar in industry and may well exist in libraries. As evidence that such an effect is present, it is noted later in this report (see Table 4) that three studies made in three rather different libraries over a period of six years showed costs of from $0.228 to $0.235 per card for preparation, production, and filing.

The total range ($0.007) is only three percent of the average cost per card. ($0.230). Such close agreement would be startling if it were found in three simultaneous studies of three nearly identical library operations. To set this agreement aside as pure coincidence seems unwarranted. It is more reasonable to assume that librarians are forced to operate under strong financial constraints and that they adjust their performance to those constraints through hiring of less well-trained personnel, increased time pressures on all personnel, etc. If this is the case, "standardized" reporting through time figures might be quite misleading unless cost figures were reported as well.

Finally, there is the question of allocating burden or overhead. Potentially, burden could present a severe problem, and occasionally it may. However, in most of the reports cited here, burden is either ignored or separately stated and there is no reason to suspect that the results given in the summaries are noticeably biased by unseen burden differences. Nevertheless, it would be of interest to determine proper overhead figures for library operations, as the switch to automation (which seems inevitable), will entail the use of more machines and fewer people, which in turn may drastically alter the overhead structure.

THE USE OF COST INFORMATION

Having noted some of the difficulties that tend to cloud cost comparisons, it is perhaps useful to investigate how cost information is likely to be used. The nature of the problem can be illustrated by two rather different situations. One is exemplified by Library "A," a large public library of some years' standing. It is considering the possibility of changing from its present manual procedures to some form of automation, and wishes to determine a reasonable strategy for implementing such a change over the next five years. Library "B," otherwise comparable to "A," has been keyboarding the catalog records of its current acquisitions for the last three years. It has now decided to convert its retrospective catalog and wishes to choose the most economic procedure for this step.

The differences in the problems facing two such libraries are basically the classic differences between strategy and tactics. Library "A," must lay out a long-term plan, taking into account the growth in its collection over the five-year period, likely changes in equipment and personnel available to it, increases in labor costs, decreases in equipment usage costs, etc. Library "B," on the other hand, is in the position of making a specific set of decisions as to whether the work should be done in-house or subcontracted; whether the Library should use punched cards, punched paper tape, or optical character-recognition devices; and so forth.

In terms of cost, Library "B," has to prepare a specific budget request for its funding agency, and it is reasonable to assume that that funding agency will require assurance that the task is to be accomplished at the minimum cost consistent with the designated quality level. Cost differences of as little as five percent may be quite important to Library "B." General cost summaries can be of use only in enumeration of the possible alternatives. Even the accounting procedures in effect in the local system will have a bearing on the final decision.

Thus, the primary utility of a general cost summary to the library about to commit itself in a tactical situation is the information it can provide about the problem statement: which cost factors other libraries have been able to identify in similar situations; which of the various alternatives may

be safely eliminated from consideration on the grounds that their present costs are considerably higher than other existing methods; and so forth. The likelihood seems remote that any general study, or, for that matter, any particular study, will be sufficiently applicable to the library now undertaking the problem to enable it to take over cost structures unchanged.

Library "A," faced with establishing a long-range plan, has much more flexibility available to it. Its interest in specific costs will be established by some gross notion as to what quantity of funds are likely to be available over the period under plan. Some procedures may be seriously considered because they are relatively new and untried and hence of potential interest to national funding agencies who would not consider funding further experiments with procedures that have been thoroughly tested. Access to good cost information of such well-tested procedures will help in establishing the likely costs for important aspects of the overall plan. Of even greater interest is the possibility that certain costs are likely to undergo substantial change over the planning period. For instance, in Reference 1 it was noted that optical character recognition may be a very attractive long-run option for catalog conversion problems precisely because it is so new, and hence has not had time to allow a sufficient number of service centers to spring up to provide truly competitive service capabilities. Computer typesetting with the new generation of hardware is in much the same category.

In both situations it is clear that what is most needed is the enumeration of cost elements on the one hand and operating cost experience on the other. Precise estimates of any one cost element are of relatively little importance, either because they are so likely to change over the long run, or because they are likely to be not appropriate to a specific application even in the short run.

Comparative cost information would therefore seem to provide a good basis for either application. The comparison forces an enumeration of cost elements precisely because one must evaluate the cost structure of each source to be sure that a reasonable comparison is possible. Reporting of the actual experience of several libraries provides a range of experience, not only over several libraries but also over time, so that the extremes reported give an indication of the variability that must be allowed for. In what follows, therefore, concentration is on the problems of cost element definition and on the reporting of as many sources as are comparable in the broad sense. Because precise estimates are not only difficult to obtain, but also unlikely to be relevant to most users, no attempt has been made to provide formal estimates either of the average cost figures or of their underlying variability.

THE COST OF CATALOGING

The preparation of catalog information for a given monograph is perhaps the most sophisticated operation in the entire catalog operation. As such it is probably the last to be considered a candidate for automation, although it is not unreasonable, even now, to consider the use of computers as aids to the cataloger. Consequently in many operations the cost of cataloging will continue to be an invariant regardless of whether automation is introduced into other aspects of the catalog operation or not. Nevertheless, it is useful to study the cost of catalogs, both to establish the relative cost of cataloging and the subsequent processing steps, and to establish the line of demarcation between the catalog step and the subsequent steps.

Any enumeration of the detailed steps involved in a complex process must be tentative. This is nowhere more true than in the cataloging operation. Fortunately the number of descriptions in detail is growing. For the cataloging operation, three sources of information were used: a detailed analysis made as part of an overall time and motion study of operations in the Lockheed Research Library (3); a detailed study of the cataloging and processing activities of the New York Public Library as a preliminary to possible automation of some of these operations (4); and a detailed study of the acquisitions, cataloging, and other processing operations for the Columbia University science libraries (5). A summary of these studies is given in Table 1.

In addition to the eight items in Table 1, the Lockheed Library study included five other items that we have chosen to include in subsequent operations.

It is generally true that professionals do not like to have their jobs subjected to the minutiae of time and motion study. There is always the ugly feeling that the creative (and most important) aspects of the job cannot be subjected to simple measurement. Nevertheless, cataloging is a continuing effort in most libraries and it is possible to establish some average production rates in terms of number of books cataloged per month or the number of minutes needed per book. The prob-

lem, as with most statistical studies, is not with the establishment of objective measurements but rather in the manner in which they are interpreted. Use of comparative statistics does not eliminate the possibility of misinterpretation but it does tend to minimize it.

The comparative studies selected for the cataloging operation, in addition to those already cited, were: a Colorado study based on average cataloging times for eleven librarians from six cooperating libraries (2), and a study of ordering, cataloging, and preparations in several Southern California libraries (6). The catalog cost information for these five studies is summarized in Table 2.

In the Lockheed and Colorado studies, basic times of each operation were studied and then "standard" time factors added to allow for nonproductive time. The standard factors increased the Lockheed times by 13 percent and the Colorado times by 48 percent. (The times in the table include these allowances.) The figures for New York were derived from their reported statements that they processed 65,000 books using 49 catalogers at a total cost of $409,500 (not including fringe benefits). The Columbia figures have been reduced by 20 percent to eliminate fringe benefits. The implied average salary for each source was obtained by dividing the total cataloging cost by the average time and multiplying by 60 to convert to cost per hour.

The simplest conclusion to reach from a study of Table 2 is that cataloging costs vary widely from one library to another. Average times differ by more than 8 to 1 and total cost varies by more than 3 to 1. The low salary for the Southern California study is presumably explained by the fact that that study was done in 1961. Adjustment of this figure for average salary increases from 1961 to 1968 would undoubtedly bring their total cost more directly in line with the other studies (Bureau of Labor Statistics shows hourly wages increased approximately 30 percent over this period). It would be interesting to know if the presumed increased salaries of the Southern California catalogers has led to a decrease in the average time they spend on cataloging. The more recent data on Colorado and New York suggest that this might be expected.

The Columbia and Lockheed time data represent, perhaps not unreasonably, the extremes in this table. The Lockheed research library is small compared to the others, and Lockheed is, of course, a private corporation, whereas the other

TABLE 1

Cataloging Cost Elements

COLUMBIA UNIVERSITY SCIENCE	NEW YORK PUBLIC	LOCKHEED RESEARCH LABORATORY
(With LC information) 1. Assign class number 2. Compare book and card, check entries in general catalog, establish subjects, etc. 3. Make necessary changes in LC proof slip, or type temporary slip giving brief descriptive information and class number 4. Completed books revised and sent for shelf listing (Without LC information) 1. Supply descriptive cataloging 2. Subject analysis, classification and authority work 3. Type workslip for processing section.	1. Review work done by searcher. Reconcile conflicts and approve new entry forms 2. Full descriptive cataloging 3. Assign subject entries 4. Assign divisional catalog designators 5. Check authority files and establish new authorities and cross references 6. Determine classmark	1. Get book and analyze for subject. Obtain Dewey and Cutter numbers 2. Check shelf list for duplicates and copy number 3a. (With LC information) Insert and type copy slip and temporary catalog card, check LC subject headings and other references. Descriptive and subject catalog book. Pencil call number on title page 3b. (Without LC information) Insert and type descriptive part only on copy slip and temporary catalog card. Write subject data only on catalog card. Pencil call number on title page 4. Tear and separate copy slips and temporary cards. Proof and correct as necessary. 5. Take report to reports cataloging 6. Travel to library, check national union catalog or other reference book 7. Count and tally titles cataloged

TABLE 2

Comparative Costs of Cataloging

LIBRARY SOURCE	DATE	AVERAGE TIME, MIN.	CATALOGING COST	IMPLIED AVG. SALARY (PER HOUR)
Lockheed	1967	10.0	–	–
Colorado	1969	28.6	$2.07	$4.34
New York	1968	39.8	6.30	5.25
So. Cal.	1961	44.8	2.23	2.98
Columbia	1967	84.0	5.85	4.17

sources represent public and university libraries. Columbia, on the other hand, is a large university library; however, the figures given are from a study of cataloging of science monographs, which may be more time-consuming.

As these cataloging cost figures will be used only as a point of comparison with subsequent operations, it is not necessary to further resolve the apparent differences. The average time for the five sources is 41.4 minutes. Assuming that a cataloger currently earns $4.50 an hour, the average cost for the five sources would be $3.11 for the unit cost of cataloging.

CARD PROCESSING COSTS

If cataloging is the least likely part of the library operation to be automated in the near future, the procedures that immediately follow cataloging are precisely opposite in character. Card preparation, production, and filing all involve time-consuming routine operations that can be done automatically, thus relieving the library community of a significant proportion of man-hours to apply to problems of greater intellectual content. Cost factors must nonetheless be considered.

As with cataloging, description of basic cost elements will vary from one library to another. For the detailed breakdown in Table 3, use is again made of the Columbia and New York Public studies previously cited. Added to them is data from an unpublished study made available by Neil Barron of Sacramento State College Library. Barron's cost elements are given in finer detail than those in the other studies reported in this section.

In Table 4, data from the New York Public Library and from the Sacramento State College Library have been grouped into three categories (preparation, production and filing) to achieve maximum compatibility with data from other sources reported in the table. These sources are: a study (7) at the University of Toronto of manual costs made in conjunction with early machine

methods; a comparative study (8) of manual methods and a special-purpose machine procedure at the Air Force Cambridge Research Laboratory Library; and results of three years of computerized card production at the Yale Medical Library (9).

Costs shown in Table 4 are on a "per-card" basis, rather than on a title basis, as differing library requirements show averages ranging from 4.6 cards per title at Sacramento to 9.8 cards per title at New York Public.

Most significant in Table 4 is the extraordinary agreement between two of the studies: the total processing costs amount to 23.2c per card and 23.5c per card for these two sources, even though the reports were prepared over a six-year period and include significant changes in the cost of labor and materials. Furthermore, these costs are reasonably constant for the individual categories in all three sources: card preparation varies from 11.4c per card to 11.6c per card; card production varies from 6.4c per card to 7.9c per card; and card filing varies from 4.2c per card to 5.2c per card. In one sense this close agreement should not be surprising. If it is indeed true that cataloging involves relatively high intellectual content that is difficult to automate, and card processing involves straightforward operations that are relatively easy to automate, it is reasonable to argue that the latter should show much less variability from one operation to the next.

The fact that the New York Public operation has significantly higher costs can be partially explained by the following observations. The NYPL costs are based on the supposition that all cards are locally produced. The other libraries indicate that a significant proportion of their work is based on the acquisition of LC cards. The breakdown for the AFCRL study is shown in Table 4 and the breakdown for Sacramento is approximately the same. Secondly NYPL is clearly the largest of the operations under consideration here, and it is not unreasonable to expect that the size of the file will

TABLE 3

Processing Cost Elements

COLUMBIA UNIVERSITY	NEW YORK PUBLIC	SACRAMENTO STATE
1. Card production	1. Receive and distribute planning sheets	1. Type master cards from handwritten slips
2. Card set completion	2. Type headings for added entries and subject entries	2. Produce subject cross reference cards
3. Sorting and preliminary filing	3. Mark designators and sort completed cards	3. Maintain guide cards
4. Shelf listing	4. Distribute cards to filing section	4. Card production and purchase
5. Typing of book pockets	5. Paint edges of cards when required	5. Complete card sets
6. Filing	6. Glue and separate batches	6. Proof
	7. Type masters for offset printing	7. Alphabetize
	8. Prepare copy for Itek masters	8. File and revise
	9. Check format of entry on masters	9. Card shifting
	10. Check letter for letter on planning sheet	10. Update existing cards
	11. Gather statistics and keep log of card preparation	11. Correction of problems
	12. Prepare Itek masters and print cards on offset	12. Withdrawals
	13. File	13. Weed order slips
		14. Assembly of statistics
		15. File temporary slips
		16. File permanent slips
		17. Shelf list shifting
		18. Blank catalog card stock

TABLE 4

Comparative Costs of Card Processing

DATE	1968	1969	1965	1963			1968
Library Cards per title	NYPL (9.8)	SSC (4.6)	ONULP (~9)	(local)	AFCRL (7) (LC cat.)	(machine)	CHY (9.3)
Preparation	0.140	0.116	0.114 ⎫	0.233	0.166	0.075	0.088
Production	⎫	0.064	0.079 ⎭				
Filing	0.186 ⎬	0.052	0.042	0.043	0.043	0.043	—
Totals	0.336 ⎭	0.232	0.235	0.276	0.209	0.118	—

(0.276 and 0.209 bracketed together: 0.228)

have an effect on the cost of filing. In fact, assuming that the NYPL cost of preparation and production is the same as that for the AFCRL's locally produced cards (27.6c) and assigning the rest of the NYPL cost to filing, the latter figure becomes 10.3c per card, or a little more than twice the average for the other three sources (4.8c per card). If this is the case, it would be of interest to know whether the problem is one of sheer size of the catalog or rather one of increased density that naturally occurs in larger files. E.g., is it more costly to file "Smith, Adrian J." in a file with 100 Smith's or 1000 Smith's?

Finally, in the two cases of partial automation (AFCRL and Yale) the cost of card preparation and production is significantly lower (7.5c and 8.8c) than that indicated for LC cards (16.6c), or the average for the three closely agreeing sources (23.2c). This observation alone should point the library community strongly towards automation of the card processing function. Nor is this observation new; both authors of the preliminary studies at AFCRL and Yale made the point more than adequately. Furthermore, as will be demonstrated shortly, the cost of filing is also reduced in an automated system.

Several factors may be contributing to the slowness of the library community to introduce changes to achieve such cost savings. First, there is inevitably a substantial initial cost involved in any automation project. Second, although the potential cost saving is a substantial proportion of the processing cost, it is still small when compared to the cost of cataloging; a librarian under pressure to reduce costs could gain more by cutting back on the time allowed for cataloging without the initial investment necessary for automation. Third, there is a persistent difficulty in finding trained personnel in the automation field. Finally, librar-

ians are certainly aware of the rapid changeover in equipment in the computing field with the concomittant costs of adapting programs to new equipment.

CASE AND SPACE

The preceding discussion has provided some notion as to the cost of obtaining the required cataloging information, encoding it on catalog cards, and entering those cards in a catalog file. These costs can be compared with other possible approaches to the problem, including those that involve some degree of automation. There are, of course, a number of associated costs that must be taken into account to obtain a full picture of the cost of card cataloging. They would include, at a minimum, the cost of the space occupied by the catalog, the purchase price of catalog filing cases, the cost to the user of consulting the catalog, and the cost to the library of maintaining the catalog in usable form.

The allocation of capital expenditure costs to a form comparable to the costs per title and the costs per card used in the earlier sections of this report raises certain difficulties. Accounting procedures vary from one institution to another. Further there is the real but difficult-to-measure problem of comparing funds of various types in a particular situation. Nonetheless, it is useful to know whether under any reasonable accounting system the cost of space and cabinets is of sufficient magnitude to make it worthwhile to consider these costs in the overall evaluation. Assuming, therefore, that a filing case capable of storing 72,000 cards fully packed costs $800 and occupies approximately 30 square feet of space, including room for aisles and access area, and further assuming that land and construction costs are approximately $30 per square foot, the total cost of the cabinet and the space it occupies would be approximately $1,700. Finally if it is assumed that on the average a catalog is approximately 60 percent full, the initial cost of space and case is approximately 4c per card. Four cents a card is not negligible, but it is only about 15 to 20 percent of the cost of producing the cards and an even smaller fraction of the total cost when cataloging is included. Hence, it seems reasonable to put this cost for space and case in the category of a secondary cost item that will favor book catalogs, microfilm catalogs, and other high-density forms. It is unlikely to be a determining factor unless other cost factors are very closely balanced.

BOOK AND CARD CATALOGS: SOME RELATIVE ADVANTAGES

Among the various cost factors involved in cataloging, the most difficult to assess objectively is the cost to the user. The problem is that no one really knows what a user does in a library, nor what impact a given change will have on its utility to him. Whether they like a card catalog or not, library users do consult it and it is thus a usable device for providing access to library materials. Equally, many libraries in times past, and again more recently, have had book catalogs, and they also are viable devices. But which is better?

A card catalog is updated by the simple expedient of entering recently obtained cards in the file. A book catalog is updated by periodically printed revisions. Hence any search for a particular item will in general require fewer specific searches in the card catalog than in the book catalog, if the proper information is available to the searcher. Card catalogs are large and costly and there are few savings over the original cost in producing a second copy. Reproducing books after the first copy is relatively inexpensive. Libraries with many branches, or a decentralized set of users, will provide better service with book catalogs. The added cost of maintaining more than a few files is heavy with cards and light with books. Whether card or book catalogs are used, the existence of a machine readable catalog provides much greater flexibility as time goes on. Revisions of cataloging practice become much simpler if the revisions can be programmed on a computer.

In sum, machine readable book catalogs appear less advantageous than card catalogs only when immediate updating is the primary criterion for comparison.

COMPARATIVE COSTS OF CATALOG CONVERSION

Table 5 (an extension and revision of Table 7 gives comparative conversion costs for three public libraries (Library of Congress (10), New York Public Library and Los Angeles Public Library), the Library of the University of California at Berkeley, the Stanford Undergraduate Library (11), the Ontario New Universities Library Project, and the Columbia-Harvard-Yale study. Although the data was gathered for the most part independently over a four-year period, it is worth making a number of internal comparisons to test for consistency.

The most outstanding comparison is between the encoding costs for the Library of Congress and those for the Los Angeles Public Library. For records of essentially the same average length (446 characters versus 450 characters) the coding costs agree to the penny! Yet the methods of production are significantly different. The Library of Congress invested heavily in the coding and editing operation and used paper tape typewriters with their relatively high rental. As a result its costs in this area are significantly higher than those for LACP. On the other hand these procedural changes resulted in significantly lower keying costs, so that the overall cost for encoding was the same.

The encoding costs of UC/B, CHY, and SUL are all very close (within three cents per title) even though there is a fair range of record size (from 180 for SUL to 317 for UC/B). These three studies probably provide a more reasonable picture of the underlying variation in cost than the unusually close figures for LC and LACP.

As a further test of consistency, average cost is plotted against average record length (in characters per record) in Figure 1. The rightmost points are for LC and LACP, and the line is simply drawn through the origin (zero dollars, zero cost) and those points. The points of UC/B, CHY and SUL cluster about the center of the line. Following is an interpretation of the other points charted.

The NYPL point of $.45 for a 300-character record is not based on actual NYPL experience, but rather on a study of information from other investigations. Its proximity to the line suggests that NYPL's analysis of existing information reaches a conclusion similar to that of this paper.

The average encoding cost used to plot the ONULP point does not contain the full rental charge reported in the ONULP study, because the entire cost of keyboard rental was charged against

TABLE 5

Comparative Conversion Costs Per Title

	MAR. 68 LC 446 CHAR.	1968 LACP ~450 CHAR.	1964 ONLUP 400 CHAR.	1968 NYPL 300 CHAR.	1966 UC/B 317 CHAR.	1964 CHY 243 CHAR.	1966 SUL 180 CHAR.
Coding/editing	$0.169	—	—	—	$0.080[1]	—	$0.044
Keying	0.207	$0.480	$0.307	$0.450	0.188	$0.198	0.183
Re-keying	0.033	0.127	0.259		0.030	0.117	0.103
Proofing	0.125	0.084	0.650[2]		0.085	0.036	0.037
Rental	0.156	0.020	0.096	0.046	—	0.036	
Conversion & List	0.359	0.084	—	0.141	0.020	0.024	0.104[3]
Edit List		—	0.508[4]	0.165	—	—	
Sort & Merge		0.036	0.580	—	—	—	0.121
Supplies	0.080	—		—	—		0.033
Supervision	0.183	—		—	—		—

[1] Includes provision for keypunch rental, and supplies
[2] Full keypunch rental absorbed by pilot project
[3] Includes use of atomatic error-detection routines
[4] Includes cost of magnetic tapes and other supplies

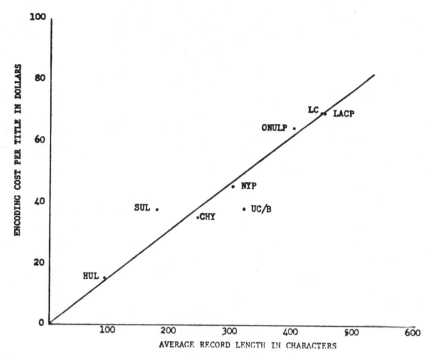

Figure 1. Encoding Costs per Title as a Function of Average Record Length.

the project although the machines were only partially utilized. The point for Harvard University Library (HUL) is based on information received in a private communication.

Although there is a significant amount from one study to another it seems reasonable to conclude that the cost of encoding is approximately $.15 per title per hundred characters.

The cost of computation is not as well-documented as the cost of conversion. Studies that reported computer costs all include the following three operational costs: The first is the cost of conversion and listing. This cost includes the cost of converting the original machine readable form (be it cards or paper tape) to magnetic tape form. In most cases a by-product of this operation was a listing (all-caps only) of the material on the tape.

The second is the cost of an edit run, including a listing in upper and lower-case. The latter was eschewed in a number of cases because of the added costs. However, many libraries would require a proper edit run and many librarians would prefer to edit from an upper/lower-case printout than from an all-caps printout.

The third is the cost of sorting and merging the tapes. Many of the early studies did not explicitly report on this cost because they were primarily concerned with the cost of converting the retrospective list. However, in an on-going operation this would be a continuing cost of some magnitude.

The available information points to a uniform cost of approximately $.02 per record for conversion and list, and approximately $.08 per record for editing. The two studies where both these costs are given indicate that a ratio of 4 to 1 is appropriate. The only study giving a ratio between the sort and merge operation and the edit operation is the NYPL study and this is based on before-the-fact-information only; the ratio is approximately 8 to 7. For convenience, one can assume that this ratio is unity, giving an overall ratio of 4-4-1. The most complete history of total computer cost is given by LC: a total of $.36 per record for 446 character records. Applying the above ratio to the LC total yields a breakdown of $.04 for conversion and list, $.16 for editing, and $.16 for sort and merge. Extending the Stanford cost of $.12 for conversion and list and editing gives a total cost for SUL of $.22 for its 180 character records. This figure is considerably more than 180/446 parts of the LC cost.

One other pertinent piece of information is available from the SUL data. In the production of the annual catalog, Stanford estimates a cost of $.121 per title for what is roughly comparable to the cost of sort and merge. This cost is then roughly 1.2 times the SUL cost for conversion and list and editing, verifying the notion that the cost of "sort and merge" is of the same general magnitude as the cost of editing.

The ratios of SIL costs to LC for encoding are .367/.690 = .532 and .225/.359 = .625 for computer time. This suggests that the means of computing average record length may be different for the two institutions. Taking the LC figures as the standard and assuming that both computing and encoding costs are strictly a function of record length, the SUL record length should be between .532 × 446 = 238 and .625 × 446 = 279. This discrepancy may be a result of one source (presumably LC) counting all delimiter and other nonprinting characters while the other does not. NYPL, indicates that the ratio of printed characters to total characters is approximately 3:4. If the SUL figure of 180 is expanded by one third, one obtains the figure of 240 which agrees well with the lower limit (based on encoding costs) given above.

The cost of sort and merge is a function of the size of the data base, not the amount of material being put into it. The Library of Congress points this out in its study (11) and report on an average month (where the data base grows for a period and then is reduced to zero.) Stanford Undergraduate Library figures are based on its second year of operation, in which 16,000 titles were added to form a total base of 41,000 titles. The actual cost of this step in the operation will therefore depend strongly on the operating strategy employed. Clearly, the number of times one has to sort and merge the entire data base should be minimized, particularly taking into account the fact that sorting costs go up faster than linearly. If the master file is arranged in n orders (author, subject, title, class number, etc.), it will generally be less expensive to sort the updating material into those n orders and make n merge runs with the sorted master files than to make a single merge with a single ordering of the master file and then sort the master file n times to obtain the required updated orderings of the master file.

MANUAL AND COMPUTER PROCESSING:

One objective of this paper is to define factors whose costs enter into calculations of relative costs of manual and computer processing of catalog in-

formation and to report these factor costs. The following paragraphs present a simplifed comparison of actual costs of manual and machine processing for a "typical" library characterized by average costs approximating those in the preceding tables.

Table 5 yields average figures for two cases: catalogs with approximately 425 characters per entry and catalogs with approximately 250 characters per entry; they may be called "full entries" and "short entries," respectively.

From Table 4, it is possible to compute similar figures for "full catalogs" and "short catalogs" by clustering the three larger cases (those having 9.8, 9.0, and 7.0 cards per title) and the three smaller cases (those having 3.0 and 4.6 cards per title). For the full catalogs the average cost of processing is 26.7c per card and 8.6 cards per title, or a total cost of $2.29 per title. For the short catalogs the average cost of processing is 20.3c per card and 3.8 cards per title, or $0.78 per title. Combining these two sets of figures gives the results in Table 6.

TABLE 6
Comparative Costs of Manual and Computerized Processing

	SHORT ENTRIES	FULL ENTRIES
Manual	$0.78	$2.29
Computer	$0.84	$1.31

Table 6 shows that an hypothesized "typical" library would be slightly better off with manual methods if it chose the short form entries, and noticeably better off with the machine if it chose the full form of the entry.

In making this quick comparison, consideration has not been given to several factors that should obviously be taken into account even in this simple example. First, there is not included either the initial cost of programming or the initial cost of converting the retrospective records. Either or both of these costs could be substantial, but as they are one-time costs and as libraries are basically long-term institutions, such costs should be written off over a relatively long period, even though they must be financed out of a given year's budget.

Second, the cost of printing the catalog is not included (assuming a book catalog is in fact to be used in the computerized system). Thus the comparison in Table 6 is between a card catalog and a catalog in machine readable form. Such a comparison is complicated by the fact that a card once filed stays in the catalog indefinitely, subject only to long-term wear and tear and a certain rate of attrition due to unauthorized removal, misfiling, and so forth, whereas the machine readable catalog must be updated periodically and supplemented by interim publications. And, of course, the comparison is also complicated by the corresponding low cost of producing a number of copies of the book catalog where this is useful for a given system.

However, to put the printing cost in some degree of perspective, one may make a quick calculation based on the production of a single book catalog using a standard upper- and lower-case print chain. At present commercially available prices this would cost between 35c and 50c per 10,000 characters, or approximately 9c per entry for the full form entries and 5c per entry for the short form entries (assuming four complete listings for author, title, subject, and class number listings). This added cost would make the comparison between manual and computerized methods even less favorable for the short form, but still substantially better for the long form entries $1.40 to $2.29).

CONCLUSION

It may be concluded that the card-processing operations in typical libraries can be automated economically in many situations today. Libraries using the short form of a catalog and having no immediate need for multiple copies of the catalog may find it desirable to wait a year or two, depending upon their local situation, the availability of trained personnel and, of course, the availability of capital to finance the initial cost of programming and retrospective conversion.

However, libraries using the full form in their catalogs, or those needing multiple copies of their catalogs, will almost certainly find that there is a substantial economic advantage to computerization at the present time. Even when allowance is made for substantial departures from the "typical" costs found in this study, it is difficult to visualize any library using full form information not finding significant economic gains in computerization.

Considering the further advantages of the greater flexibility available in machine readable records, the increased services that can be offered to the user, and the fact that machine costs are decreasing while labor costs are increasing, one is led to the conclusion that more and more libraries will move towards catalog automation.

Tables 7 to 11 appearing on the following pages are reference tables for calculating costs.

TABLE 7

Cost/Card—Library of Congress Catalog Cards (July 1968)

LC CARDS ORDERED BY/FOR	1-2 CDS ONLY	1ST COL OF 3 OR MORE ORDER	ADD'L COPIES SAME CD ORDERED SAME TM.	ALL TITLES SPECIFIC SUBJECT	SUBSC FOR ALL CDS	EXTRA CHGS/TITLE ALL ORDERS LACKING REQ INFO
1) LC#	$.22	$.10	$.06	$	$ —	
2) Author & Title	.26	.15	.06		—	
3) Series	—	.10	.06		—	
4) Subject	—	.10	.06		—	
5) Chinese/Japanese/Korean	.22–.27	.10–.15	.06		.04	$.04
6) Motion Pictures & Filmstrips	.22–.27	.10–.15	.06	.10	.04	
7) Phonorecords	.22–.27	.10–.15	.06	.10	.04	
8) Revised & Cross Ref.	—	–	–		.04	
9) Anonymous		$.04				

Source—LC cds, July 1968

TABLE 8

Catalog Card Costs

CARDS	COST/CARD		COST/HOUR	TIME
LC Cards	$.22-.27 (min order 1-2 cds) .10-.15 (1st cd—3 more order) .04-.06 (add'l copies same cd-same order)	} $.04 extra chg all orders lacking req. info.		
Blank Cards	<3-<4 for $.01			
Original Card Preparation	$.20-2.34		$2.40-4.70	5-30 min/cd
Card Checking Before Filing	$.21		$4.20	3 min/cd
Correcting Detected Errors	$.12		$2.40	3 min/cd
File	$.024 .03 .047		$2.40 3.00 4.71	100 cds/hr 100 cds/hr 100 cds/hr
Store	$.01			
Reproduce	$.0023-.00208 (AB Dick Offset Press = $.125/bk(54-60 cds) .045 (Xerox—1K-100K cds)			

TABLE 9

(Estimated) Annual Cost of 1000 Sq Ft of Storage Space

1) Minnesota State Dept. of Education (1968)—$520*
2) R&D Estimate**

$$\frac{\text{1968 Construction Cost}}{\$30 \text{ sq ft} \times 1000 \text{ sq ft}} = \frac{\$30,000}{100 \text{ yrs (life of bldg)}} = \$\ 300/\text{yr}$$

$$+ \text{ Maintenance Costs, clean up, etc. (\$1 yr/sq ft)} = \frac{\$1000}{\$1300/\text{yr}}$$

$$\frac{\text{1974 Construction Cost}}{\$50 \text{ sq ft} \times 1000 \text{ sq ft}} = \frac{\$50,000}{100 \text{ yrs (life of bldg)}} = \$\ 500/\text{yr}$$

$$+ \text{ Maintenance Costs, clean up, etc. (\$ yr/sq ft)} = \frac{\$1000}{\$1500/\text{yr}}$$

*Source—Private communication
**Source—E. Graziano, Univ. Calif. at Santa Barbara

TABLE 10

Card Catalog Cost/Year

Given the following variables, 1 card catalog case with a maximum card capacity of 72,000 cards (purchase price—$789)—the cost/card to store would be $.01.

	ESTIMATED COST SQ FT RENTAL @ $.42 SQ FT/MO	CONSTRUCTION COST $30/SQ FT ÷100 YRS LIFE BLDG	MAINTENANCE EST. @ $1/SQ FT	COST/YR
Cabinet (6 sq ft)	$30.23	$1.80	$ 6.00	$ 38.04
Room for Users (16 sq ft)	80.64	4.80	16.00	101.44
Aisles (3 sq ft)	15.12	.90	3.00	19.02
Catalog Table (5 sq ft)	25.20	1.50	5.00	31.70
				$190.20
			+72,000 cards @ $1.01 (to store)	720.00
			TOTAL COST/YR	$910.20

TABLE 11
Card Catalog Maintenance Costs

REQUIREMENT SPACE		ESTIMATED COST/SQ FT	COST/MO	COST/YEAR
Card Catalog Cabinet	− 6 sq ft	$.42	$ 2.52	$ 30.24
Room for Users	−16 sq ft		6.72	80.64
Aisles	− 3 sq ft		1.26	15.12
Catalog Table	− 5 sq ft		2.10	25.20
	30 sq ft		$12.60	$151.20

Source—E. Graziano, Univ. Calif. at Santa Barbara and R&D Consultants Co.

ACKNOWLEDGMENTS

The work reported in this paper was supported by the U. S. Office of Education under Contract Number OEC-9-8-00292-0107.

Mrs. Henriette Avram (Library of Congress) and Mr. Neil Barron (Sacramento State College, Sacramento, California) made important contributions of cost figures and other technical data used in this report. Various State Libraries supplied detailed cost information.

BIBLIOGRAPHY

A 400-item bibliography on cost and automation is available from the National Auxiliary Publication Service of ASIS (NAPS 00696).

REFERENCES

1. Dolby, J. L.; Forsyth, V. J.; Resnikoff, H. L.: *Computerized Library Catalogs: Their Growth, Cost and Utility* (Cambridge, Mass.: M.I.T. Press, 1969).
2. Dougherty, Richard M.: "Cost Analysis Studies in Libraries: Is There a Basis for Comparison," *Library Resources and Technical Services,* 13 (Winter 1969), 136-141.
3. Kozumplik, William A.: "Time and Motion Study of Library Operations," *Special Libraries,* 58 (October 1967), 585-588.
4. Henderson, J. W.; Rosenthal, J. A.: *Library Catalogs: Their Preservation and Maintenance by Photographic and Automated Techniques* (Cambridge, Mass.: M.I.T. Press, 1968).
5. Fasana, Paul J.; Fall, James E.: "Processing Costs for Science Monographs in the Columbia University Libraries," *Library Resources and Technical Services,* 11 (Winter 1967), 97-114.
6. MacQuarrie, Catherine: "Cost Survey: Cost of Ordering, Cataloging, and Preparations in Southern California Libraries," *Library Resources and Technical Services,* 6 (Fall 1962), 337-350.
7. Bregzis, Ritvars: "The ONULP Bibliographic Control System: An Evaluation," In University of Illinois Graduate School of Library Science: *Proceedings of 1965 Clinic on Library Applications of Data Processing* (Urgana: University of Illinois, 1966), pp. 112-140.
8. Fasana, Paul J.: "Automating Cataloging Functions in Conventional Libraries," *Library Resources and Technical Services,* 7 (Fall 1963), 350-365.
9. Kilgour, Frederick G.: "Costs of Library Catalog Cards Produced by Computer," *Journal of Library Automation,* 1 (June 1968), 121-127.
10. Avram, Henriette: *The MARC Pilot Project* (Final Report on a project sponsored by Library Resources: Chapter VIII: "Cost Models" (Washington, D. C.: Library of Congress, 1968).
11. Johnson, Richard D.: "A Book Catalog at Stanford," *Journal of Library Automation,* 1 (March 1968), 13-50.

VI

COPYRIGHT

In the article which follows, the authors refer several times to the principle of "fair use." Because "fair use" is important to an understanding of the problem, some readers may wish to consult the article by Verner Clapp (listed in the section on additional readings). Most librarians are quite familiar with the subject.

The principle of "fair use" is one of long standing, one which librarians prefer to retain in the age of the computer. Whether this can be done is problematical. That the "fair use" concept has been abused in the age of Xerography is beyond argument; whether the abuse has led to serious economic losses to authors and publishers is debatable. But within the present state of affairs, if the concept were not abused the right of the public to information would be seriously impaired. Some would argue that the economic loss is far from large enough to warrant interference with the rights of the public to information, and the latter is surely no less an important objective of a copyright law.

The authors of the article on the computer and copyright have provided an admirable introduction to the physical properties of the computer as these relate to the copyright issues. With respect to the issues the authors work towards a recommendation by separating the inputs and the outputs. While not so tolerant of abuses as others, we cannot fairly say that these authors have disregarded the rights of the public to know. On the other hand, their sympathy for the rights of authors and publishers lead them to the conclusion that control at the output stage is not realistic.

However, control at input is not free of problems. In some kinds of situations, the user is not sure of what or how much use he can make of the material. Many users of reprography machines find on reflection little use for material that has been copied. The authors of the article here reprinted argue, however, that many libraries purchase books which prove later to be seldom used.

In order to get around the problem of the author who refuses to grant permission to have his work put into the computer, or of the author who cannot be found, the proposal is made that a work published in any form must be made available. This, however, raises two problems: what is a published work, and what of the author who seeks to circumvent compulsory permission by asking for an exorbitant fee? The first of these problems is not discussed by our authors. As for the second, they would avoid fee schedules, but instead provide a system of arbitration.

From the viewpoint of librarians, this article compels interest in its consideration of information transmitted to the homes of users via television-like screens. This brings to mind a new service which libraries might then offer, transmitting information directly into the homes of subscribers. Would librarians accept this challenge, or would they permit commercial operations to monopolize the service?

Information Storage and Retrieval by Computer—
An Emerging Problem for the Law of Copyright

by Steven Allen, Sharon Green, Jerald Friedman, Bruce E. Harrington and Lawrence R. Johnson

As the name implies, computerized information storage and retrieval systems utilize computers to store and retrieve information, either in printed or electronic form. Although primitive systems are already used in the business world to store and retrieve business documents, they present no threat to the copyright owner because they do not use copyrighted materials. However, the use of copyrighted abstracts in information storage and retrieval systems is extant and contemplated. Law Research, Inc. has a computerized research service for lawyers.[1] And only recently, the Department of Defense requested permission from the Society of Photographic Scientists and Engineers to input the Society's scientific and technical abstracts.[2] We will only tangentially address the problems presented by these current uses, concentrating instead on prospects for the future.

The real problem for copyright will arise with the development of sophisticated computerized information storage and retrieval systems, an entirely different use of computers which may revolutionize information dissemination as we now know it. This new computer application in information dissemination threatens to replace printed works completely. In such a system, entire works would be stored in a computer in electronic rather than printed form. At the request of a user, the work would be retrieved from the computer's memory (storage area) and printed out in hard copy—a paper copy—or displayed on cathode ray tubes, similar to television screens. This "output" could conceivably emanate from one central computer (a national information center) to homes and offices throughout the country. Each home or office would have a viewer-printer console in place of a library. The console would receive electronic impulses from the central computer over telephone lines and cables, such as those used by cable antenna television,[3] or microwaves.

Receiving information at home through this network may someday be simpler than placing a telephone call. The computer could receive multiple requests, retrieve the information, and send out any number of information units simultaneously.

Further, as the information is displayed on his home console, the viewer may instruct the console to print out a hard copy of selected parts of the material displayed. Suppose that John Smith is preparing a speech for his local Toastmaster's meeting. John sits at his console viewer, and dials in a request for Chinese proverbs, from which he hopes to glean an opening sentence which will also set the theme for his talk. As the proverbs appear on his screen he picks up a light pen—a cartridge the size of a fountain pen, with a photoelectric cell in the tip. John touches the first letter of each proverb he would like to re-read before making a final choice. The selected messages are stored temporarily in his home console. If John finds a proverb he wants to use, he may instruct the console to print it out immediately; but if he is uncertain he may instruct the console to again display the proverbs he has previously indicated with his light pen. On re-reading he may then choose one or several for printout in hard copy.

The application of this technique to legal research is a matter for happy contemplation.[4] Add the possibility that portable consoles may be developed, and we may envision attorneys carrying all of their legal literature to court with them.

Although sophisticated computer information storage and retrieval systems will not be commercially available in the next few years, they may become a reality within our lifetimes. Since this dramatic change in the method of dissemination of information creates very unique problems for copyright law, we will focus on computer use of copyrighted material in the context of such a system. Some of the technological barriers which must be overcome will first be pointed out; then we will turn to the problem of affording protection, economic and otherwise, to authors, when their works are stored in computers rather than libraries, and sold as communication services rather than bookvendor's goods.

THE TECHNOLOGICAL NEEDS OF AN INFORMATION STORAGE AND RETRIEVAL SYSTEM

Input

Data is the "stuff" upon which computers operate. Data and directions in the form of programs must be fed, or input, into the computer system and transformed into electronic machine readable form before the computer can act. An information storage and retrieval system utilizing a central computer system, *e.g.*, a computerized library serving all nine branches of the University of California, would require a rapid, low cost means of data input.

Until recently, the most common input device was the typewriter keyboard of a cardpunch machine. Human operators punch data on computer cards (the familiar IBM card, for example), which are then fed into the computer. While punched cards are a simple and flexible means of input, their use for mass information input is not possible due to the labor cost involved. If one wished, for example, to input all the books in a library, the job would be comparable to retyping the entire collection twice; duplication is necessary in order to verify the cards for errors.[5]

Punched card input has been supplanted by more sophisticated input devices, such as typewriter consoles which communicate directly with the computer, thus avoiding the use of cards. Though data is input directly, the input rate is still dependent on the typing speed of the human operator.[6] So long as the input device is primarily a keyboard, a mass information system requiring input of millions of words per hour is impossible.

Within the last three years a device called an optical scanner has been developed which may greatly increase the practicability of mass input. The optical scanner, when perfected, will be able to ingest large amounts of data by merely scanning printed pages, translate it into machine readable form, and store the "translation" automatically.[7] Today's optical scanners are primitive, and still in the experimental stage.[8] Until the optical

scanner is commercially feasible, information storage and retrieval systems will be unable to exploit the full capabilities of the computer. So long as input is dependent upon the speed of human operators to translate written material into machine readable form, the use of computers will be limited to indexing and retrieving documents stored on microfilm or microfiche.[9]

No national network is likely to be created while these forms of storage are used. Microfilm and microfiche are costly due to the retrieval time required. After a request is made to the computer, the machine indicates which external microfilm or microfiche file contains the material. It then suspends its processing on that request until the required file is brought (mechanically or manually) to the computer. Since computer cost is measured in time units, the user must also pay for the "waiting time."

Furthermore, if microfilm or microfiche storage is used, computers cannot perform content analysis; that is, they cannot "read" documents, either to index them automatically as they are stored, or to determine whether particular documents are relevant to the user's request.

Memory Storage and Access Techniques

After data is input, the computer may direct it to either the internal memory core (internal storage) or to tapes, discs or drums (external storage). A storage system with optimum efficiency would be inexpensive and would have large storage capacity and rapid access to stored data.[10]

Data access time is the time expended while the computer probes its memory and retrieves the requested data. Computer processing is held in abeyance during the memory probe; therefore, if lengthy memory probes are required, costly computer time is wasted. Where data is recorded on magnetic tape, access is sequential, *i.e.*, when the computer probes the tape for the requested data, the tape must be wound to the "address" of the desired data before it may be retrieved. If the data is recorded near the outer end of the tape, access time is minimal. But if it is stored near the inside end of the tape, the process could take up to two minutes.

(1) Internal Storage

In contrast to sequential access storage, random (direct) access features approximately equal retrieval time for any unit of stored data. Most random access storage is internal, but some forms of external storage are nearly random access, *e.g.*, disc and drum storage. Since programs must be immediately available for computer operations, they are generally stored in the internal memory, leaving little internal storage space available for raw data. Internal storage is also too costly at present to be used for mass information storage.

The general repository for mass data today is external storage, which has a low cost and high capacity but slow retrieval time. However, extensive research in chemical storage techniques[11] is underway in an attempt to produce increased internal storage facilities at lower cost. These techniques would use chemical compounds and compositions as the storage medium. Laboratory results have yielded a high storage density, but astronomical production costs make such high density storage commercially impractical at this time.

Though increased internal storage density and reduced storage costs may someday make internal storage of raw data possible, computer systems will continue to rely on external storage of mass information for the foreseeable future.

(2) External Storage

We have mentioned one form of external storage—facsimile storage in microfilm or microfiche form.[12] The most common form of external storage is magnetic tape, similar to common audio recording tape, on which data is sequentially recorded in machine readable form (electronic impulses). Access time approaches a turtle's pace when compared with access to internally stored data.[13]

In 1956, a new form of external storage was introduced which had random access features—a magnetic disc storage unit.[14] The unit is made up of a number of metal discs permanently fixed one inch apart on a vertical shaft. The discs resemble a stack of phonograph records. Pickup heads move horizontally across the disc surfaces to reach given data addresses. The system is sequential insofar as the disc must be turned (at speeds over 2,000 revolutions per minute) to enable the head to reach the proper location. As more and more heads are affixed for each surface the system becomes more nearly random access. Due to the expense of these pickup heads, the system is more economical where only one head is used, but random access is then lost. For the foreseeable future, magnetic discs will be the primary media for high density external storage.

Disc pack libraries might well solve many of the storage problems of a rudimentary information system, but their capacity is too limited to provide the basis for a national information center.[15] Existing memory systems are too costly for the kind of mass information storage necessary to "computerize" libraries. But even if inexpensive mass storage is developed in the near future, a severe problem would be encountered in outputting the information a user has requested.

Output

Processed data may be output from a computer system in the form of hard copy printout or as visual images on a cathode ray tube. Printout affords a permanent record of the processed data and is the most efficient method of volume data transmission.

A totally efficient output system would be able to handle an uninterrupted flow of data from the computer through the output device. A less optimum system is restrained by a data "backup" at the point of output. Data output in all phases of computer development has been characterized by this backup phenomenon. The backup is attributed to the inability of the output device to function at the same speed as the computer.

The first output device was a computer controlled electric typewriter. This electromechanical typewriter is the least efficient means of output transmission. The speed of hard copy output greatly increased when line printers were developed ten years ago. As the name indicates, line printers print line-by-line[16] in contrast to the conventional typewriter which prints character-by-character. But mechanical limits on the speed of output have caused computer engineers to turn to other modes of output, based on radically different scientific principles. Two of these are high speed thermal printing, and cathode ray tube viewing and printing devices.

Thermal printing converts electrical signals into heat to produce a printed output on paper.[17] This process, involving no major moving parts, is not subject to the mechanical problems and noise associated with impact printers such as the line printer. But the inability to make unlimited multiple copies of the printout presents economic barriers to its commercial use.

The cathode ray tube is an all-electric output device. It may be used as an intermediate device to final printout, and as a viewing monitor. In the former application, the cathode ray tube generates the characters which are then imposed upon light-sensitive paper passing in view of the continuously changing character display. This device can output an amount equal to twenty pages of typeset book per minute.[18] Cathode ray tube printers do not as yet provide multiple copies, but one can anticipate that a hybrid output-reprography device will be developed which could accept data flow directly into a reprography machine for unlimited copy printout.

The basic technological problems in developing a national information center, which would serve individuals at home or office locations, have been set out above. The problem of input may be solved quite early—already visual scanners are used with some limited success. Efficient output transmission to users also appears to be within the reach of today's technology. The problem of mass internal storage, or mass random access storage of some sort, will not be so readily solved.

If the technology does lead to an entirely new computerized system for the dissemination of information, the impact on copyright will be such that the focus of protection may be directed toward entirely new areas. As we will point out, some of the author's problems relating to censorship or distortion of his works may force copyright law into the area of protection known on the Continent as "moral rights."[19]

However, one feature of copyright protection will not change—protecting the author's economic expectations. In computer use of copyrighted works this problem becomes primarily one of administration. But computer use will also require a serious examination of what we are trying to protect, and the extent to which we can afford protection consistent with encouraging the dissemination of writings.

PROBLEMS AND SOLUTIONS

Economic Problems

Computer information storage and retrieval systems will create a revolution in information dissemination. Examining the alternative solutions now may enable us to develop a larger number of alternatives for the solution to future problems. If the alternatives are not explored with some degree of detachment today, we may find that the force of circumstances will demand an immediate and ill-considered choice in the future. At that point the opportunity for planning will be lost, and we will be relegated to putting out bonfires.

Economic solutions will effect the speed of the changeover. For example, if computer use of copyright materials is accommodated by forcing all copyright owners to permit the use of their works in computers upon payment of a statutory fee, the death of the book in hard copy form may come about much sooner.

One publisher has argued that one purpose of copyright protection is "protection of the form in which a work has been created."[20] While the statement is undoubtedly true, in the conventional sense that a copyrighted book may not be made into a play or motion picture without permission, it is difficult to justify a policy which would insure the maintenance of an obsolete hard copy form if dissemination is more effective through computer networks.

Publishers who are fearful of being prematurely retired are using copyright arguments to preserve themselves. Although the issue is often phrased in economic terms, the stakes are higher than merely insisting on payment for the use of their works. Without question some publishers, who are also copyright proprietors, are mainly concerned with preserving hard copy dissemination.

The argument has been made that by discarding the book form we are throwing away something beautiful. "There are two things there's nothing like—a dame and a good book. I love both just the way they are, even if hardware *is* more efficient."[21] Undoubtedly there are pleasurable sensations associated with turning the pages of a book, but as children are taught to read from a console screen, they are likely to be annoyed with the effort and slowness of page turning. In any event, the scientific community, with urgent information demands, is unlikely to mourn the passing of page flipping.

Underlying the administrative system we develop for licensing works, and for collecting payments will be a decision to promote or hinder the death of the hard copy publisher. If the demise comes slowly, as it must to the extent that technological needs must first be met, publishers may adapt to a new role. They are not tied to the printing process. Publishers rarely print their own material; they function as packagers of the written merchandise, selecting the material to be published and then editing, advertising and marketing it. With the advent of computers the necessity for these steps will remain, but they will take on a much different form.

Someone will still have to read manuscripts and decide which ones will be "published." If there is a single national information network, a single bureaucracy may be given this role—presenting grave dangers of censorship. More likely, the national system will "sub-contract" out the editorial process to existing publishers. Another alternative might be to require the central information system to sell computer facilities to private publishers, thus preserving the private enterprise publisher as a merchandiser. The publisher would select the material to be disseminated, as he does today, but in place of sending the edited manuscript to a printer he would have it recorded in machine readable form and then pay the central computer network to input it in the memory center, thereby making it available to users. The publisher would then have to create a demand for the work which he had thus published; we might experience the odd phenomenon of having computerized books advertised on television.

Copyright owners envision a substantial reduction in the number of purchasers for their works when computerized information systems are developed. Their fears are justified in the case of "fact works" such as dictionaries and encyclopedias. Because they foresee that one day there may be only one purchaser—a national information center—copyright owners are insistent on payment at the time of input. On the other side are the potential users, including government agencies, whose position is that they are willing to pay for the use of copyrighted material, but that while their systems are in the embryonic stage they should be allowed free input. They are fearful that the cost of inputting material which may not even be useful will be so costly, both in terms of royalties and in terms of the effort involved in obtaining permissions, that they will be unable to begin their studies. This position was articulated by Mr. Anthony G. Oettinger, President of the Association for Computing Machinery and Professor of Linguistics and Applied Mathematics at Harvard University, in the following manner:

> I have as yet no idea how much of what I buy, rent borrow or produce myself I will eventually keep and either use in my classroom, publish conventionally or disseminate by less conventional means now still in the experimental stage.
> . . . [If input is infringement] I would have not only to acquire and evaluate materials, but in each instance, *before* experimenting with them, seek out the owner of a copyright, if any, make formal requests for permission to use the material, pay royalties if any are due, etc. All this before any material could actually be used and, in fact, before I could find out whether

or not the material was useful! The delays, the frustrations, and chaos inherent in such a process now seems so formidable that . . . I would be tempted to return to the safer occupation of copying out manuscripts with a goose quill pen.[22]

(1) Imposing Liability on Input

Is input of copyrighted material without permission of the copyright owner an infringement under present law? Before examining this question, we note preliminarily that output is undoubtedly an infringement. Under section 1 (a) of the Copyright Act, the owner has the exclusive right "to print, reprint, publish, copy, and vend the copyrighted work . . . ." Where a computer disgorges printed reproductions of a copyrighted work as output, there would be no difficulty in finding the presence of an infringing copy under this subsection.

Unfortunately, the answer is not nearly as simple in the case of the input process. If a computer system takes extensive portions of a copyrighted work verbatim, the rights of the author or publisher may well rest, under the current law, upon such an arbitrary distinction as whether the potential infringer has chosen a "readable" or visually perceptible means of recordation such as printed punched cards, or humanly unintelligible recordings such as magnetic tape.

In most instances a preliminary sequence of events precedes a computer's consumption of data. It may be possible to find infringement in at least one of these early stages. Section 1 (b)[23] grants to the copyright owner the exclusive right to "translate the copyrighted work into other languages or dialects, or make any other version thereof." Although it has not as yet been extended to translations in machine readable form, the translation right has been extended beyond translation into foreign languages in the conventional sense.[24]

In *Addison-Wesley Publishing Company v. Brown*[25] the court found the plaintiff's copyrighted physics text book had been infringed by defendants who published answers to the problems in the plaintiff's book. The plaintiff argued that the defendant had taken his expression because, in supplying the answers, the defendants of necessity had translated the plaintiff's textbook hypotheticals into "the language of the mathematician and the physicist."[26]

The court held for the plaintiff on other grounds,[27] but went on to say that if copyright infringement had been the sole issue

> ...the Court would be constrained to hold in the con-
> text of our dawning space age that each science as it
> moves into new areas of research and discovery must
> needs invent its own Esperanto. Plaintiffs' argument
> based on the claimed existence of a language or
> jargon into which the sense of the problems has been
> converted would, in such event, persuade. [28]

An equally liberal court may well find that recording a copyrighted work on computer readable
magnetic tape constitutes an infringement under
the translation right.

Whether magnetic tape records constitute copies
under section 1 (a) turns on a case decided in
1908. *White-Smith v. Apollo*[29] held that perfo-
rated piano rolls which reproduced songs printed
in copyrighted sheet music were not infringements
of the copyrighted works because the piano rolls·
were not "copies" under the Copyright Statute.
The Court gave two reasons for determining that
piano rolls were not copies. First, the Copyright
Act required that two copies be deposited with
the Librarian of Congress in order to obtain
statutory copyright. The copies must be duplicates of the original work.

> If the copyrighted work is sheet music, a duplicate of
> the sheet, that is, another sheet bearing the same
> notations, must be deposited. This proposition is still
> generally the law, and is certainly a logical require-
> ment. The piano roll did not meet this requirement
> because it was an undecipherable sheet of perfo-
> rated paper which was definitely not a duplicate
> original of the copyrighted sheet music and did not
> even produce a duplicate of the copyrighted sheet
> music when played—it produced sounds, not the
> original readable material. [30]

Secondly, the Court felt that the piano rolls were
a part of the machine within the meaning of the
statute.

The majority opinion defined a copy under the
Copyright Act as a reproduction or duplication of
the original work, "a written or printed record . . .
in an intelligible notation,"[31] *i.e.*, readable with
the unaided eye.

Apollo may be distinguished in the case of computer tapes and other magnetic recording devices.
The computer does not normally communicate
expressions through sounds, and is capable of reproducing a printed copy of the original work
from the tape. Secondly, as noted earlier, the
Register of Copyrights will accept these forms of
programs for deposit if they are accompanied by
printed copies.[32]

Ignoring the history of the *Apollo* case,[33] and

resorting to "mechanical jurisprudence," some
authors have argued that the "intelligible notation"
test as applied to machine readable forms dictates
that translation of copyrighted works to electronic
signals is not a copy and therefore not an infringement.

> In 1908 the United States Supreme Court held that
> a perforated roll of paper which operated a piano
> was not a copy of a printed musical composition.
> The reason given is that only a person of great pa-
> tience and skill could read a perforated roll. The court
> also said that a cylinder of a music box and a record
> of a phonograph are not copies. The reasons given
> by the court apply equally to printed literary works
> of all kinds. They also apply to punched cards and
> magnetic tapes.[34]

This approach ignores the real issue, which is
whether computer input ought to be an infringement in light of its effect on the interests of the
author of the original work. The "intelligible
notation" test established by *Apollo* is the chief
impediment to protection from computer use of
copyrighted material. If the law of copyright
persists in its obedience to *Apollo* it will be
woefully inadequate to provide any meaningful
proprietary rights for authors in the computer
era.

There are signs that courts are attuned to the
economic realities of the new technology. For
example, in *United Artists Television, Incorporated v. Fortnightly Corporation*[35] the plaintiff claimed infringement of his exclusive rights
under Section 1 (d) and 1 (c)[36] of the Act to
make a transcription or record "by or from which,
in whole or in part, . . . [the copyrighted work]
may in any manner or by any method be exhi-
bited, performed, represented, produced, or reproduced."[37] The act of infringement claimed by the
plaintiff consisted of sending messages by cable
antenna television (CATV). Plaintiff's expert
witness stated that CATV stores information in
the coaxial cables of the system "during the time
the audio and video signals are being propagated
through the cables; . . . 'the physical reality of
the electromagnetic field containing the sights
and sounds of the program is every bit as real
as a piece of paper with print on it or a photo-
graph.' "[38]

This kind of a technical argument is equally
applicable to the electronic storage of messages
within a computer system. Section 1 (c) refers
to "non-dramatic literary" works, a designation
sufficiently broad to include technical and
scientific works stored in a computer. Judge
Herland did not decide the validity of this argu-

ment in the *Fortnightly* opinion, for he held that the defendant had infringed the plaintiffs' performing rights.[39] Nevertheless, he commented that the argument was "not without force."[40] An equally learned judge might well find infringement in computer input under a similar argument.

A related issue is whether the computer makes an additional copy when it performs an internal operation on a copyrighted work already stored in machine readable form. During the processing operation, the computer picks up signals from memory storage and holds a duplicate of them internally. The signals are removed from the system when the job is completed. Under the *Fortnightly* argument, it may be possible to find an infringement at the time the work is input, and an additional infringement every time the computer processes or manipulates a work already input. The proposed Copyright Revision Bill precludes a finding of infringement at the latter stage, under the definition of when a work is "fixed" in section 101.[41] A "copy" is any "material object in which a work is fixed;"[42] and a work "is fixed" in a tangible medium of expression when its embodiment in a copy . . . is sufficiently permanent or stable to permit it to be perceived, reproduced, or otherwise communicated for a period of more than transitory duration."[43] This section[44] was proposed to cover just the problem raised— whether the manipulation process of a computer could be said to create a copy—and the Revision Committee's determination was that such manipulations would not be considered copying.

The government agencies most concerned with rapid dissemination of scientific and technical information are among those urging that information systems be allowed free input of copyrighted works. The Committee on Scientific and Technical Information (COSATI), a committee of the Federal Council for Science and Technology, with members from various executive departments, including the Department of Commerce, the Atomic Energy Commission, the National Science Foundation, and the Department of Defense, and observers from USIA and the CIA, among others, was formed as a policy development group. Of special concern to COSATI is the development of "a sound concept of a national system for scientific and technical information."[45] COSATI has concerned itself with the many problems of setting up a national information system for technical and scientific works, including the development of uniform standards of technology so that

various units of the system may work in conjunction with each other.[46]

The COSATI group was silent on the copyright problems during the House hearings on the Copyright Revision Bill, and the Bill as passed by the House would make input an infringement under the definition of "copies" in section 101:

> "Copies" are material objects, other than phonorecords, in which a work is fixed by any method now known or later developed, and from which the work can be perceived, reproduced, or otherwise communicated, either directly or with the aid of a machine or device. The term "copies" includes the material object, other than a phonorecord, in which the work is first fixed.[47]

As noted by Representative Robert W. Kastenmeier, Chairman of the House Judiciary Subcommittee, "The bill was gone over with a fine tooth comb, but not once did anyone mention the word computer."[48] The Senate subcommittee, under the chairmanship of Senator John L. McClellan, left section 101 intact, and had prepared to conclude its hearings on April 28, 1967; but at the request of Dr. Donald Horning, Director of the President's Office of Science and Technology, Senator McClellan agreed to have the subcommittee hear testimony from government agencies concerning the impact of the copyright revision legislation on the use of computer systems.[49]

COSATI's Ad Hoc Task Group on Legal Aspects Involved in National Information Systems issued a report on April 29, 1967, entitled "The Copyright Law as it Relates to National Information Systems and National Programs." Addressing attention to the question of when to charge for computer use, the ad hoc report reviewed arguments for and against assessing liability at the point of input and recommended that until the matter is finally settled by legislation, no copyright fees should be levied on input. The report stated, "to refrain from charging a copyright toll at the input stage will not significantly affect publishers' or authors' revenues at the present time. . . . For these reasons, we believe that the present bill should make clear that a copyright royalty need not be paid during the moratorium period in order to put such material into a computer system.[50]

The computer use problem became one of the major issues during the Senate subcommittee hearings, and Senator McClellan, in response to the hurdle this problem raised against the passage of any general copyright revision legislation, introduced a bill[51] to establish a national commission with a three year life to study computer use problems. The moratorium period referred to in the COSATI report is the term during which the commission would conduct its study. The National Commission Bill was passed by the Senate, but at the time of this writing has not been passed by the House. The status of input liability during the moratorium period has therefore not been decided.

A good deal of the disagreement concerns whether input should be the point at which copyright liability attaches, and we will discuss the arguments made on both sides.

Since it is possible that the output of a computer will largely consist of fair use portions of copyrighted material copyright owners argue that input should be an infringement because otherwise they may never be paid for the use of their material. A computer system offers a service to the public. To the extent that it has a large repository of copyrighted works it is a more desirable service—the fact that the works are in the system enhances the marketability of the service. In a sense, the computer owner who has free input offers his repository for public use without payment to the copyright owners, whose works form part of his saleable product. He is making money from the exploitation of those works, even though he may never printout more than "yes" or "no" answers.

On the other hand, to require a research team to pay royalties for the input of nine or ten volumes, which they will use to process one problem, or compile one concordance, and then will remove from the computer's memory, would not present the same situation. Clearly the research team could manually go through the works and compile a concordance without permission from the copyright owner. The concordance would be independently copyrightable, and unless it borrowed so heavily from the original works that it constituted a derivative work,[52] the copyright could be obtained without consent of the owner of the material from which it was compiled. "One use" input is a very difficult problem to resolve—and we will return to it again.[53]

The copyright owner also argues that input should be infringement because input to a single system may be the only "sale" he can make. Today there may be several thousand buyers for a seldom-used technical book, but if scientific users can turn to a computer network which has input a copy, the several thousand buyers are reduced to one. If the publisher is not paid when the book is input, but is paid only on output, he may still suffer an economic loss. For example, today he may be able to sell copies of his work to 3,000 libraries, even though his work may attract only dust in some libraries; in the future one copy would go into a computer, and in a period of, say, ten years, only 500 requests for printouts might be made. Today he is apparently selling the work for more than it is worth, and is reaping an economic advantage from the fact that buyers cannot evaluate the eventual worth of the books they purchase. But it may well be the case that the amount the 3000 libraries collectively pay for the book represents its true value—the book would not be published and the ideas it contains not disseminated if the compensation were less. It may be less efficient for 3000 libraries rather than for one computer network to offer the work to patrons, but if the inefficient system is the only one which will produce the work, then perhaps the price it will pay should be the price the more efficient system should be required to pay.

If liability for use is not levied at the point of input, the copyright owner may be faced with a policing impossibility similar to the one which exists today in the photocopying field. Being unaware of which computers have input his works, the copyright owner will be helpless to discover output for which he has not been paid. Uncovering reproductions without any knowledge of where the work has been input is much more difficult than discovering unlicensed input. The copyright proprietor can investigate infringing input by requesting copies of the work through third persons from computer services which he suspects have stored his work without permission. But he cannot determine each infringing act of output unless a "governor" reports to him from each output device.

It has also been asserted that the possibility of establishing a workable licensing system is lessened if free input is permitted. To the extent that copyright owners are forced to assume the burden of policing the system, computer centers will be reluctant to support a licensing scheme. They will have the advantage in a "try and catch me" system. On the other hand, if such centers are *precluded* from using materials without permission, then the burden of obtaining permission is such that the centers will also favor the development of a systematized licensing procedure.

If we allow free input, how shall we resolve the inevitable dispute which will arise when the computer center is refused permission to output a work which it has gone to considerable expense to store? The obvious possibility is that the computer network will go ahead and output the work without permission—challenging the copyright owner, in effect, to detect their acts. A systematic licensing system for input appears preferable to a situation where the copyright owner will try to extract an exorbitant fee for output, in effect charging the computer owner as much for the first output as he feels he should have received for the input of his work in the first place. Clearly, it would be easier on the nervous systems of both sides if permission were negotiated at the point of input.

We now turn to the computer users' arguments. They state that a good deal of input would be considered fair use, and that imposing liability for all input abolishes the fair use doctrine.[54] If fair use is strictly defined in economic terms—as a use which will not prejudice the sale of the original work—then the area of fair use in computer input is probably much more constricted than most computer people realize. It is clear that computer input has a different economic impact than traditional forms of copying. Illustrative is the example of the technical work which is today sold to 3000 libraries, but which would only be used 500 times in ten years in the computer. The fair use doctrine may be applicable to the research team which will make one use of the material and then "erase" it from the computer memory, but where the material will be permanently stored in a computer service, the economic impact on the original work will nearly always take this input outside the scope of the fair use doctrine. This is equally true where only a small portion of the work is input. It is questionable whether there can be "trivial input"; if the work is valuable enough to input and store, it would appear that the value is such that the input is not a fair use.

Users are seriously disadvantaged today if input can only be accomplished with the author's permission. Since there is no systematic way to get permission, the burden is on the user to find the copyright proprietor and communicate with him. For this reason COSATI proposed free input during the moratorium period. However, the burden is not so great in the case of current scientific works—the registered address of the copyright holder would most probably be current. If the copyright owner does not respond to a request for permission within a reasonable period of time, it may be justifiable to allow input without liability

in this limited circumstance during the moratorium period.

Scientists argue that they cannot predetermine what they will use, and therefore should only be charged for material actually used regardless of input. But it would not seem unreasonable to require them to make the choice before input. Libraries buy books no one will use, but the argument that they should not have to pay for works on their shelves which no one wants is less than persuasive. We conclude that input should be an infringement unless the copyright holder's permission is obtained. This conclusion is based primarily on economic factors, but, as we will indicate in a subsequent subsection,[55] noneconomic factors also require that input be an infringement. Passage of the Revision Bill in its present form would assure this result,[56] but in the event the bill is not passed, the courts already have the tools to make input an infringement.[57]

(2) Collection of Payment for Computer Use of Copyrighted Material

Both computer users and copyright owners have an interest in developing a systematic procedure for obtaining licenses and making payment for computer use of copyrighted works. The public interest would also be served by the development of such a system, for the computing industry would be encouraged to set up information storage and retrieval networks.

Payment for computer use of copyrighted material may be collected upon input, output, or at some phase of operation within the computer. The latter, while it might provide the most equitable system, by actually determining the amount and type of use made of the copyrighted works, is not technologically or administratively feasible at any reasonable cost.[58] Thus, this section will deal with suggestions for collection at the time of input and at the time of output or printout. The problems of distributing payments once they are collected are identical to the distribution problems found in the proposed solutions to photocopying of copyrighted works discussed in the reprography section.

In determining how best to set up a system of clearance and payments for computer use of copyrighted material, one of the threshold determinations which must be made is whether the copyright owner will be required to permit use of his work in computers, or will be free to refuse such use. The issue can be stated in terms of whether the statutory scheme should include a compulsory licensing provision for computer use of copyrighted works. The present law relies solely on voluntary licensing. The computer owner who wishes to obtain a license must now contact the author and negotiate for the use of the writings. This can be difficult, since the copyright owner may be a corporation which no longer exists or an author who has moved to a new address.

For example, one company, which desired to produce an abstract of all the spectrographs of different elements from published sources in various journals,[59] wrote to the copyright owners to obtain licenses for such use. The company was unable to obtain permissions, not due to disagreement over payment rates, but because it was unable to get a response from the owners or because the response indicated that the journal did not own the copyright and was unaware of the address of the author who had retained copyrights. The need for this compilation was evident, yet the obstacle erected by copyright law prevented its development. In such cases the argument for compulsory licensing is strong.

A statutory licensing scheme may become "compulsory" at any one of three points: (1) when a work is published in any form; (2) when a work is published in machine readable form; or (3) when an author chooses to register a work for computer use. The most complete proposal to date for the collection of royalties for computer use of copyrighted works would follow the last alternative. Norton Goodwin,[60] an attorney and a member of the Publications Board of the Society of Photographic Scientists and Engineers, suggested this system of voluntary entry. Under his system, copyright liability would be imposed on output.[61] Each author would register with the Copyright Office, and would receive from that office a seven-digit "registrant identification number." He would be required to file his postal address and keep it up to date after registering.

When an author translated his work into machine-readable form, he would divide it into units. The author could designate each sentence, paragraph, page, chapter, etc. an independent unit. Under Goodwin's proposal the author would receive a statutory fee of ten cents for each unit output by a computer. A code number which included the author's identification number and the copyright expiration date would be inserted at the end of each unit.

As the computer printed out the work, a recording device would pick up the unit code number each time it appeared. If the copyright had expired, the computer would not record the number. Quarterly payments would be mailed to the author directly, according to the number of his code units which appeared in the computer's registry. Thus, if twenty of an author's units had been printed out in a given quarter, he would receive two dollars from the computer owner. The virtue of this plan is that each registered author would be paid for exactly the amount of his work printed out.

There are, however, difficulties with the system. First, the system would permit free input. The Goodwin proposal could be modified to provide for payment on the input level, but it appears that payment on input would be more feasibly regulated by a system similar to the collection of payments for performing rights, such as ASCAP[62] and BMI now use. They are able to negotiate blanket licenses—permitting the use of all the works in the catalogue, or all the works of one author. This flexibility is desirable where works are input for different purposes. The collection agency may charge a minimal fee to a scientist who wants to input works for one processing. Permission may even be granted without charge, as is the practice of ASCAP and BMI in the case of organizations wishing to use its songs for fund raising programs.[63]

Second, under Goodwin's system, authors could refuse to license their works for "translation" into machine readable form. If authors have the legal power to prevent use of their works, the time and expense of locating and negotiating with them will certainly inhibit the development of computerized information storage and retrieval systems.

A better system would provide statutory compulsory licensing *requiring* authors to license all works for computer use which have been published in any form. A variant of this statutory scheme could provide for a "restricted list" of works which could not be used without authors' permission.[64] This would put the burden on the copyright owner to take affirmative action to prevent compulsory licensing. However, this "exemption" could be abused if all or most applications for copyright in the future included a request for "restricted listing" as a matter of course. One would not expect this to occur in the scientific and technical writing field, since authors of journal articles are rarely paid for their work.[65] But if the threat of this abuse is realistic, then the duration of the "restricted" classification might be shortened to three or four years by the statute.

We would recommend the development of a statutory scheme making unlicensed input an infringement. Such legislation would prevent computer use from becoming a repetition of the reprography problem; unlicensed input would be easier to detect than unlicensed printout, and the copyright owner's rights would be more practically enforceable.

However, if copyright owners are given the right to impose liability on input, some counterbalancing consideration should be given to the interests of the users. A form of compulsory licensing is necessary to prevent copyright owners from withholding works from computer systems. We would suggest a compulsory licensing provision which requires works published in any form—not just in machine readable form as Mr. Goodwin suggests—to be licensed for computer use.

We would not suggest, as a concomitant provision, however, that there be a predetermined statutory fee. We believe that a fee and collection system should not be embodied in the legislative scheme because unknown factors may create future problems requiring a change in the system. If the system could only be changed by congressional action, information services might be seriously harmed by legislative delay. The flexibility of a voluntary system would be beneficial to the users, the owners, and the public.

A more flexible plan might be developed to provide for compulsory arbitration in the event copyright holder and computer user cannot agree on the proper input fee. The input requirement would prod the users, and the compulsory licensing provision would spur the copyright owners, toward developing a system for licensing and payment. Arbitration would be necessary only when they were unable to agree on fees. A private voluntary agency patterned on the ASCAP-BMI model could easily develop, given the above statutory scheme. Such an agency could make licensing easier and speedier than use-by-use negotiation with individual authors. The agent-association offers the advantage of permitting the negotiation of fees and development of collection procedures on an institutionalized basis. In short, the best legislative solution may well be one which will force the owners and users to work out their own collection and payment system.

Non-economic Problems

Preventing Distortion of a Work

When copyrighted works are used in computer systems, accidental distortion may result from de-fective storage. For example, where tape has collected dust particles, the head cannot properly pick up the signals recorded on the surface. Also, if the edge of a tape is damaged, some of the electronic charges "drop out" and the message stored in the computer's memory is changed. There are techniques available to minimize these possibilities —service companies can rehabilitate tapes, and tape cleaning machines exist. Relying on the computer industry itself to detect and remedy these kinds of distortions would not seem unreasonable. Computers are valuable only insofar as they are accurate. Errors are costly to users[66] and it is in the economic interest of the industry to provide distortion-free storage methods.

Deliberate distortion is a problem not as easily solved. Deliberate distortion may be successful in two ways: input distortion, and altering works after input. Input distortion may be the easier to prevent. The use of optical scanners would discourage such distortion because it appears impossible to create a scanner which would alter works as it "translates" from natural language to machine-readable form. However, it is possible that someone would expose an altered work to the scanner. Copyright law may play a role in the detection of input distortion by requiring that the author have access to a printout of his work to check it for errors. This procedure would not impose an economic burden on the computer facility, because a printout would normally be made to "proof read" the input.

Where deliberate changes are made in the work *after* input the most difficult detection problem is presented. There are two ways in which this may occur. Alterations may be made by someone with the intent to distort or change the meaning of a work. There is no policy justification for allowing this kind of censorship by someone other than the author. But it does not follow that the law should prohibit all changes after input.

A simple example will illustrate this. At a recent conference on libraries at Woods Hole, Marvin Minsky is reported to have suggested that the future systems should enable him to "correct" his articles as he learns more about what he is doing. Rather than write more articles, he can bring the old ones up to date. The reader would always have the latest, best knowledge on the subject. While this may be very convenient for the scientist, it could really foul things up in the humanities. Playwrights could make continual modifications to their scripts as new thoughts occurred to them. For that matter, imagine the poor historian of science or literature, trying to piece out whatever happened![67]

There are strongly conflicting policies regarding whether an author ought to be allowed to change his work after "publication" by computer input. Under the Gutenberg system, as ideas were refined an author published new articles and a record was thereby made of the development of the ideas. There is value in being able to trace the history of a concept, or the course of a writer's development. But do we want to require such record-keeping? If we think record-keeping desirable, the function may be adequately filled by requiring deposit of the original with the Copyright Office, along with any subsequent modifications. Then the public interests in having the most current thinking represented in the computer network and in preserving writings for historical research are satisfied.

Some writers' early works were their most significant, and allowing the author to destroy those works through later changes (perhaps as the writer approaches senility) may be detrimental to the interests of the public. However, an author may have strong personal motives for wanting to destroy an earlier work.

> And there was Irwin Shaw, and the terrifying *Bury the Dead*, which convinced us that but for propaganda there would be no wars. (Irwin, a few years later, became the best soldier that the Dramatists Guild would produce. By that time he had taken *Bury the Dead* off the market, refusing to allow its further public presentation).[68]

This example poses the problem of whether a change in personal philosophy entitles an author to destroy an earlier work which contradicts his present beliefs. The Gutenberg system tends to solidify, preserve, and prevent retraction of early works, because of the physical presence of many copies. This will not be true where works are stored in computer memory systems. Thus, a new and very difficult problem for copyright law looms on the horizon.[69]

Where someone other than the author changes a work for the purpose of correcting errors, the act may be distinguished from intentional "censoring" although the effect may be the same in some instances. Suppose that a scientist determines that smoking two cigarettes a day will result in no greater likelihood of cancer than not smoking at all, and that smoking two packs per day increases the likelihood of cancer fourfold over smoking one pack a day. His paper is input into a computer. Then other studies are made, which all contradict his findings regarding smoking two cigarettes per day. The computer may be instructed in the interest of accuracy, to alter its memory cells to reflect the "established fact" that smoking even a few cigarettes is correlated with a greater likelihood of cancer. The scientist's article may still be retained in its corrected form because the comparison which it makes between smoking a pack of cigarettes and two packs of cigarettes a day is valid; the only error is in the conclusion, later disproven, that smoking two cigarettes a day has no deleterious effect.

If the author has a right to protect the integrity of a work bearing his name, printing out the "corrected" work and identifying it as his would seem to be a violation of that right. Printing out the work without reference to the author should not be permitted for "an important way in which copyright protects the public interest, and at the same time the private interest, is that it causes the *sources* of information to be identified.[70] An alternative procedure might be to print out the original work, and include within the printout the opposing arguments, which are identified as those of another author. This may, however, disturb the integrity of the work, because the reader would not get the full expression and continuity of the author's thoughts.

A permissible method of making corrections would be to list them at the end of the printout, citing other available writings. The basis of copyright law is to promote the dissemination of ideas; citing counter arguments at the end of a work would not seem to conflict with this policy. However, there is as yet no uniform method of citation outside of the legal field.[71] Nevertheless, someone who offers a computer service will want to give users all the information relevant to the request, and this desire may provide the impetus to develop uniform methods of citation.

Insuring Access to Users—Indexing and Dissemination

Indexing—A computer may be utilized to automatically index material which is stored internally in machine language. Where information is stored in microfilm and microfiche, automatic indexing is impossible, for, as we have seen, a computer can only "read" material stored in machine language form. Nor, can it perform content analysis, *e.g.*, it cannot read words or word combinations in order to classify documents. Where material is stored in microfilm or microfiche, the computer can follow an index embodied in a program but cannot compose such an index. Using a computer to retrieve documents which are pre-indexed is faster than using an ordinary card file index to locate library materials, but only a minor part of the computer's capacity to organize and locate material would be utilized.

Full use of the computer's capabilities can only be obtained by causing it to index by ideas, that is, to classify the *messages* contained in documents, not merely the author and title. In contrast, non-computer library indexing systems such as the Dewey Decimal System[72] organize the documents themselves, and not their information content. The numerical divisions in the Dewey system are made on the basis of subject matter categories, but this categorization only determines the location or address of the book in a library in relation to other books; it makes no division within individual works, and no comparison among works beyond the single address given to each.

Computer classification through content analysis would organize all of the information stored in the system without regard to the individual works in which it is embodied; that is, it would enable the user to find information even though he is ignorant of the particular publication containing that information. Computer classification will ultimately enable the user to make requests based upon his information needs rather than on his knowledge of the author or title of a work.

There has been a great deal of difficulty in developing computerized classification systems for information retrieval. In a library, the Dewey Decimal system is workable because the librarian knows *where* he put specific books; if the user is unable to find a particular book the librarian can assist him. Books are pre-identified units labeled by title and author. But when books are broken down into information units the "librarian" who so divides the book must create new units. Before the computer, which is acting as a librarian in storing these created units, can be asked for a particular item of information, both computer and user must "share" a common "language." The user must have some understanding of the classification system which the programming "librarian" has used. The problem is something like finding cases on a particular point of law through the use of a key word index, but much more difficult. If a lawyer wants to find case law on the emancipation of minors he might look through an index under "emancipation" or under "minors" and not find what he wants. He must continue searching until he finally looks under the "parent and child" subject heading. If such a system were put into a computer, the material would be available only if

the person quizzing a computer asked for a class of material already existent in the computer's system of classification. If the computer cannot "find" the proper material from the user's request, the burden is on the user to rephrase his request to accord with the computer's classification system.

Automatic classification has reached only the experimental stages.[73] Classificationists are attempting to devise systems of classifying the information content of documents based on word patterns or word frequencies occurring in particular works. The experiments have so far been restricted to documents within a specific subject matter (*e.g.*, nuclear fission).[74] These systems attempt to use the patterns which the computer extracts in order to develop a classification system based on the word structure of the documents stored rather than solely upon human evaluation of the information content.[75] Human judgment must still determine which terms, among those extracted by the computer, should be used as index terms or keywords. If a relevant document within the group cannot be retrieved by phrasing a request from the index terms selected by the human classifier, the classification system must be modified to correct the defect.

Presently, publishers object to computer indexing of material. They fear that computer classification might "hide" some works by classifying them in such a way that they cannot be found. But insofar as the computer uses the words in documents themselves as the source of information classification the possibility of error is less likely. Moreover, "if the indexing task in the automatic system is itself automatic, inconsistencies normally introduced by a large number of human indexers are also avoided.[76] Where several types of automatic indexing (*e.g.*, key word and index phrases) are used simultaneously within the system, there is even less likelihood that a document with information relevant to the user's request will not be retrieved.[77]

It is possible that information can be deliberately secreted and made inaccessible to users by an instruction to the computer to index any materials on a specific topic, *e.g.*, communism, under a nonsense title like "itletay" which no one would ever request. This the copyright law ought to prevent by giving the author the right to sue for misuse of his work if it is so "buried."

More difficult to control is *programming* for the purpose of censorship.[78] After documents have been classified, the computer program may be instructed not to retrieve documents within a certain classification. The government in effect does this with "top secret" material. Unless a user has the required "code key," he cannot retrieve material so designated.[79] While it is conceded that the government may justifiably classify some material in the interests of national security, it is difficult to control the natural tendency to classify too much rather than too little. Where there is no independent review of these determinations, the censor is his own supervisor. The obvious difficulty is that no one knows what is classified.

For example, a study on the causes of revolutions in modern Latin American countries, undertaken by a federally funded research project, might be classified top secret "in the interests of national security." Yet such a designation would operate to prevent a scholar studying the development of revolutions in Latin America from examining material relevant to his research. When the possibility is presented that the government or one of its agencies will operate an information network or a national information system by computer,[80] the dangers of censorship are apparent.

Private censorship may be equally dangerous. For example, suppose that a company with diversified interests owns a computer information storage and retrieval center whose users are private individuals. It also has substantial investments in Texas real estate, which it hopes to develop as producing oil fields. A doctoral thesis is written by a geologist, demonstrating that land with a given characteristic will never produce oil—a determination which had never been made before. He offers the manuscript to the computer center for "publication." After it is purchased by the computer division, the executives of the company discover that their land obviously has the characteristics described in the thesis. After inputting the thesis and providing the author a copy of the printout, the computer could be programmed to deny access to this work to all but authorized personnel of the company.

The copyright law can provide the author with a sword to prevent such censorship by giving him the right to insist on dissemination if he has not specifically waived it by contract, and adequate remedies, such as punitive damages without the necessity of showing actual damages. The author could detect the "burial" of his work by having a third party request the information from the computer center.

Dissemination—The dissemination of "writings" and thus the distribution of information to the public, is one of the two primary goals of copyright law. Though the other goal—protecting

authors—should be seriously considered, copyright law should be concerned with information dissemination in general and not merely with protecting the interests of authors. With this view in mind, we conclude our presentation on a sociological note.

If the new technology ultimately results in the creation of national or even local computer networks which communicate written works to homes and offices through consoles, printing may be replaced as a means of communicating information. Two basic modes of communicating from the computer to the user may be utilized: (1) hard copy printout by high speed thermal printing, and (2) ephemeral images projected on cathode ray tubes. It is possible that most homes would have both devices—the screen to communicate with a central computer information center for reference and entertainment information, and home printers for circulation of newspapers and magazines, though the latter might ultimately be completely replaced by ephemeral images. As we have seen, the nature of periodicals could change significantly because each user may in effect become his own publisher by "ordering" only the transmission of subject matter of interest to him.

The copyright owner in such a situation would be economically protected by payment through the computer system, accompanied by whatever legislators and courts find necessary to safeguard his interests. But there is another interest, now served by the system of printing, which may suffer. Today those in economically disadvantaged groups are able to satisfy their needs for information through newspapers and pulp magazines. These are inexpensive due to their large distribution and advertising income—income which would not continue if higher income groups began to replace them with computer communications. While newspaper and pulp printing would not immediately disappear, one could expect their cost to rise as circulation drops. If lower economic groups were unable to afford home consoles and printers, the new dissemination would tend to further ghettoize low income groups and make learning more difficult for them. For instance, if most reading matter were available only on machines, the poor child trying to learn to read would be put in the same position as a child taking piano lessons without a piano at home.

Computer console "libraries" could be developed, but providing consoles for homes in the poverty areas would be a more positive step toward assuring low income groups the same opportunities for learning and personal development that the more advantaged groups have. For example, one of the difficulties minority children have upon entering school is the lack of cultural exposure—many do not know the names of colors, partly because their parents do not know them, and partly because there is no source of information in the home other than the parent. The presence of an information center in each home could drastically change this situation. As the child learned to read, all of his interests could be satisfied as they arose, and his questions could be answered immediately through the console.

Computer consoles for the poor might come about either as a result of governmental action or through advertising. If private enterprise initiates transmission from computers to home consoles, the financing might well come from advertising somehow appended to the material transmitted. And if the computer utility is expanded to enable users to order their groceries and other consumer commodities by computer communication, advertising would certainly be a part of such communications.

But if no practical way is found to combine advertising with information dissemination in this new medium, the cost might be such that the federal government would be the only source capable of financing the system. Should the government initiate a national information system directed to home users, it is at least possible that consoles would be provided for those who could not afford them. In a privately financed network, advertising might support the costs of transmission to such an extent that the consoles would be available to the poor, as is presently the case with television. But there is an important difference which makes the analogy between television and a console system misleading: television is an entertainment medium; there is a larger demand for home entertainment than for home education and information services. This is especially true among the poor where the felt need for information is minimal, and therefore the danger exists that they may isolate themselves from access to the central information system. Any change in copyright law which facilitates the technical changeover to home console information dissemination should be considered in the light of its effect, especially during an interim development period, on low income groups.

ADDENDUM

After this project had been sent to the printer, the Committee to Investigate Copyright Problems (CICP) issued a report[81] of the results of a sixty-six library study of photocopying involving a survey and personal interviews with representatives of fifty-nine of the libraries, and a six library study involving recordation of all copying transactions in each library for a one month period. The report notes: "Almost every librarian interviewed considered the making of a single copy of any part of a copyrighted work as within the meaning of 'fair use.'[82] It concludes that fair use "provides no protection to the copyright owner because there is no effective control. It has become a euphemism for single-item copying.[83]

Analysis of the material copied, mainly from the more exact six library study of recorded copying transactions, indicated that "library copying is mainly from journals, and mainly from non-profit journals."[84] The ratio of journal titles to book titles copied was more than nine to one.[85] Scientific and technical journals were the main materials copied.[86] And, "on the average over 80 per cent of the copying from copyrighted matter occurred in the first five years; and 90 per cent in the first ten years."[87] "The stress on recency is subject-sensitive and mission-sensitive. It is greater for the sciences than for the humanities."[88]

These results are consistent with our expectations, lending force to the suggestion that a clearinghouse might first focus on protection of recent scientific and technical journals copied in governmental, industrial, academic, and other institutional libraries. The sixty-six library study showed that of the forty-two libraries reporting on the type of machine they used, twenty-nine used xerography for multiple copy reproduction.[89] Thus a tax on this type of machine might also be a feasible, though seemingly discriminatory, way to collect payment for much of the copying occuring in libraries.

Question 42 of the sixty-six library survey— "What would be the library's response to or attitude toward the concept of a clearinghouse for royalties?"[90]—was "reported verbatim and without interpretation."[91] By our count, the positive and negative responses are about equal. This would indicate substantial resistance to the idea of payment, which both we and the report have concluded to be necessary. But most of the negative responses seem based on a misunderstanding of the law of fair use. The following response is typical: "Since most of our copying is done under the 'fair use' provisions, we see little need for the establishment of a clearinghouse."[92] The report noted at the outset that there was widespread and misplaced reliance by librarians on the *Report of the Joint Libraries Committee on Fair Use in Photo-*

copying[93] as "authority for this belief."[94] Should the Williams and Wilkins suit against the National Library of Medicine[95] be successful, or should Congress pass legislation making it clear that single copy-making is not per se a fair use, this resistance might be substantially lessened.

The forty-two responses to question 43—"If a clearinghouse were to be established, what type of control or sponsorship would you favor for organization?"[96]—indicated what might have been expected. There were many points of view, none commanding even a significant plurality.[97] The choices among proposals are difficult and, if making a choice is to wait for a consensus, the CICP Report adds weight to the proposition that a clearinghouse may be delayed indefinitely.

FOOTNOTES

[1] Interview with Arthur Greenbaum, Attorney, in New York City, Sept. 25, 1967.

[2] Interview with Norton Goodwin, Attorney, Member of the Publications Board of the Society of Photographic Scientists and Engineers, in Washington, D.C., Sept. 19, 1967.

[3] Interview with Barbara Ringer, Assistant Register of Copyrights, in Washington, D.C., Aug. 30, 1967.

[4] Several firms offer computerized research service to attorneys, many of whom have been disappointed with the quality of the service in its present state.

[5] "[Punched cards] permit permanent storage of data and are amenable to checking for errors, and in the case of an error, correction may be made simply by substituting a correct card for an incorrect one. On the other hand, use of cards is expensive. Although the dollar cost of an individual card, or even the cost per bit of the materials used, is low, the expense comes about due to the extreme slowness in processing. [The cost] is approximately three-tenths of a cent per bit for punching, and an equal amount for verification . . . .

"The handling of the cards as input data is also slow. Modern card reading equipment can handle up to 1,000 cards per minute, but even this is only about 1,000 characters a second, a speed three orders of magnitude or more slower than the capabilities of the data processing system to handle the data." C. Fanwick, Trends in Computer Hardware 11 (1966) (unpublished professional paper on file UCLA Law Review Office).

[6] Instantaneous input makes error correction or data alteration practically impossible. Additionally, input data, while typed simultaneously on sheets of paper, is not available for future machine use without again being input through the typewriter. Data cards, on the other hand, store data in machine readable form and are on hand for direct computer input. These objections have recently been alleviated by typewriter input to magnetic tapes. The subsequent tape input to the computer is an order of two magnitudes faster than card reading devices (over 100,000 characters per second), and a permanent machine readable record is available for storage. However, the human operator is still needed at the initial stage of off-line input.

[7] The operation is similar to mechanical reading of bank checks by optical scanners which ingest the customer's account number. However, bank check printing is done with magnetic ink and the numerical characters are designed specifically for scanner use.

[8] The most sophisticated scanners can handle 2,000 characters of print per second, but can recognize less than a dozen different fonts, *i.e.,* printing styles such as italics or roman. Moreover, scanner recognizable fonts do not have mixed upper and lower case characters. Control Data Corporation, the leading developer of the optical scanner, describes the scanner's present and future capabilities as follows:

"While the potential capability of optical character recognition is quite extensive, the present practice of commercial equipment is limited to reading one or a small number of fonts and usually these fonts have been specifically developed to enhance the accuracy of machine recognition.

"The problem of scanning without limitation of font style is in fact a two prong problem in which the variations of print quality are even more important than the variations in style. While there are a number of opportunities for performing this fantastic task of reading an entire library, this capability is, to [our] knowledge, quite beyond not only commercial equipment but also those techniques which can be demonstrated in the laboratory. This is not to say that the task is impossible, but rather that it is not economical at the present state of the art and that it is doubtful that it will become so in the near future." Letter from Rabinow Engineering Div., Control Data Corp., Rockwell, Maryland, to UCLA Law Review, Nov. 23, 1967.

[9] Microfilm or microfiche has long been used in document retrieval.

[10] Specifically, data storage efficiency is evaluated by three criteria: (1) capacity of the storage bank; (2) accessibility of the stored data; and (3) cost per unit of stored data. These variables have generally been incompatible, resulting in a number of differing storage media which satisfy one or two criteria at the expense of the others. A high capacity storage bank may have a slow access time, while most random, high speed access media are characterized by relatively small data capacity and high per unit storage cost. Computer systems employ varying combinations of each storage medium in an effort to produce optimum storage efficiency for the given memory demands of a computer's application.

[11] One method involves a chemical plating in which the actual structure of a chemical composition is charged either positive or negative. A storage density approaching 100 words per square inch plus a favorable access time has been recorded under laboratory conditions. But presently produced commercial plating capacity is limited to a modest ten words per square inch.

The second chemical storage technique involves a light-sensitive chemical similar to the charged phosphorus in today's color television screen. A standard twenty-five inch screen has approximately 450,000 tiny "dots" (actually chemical ions) which are controlled to produce the color image. Similar ion dots are the basis of the projected memory system. Contact with light or heat will cause color change in a dot and data will thereby be stored. There will be a form of contact with the dots which in effect asks, "Are you light or dark, and what shade?" While the projected storage density for light-sensitive chemicals is 200,000 words per square inch with a cost approaching .01 cent per word, ion chemical storage is in the preliminary stages of development and will not be available commercially in the near future. Fanwick Interview, *supra* note 137.

[12] *See* text following note 9 *supra*.

[13] It may take as long as two minutes to turn a tape reel to the desired bit of information. When the machine finds the information, it takes approximately eighty microseconds to read and transfer the data to the processing center. Comparatively, random access internal storage cores recently developed by Lockheed Electronics Co. have a retrieval time of less than 500 nanoseconds (500 billionths of a second). The low retrieval time of internal storage is offset by capacity limitations (low storage density) and a high cost per unit storage relative to most external storage costs. The "best" internal memory banks have less than a 75,000 word capacity and a cost of approximately seventy-five cents per character.

In contrast, present tape capacity exceeds 2,000 characters per square inch. This staple of mass memory offers low cost (thirty-five cents per character) external storage, and is the basis of much data storage in large scale scientific systems.

[14] The system is called RAMAC. *See* Hoagland, *Mass Storage Revisited*, 31 AFIPS Conf. Proc. 255, 257 (1967).

[15] A recent development by Ampex Corp. promises to increase the number of computer document retrieval systems. The system, called "Videofile," stores documents as television recordings on magnetic video tape, similar to the "stop-action" storage system employed in televised sports events. Capacity is 500,000 legal pages per fourteen inch diameter reel. Output is provided to either individual television viewing stations or to conventional electrostatic line printers.

Photographic storage also promises to play a substantial role in future external storage systems. While photographic storage is only in an embryonic laboratory state, the gestation period to commercial reality could be within the next ten years. Already a prototype system has been developed to serve as a dictionary storage unit for language translation. It boasts a storage density of 27,500 characters per square inch and an access time of about fifty milliseconds. The non-erasable quality of photographic storage may be a disadvantage to a system application requiring continuous updating or purging of stored data. However, information libraries would not require such a flexible memory system. Non-changeable historic fact, novels, textbooks, poems, magazines, and journals are just a small sampling of data which could be stored in mass photographic memory banks. The commercial development of such memory systems would be a major step toward computerized information dissemination. It may be expected that photographic storage will be adopted on a card basis, especially when updating of information is necessary.

"Changes to data will then be made by substitution of new cards for old. When it is considered that one card, such as an IBM punch card, can hold many millions of bits of data [approximately fifteen million on a conservative estimate] it is seen that updating may well be a matter of repeating most of the data on a card but changing only a small percentage of it." C. Fanwick, *supra* note 197, at 23.

While beam address photographic storage occupies the limelight of memory research and development, it was the consensus of computer experts interviewed at the 1967 Fall Joint Computer Conference Anaheim, California, that mass data storage within the next ten years would be centered on (1) magnetic random disk storage and (2) non-machine language microfilm or microfiche storage.

[16] A typical line printer outputs 120 characters per line at a maximum rate of 2400 lines per minute or 4800 characters per second. This printing rate approaches the maximum limit of electromechanical printing, a limit dictated by inability to coordinate paper and ribbon flow with print head impact at speeds much greater than 2400 lines per minute.

[17] The thermal printer developed by National Cash Register, Inc., for the U. S. Army Electronics Command makes copies by transfer under pressure on paper which is heat sensitive. "A very desirable feature of this copy process is that only plain paper is needed to make copies thus reducing the operating cost. Three copies can be made in the printer and three more by a copy roll box which was also delivered with the printer. Papers capable of producing up to 20 legible copies have been tested." Joyce & Homa, *High-Speed Thermal Printing*, 31 AFIPS Conf. Prod. 261, 265 (1967).

[18] *See* C. Fanwick, *supra* note 5, at 16.

[19] *See* Melville B. Nimmer, *Copyright*, §110, at 442

[20] Benjamin, *Computers and Copyright*, 152 Science 181, 182 (1966).

[21] Horne, *One Plasma Sandwich, Hold the Plasma*, 9 Scholarly Books in America 2, 4 (1967).

[22] Oettinger, *Statement Prepared for Submission to the Subcommittee on Patents, Trademarks and Copyrights*, Monitor, May, 1967, at 4.

[23] 17 U.S.C. § 1(b) (1952).

[24] *See* Nimmer, *supra* note 19, § 8.31, at 20 to the effect that "code words without established meanings . . . may qualify as 'writings' under the Copyright Clause."

[25] 223 F. Supp. 219 (E.D.N.Y. 1963).

[26] *Id.* at 226.

[27] The holding appears to be based on a theory of misappropriation of the plaintiff's work.

[28] 223 F. Supp. at 226

[29] 209 U. S. 1 (1908).

[30] *Computers, Copyrights, and the Law Prior to Revision*, Address by Arthur J. Greenbaum, Current Copyright Problems Seminar sponsored by the Practising Law Institute, in New York City, July 19, 1967 (mimeo on file in UCLA Law Review Office).

[31] 209 U. S. at 17.

[32] Copyright Office Announcement SML-47, *supra* note 131.

[33] At the time of the decision, a composer derived most of his income from sheet music; mechanical reproduction was not prevalent, and denying him protection from unauthorized reproduction in that medium was not, therefore, a significant economic detriment. *See generally* Comment, *Scope of Protection for Computer Programs Under the Copyright Act*, 14 DePaul L. Rev. 360 (1965).

[34] Lawlor, *Copyright Aspects of Computer Usage*, 7 Communications of the A.C.M. 572, 574 (1964)

[35] 225 F. Supp. 177 (S.D.N.Y. 1966), *aff'd* 377 F.2d 872 (2d Cir. 1967), *cert. granted*, 389 U. S. 969 (1967). For a discussion of the effect of *Apollo* on disc-television *see* Boardman, *"Disc-Television": Some Recurring Copyright Problems in the Reproduction and Performance of Motion Pictures* (mimeo on file in UCLA Law Review Office).

[36] 17 U.S.C. § 1(c), (d) (1947).

[37] 17 U.S.C. § 1(d) (1947); § 1(c) has similar language.

[38] 225 F. Supp. 177, 199 n.9 (1966).

[39] *Id.* at 214.

[40] *Id.* at 199.

[41] H. R. 2512, S. 597, 90th Cong., 1st Sess. § 101 (1967).

[42] *Id.*

[43] *Id.*

[44] The definition of "fixed" in section 101 was sponsored by John Banzhaf III, President of Computer Program Library Co.

[45] Office of Science and Technology, [1965-66] Report on the Activities of the Federal Council for Science and Technology 29.

[46] Among the notable achievements of COSTAI are three publications: COSTAI Subject Category List (1967); Federal Microfiche Standards (1967); and Standards for Descriptive Cataloging of Government Scientific and Technical Reports (1967). *Federal Microfiche Standards* gives specifications for the outside dimensions of fiche, reducing ratio, image-frame size, and frame separation. *See generally* Barry, *Committee on Scientific and Technical Information Coordinates Inter-Agency Information Systems,* 12 Navy Management Rev. 3 (1967).

[47] H. R. 2512, S. 597, 90th Cong., 1st Sess. § 101 (1967).

[48] Zurkowski, *The Post-Gutenburg Era* 1 (unpublished mimeo on file in UCLA Law Review Office). Mr. Zurkowski is Representative Kastenmeier's legislative assistant.

[49] *Hearings on S. 597*, *supra* note 8, at 1103-04.

[50] COSATI, The Copyright Law as it Relates to National Information Systems and National Programs 15 (1967).

[51] S. 2216, 90th Cong., 1st Sess. (1967).

[52] "Compilations or abridgments, adaptations, arrangements, dramatizations, translations, or other versions of works in the public domain or of copyrighted works when produced with the consent of the proprietor of the copyright in such works, or works republished with new matter, shall be regarded as new works subject to copyright under the provisions of this title; but the publication of any new works shall not affect the force or validity of any subsisting copyright upon the matter employed or any part thereof, or be construed to imply an exclusive right to such use of the original works, or to secure or extend copyright in such original works." 17 U.S.C. § 7 (1947).

[53] *See* text following note 58 *infra*.

[54] Goodwin Interview, *supra* note 2.

[55] *See* pp. 1017-26 *infra*.

[56] Section 101 defines "copies" in the following manner: " 'copies' are material objects . . . in which a work is fixed by any method known or later developed, and from which the work is first fixed. . . .A work is 'fixed' in a tangible medium of expression when its embodiment in a copy . . . is sufficiently permanent to permit it to be perceived, reproduced, or otherwise communicated for a period of more than transitory duration." H.R. 2512, S. 597, 90th Cong., 1st Sess. § 101 (1967). Under these definitions computer input of a work would constitute a copy.

[57] *See* text accompanying notes 35-39 *supra*.

[58] This point is disputed by Norton Goodwin. See his proposal in *Hearings on S. 597*, *supra* note 8, at 737-40. However, a number of computer experts were asked about the cost of recording the source of material processed within the computer each time it was used and, without exception, they stated it could not be done today for less than twenty cents per recording. Anonymous Interviews, 1967 Fall Joint Computer Conference, Anaheim, California, Nov. 14-16, 1967.

[59] Interview with Gerald Sophar, Executive Director, CICP, in Washington, D.C. Sept. 1, 1967.

[60] Goodwin Interview, *supra* note 2.

[61] *See* note 48 *supra*.

[62] Finkelstein, *supra* note 79, at 2.

[63] 17 U.S.C. § 104 (1947) provides that an unauthorized performance of a musical or nondramatic literary work is an infringement only if the performance is for profit. However, in the case of musical works it is not necessary that an admission be charged to constitute a performance for profit. The test is generally whether a commercial advantage is or can be expected from the performance. Kaye Interview, *supra* note 85.

17 U.S.C. § 104 (1947) also exempts non-profit musical performances by schools and churches. In the gray areas, e.g., a fraternity musical program to raise funds which will be used to send underprivileged children to summer camp, the performing rights societies will normally grant free licenses. *Id.*

[64] ASCAP has a provision for restricted listings. The works on restricted listing are usually works involved in a pending infringement action.

[65] Sophar Interview, *supra* note 59.

[66] "[E]xperience indicates an average of 25 to 30 errors per reel of tape in use in the typical library today. These errors generate 'write-skips' costing you anywhere from 3 to 18 cents each. Read *errors* are even worse—you may have to rerun the whole job. Let's assume a computer tape library of 400 reels of tape with 28 errors per reel average, then total library errors is equal to 11,300! Now let's talk dollars, with 11,300 existing errors at, say 5 cents each, and, an estimated usage for each reel of tape at 75 times per year, we have a total cost to you, of, would you believe? $42,375.00 per year!!" General Kinetics, Inc., The Financial View (1967) (advertising brochure).

[67] Stone, *Transformation and Organization of Information Content: Contribution of Psychology* in [1965 Proceedings] International Federation for Documentation 83, 85 [hereinafter cited as 1965 Proceedings].

[68] R. Ardrey, The Territorial Imperative 36 (1966).

[69] The so-called moral rights are usually protected in the United States under the law of unfair competition. "We have always recognized the author's right to first publication, and this right includes the right to prevent distortion of the work." Interview with John Schulman, Attorney, in New York City, Sept. 5, 1967.

In the United States, whether an author can alienate the right to prevent distortion raises no difficult problems; it is treated as a matter of contract. In Europe, the moral right is separable from the copyright and is vested in the author. For example, under French law, authority to make changes in a work when producing a movie from it is given to the director, as agent of the author. *Id.* Moral rights are discussed in Nimmer, *supra* note 45, § 110, at 442.

[70] Jovanovich, *Information as a Property*, California Monthly, April-May, 1967, at 23.

[71] Lipetz, *The Effect of a Citation Index on Literature Use by Physicists*, in 1965 Proceedings, *supra* note 259, at 107.

[72] For a comprehensive analysis of the logic theory on which the Dewey Decimal System is based *see* Richmond, *Transformation and Organization of Information Content: Aspects of Recent Research in the Art and Science of Classification* in 1965 Proceedings, *supra* note 67, at 87.

[73] "There are four main types of experimental classification systems based on probability methods, all of which have been designed or used with small samples in very specific subject fields:

A

"list work frequencies (machine)
select index terms from list (man)
search documents for these index terms
  & record occurrence per document
  (machine)
treat results to create groups of weighted
  terms (man-machine)
    —data matrix (doc.-term)
    —correlation matrix (term-term) for
    word pairs
    —factor analysis, etc.
terms in group list constitute a class
  name classes (man)

B

"select class categories (man)
divide docs. according to these categories
  (man)
select index terms from these documents
  & calculate frequency (machine)
select index terms with list (man)
identify index terms with categories via
  data matrix (category-term) & calculate prediction value of each term for
  its categories (attribute numbers)
  (man-machine)
search documents for selected index
  terms, assign attribute numbers, rank,
  identity category (machine)
a class is identified by the first item of a
  group of ranked index terms pertaining
  to a document

C

"select keywords from authoritative list
  & put into some order (man)
search documents for these keywords
  only (machine)
make keyword pattern for each doc. by
  indicating presence or absence of these
  keywords in fixed order (machine)
treat pattern to yield "ordering ratio"
  (fixed probability listing for each combination of words)
  for each pattern (man-machine)
    —matrices (several in series)
    —latent class analysis
a class consists of an indefinite-sized
  group of keywords in a fixed pattern
1965 Proceedings, *supra* note 67 at
  95.

D

"select index terms from document
  (man)
treat to create groups or clumps (man-
  machine)
    —data matrix (doc.-term)
    —co-occurrence matrix (term-term)
    for word pairs
    —algorithm for group information
terms in group membership (clump) constitute a class; one term may occur in
  several groups"

[74] *Id.* at 71.

[75] *Id.* at 71.

[76] Salton, *The Evaluation of Computer-Based Information Retrieval Systems*, in 1965 Proceedings, *supra* note 259, at 125.

[77] Statement of Kenneth Janda, Professor of Political Science, Northwestern University, at group discussion following his address at the 1967 Fall Joint Computer Conference, in Anaheim, California, Nov. 15, 1967.

[78] Interview with Bella Linden, Counsel for the American Text Book Publishers' Institute, in New York City, September 5, 1967.

[79] Interview with Byron R. Fry, Associate Director, UCLA Computer Processing Center, in Los Angeles, October 13, 1967.

[80] *See generally,* Cosati, Toward a National Information System (1965).

[81] Committee to Investigate Copyright Problems Affecting Communication in Science and Education, Inc., The Determination of Legal Facts and Economic Guideposts with Respect to the Dissemination of Scientific and Educational Information as it is Affected by Copyright—A Status Report (1967) (compiled under contract with the Office of Education, U.S. Dept. of Health, Education, and Welfare) [hereinafter cited as Status Report].

[82] *Id.* at ii.

[83] *Id.* at 81.

[84] *Id.* at 68.

[85] *Id.* at Table I. This ratio seems heavily influenced by the fact that one library's copying of journals accounted for well over half of the total while the copying of books in that library accounted for less than an eighth of the total.

[86] This conclusion is based on the finding of the sixty-six library study that journals published not-for-profit are those most copied. (*Id.* at 67), and the fact that eighty-four per cent of the libraries reporting in the sixty-six library study "reported between 41 per cent and 100 per cent of all material copied as scientific and technical. This result reflects in part the choice of libraries, *i.e.*, a non-random sample." *Id.* at 77.

[87] *Id.* at 65. This result is based on data from four of the libraries in the sixty-six library study, *Id.* at Table V.

[88] *Id.* at 83.

[89] *Id.* at Survey Table XXIII.

[90] *Id.* at 51.

[91] *Id.*

[92] *Id.* at 52.

[93] Joint Libraries Committee on Fair Use in Photocopying, Fair Use in Photocopying: Report on Single Copies (1961).

[94] Status Report ii.

[95] *See* note 20 *supra.*

[96] Status Report 54.

[97] *Id.* at Survey Table XXXXIII.

VII

INFORMATION RETRIEVAL TESTING

Beyond question, the main tests of information retrieval have been conducted by Cleverdon at Cranfield, by Salton at Cornell, by Saracevic and others at Case Western Reserve, and by Lancaster in his evaluation of the Medlars system.

In time the results of these experiments may greatly influence subject indexing, especially in non-conventional circumstances. For example, librarians may before long need to index data collections and data programs. Based on the results of these tests, it is unlikely that a controlled list of subject headings will be adopted without serious consideration of an indexing system based on clue words found in the description of the data, buttressed by a synonym dictionary.

Because of Salton's use of the term "automatic" indexing, it is important to understand what is meant by the term. In traditional indexing a book is investigated, its subject matter is decided upon, and the indexer then turns to an established, controlled list of subject headings in order to enter the book into the retrieval system. This, indeed, is the procedure used in producing *Index Medicus,* the printout version of Medlars. Medlars goes beyond this stage in its magnetic tape version in the number of subject headings assigned and by the greater flexibility in searching provided by the computer.

The retrieval languages tested at Cranfield by Cleverdon involved three indexing languages. One need not detain us, while the other two are well understood by librarians, namely, an indexing language based on a set of controlled terms (such as is the LC list of subject headings), and another language in which the entries were taken from clues provided within the text of the articles being indexed, which is to say, an uncontrolled indexing language.

Cleverdon applied a considerable variety of recall and precision devices to each of these languages; in the end it was evident from his results that most devices were ineffective and that the controlled language even when associated with its most beneficial devices were inferior to the indexing which was uncontrolled. This was especially true of the uncontrolled language aided by a dictionary of synonyms.

Saracevic's approach was such that little attention was given to the difference between controlled and uncontrolled languages, so that we can move directly to the explanation of what Salton means by automatic indexing. Salton's main thrust is toward the words and phrases found within the material being indexed. Unlike the traditional cataloger who asks first, what does this title deal with, Salton looks at word frequency, at the combinations in which words appear, and the similarity of words used in different articles. These are aided by devices, or special dictionaries, including dictionaries of synonyms. To make a search for a user, Salton takes the question propounded by the user and seeks to match the clues supplied in the question with the clues found in the text, both having been put into machine readable form and fed into the computer.

There is no danger presumably of downgrading automatic indexing unduly if one quotes Salton: "One might interpret the results of the SMART-Medlars comparison by saying that the conventional and the automatic indexing procedures produce equally poor results."

I have put my own article on retrieval testing at the head of this section because it serves as a summary and as an introduction to the four that follow.

Information Retrieval from the Management Point of View

by Louis Kaplan

Several conclusions may now be drawn by management, based on results derived from several "laboratory" experiments in information retrieval. A major finding is that a controlled indexing language (controlled by an authority list of headings) will not provide more effective retrieval than will the uncontrolled type. Automatic indexing, using semantic and syntactic devices, does not improve upon the performance of a manual system. Increasing the number of subject entries per document (with or without computer) will increase the number of retrievals relevant to a question, but will at the same time disproportionately increase the number of nonrelevant references.

INTRODUCTION

A number of investigations conducted recently by documentalists have grave implications for those library administrators contemplating the development of a large-scale information system. In this paper some well-known experiments are discussed, and the results evaluated from a management point of view. During the past few years a number of significant tests of information retrieval systems have been conducted, of which three are perhaps most important to librarians: the work by Cleverdon and his associates at the College of Aeronautics in Cranfield, England; by Saracevic, Rees, and others at the Center for Documentation and Communication Research at Case Western Reserve University; and by Salton and his co-workers in the Department of Computer Sciences at Cornell. These information scientists have indisputably advanced our understanding of information retrieval; on the other hand, their efforts to optimize retrieval have not met with undivided success. Furthermore, from the library management point of view, the depth of indexing employed, the construction of thesauri, and the sophisticated devices introduced seem terribly expensive. Nevertheless, it would be a mistake for librarians to ignore the implications of the work done by these information scientists.

BRIEF DESCRIPTION OF THE TESTS UNDER DISCUSSION

The Cranfield Tests

The Cranfield tests emphasized the significance of language devices which influence recall and precision, such as roles, links, interfixing, partitioning; also studied was the influence of the number of coordinate terms in a search question and the depth of indexing.[1]

Three indexing languages were tested: single-terms, concepts, and a controlled language, all in the subject field of aerodynamics. With each language several recall devices were tested, and for each of the languages several precision devices were used, including coordination.

The Case Western Reserve Tests

Several indexing languages were tested by Saracevic and his team.[2] Those that need be referred to in this context are: (a) keywords assigned by indexers (that is, in the language of the text) and (b) a language based on the so-called "telegraphic abstracts" (a language employing a number of formal recall and precision devices).

The tests conducted at Case Western Reserve

SOURCE: Reprinted from *College and Research Libraries,* 31: 169-73 (May, 1970) by permission of the publisher. Copyright 1970 by the American Library Association.

University emphasized the influence of the manipulation of search questions. Depth of indexing was tested by treating full texts, abstracts, and titles as independent variables. A third major variable was the indexing languages.

SMART

The SMART system (originally established at Harvard, now at Cornell) is described in a recent text by Gerald Salton and in a number of reports entitled *Information Retrieval System,* coming most recently from the Department of Computer Sciences at Cornell.[3] Unlike MEDLARS, where machine manipulation follows manual indexing, SMART indexing depends as well upon machine manipulation of the documents prior to the actual retrieval process. Each search question and each document is manipulated from the viewpoint of word and phrase frequency and from the viewpoint of establishing, by frequency studies, clusters of related documents.

In addition, dictionaries are provided to reduce the variety of words by compounding stems and suffixes; for example, one dictionary makes it possible to recognize the singular and the plural of a word as a single term, and words such as economize, economical, economies are also gathered up as a single term. Semantic relationships are established by means of a dictionary of synonyms, and the hierarchical relationships are established in a classified system. The syntactic relationship between phrases is controlled by phrase dictionaries, for example, library schools and schools of librarianship. The emphasis in SMART, then, is on the influence of these dictionaries on the document search and in the manipulation of the search questions. These dictionaries are studied independently and also with respect to their cumulative effect. Thus the SMART system identifies the single best dictionary, as well as those which in combination prove most efficient with respect to recall and precision.

RESULTS OF TESTS

The Inverse Relationships of Recall and Precision

There is general agreement that there is usually an inverse relationship between recall and precision, that is, while recall can be raised to 100 percent, the cost in the number of nonrelevant documents retrieved is great. The nearer one approaches 100 percent recall, the greater proportionately is the drop in precision.

Automatic indexing. Using SMART methods Salton came to the conclusion that, "Fully automatic text analysis and search systems do not appear to produce a retrieval performance which is inferior to that obtained by conventional systems using manual document indexing and manual search formulations."

Precision and recall devices. Precision devices, except for coordination, proved of little value. Of the various recall devices, the use of synonyms proved significant, while the hierarchical (classified) proved less effective than had been supposed. At Case Western the use of role indicators proved to be significant only when the full text was available to the indexers; with abstracts, role indicators and other retrieval devices were not superior. At Cranfield, the controlled language performance was not improved by manipulating it hierarchically.

At Cranfield a surprising outcome was the realization that the uncontrolled single term natural language of the text was little improved by most recall or precision devices. At Cornell, it was found that the cumulative effect of all the dictionaries was more effective than any lesser combination.

In summary, in any system a significant recall device is the dictionary of synonyms, but the hierarchical element is not of major significance. Coordination is a powerful retrieval procedure.

Controlled languages. At Cranfield, a rank order of thirty-three indexing languages and devices was published, indicating their power of recall. The top seven languages were all uncontrolled. The best controlled language ranked tenth; its recall ratio was 61 percent compared to 65 percent for the best of the uncontrolled languages. The statistical difference between them is regarded as significant.

SOME OBSERVATIONS FROM THE MANAGERIAL POINT OF VIEW

Cost Factors

Information scientists have not seriously attacked the question of the cost of the various indexing languages.[4] It would appear, given the emphasis placed on the indexing languages at Cranfield and the search strategy at Western Reserve, that a number of those engaged in the testing were probably well acquainted with the subject matter of the tests. Despite this, Saracevic reported that the single greatest and most important variable was the quality of the indexing. A study of MEDLAR failures shows that with respect to recall, 72 percent of the failures can be attributed to faulty indexing or to faulty search strategy, while with respect to precision the number attributable to these two factors was 45 percent. From these bits of evidence the relative insignificance of the indexing system and language, compared to the indexing itself, and the imaginativeness of the search strategy, rises to haunt us. Furthermore, realizing that automatic indexing is not now superior to manual indexing, and guessing at the cost of this kind of indexing, the prospects are anything but bright.

Depth of Indexing

Also significant is the considerable depth of indexing employed in these tests, depth considerably greater than is provided by conventional subject catalogers. At Western Reserve, the number of indexing terms extracted from the full text ranged from thirty-six to forty, while twenty-three to thirty were taken from the abstracts.

The significance of the depth of indexing can be seen in the statistics supplied by Cranfield in tests run on the single-term, natural language indexing language: with fourteen index terms, the recall ratio was 62.8; twenty-two terms produced a ratio of 63.5; and thirty-three terms produced a ratio of 65. However, there is a law of diminishing returns with respect to the depth of indexing. When an average of sixty terms were taken from abstracts, the recall ratio dropped to 60.9.

Automatic Indexing

Turning to automatic indexing, of considerable significance from the managerial point of view is the fact that the intellectual effort required is considerable and of great significance with respect to the results. In the absence of a good dictionary of synonyms, the results can be disappointing, while the time required to compose a dictionary is an imposing consideration, as Salton has noted.

On the average, using all the devices available, SMART performs as follows:

Recall Ratio	Precision Ratio
10	85-95
50	60-80
100	30-45

As Salton himself has admitted, these are not satisfactory levels of performance.

Coordinate Indexing

The first Cranfield study (1962) tested four indexing systems, of which one was a coordinate system, best known as Uniterms. As summarized by Cleverdon, "It achieved the best overall figures in the test, it presented no difficulties for the technical searchers. . .and was notably successful with short indexing times. It appears to have as good a relevance figure as any other system."

Nevertheless, the Cranfield group refuses to concede any natural advantage to Uniterms (a "post-coordinate" system) over the others tested (the "pre-coordinate" types). The capability of retrieving any combination of terms is a feature of a post-coordinate system, yet "the results of the investigation show that this advantage, though it existed, was not large." Also: "the difference between the two types of system is therefore shown to be not a fundamental difference but merely one of cost or convenience, and it has not been proven as yet on which side the advantage lies."[5]

It should be made clear in this connection that the Uniterm index system tested at Cranfield was devoid of various precision devices which are a feature of other coordinate indexing systems (such as the metallurgical index at Case Western Reserve). In the presence of such precision devices, the recall ratio found at Cranfield presumably would have been lowered.

The argument has been made that a Uniterm system will break down if used with a large collection of documents.[6] Cleverdon disputes this, though neither disputant can argue from experience. Still another theoretical argument against the Uniterm system is that it might prove less effective with social science and humanistic materials than with materials in the natural sciences.

Computer Manipulation of a Manual-Based System

Such a system is MEDLARS; it is not an automatic system in the sense of the SMART system. In the MEDLARS system, other than the machine search itself, the indexing operations are performed manually. The MEDLARS system, on the average, provides the user with about 60 percent of the relevant documents in the collection, but of the total documents retrieved, about 50 percent will not be relevant.

It is widely believed that computer manipulation when applied to a controlled indexing language will greatly improve its efficiency. This is not true; even if more subject terms per document are posted, the overall efficiency of a controlled indexing language will not be significantly improved by computer manipulation, assuming that improvement of the recall factor alone is not enough.

This raises a perplexing question. Are all our users equally allergic to an increase in the number of nonrelevant documents, given an increase in the number of relevant ones? For example, in this regard are historians to be equated with chemists? With economists?

Another perplexing question is this: librarians suspect that scholars do not use the subject catalog extensively, and most often use it with respect to subjects outside their own specialty. Is this mainly because the subject catalog is inadequate, or because their more urgent retrieval needs lie in nonmonographic documents not now indexed in our subject catalogs?

Search Strategy

Also of importance is the amount of manipulation of questions (commonly termed search strategy) that took place in these experiments. In university libraries few questions are manipulated to the extent that took place in the tests under discussion. In the Cranfield tests and at Case Western the manipulation of the questions was extensive. At Case Western each question was searched in four different ways, namely: (1) the searchable terms found in the question itself; (2) to (1) is added terms taken from a thesaurus; (3) to (1) is added terms taken from encyclopedias and sources other than the thesaurus; (4) a combination of (2) and (3).

The considerable influence of these four manipulations can be seen in the number of relevant and nonrelevant documents retrieved:

	(1)	(2)	(3)	(4)
Relevant	106	130	180	192
Nonrelevant	124	197	509	598
Recall Ratio	.43	.52	.72	.77
Precision Ratio	.54	.48	.34	.33

At Cornell, various semantic and syntactic procedures are applied both to the questions and to the documents; to put it otherwise, the heart of the SMART system is the correlation coefficients by which terms in the question are matched with terms from the documents.

Except in libraries serving a small group of users, in a manual setting this kind of question manipulation will not be possible unless highly skilled librarians in considerable numbers are employed. In the automatic system the manipulation of the questions is mandatory.

Whether the costs of sophisticated information systems can be justified in either the manual or the automatic mode remains to be seen. At the moment we have no idea what costs would be incurred by systems such as the SMART system in the setting of a large library with a large number of scholars engaged in research. As for making the system available to undergraduates, this involves an entirely different order of cost magnitude.

REFERENCES

1. Cyril W. Cleverdon, *Factors Determining the Performance of Indexing Systems* (Cranfield, England: College of Aeronautics, 1966), 2v.
2. Tefko Saracevic, *An Inquiry into Testing of Information Retrieval Systems* (Cleveland, Ohio: Center for Documentation and Communication Research, Case Western Reserve Univ., 1968).
3. Gerald Salton, *Automatic Information Organization and Retrieval* (New York: McGraw-Hill, 1968).
4. Frank B. Rogers, "Costs of Operating an Information Retrieval Service," *Drexel Library Quarterly* 4:271-78 (Oct. 1968).
5. Cyril W. Cleverdon, *Report on the Testing and Analysis of . . . Indexing Systems* (Cranfield, England: College of Aeronautics, 1962), pp. 101-02.
5. Arthur D. Little, Inc., *Centralization and Documentation. Final Report to the National Science Foundation.* 2d ed. (Cambridge, Mass.: 1964).
7. Cleverdon, *Report.*

Automatic Text Analysis

Automatic document indexing and classification methods are examined and their effectiveness is assessed

by G. Salton

Over the years, linguists and philosophers of language have deplored the fact that no adequate theory exists to account for many of the important phenomena connected with the natural language. The lack of such a theory has in particular made it impossible to construct linguistic models which would completely and accurately represent the structure of the natural language, and this in turn has led to predictions that computers, which must rely on some model specifying the processing rules, would have only a relatively minor role in the analysis of written texts (1).

While remarks concerning the lack of appropriate linguistic theories and models are entirely justified, the many experiments conducted over the last few years in the general area of automatic text processing, including automatic document indexing and classification and automatic text analysis, provide evidence that computer-based text processing is practicable and useful for many kinds of applications. In fact, the indication is that some of the automatic content analysis and text processing methods not only are relatively easy to implement but can be used in an automatic information storage and retrieval environment to produce a retrieval effectiveness at least equal to that obtained by the conventional, mostly manual procedures used in the past.

In this article the principal experiments in automatic text analysis are briefly reviewed, and an indication is given of developments to be expected in the future.

GENERAL METHODOLOGY

The first serious work in automatic text analysis dates back to the middle and late 1950's, when Luhn argued that the vocabulary contained in individual document texts would necessarily have to constitute the basis for a useful content analysis and classification (2, 3). Several possible indexing methods were proposed by Luhn, including, for example, the following (2, p. 315):

... a notion occurring at least twice in the same paragraph would be considered a major notion; a notion which occurs also in the immediately preceding or succeeding paragraph would be considered a major notion even though it appears only once in the paragraph under consideration; notations for major notions would then be listed in some standard order.

Luhn further suggested that the inquirer's "document" (that is, the search request) be encoded in exactly the same manner as the documents of the collection, so that queries and documents could appropriately be matched.

These early ideas were not universally appreciated, partly because they could not be applied uniformly to all query and document texts—many counterexamples were produced to show that a given methodology would not operate under certain circumstances—and partly because the automatic procedures were never adequately tested. Nevertheless, a good deal of work has been done to refine and expand the original ideas, and several operational automatic content analysis systems are now in existence. The following types of operations are often used.

1) Expressions are first chosen from the document or query texts; often this implies the identification or generation of words, word stems, noun phrases, prepositional phrases, or other content units, with certain specified properties.

2) A weight may be assigned each expression on the basis of the frequency of occurrence of the given expression, or the position of the expression in the document, or the type of entity.

3) Expressions originally assigned to documents may be replaced by new expressions, or new expressions may be added to those originally available, thereby "expanding" the set of content identifiers; such an expansion may be based on information contained in a stored dictionary, or, alternatively, it may be based on statistical co-occurrence characteristics between the terms in a document collection, or on syntactical relations between words.

SOURCE: Reprinted from *Science*, 168: 335-343 (17 April 1970) by permission of the publisher. Copyright 1970 by the American Association for the Advancement of Science.

4) Additional relational indicators between expressions may be supplied to express syntactical, or functional, or logical relationships between the entities available for content identification.

The result of such an automatic indexing process is then similar to that outlined by Luhn in the sense that each document or search request is identified by a set of terms. However, these terms may consist of complete phrases which do not necessarily originate in the document to which they are assigned; moreover, each term may carry a weight reflecting its presumed importance for purposes of content analysis.

It is impossible in a brief article such as this to discuss the many strategies that have been proposed for automatic indexing (4). Instead, the experimental evidence derived from many of the recent studies in automatic indexing and text analysis is examined, and conclusions are drawn concerning the effectiveness of the various techniques.

INDEXING EXPERIMENTS

Most of the early experiments in automatic indexing did not include any kind of retrieval test but consisted principally of a comparison between automatically derived index terms and preestablished manually assigned subject categories. Typically, a manually indexed document collection would be taken, and an attempt would be made to duplicate by automatic means as many of the pre-assigned terms as possible. Three types of studies may be distinguished, depending on the testing device actually used: (i) title word studies, (ii) studies involving comparisons of automatically generated and manually assigned terms, and (iii) studies based on automatic assignment to known subject classes.

The title word studies use as a criterion the similarity between entries derived from document titles and from manually assigned subject headings. Montgomery and Swanson (5) used an issue of *Index Medicus* containing title citations in biomedicine cross-filed under the various manually derived subject headings and concluded that, for 86 percent of almost 5000 titles, a correlation existed between the subject heading assigned in *Index Medicus* and the document title ("Correlation" was defined as an actual match between word stems, or a match between rather loosely defined synonymous terms). In a somewhat related study based on use of the chemical literature, Ruhl (6) found that 57 percent of the titles ex-

amined contained all the important concepts (or their equivalents) listed for these documents in the subject index of *Chemical Abstracts,* while only 12 percent of the titles missed three or more important subject headings. Similar results were found by Kraft (7) for the legal literature: only about 10 percent of the document titles examined did not contain any key words useful for indexing purposes, while 64 percent of the title entries contained one or more of the subject heading words included in the *Index to Legal Periodicals,* and an additional 25 percent of the titles contained "logical equivalents" of the subject headings.

While results of this type are not directly usable, particularly in the absence of tests in a retrieval environment, the evidence nevertheless suggests that simple automatic word-extracting methods are not necessarily worthless. Furthermore, the counter-evidence cited by O'Connor (8), who finds a correlation between assigned subject headings and title words ranging from a low of only 13 percent to a high of only 68 percent, was produced with a very strict definition of synonymy (that is, the terms were required to be strictly synonymous in order to be considered equivalent) which is not necessarily desirable either for indexing or for retrieval (8).

The next set of experiments consists of a comparison between automatically generated and manually assigned sets of index terms. Such term set comparisons are often performed by matching a set of automatically generated index terms with the available manually assigned terms. An evaluation coefficient such as q may be used to measure the amount of overlap between vocabularies, where

$$q = \frac{c}{a + m - c}$$

[Here c represents the number of common term assignments, a is the number of automatically derived terms, and m is the number of manually assigned terms (9).]

Various tests of this general type have been performed (10, 11), and the consensus is that about 60 percent agreement between manually and automatically produced terms is obtainable. In one test involving the automatic assignment of phrases to documents, as many as 86 percent of the automatically assigned phrases were found by human judges to be acceptable subject heads, the "overassignment" (that is, the assignment of extraneous phrases) being of the order of 14 percent, and the "underassignment" (that is, proper content indicators not recognized by the machine) being of the order of 11 percent (*12*). A related approach, consisting of a comparison between automatically derived document affinities based on similarities in the bibliographic citations attached to the documents with document affinities based on overlapping sets of manually assigned subject headings, also indicates a considerable amount of agreement between the automatic and manual procedures (*13*).

The last set of experiments (apart from tests in a retrieval environment) involves automatic classification of documents into subject categories (rather than assignment of index terms to documents) (*14*). This is often accomplished as follows. A *test* collection is used manually to classify documents into subject categories and to compute similarity parameters between a given subject category and the vocabularies of documents contained in that category. These parameters are then used automatically to classify a *control* collection consisting of new, incoming documents (*15, 16*). It is found that, for the original test documents, an automatic assignment to subject categories is about about 80 to 90 percent effective (that is, the correct category is chosen in about 80 to 90 percent of the cases). For control items—documents not used in deriving the test parameters—the effectiveness of the automatic classification based on document vocabularies drops down to about 50 percent.

O'Connor (*16*) remarks that the percentage of correctly classified documents increases when more refined classification parameters are used (from 76 percent when key words alone are used to 92 percent when certain relationships between key words are also utilized); at the same time, the number of incorrectly classified items which are wrongly included in a category also increases from 13 to 18 percent. This tradeoff between the number of correct and incorrect responses—as the first goes up, the second goes up also—is characteristic of retrieval system performance.

RETRIEVAL EXPERIMENTS

The indexing experiments described above were not performed within a normal retrieval situation, and involved reliance on criteria supplied by human experts for purposes of evaluation. In a retrieval environment, on the other hand, it is possible to use as a criterion of system effectiveness the ability of the system to satisfy the user's need for information by retrieving wanted material and rejecting unwanted items. Two measures have been widely used for this purpose, known as "recall" and "precision," and representing, respectively, the proportion of relevant material actually retrieved and the proportion of retrieved material actually relevant. Ideally, all relevant items should be retrieved and all nonrelevant items should be rejected; such a situation is reflected in perfect recall and precision values, equal to 1.

It should be noted that both the recall and the precision figures achievable by a given system are adjustable, in the sense that a relaxation of search criteria (a broader search formulation) often leads to high recall, while a tightening of search criteria (a narrower search formulation) leads to high precision. Unhappily, experience has shown that, on the average, recall and precision tend to vary inversely: the retrieval of a greater number of relevant items normally also leads to the retrieval of a greater number of irrelevant ones. When recall and precision are plotted against each other, a monotonically decreasing curve of the type shown in Fig. 1 reflects the average performance characteristic of a retrieval system.

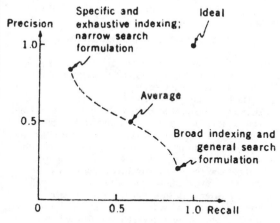

FIGURE 1. Typical recall-precision graph reflecting performance characteristics of retrieval systems.

In practice, a compromise is usually made, and a performance level is chosen such that much of the relevant material is retrieved while the number of nonrelevant items also retrieved is kept within tolerable limits. Thus, in what is probably the most exhaustive evaluation of an operating retrieval system involving the use of manually indexed documents (in this case the Medlars system at the National Library of Medicine), Lancaster (*17*) reports an average recall of 0.577 and an average precision of 0.504 (*18*). Additional evaluation results are to be found in the extensive literature dealing with the evaluation of operating manually based retrieval systems (*19*).

The first comparison of conventional retrieval (retrieval of manually indexed documents) with automatic text processing systems appears to be the one made by Swanson in the late 1950's, using 100 documents and 50 queries (*20*). Three indexing and analysis systems were used: (i) conventional retrieval based on a subject heading index; (ii) retrieval based on specifications provided by words and phrases automatically extracted from the document texts; and (iii) retrieval based on use of a thesaurus in addition to the words obtained from the documents. A measure similar to the "recall-precision" measure was used to evaluate system performance; it varied directly with the relevance weight of the retrieved items and included in addition a penalty factor for retrieval of irrelevant material.

The test results indicated that the average retrieval performance of a system based on automatic text analysis was superior to the performance of the standard system based on manual indexing. Since Swanson provides the first of a long series of results all tending to prove the same point, it is worth quoting from his report (*20*):

> The first conspicuous implication of the result is that the proportion of relevant information retrieved under any circumstances is rather low.
> The second implication of the data is the apparent superiority of machine-retrieval techniques over conventional retrieval within the framework of our model, Conventional retrieval was carried out under the favorable conditions of a highly detailed and specific subject-heading list, tailored to a sample library. . . .
> It is expected that the relative superiority of machine text searching to conventional retrieval will become greater with subsequent experimentation as retrieval aids for text searching are improved, whereas no clear procedure is in evidence which will guarantee improvement of the conventional system. . . . Thus even though machines may never enjoy more than a partial success in library indexing, a small suspicion might justifiably be entertained that people are even less promising.

In view of the test results produced by far more extensive experimentation reported below, these prophesies appear to have been remarkably accurate.

Swanson's original results were confirmed in an extension of the test in which, for the first time, natural-language queries were used (instead of manually constructed query formulations) (*21*).

Documents were retrieved in decreasing order of similarity to the queries, the similarity score for an article being computed by summing the weights of those words in the article which coincided with the query words. With such a ranked list of retrieved documents, it is then possible to compute recall and precision values following the retrieval of each document (or each nth document); this produces a sequence of recall-precision pairs which can be plotted as a curve similar to that of Fig. 1. Swanson concludes his study by stating (*21*):

> . . . though these results [that automatic text processing using an automatic thesaurus is more accurate than the human process of assigning appropriate subject index terms to documents and queries] may violate one's sense of intuition, there is no good theoretical reason to believe that they ought to have come out differently.

Various later studies also included elements of automatic text analysis, including full text search (*22*), the use of phrase dictionaries and syntactic analysis procedures (*23, 24*), statistical term associations (*25, 26*), and automatically constructed term groupings (thesauri) (*27*). In each case the intent is to show that one or another of the proposed automatic language analysis methods operates more successfully than either a manual indexing process or an automatic process based on a less sophisticated approach. In general, the case is made that the use of manually constructed thesauri or of automatic term associations or term groups is useful in a retrieval environment. [In the one case where an automatic phrase-matching procedure appeared not to produce reasonable results, the test conditions were peculiar, since the texts processed in the experiment were not the same as those used to determine the relevance of a given document to a query (*24*); furthermore, retrieval appears to have been based on the presence, or absence, of a single matching phrase or sentence fragment, so the test results are difficult to interpret effectively.]

Most of these studies are somewhat fragmentary, and a detailed report of their findings is not given here. Instead, the test environment and results of the Aslib-Cranfield and SMART retrieval experiments, both of which include a large range of automatic text analysis methods, are described in some detail in the next section.

RETRIEVAL SYSTEM EVALUATION

The work described above generally consists in implementing a particular type of text analysis process, and in testing it through use of a sample document collection and a set of sample queries. Both the Cranfield experiments, undertaken in England by Cleverdon and his associates, and the SMART project, based at Cornell and Harvard universities, have gone beyond that in the sense that a whole range of automatic text analysis methods were systematically tested, and that, at least in the case of SMART, the experimentation was extended to many different document collections in diverse fields, including documentation, computer engineering, aerodynamics, and medicine.

The Cranfield II experiments [not to be confused with the earlier Cranfield I tests designed to compare four conventional systems based on manual indexing (28)] were designed to measure a large variety of index-language "devices" that are potentially useful in the representation of document content. These devices include the use of synonym dictionaries, hierarchical subject classifications, phrase assignment methods, and many others. All the indexing tasks were performed manually by trained indexers, starting with the simple "single term" methods and proceeding to more complex methods involving use of a controlled vocabulary and various types of dictionaries. The indexing rules were carefully specified in each case, and were always based initially on the text of the documents or of the queries; the indexers were therefore simulating potential machine operations, and the evaluation results may thus be applicable to automatic indexing procedures.

A collection of 1400 documents in aerodynamics was available (the Cranfield collection) together with 279 search requests prepared by aerodynamicists. Three main indexing languages were tested, known respectively as "single terms," "controlled terms," and "simple concepts." The single terms are content words chosen from document texts;

controlled terms are single terms modified by "look-up" in a manually constructed subject authority list; and simple concepts are terms concatenated to form phrases. The test consisted in determining the retrieval effectiveness of these languages when used with the indexing devices referred to above. It was expected that some linguistic devices (the "recall devices"), including synonym dictionaries, concept associations, and term hierarchies, would broaden document and query identifications, thereby improving recall, while others (the "precision devices"), such as the assignment of term weights and the specification of relational indicators between terms, would narrow the content identifications, or make them more specific, thereby improving precision.

The evaluation process was based on a computation of recall and precision measures at various "coordination levels" (29)—that is, for various degrees of matching between queries and documents—followed by an averaging of results over all the search requests used. The output was then presented as a set of recall-precision tables and graphs. In addition, a global "normalized recall" measure, consisting, for each system, of a single value, computed in a manner somewhat analogous to computation of the "normalized" measures used in the SMART system (30), was used to rank the various systems in decreasing order of effectiveness. The detailed retrieval results (31, 32) cannot be reproduced here. However, a summary of the main results is contained in Table 1 where the three language types are arranged in decreasing order of effectiveness according to the average normalized recall score obtained.

It may be seen from Table 1 that the simple, uncontrolled indexing language involving single terms produces the best retrieval performance, while the controlled vocabulary and the phrases (simple concepts) furnish increasingly worse results. To quote

TABLE 1

Order of effectiveness of three types of indexing languages. [Adapted from Cleverdon and Keen (31, fig. 8.1 T, p. 253)]

TYPE OF INDEXING LANGUAGE	RANK ORDERS FOR METHODS USING INDEXING LANGUAGE	AVERAGE SCORE FOR LANGUAGE
Single terms: content words manually chosen from full document	1, 2, 3, 4, 5, 6, 7, 12	64.15
Controlled terms: single terms modified by look-up in manually constructed thesaurus or authority list	10, 11, 15, 17, 18, 19	60.34
Simple concepts: single terms concatenated into standard noun phrases reflective of document content	8, 9, 21, 22, 23, 24, 25, 26, 27, 28, 29, 30, 31, 32, 33	54.55

from Cleverdon and Keen (*31*):

> ... quite the most astonishing and seemingly inexplicable conclusion that arises from the project is that the single term index languages are superior to any other type ...
> ... of the six controlled term index language; ... on the other hand, the single gave the best performance ... as narrower, broader, or related terms are brought in, ranking orders ... decrease ...
> ... the conceptual terms of the simple concept (phrase) index languages were over-specific when used in natural language; ... on the other hand, the single terms appear to have been near the correct level of specificity; only to the relatively small extent of grouping true synonyms (using a synonym dictionary) and word forms (using a suffix cut-off process to generate word stems) could any improvement in performance be obtained. ...

In other words, the surprising conclusion is that, on the average, the simplest indexing procedures which identify a given document or query by a set of terms, weighted or unweighted, obtained from document or query texts are also the most effective. Of the many procedures tried in an attempt to increase recall or precision, only the use of a synonym dictionary which groups related terms into concept classes produces a better performance than the original, unmodified terms. It goes without saying that single term indexing is easier to implement automatically than the more sophisticated, seemingly less effective alternatives.

One might be tempted to dismiss the Cranfield results by ascribing them to some peculiar test conditions were it not for the fact that the extensive evaluation work carried out for some years with the SMART system points in the same direction (*33, 34*). The SMART system is an experimental, fully automatic document retrieval system, operating with an IBM 7094 and a 360/65 computer. Unlike most other computer-based retrieval systems, the SMART system does not rely on manually assigned key words or index terms for the identification of documents and search requests, nor does it use primarily the frequency of occurrence of certain words or phrases included in the texts of documents. Instead, an attempt is made to go beyond simple word-matching procedures by using various intellectual aids in the form of synonym dictionaries, hierarchical arrangements of subject identifiers, statistical and syntactic phrase-generation methods, and the like, in order to obtain the content identifications useful for the retrieval process.

The following facilities incorporated into the SMART system for document analysis appear of principal interest.

1) A system for separating English words into stems and affixes (the so-called suffix "s" and stem thesaurus methods) used to construct document identifications consisting of the stems of words contained in the documents. Such a stem analysis is, preferably, applied only to those words whose frequency of occurrence in a given document is unexpectedly high, as compared with their frequency of occurrence in the literature at large (*10, 25*).

2) A synonym dictionary, or thesaurus, which can be used to recognize synonyms by replacing each word stem by one or more "concept" numbers; these concept numbers then serve as content identifiers, instead of the original word stem.

3) A hierarchical arrangement of the concepts included in the thesaurus which makes it possible, given any concept number, to find its "parents" in the hierarchy, its "sons," its "brothers," and any of a set of possible cross references. The hierarchy can be used to obtain more general content identifiers than the ones originally given (by going *up* in the hierarchy), more specific ones (by going *down*), and a set of related ones (by picking up brothers and cross-references) (*33*).

4) Statistical association procedures which use similarity coefficients based on term co-occurrences within the sentences of a document, or within the documents of a collection, to determine the "associated" terms. Such association methods then produce for each term a "profile" of associated terms, from which in turn a second-order profile containing still further associations can be obtained, and so on (*35*); the original terms and their associations may then be used for content identification.

5) Syntactic analysis methods which make it possible to compare the syntactically analyzed sentences of documents and search requests. The syntactic analysis used to identify the phrases or sentence structures to be matched may be formal in the sense that it is based on a complete phrase structure or transformational grammar of the language, or the analysis may be of an ad hoc nature, based principally on recognition of certain function words from which prepositional and other phrases are then derivable (*36*).

6) Statistical phrase-matching methods which operate like the syntactic phrase procedures—that is, through use of a dictionary to identify phrases used as content identifiers. However, no syntactic analysis is performed in this case, and phrases are defined as equivalent if the phrase components match, regardless of the syntactic relationships between components.

7) A dictionary system, designed to revise the several dictionaries included in the system, such as the word stem dictionary, the word suffix dictionary, the common word dictionary (for terms to be deleted during analysis), the thesaurus (synonym dictionary), and the statistical and syntactic phrase dictionaries.

8) An automatic document classification system which groups documents with similar content identifiers into document clusters in such a way that a given file search can be confined to certain document clusters instead of being extended to the complete file.

9) A user feedback system which modifies document and query identifiers, on the basis of information supplied by the customers during the search process (*37*).

Stored documents and search requests are processed by the SMART system, without any prior manual analysis, by one of several dozen combinations of these and other automatic content analysis methods, and those documents which most nearly match a given search request are extracted from the document file in answer to each request.

In Table 2, a sample analysis produced by the

TABLE 2

Thesaurus analysis for English query Q 13 B: "In what ways are computer systems being applied to research in the field of the belles lettres? Has machine analysis of language proved useful, for instance, in determining probable authorship of anonymous works or in compiling concordances?"

CONCEPT NOS.	WEIGHT	SAMPLE TERMS IN THESAURUS CATEGORY
3	12	Computer, processor
19	12	Automatic, semiautomatic
33	12	Analyze, analysis, etc.
49	12	Compendium, compile
65	12	Authorship, originator
147	12	Discourse, language
207	12	Area, branch, field
267	12	Concordance, KWIC†
345	12	Bell
*		Anonymous, lettres

*Query terms not found in thesaurus. †KWIC, "Key Word in Context."

SMART system, with a thesaurus process, is shown for query Q 13 B. The original query text is given, together with the resulting set of weighted (*38*) concept numbers (terms). Listed opposite each concept number is a sample of the terms appearing in the thesaurus under that concept category.

The SMART system organization makes it possible to evaluate the effectiveness of the various processing methods by comparing the output ob-

tained from a number of different runs. This is achieved by processing the same search requests against the same document collections several times, while making selected changes in the analysis procedures between runs. By comparing the performance of the search requests under different processing conditions, it is possible to determine the relative effectiveness of the various analysis methods. The evaluation is then performed by averaging performance over many search requests and plotting recall-precision graphs of the type shown in Fig. 1. The effectiveness of a given method is reflected by the nearness of the corresponding curve to the upper right-hand corner of the graph, where both recall and precision are high.

Extensive evaluation results obtained with the SMART system have been published for collections in computer engineering, medicine, documentation, and aerodynamics (*33, 39, 40*). In each case, recall-precision graphs are drawn for the performance of two or more analysis and search procedures, averaged over many search requests, and the statistical significance of the differences in performance for any two methods is computed. A typical example, showing differences in performance for an antomatic word stem analysis and an analysis involving use of a stored synonym dictionary (or thesaurus) to transform weighted word stems into weighted thesaurus classes is shown in Fig. 2. It may be seen that, for the collection of 780 documents in computer engineering used with 35 search requests, the synonym recognition afforded by the thesaurus produces an increase in precision of about 10 percent for any given recall point.

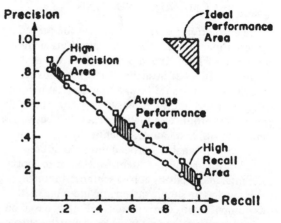

FIGURE 2. Recall-precision graph illustrating word stem and thesaurus performance (averages for 780 Institute of Radio Engineers documents). (Circles) Word stem; (squares) thesaurus-3.

It is not possible to reproduce here in detail the evaluation results obtained for many hundreds of runs. A few quotations from the published conclusions (slightly paraphrased to avoid introducing new terms not otherwise needed) may suffice (*40*, pp.33–34).

> The order of merit is generally the same for all three collections [that is, computer engineering, aerodynamics, and documentation].
> The use of unweighted terms [weights restricted to 1 for terms that are present, and 0 for those that are absent] is always less effective than the use of weighted terms.
> The use of document titles alone is always less effective for content analysis purposes than the use of full document abstracts.
> The thesaurus process involving synonym recognition always performs more effectively than the word stem methods where synonyms and other word relations are not recognized.
> The thesaurus and statistical phrase methods are substantially equivalent in performance; other dictionaries, including term hierarchies and syntactic phrases, perform less well.

These results indicate that, in automatic content analysis systems, weighted terms should be used, derived from document excerpts whose length is at least equivalent to that of a document abstract. Furthermore, synonym dictionaries should be incorporated wherever they are available. The principal conclusions reached by the Cranfield project are also borne out by the SMART studies: that phrase languages are not substantially superior to single terms as indexing devices, and that sophisticated analysis tools are less effective than had been expected.

COMPARISON OF AUTOMATIC AND MANUAL INDEXING

The evaluation results described in the preceding section appear to raise as many questions as they answer. (i) What is the explanation for the finding, the reverse of what intuition leads one to expect, that simple automatic term extraction, combined with weighting and dictionary "look-up" methods, apparently produces a higher retrieval effectiveness than more sophisticated, semantically more complete, content analysis procedures such as complete word recognition, identification of pronoun referents, and analysis across sentence boundaries? (ii) How do the simple automatic indexing methods compare with conventional methods based on manual term assignment? (iii) How can the automatic procedures be improved (given that the performance range exemplified by the output of

Fig. 2 is not as high as one would hope)? (iv) How would the automatic indexing process cope with the practical problems of automatic document input and of foreign language processing? (v) What is likely to be the future of automatic document processing? These questions are now treated in order.

The problem of rationalizing research results different from those one intuitively expects is always a difficult one. In the present case, however, some reasonable arguments are readily available.

First, it must be remembered that the problem of automatic documentation is not comparable to automatic translation or to automatic question answering, in that a retrieval system is designed only to lead a user to items likely to be related to the subject in which he is interested. A somewhat gross rendition of document content, consisting mostly of the more salient features, may therefore be perfectly adequate, in place of the line-by-line type of analysis needed, for example, for translation.

Second, a retrieval system is designed to serve a large, sometimes heterogeneous user population. Since users may have different needs and aims, and since their search requests may range from survey or tutorial type questions to very detailed analytical queries, an excessively specific analysis may be too specialized for most users.

Finally, in the evaluation procedures used to judge retrieval effectiveness, a performance criterion averaged over many search requests is used. This implies that analysis methods whose overall performance is moderately successful are given preference over possibly more sophisticated procedures which may operate excellently for certain queries but far less well for others. In practice, it may turn out that, for each query, a specific type of sophisticated analysis will be optimal, whereas, for the average query, the simpler type of indexing is best.

In explaining the test results, one might also argue that the evaluation results are inherently untrustworthy, first because they were obtained with small collections, often outside an accepted user environment and, second, because the recall and precision results are unreliable since they are based on subjective judgments of the relevance of the documents to the queries. Concerning the first point, it can be said that, although the tests were in fact conducted with collections of small size (less than 1500 documents each), the evaluation results are remarkably consistent over many collections in diverse subject areas; furthermore, the total test environment has included several thousand documents and several hundred queries. There is therefore no likelihood that such consistent results could have occurred by chance.

The second point appears, on the surface, more serious. It is a fact that recall and precision measures require a prior determination of relevance; that is, for each query it is necessary first to identify the set of relevant and nonrelevant items before the evaluation measures can be generated. Relevance assessments must be made by human subjects—preferably by the requester himself—and they will vary from one assessor to another. Studies of the relevance assessment process have indicated that the overall agreement between assessors may not be greater than about 30 percent (41, 42). Nevertheless, the conclusion that the recall and precision values are therefore unreliable is unwarranted. In fact, a recent study performed with four different sets of relevance assessments and a collection of 1200 documents in library science has shown that the average recall and precision curves are almost identical, even though the relevance sets are completely dissimilar. The explanation is that, for those documents which are most similar to the queries and which are therefore retrieved early in the search, the assessments are in almost perfect agreement; these documents are also the ones which principally determine the shape of the recall-precision curves in the nonzero regions, and which are therefore responsible for the relative invariance of the test results (42).

It appears, then, that reasonable arguments can be furnished to support the principal test conclusions, and that appropriate answers can be made in response to the more obvious objections. Finally, one must examine any counterevidence that may be available. Although systematic tests of automatic indexing procedures have not been made outside of the SMART and Cranfield environments, some data are available which appear not to be in agreement with the results reported above. For example, Saracevic reports that, in a test involving the use of 2600 documents in biomedicine and 124 queries, use of a thesaurus for term expansion was found not to be effective (43). It is not clear whether the fault, in this case, lay with the type of thesaurus [the SMART results apply only to certain types of thesauri, constructed in accordance with a specific set of principles (33, 40)] or with the type of analysis (a different analysis process was used for documents on the one hand and for queries on the other). Furthermore, because the results were cumulated for five different analysis procedures instead of being individually displayed, the output is not strictly comparable to the SMART or Cranfield data, and the results are difficult to assess.

The same is true of the test results obtained by Jones and his associates (12) using 22 queries each specified by a single phrase (or "content-bearing unit"). Here, a very high search precision (0.84) is reported for the phrase-matching process, but no recall values are given; the cited performance may thus correspond to a system operating at the left-hand end of a normal recall-precision curve. Furthermore, the queries, each consisting of a single two-word phrase, are probably not typical of queries normally received in information centers, and are in any case not comparable to the natural-language queries processed by SMART and Cranfield.

To summarize, there is no obvious evidence for distrusting the main results of the automatic indexing studies outlined above.

In some of the early text processing experiments it was seen that the automatic document search procedures were producing retrieval results at least equivalent to those obtained with conventional manual indexing (20, 21). Furthermore, the later tests conducted in an automatic retrieval environment indicate that the simple, single-term methods, which are easiest to implement on a computer, are also the most effective. It is interesting to try to determine under these circumstances how the automatic SMART procedures compare with standard manual indexing methods. The evidence here is not wholly conclusive, since the SMART processing is necessarily performed with small document collections. However, whatever evidence exists shows that the automatic indexing procedures are not inferior to what is now achieved by conventional, manual means.

For example, an initial comparison between the manual indexing used at Cranfield and the automatic processing of abstracts performed by SMART shows that the results obtained by the two systems are not statistically different (31, 40). To check these results, a comparison was made between the test results obtained by Lancaster for the manually based Medlars system (17) and the results for the SMART system. Specifically, for 18 of the Medlars queries used earlier by Lancaster, document abstracts were keypunched, and the retrieval process was repeated by means of the automatic text searching methods incorporated in SMART (44). The results indicate that, for that subcollection, a slightly higher average recall is obtained by SMART (0.69 as compared with 0.64 for Medlars), whereas Medlars achieves a somewhat higher precision (0.61 for SMART and 0.62 for Medlars). In any case, the intuitive feeling that the conventional indexing would necessarily be superior is again not confirmed.

One might interpret the results of the SMART-Medlars comparison by saying that the conventional and the automatic indexing procedures produce equally poor results (a recall and precision performance between 0.55 and 0.65, as compared with a possible maximum of 1). The reasons for the relatively poor performance of the automatic methods are clear when one considers the simplicity of the content analysis procedures used. For the manual indexing process, Lancaster reports the following main sources of failure (*17*): (i) index language problems (lack of specific terms or false coordination of terms); (ii) search formulation (query formulation too exhaustive or too specific); (iii) document indexing (document indexing insufficiently exhaustive, or too exhaustive, or important terms omitted); and (iv) lack of user-system interaction during the search process. The first three sources of failure all have to do with the query or document indexing process. The last inadequacy, however, appears to be one that can be remedied immediately.

For this reason, interactive search procedures have been incorporated into several recently implemented retrieval systems. The SMART system, in particular, attempts to meet the user problem by performing multiple rather than single searches. Thus, instead of submitting a search request and obtaining in return a final set of relevant items, a partial search is first made and, on the basis of the preliminary output obtained, the search parameters are adjusted before a second, more refined search is attempted. The adjustments made may differ from user to user, depending on individual needs, and the search process may be repeated as often as desired.

Various strategies are available for improving the results of a search by means of user feedback procedures (*37, 45, 46*). The first is based on a selective printout of stored information to be brought to the user's attention during the search process. For example, a set of additional, possible search terms related to those initially used by the requester may be extracted from the stored dictionary and presented to the user. The user may then be asked to reformulate the original query after selecting those new associated terms which appear to him most helpful in improving the search re-

sults. Typically, the statistical term associations discussed above can be used to obtain the set of related terms, or the sets of associated thesaurus classes can be taken from the thesaurus. This "search optimization" procedure is straight-forward, but leaves the burden of rephrasing the query to the user (*45*).

A second strategy consists in automatically modifying a search request by using the partial results from a previous search. The user is asked to examine the documents retrieved by an initial search, and to designate some of them as either relevant (R) or irrelevant (N) to his needs. Concepts from the documents termed relevant can then be added to the original search request if they are not already present, or, if they are, their importance can be increased through a suitable adjustment of weights; contrariwise, terms from documents designated irrelevant can be deleted or given a lower weight (*37, 45-47*). An illustration of such a "relevance feedback" process is shown in Fig. 3, where a query first retrieves a document identified as nonrelevant (Fig. 3a). The query-updating process which follows then shifts the query in such a way that a new search operation retrieves some relevant documents (Fig. 3b). These documents, in turn, are used to generate two subqueries, which are then successful in retrieving all relevant items (Fig. 3c).

A good deal of work has been done to improve this type of feedback operation, and evaluation results indicate that the process is considerably more effective than the standard one-pass search process. Figure 4 is a typical feedback evaluation graph showing averages for 200 documents and 42 queries in aerodynamics. Here an initial one-step search process based on a word stem analysis is compared with a feedback procedure based on the display of abstracts of previously retrieved documents; such a display is then used for manual updating of queries. The results of such manual updating are in turn compared with one iteration of the automatic relevance feedback process. It may be seen in Fig. 4 that the automatic updating procedure is more effective than the manual one, and that an improvement of about 20 percent in precision is obtained through the feedback procedure. Moreover, this type of improvement in retrieval effectiveness has been duplicated for all collections so far processed (*45-47*).

Two other practical points—document input and foreign language processing—require discussion, since it is sometimes claimed that no automatic indexing process would be viable without consider-

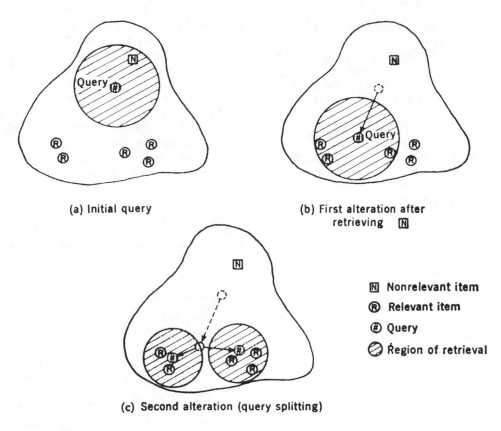

(a) Initial query

(b) First alteration after retrieving Ⓝ

(c) Second alteration (query splitting)

Ⓝ Nonrelevant item
Ⓡ Relevant item
⊕ Query
⊘ Region of retrieval

FIGURE 3.   Typical query transformations resulting from relevance feedback.

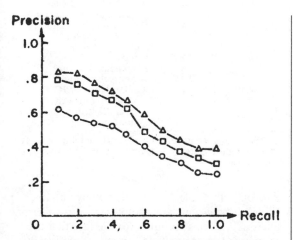

FIGURE 4.   Recall-precision graph illustrating the performance of abstract display and relevance feedback. (Circles) Original queries (word stem); (triangles) relevance feedback (word stem), one iteration; (squares) abstract display (word stem).

ation of these questions. The input problem is particularly acute in an environment which includes automatic indexing, since document ex-

cerpts of at least abstract length should be available for analysis. Obviously, if all the material contained in an abstract (or, possibly, in the full text) requires manual keypunching, the main benefits of the automatic analysis procedure may be lost. No overall solution appears immediately available. However, the use of automatic character recognition equipment and of automatic typesetting processes is becoming more widespread, with the result that document input products that can be automatically read may well become generally available with each document before long.

Concerning the foreign language problem, the situation is less difficult than might appear to be the case. It is true that, in certain subject areas, up to 50 percent of the pertinent documents are not written in English [this is true of the documents in biomedicine processed at the National Library of Medicine (*17*)] . The English-language analysis methods will obviously not be applicable for these documents. However, it is also true that 90 percent of these documents are in one of only six or seven languages, most of them being in French, German, and Russian.

Some experiments were recently conducted with the SMART system and a collection of about 500 German documents in the field of library science. A multilingual thesaurus (Fig. 5) was prepared

230 ART	ARCHITEKTUR
231 INDEPEND	SELBSTAENDIG
	UNABHAENGIG
232 ASSOCIATIVE	
233 DIVIDE	
234 ACTIVE	AKTIV
ACTIVITY	AKTIVITAET
USAGE	TAETIGKEIT
235 CATHODE	DIODE
CRT	VERZWEIGER
DIODE	
FLYING—SPOT	
RAY	
RELAIS	
RELAY	
SCANNER	
TUBE	
236 REDUNDANCY	
REDUNDANT	
237 CHARGE	EINGANG
ENTER	EINGEGANGEN
ENTRY	EINGEGEBEN
INSERT	EINSATZ
POST	EINSTELLEN
	EINTRAGUNG
238 MULTI—LEVEL	
MULTILEVEL	
239 INTELLECT	GEISTIG
INTELLECTUAL	
INTELLIG	
MENTAL	
MIND	
NON—INTELLECTUAL	
240 ACTUAL	PRAXIS
PRACTICE	
REAL	

FIGURE 5. Excerpt from multilingual English-German thesaurus.

manually by translating the English version of an existing thesaurus into German. From Fig. 5 it may be seen that the same concept-class number represents both an English word class and the corresponding German class. The translation test performed consisted in processing a set of original English language queries against both the English and the German document collections; the test was then repeated by processing the English queries manually translated into German against the same two collections (English and German). The test results indicate that no significant loss in performance results from the process of query translation (48).

A sample German query processed through the German thesaurus is shown in Table 3. A com-

TABLE 3

Thesaurus analysis for German query Q 13 B: *"Inwieweit werden Computersysteme sur Forschung auf dem Gebiet der schönen Literatur verwendet? Hat sich maschinelle Sprachenanalyse als hilfreich erwiesen, um z. B. die vermutliche Autorenschaft bei anonymen Werken zu bestimmen oder um Konkordanzen zusammenzustellen?"*

CONCEPT NOS.	WEIGHT	SAMPLE TERMS IN THESAURUS CATEGORY
19†	12	Computer, Datenverarbeitung
3†	12	Automatisch, Kybernetik
21	4	Artikel, Presse, Zeitschrift
33†	6	Analyse, Sprachenanalyse
45	4	Herausgabe, Publikation
64	4	Buch, Heft, Werk
65†	12	Autor, Verfasser
68	12	Literatur
147†	6	Linguistik, Sprache
207†	12	Arbeitsgebiet, Fach
267†	12	Konkordanz, KWIC
‡		schönen, hilfreich, vermutlich, anonymen, zusammenzustellen

*For translation, see Table 2. †Common concepts with English query. ‡Query terms not found in thesaurus.

parison with Table 2 shows that a large number of "English" concepts are also present in the German analysis, and this accounts for the fact that the thesaurus translation is successful. The foreign language problem appears not to present a major roadblock to development of an automatic document processing system.

A large number of automatic text analysis and indexing experiments have been examined. All the available evidence indicates that the presently known text analysis procedures are at least as effective as more conventional manual indexing methods. Furthermore, a simple indexing process based on the assignment of weighted terms to documents and search requests produces better retrieval results than a more sophisticated content analysis based on syntactic analysis or hierarchical term expansion. Such a simple automatic indexing procedure is easily implemented on present-day computers, and there are no obvious technical reasons why manual document analysis methods should not be replaced by automatic ones.

While automatic document analyses appear, therefore, to be at least as efficient as presently used manual methods, it is unfortunately the case that all known indexing procedures—whether manual or automatic—produce relatively mediocre results. One of the most fruitful ways of upgrading retrieval performance consists in using multiple searches based on user feedback information furnished during the search process. Interactive search methods should then lead to a retrieval effectiveness approaching a recall and precision of about 0.70 instead of the present 0.50 to 0.60. Some tentative extrapolations appear to indicate that an increased sophistication in indexing and search methodology may eventually lead to "optimal" systems for which the average recall and precision values would approach 0.80 (*42, 49*).

No obvious advances leading to additional large-scale improvements in retrieval effectiveness are likely to be made soon. For this reason, the known automatic document analysis and search procedures described in this article may well become the standard tools in most mechanized information systems of the future.

FOOTNOTES

1. Y. Bar Hillel, in *Digitale Informations-wandler,* W. Hoffman, Ed. (Vieweg, Brunswick, Germany, 1962).

2. H. P. Luhn, *IBM J. Res. Develop.* 1, No. 4 (1957).

3. ——, "Potentialities of Auto-Encoding of Scientific Literature," *IBM Res. Cent. Rep. No. RC-101* (1959).

4. J. O'Connor, *J. Ass. Comput. Mach.* 11, 437 (1964); M. E. Stevens, "Automatic Indexing: A State of the Art Report," *U.S. Nat. Bur. Stand. Monogr. 91* (1965); ——, V. E. Giuliano, L. B. Heilprin, Eds., "Statistical Association Methods for Mechanized Documentation," *U.S. Nat. Bur. Stand. Monogr. 269* (1965).

5. C. Montgomery and D. R. Swanson, *Amer. Doc.* 13, 359 (1962).

6. M. J. Ruhl, *Amer. Doc.* 15. 136 (1964).

7. D. H. Kraft, *Amer. Doc.* 15, 48 (1964).

8. J. O'Connor, *Amer. Doc.* 15, 96 (1964).

9. H. Fangmeyer and G. Lustig, "The Euratom automatic indexing project," paper presented before IFIP [International Federation for Information Processing] Congress 68, Edinburgh (1968).

10. F. J. Damerau, "An Experiment in Automatic Indexing," *IBM. Res. Cent. Rep. No. RC-894* (1963).

11. M. E. Stevens and G. H. Urban, in *Proceedings, Spring Joint Computer Conference* (Spartan, Washington, D.C., 1964), pp. 563–575; T. N. Shaw and H. Rothman, *J. Doc.* 24, No. 3 (1968).

12. P. E. Jones, V. E. Giuliano, R. M. Curtice, "Papers on Automatic Language Processing—Development of String Indexing Techniques," *Arthur D. Little (Cambridge, Mass.) Rep. ESD-TR-67-202* (1967), vol. 3.

13. M. M. Kessler, *Amer. Doc.* 16, 223 (1965).

14. R. M. Needham, *Mech. Transl.* 8, Nos. 3 and 4 (June-Oct. 1965); L. B. Doyle, *J. Ass. Comput. Mach.* 12, No. 4 (1965); H. Borko and M. D. Bernick, *J. Ass. Comput. Mach.* 10, No. 2 (1963).

15. M. E. Maron, *J. Ass. Comput. Mach.* 8, 404 (1961).

16. J. O'Connor, *J. Ass. Comput. Mach.* 12, 490 (1965).

17. F. W. Lancaster, "Evaluation of the Operating Efficiency of Medlars," *Nat. Libr. Med. Final Rep.* (1968).

18. These figures imply that an average search processed by Medlars manages to retrieve almost 60 percent of what is wanted, while only half the retrieved items are not relevant; in view of the large document file being processed—over 600,000 items—this is a remarkable achievement.

19. P. Atherton, D. W. King, R. R. Freeman, "Evaluation of the Retrieval of Nuclear Science Document References Using UDC as the Indexing Language for a Computer Based System," *Amer. Inst. Phys. Rep. AIP-UDC 8* (1968); F. H. Barker and D. C. Veal, "The Evaluation of a Current Awareness Service for Chemists," *Chem. Soc. Res. Unit Inform. Dissemination Retrieval Rep.* (1968); C. D. Gull, in *Coordinate Indexing,* M. Taube *et al.,* Eds. (Documentation, Inc., Washington, D.C., 1963); L. B. Heilprin and S. S. Crutchfield, in *Proceedings, 1964 Annual Meeting of ADI [American Documentation Institute]* (Spartan, Washington, D.C., 1964); M. R. Hyslop, *ibid.*; W. F. Johanningsmeier and F. W. Lancaster. "Project SHARP Information Storage and Retrieval System: Evaluation of Indexing Procedures and Retrieval Effectiveness," *U.S. Bur. Ships Rep. NAVSHIPS 250-210-3* (1964); D. W. King, *J. Chem. Doc.* 5, 96 (1965); D. B. McCarn and C. R. Stein, in *Electronic Handling of Information: Testing and Evaluation,* A. Kent *et al.,* Eds. (Thompson, Washington, D.C., 1967), pp. 110-122; E. Miller, D. Ballard, J. Kingston, M. Taube, in *Proceedings. International*

Conference on Scientific Information (National Academy of Sciences–National Research Council, Washington, D.C., 1959), vol. 1, pp. 671-685; B. A. Montague, *Amer. Doc.* **16**, 201 (1965); National Academy of Sciences Ad-Hoc Committee of the Office of Documentation, "The Metallurgical Searching Service of the American Society of Metals–Western Reserve University: An Evaluation," *Nat. Acad. Sci. Nat. Res. Counc. Publ. 1148* (1964); J. A. Schuller, *Aslib Proc.* **12**, 372 (1960); J. Tague, *Effectiveness of a Pilot Information Service for Educational Research Materials* (Center for Documentation and Communication Research, Western Reserve University, Cleveland, 1963).

20. D. R. Swanson, *Science* **132**, 1099 (1960).

21. ____, in *Proceedings IFIP [International Federation for Information Processing] Congress 62,* C. Popplewell, Ed. (North Holland, Amsterdam, 1963), pp. 288–293.

22. E. M. Fels, *Amer. Doc.* **14**, No. 1 (1963).

23. B. Altmann, *Amer. Doc.* **18**, No. 1 (1967).

24. J. S. Melton, "Automatic Processing of Metallurgical Abstracts for the Purpose of Information Retrieval," *Center for Communication and Documentation Research, Case Western Reserve University, Cleveland, Final Rep. NSF-4* (1967).

25. S. F. Dennis, in *Information Retrieval–a critical view.* G. Schechter, ed. Thompson, Washington, D.C., 1967.

26. V. E. Giuliano and P. E. Jones, "Study and Test of a Methodology for Laboratory Evaluation of Message Retrieval Systems," *Arthur D. Little [Cambridge, Mass.] Rep. ESD-TR-66-405* (1966).

27. K. Sparck Jones and D. M. Jackson, "The Use of Automatically Obtained Keyword Classifications for Information Retrieval," *Cambridge [England] Language Research Unit Final Rep. ML 211* (1969).

28. C. W. Cleverdon, in *Proceedings, International Conference on Scientific Information* (National Academy of Sciences–National Research Council, Washington, D.C., 1959), vol. 1, pp. 687–698; ____, "Testing and Analysis of an Investigation into the Comparative Efficiency of Indexing Systems," *Cranfield (England) Res. Proj. Rep.* (1962).

29. A document exhibiting *n* terms in common with a given query is said to be retrieved at coordination level *n*.

30. G. Salton, in *Proceedings, FID Congress 1965* (Spartan, Washington, D.C., 1966).

31. C. W. Cleverdon and E. M. Keen, "Factors Determining the Performance of Indexing Systems," *Aslib Cranfield (England) Res. Proj. Rep.* (1966), vols. 1 and 2.

32. C. W. Cleverdon, *Aslib Proc.* **19**, No. 6 (1967).

33. G. Salton, *Automatic Information Organization and Retrieval* (McGraw-Hill, New York, 1968).

34. ____ and M. E. Lesk, *Commun. Ass. Comput. Mach.* **8**, No. 6 (1965); G. Salton, *IEEE (Inst. Elec. Electron, Eng.) Spectrum* **2**, No. 8 (1965).

35. H. E. Stiles, paper presented at the 3rd Institute on Information Storage and Retrieval, American University, Washington, D.C., 1961.

36. P. B. Baxendale, *IBM J. Res. Develop.* **4**, No. 2 (1958); D. J. Hillman and A. J. Kasarda, in *Proceedings AFIPS Spring Joint Computer Conference* (AFIPS Press, Montvale, N.J., 1969).

37. G. Salton, in *Proceedings IFIP [International Federation for Information Processing] Congress 68* (North-Holland, Amsterdam, 1969).

38. In the SMART system the term weights are based on the frequency of occurrence of each term in a document, as well as on individual term characteristics derived from the word stem or from thesaurus dictionaries.

39. G. Salton, *Amer. Doc.* **16**, 209 (1965); ____ *et al.,* "Information Storage and Retrieval," *Dep. Computer Sci. Cornell Univ. Rep. Nos. ISR-11, ISR-12, ISR-13, ISR-14, and ISR-16 to Nat. Sci. Found.* (1966–1969).

40. G. Salton and M. E. Lesk, *J. Ass. Comput. Mach.* **15**, 8 (1968).

41. C. A. Cuadra and R. V. Katter, *J. Doc.* **23**, No. 4 (1967); A. M. Rees and D. G. Schultz, "A Field Experimental Approach to the Study of Relevance Assessments in Relation to Document Searching," *Cent. Doc. Commun. Res. Case Western Reserve Univ. Final Rep. to Nat. Sci. Found.* (1967).

42. M. E. Lesk and G. Salton, *Inform. Storage Retrieval* **4**, No. 4 (1968).

43. T. Saracevic, "The Effect of Question Analysis and Searching Strategy in Performance of Retrieval Systems: Selected Results from an Experimental Study," *Comp. Syst. Lab. Rep. No. CSL:TR:5, Cent. Doc. Commun. Res. Case Western Reserve Univ. Cleveland* (1968).

44. G. Salton, *Amer. Doc.* **20**, No. 1 (1969).

45. M. E. Lesk and G. Salton, in *Proceedings AFIPS Spring Joint Computer Conference* (AFIPS Press, Montvale, N.J., 1969).

46. E. Ide, "Relevance Feedback in an Automatic Document Retrieval System," *Dep. Computer Sci. Cornell Univ. Rep. No. ISR-15 to Nat. Sci. Found.* (1969).

47. G. Salton, in *Mechanized Information Storage, Retrieval and Dissemination,* K. Samuelson, Ed. (North-Holland, Amsterdam, 1968), pp. 73–107.

48. ____, "Automatic processing of foreign language documents," *J. ASIS [Amer. Soc. Inf. Sci.],* in press.

49. C. W. Cleverdon, "The Methodology of Evaluation of Operational Information Retrieval Systems based on the Test of Medlars," *Cranfield (England) Res. Proj. Rep.* (1968).

50. This study was supported in part by the National Science Foundation under grant GN-750.

The Testing of Index Language Devices

by Cyril W. Cleverdon and J. Mills

INTRODUCTION

The evaluation of information retrieval systems has recently become an important matter. In the past, however, most reports or proposals on this type of work appear largely to have ignored the efficiency of operation of the central core of an IR system, namely those operations concerned in the compilation and use of the index. The only aspects to receive consideration are the physical form of the index and the design of thesauri or classifications. The former activity has been slanted towards the use of computers and has tended to assume that this type of equipment will, *ipso facto,* give an improved performance but has made no attempt to justify cost factors which may be one hundred times that of conventional techniques. Work on thesauri and classifications, where it has been practical in nature, appears to consist of compiling lists of terms which go out of favour as quickly as any list of subject headings in the past; the more popular theoretical approach is the setting up of models or the use of increasingly abstruse and complex algebras. From the results and conclusions of the experimental work at Cranfield, it would seem that many of these investigations are comparatively trivial.

In this paper we set out the fundamental operations involved in compiling and using an index, show how the various factors can influence the operating efficiency, and consider the methods to be used in the present Aslib Cranfield investigation.

DEFINITIONS

As the analysis of indexing has become more detailed, there has been an increasing requirement for the more precise definition of the various operations. We have endeavoured to use terms in their conventional meanings wherever possible, but it has frequently been necessary to modify, or to find new terms.

An *information retrieval system* is the complete organization for obtaining, storing and making available information. This could be a definition of a conventional library, but an IR system would be expected to exploit the information in a positive manner and to have extra facilities such as people on the staff capable of evaluating information before it is passed to the inquirer. It would be expected to have a *subject index* to the items in the store, the index being the physical equipment which permits of the retrieval of references in the searches. The index may be in the form of a card catalogue, a printed list, a set of peek-a-boo cards, a computer, or any other convenient equipment. The arrangement within the index will depend upon the *index language** and this may be a straightforward alphabetical arrangement of terms, or a classified arrangement of terms or any variation of these methods. The index language may be used in a *pre-co-ordinate* or *post-co-ordinate* manner. The former implies that the co-ordination of separate concepts is done at the time of indexing and the entries in the subject index will show this co-ordination. The latter implies that the co-ordination of concepts is done at the time of searching, so the entries in the subject index will refer only to single elements.

The *vocabulary* of the index language is the complete collection of sought terms in the natural language, including all necessary synonyms, that are used in the set of documents and are therefore required for entry points to the index language. An *index term,* on the other hand, is an actual term or heading used in the index language, and may be a word or words, as with alphabetical subject indexes, unitermindexes or zatocoding, or may be notational elements, such as a group of numbers in the Universal Decimal Classification, or may be nonmeaningful groups of letters, as in the Western Reserve University Metallurgical Index.

Concept indexing is the intellectual process of deciding which are the concepts in a particular document that are of sufficient importance to be included in the subject index. Conventionally, this involves a 'Yes' or 'No' assessment, for a concept either is, or is not, considered worthy of inclusion in the subject index. It is possible for the indexer to indicate the relative importance of different concepts in a document by *weighted indexing,*

SOURCE: Reprinted from *Aslib Proceedings,* 15: 106-130 (April, 1963), by permission of the publisher.

which involves the assignment to each concept of a weighting number.

The *exhaustivity* of the concept indexing is a comparative term; at a high level it implies that an entry is made for every possible concept in a document. At a low level it implies that a selection has been made and a smaller number of concepts have been used. *Specificity* is also a comparative term. A concept can be translated into an indexing language in such a way that the index term is co-extensive with a concept. This is a high level of specificity and implies that the index term covers the concept but nothing else besides the concept. Alternatively, the translation can be to a less specific (often called 'broader') index term which includes the concept being indexed as well as other concepts.

Syntactic indexing implies the use of headings which display the relationship between the various elements, as distinct from those which merely show the existence of several attributes relevant to the subject indexed.

A *search programme* is the formalization of the search request and it can show the same characteristics as outlined above for indexing, i.e. it entails a statement of the concepts, which can be at varying levels of exhaustivity, and can be translated into indexing terms of varying specificity.

The *operating efficiency* of an index language will depend upon its performance as regards recall and relevance. *Recall ratio* equals $\dfrac{100R}{C}$, where C equals the total number of documents in the collection which have an agreed standard of relevance to a given question, while R equals the number of those relevant documents retrieved in a single search. On the other hand, *relevance ratio* equals $\dfrac{100R}{L}$, where L equals the total number of documents retrieved in a single search. Operating efficiency is affected by the exhaustivity and specificity of the indexing, as well as the search programme, and by varying any of these factors, one will obtain a performance curve which plots recall ratio against relevance ratio. *Economic efficiency* deals with the performance of the complete index.

A *set of documents* is any collection of documents which are, or will be, used as the basis of a single subject index. The set can be large or small, restricted to an organization's research papers, or be a heterogeneous collection of journal articles, research reports, patents, etc., in many different languages, but homogeneous in that they will be used as the raw material of a single index. A *set of questions* is a collection of questions to be put to a single subject index, either at present, or at any time in the future when the index is still intended to be operating.

THE PREPARATION OF AN INDEX

Assuming there is agreement concerning the set of documents to be indexed, the following operations have to be carried out in compiling and using an index:

1. Assess the subject matter of each document in relation to the requirements of the users, and decide which subjects should be included in the index. This is concept indexing, and is at present, and for the foreseeable future, an intellectual operation. With a pre-co-ordinate index, it is also necessary to decide on the appropriate combinations of concepts and, if the index language is to show relationships, the syntax.
2. Translate the subject concepts into the index language. This is a clerical task, except in those cases where a new term has to be added to the vocabulary of the index language.
3. Place the indexing decisions into the index, which may involve preparing and filing catalogue cards, punching holes in a card or cards, or making marks on tape. This again is a clerical process.
4. Make a concept analysis of the question and decide on the priority of alternative search programmes. As with concept indexing, this is an intellectual process.
5. Translate the search concepts into the index language, a purely clerical task.
6. Operate the physical retrieval mechanism of the index.

The Aslib Cranfield Project has been primarily concerned with operations 1, 2, 4 and 5, and it has only been due to the necessity of having the index in the physical form that we have been involved with 3 and 6. It is certain that these two latter points play no part in deciding on the operating efficiency, except in so far as that one technique might be more, or less, prone to clerical errors than another. They can, however, significantly affect the economic efficiency of an index.

Involved in these operations is the variable of the index language. Whichever type of index language is used, it is certain that all the stages 1 to 6 have to be carried out. More important is it to note that the only two operations which have a true intellectual content are completely divorced from any consideration of the index language.* The basic concept analysis of the document and the basic concept analysis of the question, with the auxiliary decision of which concepts should be included in the index or the search programme, will be the same irrespective of which index language is used. It is probably the case that many indexers tend to think in the terms of the index language and their concept indexing decisions may be thereby influenced, but fundamentally it is true that concept indexing is a separate process which should not be affected by the index language.

INDEX LANGUAGES

The common basic requirement of all index languages is a complete vocabulary of all the sought terms, including all necessary synonyms, that are used in the indexing of a set of documents. This may be likened to an uncontrolled set of uniterms, and must be the basic structure for all index languages; and, whatever ultimate form an index language may take, it can only operate at maximum efficiency by having such a vocabulary. To this basic structure can be added a number of devices which are intended to improve the recall ratio or the relevance ratio. These devices (see Vickery[1]) can be listed as follows:

A. *Devices which, when introduced into an uncontrolled vocabulary of simple terms, tend to broaden the class definition and so increase recall*

1. Confounding of true synonyms.
2. Confounding of near synonyms; usually terms in the same hierarchy.
3. Confounding of different word forms; usually terms from different categories.
4. Fixed vocabulary; usually takes the form of generic terms, but may use 'metonymy' for example, representing a number of attributes by the thing possessing them.
5. Generic terms.
6. Drawing terms from categories and, within these, facets; this controls the generic level of terms, and to a certain degree controls synonyms.
7. Representing terms by analytical definitions (semantic factors), in which inter-relations are conveyed by relational affixes or modulants; the generic level will usually be more specific than when control is by categories.

8. Hierarchical linkage of generic and specific terms, and, possibly, of co-ordinate terms.
9. Multiple hierarchical linkage, i.e. linking each term to a number of different generic heads. It should be noted that devices 8 and 9 are not usually (as the others are) methods of class definition determing the structure or constituents of individual subject descriptions; they are ancillary devices (manifested as systematic sequence, or classified arrangement, as a thesaurus, as a network of *see also* references, etc.) indicating the existence of classes wider than these individual descriptions.
10. Bibliographical coupling, and citation indexes; these, also, are ancillary devices which indicate the existence of wider classes, the latter reflecting the use made of the documents and a probability of relevance arising from this.

B. *Devices which tend to narrow the class definition and so increase relevance*

11. Correlation of terms: although implicit in some form in all practical indexing, this device is not inevitable; i.e. the use of a single term to define a class may retrieve quickly and economically, if the term is sufficiently rare in the context of the system.
12. Weighting, i.e. attempts to express the particular relevance of each concept used in indexing a document to the whole document. It may take two forms:
   i. An attempt to assess subjectively the relative 'information content' of each term within the context of the system;
   ii. An objective measure, based on statistical counting of the word frequencies, etc.
13. Indicating connections between terms (interlocking):
   a. Without explicit expression of particular relations (interfixing); this may take at least three forms:
      i. Partitioning of the document; e.g. if the same document deals with the Conductivity of titanium and the Hardness of copper at a particular temperature, partitioning makes it clear that the document has at least two separate 'themes'.
      ii. Interfixing within a theme (or 'information item'); e.g. Lead (1) Coating (1) Copper (2) Pipes (2) makes it clear that the subject is the Lead coating of copper pipes and not the Copper coating of lead pipes.
      iii. If terms are recorded physically in a lin-

ear sequence, a citation order (a regulated sequence in which terms from different categories are cited), will convey relations.

b. With explicit expression of particular relations; this is necessary in cases where simple interfixing cannot cope with the possible ambiguities; e.g. to distinguish which particle is the projectile, which the target, and which the product, in a report in nuclear physics. Two forms are usually recognized:

   i. Role indicators: these are usually limited in number and express the basic or most common relations found in the subject field concerned; e.g. Product, Starting material.

   ii. Relational terms: these are more freely developed, the name of a relation being used in the same way as any other term. It may, however, be cited only in the framework of a limited number of fundamental relations, as in Farradane's system.

A third form sometimes to be found in conjunction with a, iii above is that of distinctive facet indicators which convey clearly the exact category to which the next term belongs.

Any operating index language is an amalgam of some of these devices; for example a modern faceted classification uses hierarchical linkage within its facets, combines (correlates) terms from different categories (according to a strict citation order so as to maximize the mutual exclusiveness of its classes), provides a degree of multiple hierarchical linkage through its relative alphabetical index, controls synonyms, may control near synonyms, and may confound word forms to a mild degree.

A machine-orientated retrieval system may use correlation as its basic device, but supplement this with confounding of synonyms, confounding of near synonyms, of word forms, show hierarchical and multiple hierarchical linkage to some degree (often via a thesaurus), and use links and roles.

A simple, manual Uniterm system will use correlation as its basic device, but may add to this the confounding of true synonyms, of near synonyms and (possibly) of word forms, a modest degree of hierarchical linkage, and roles.

PERFORMANCE MEASUREMENT

The technique evolved in the Aslib Cranfield tests for the measurement of operating efficiency depends on two factors—the percentage of relevant documents retrieved as against the total of relevant documents in the collection (recall ratio), and the percentage of relevant documents among those actually retrieved (relevance ratio). The original Aslib Cranfield project established the former by conducting searches for questions which had been based on documents known to be in the collection, and the result of this showed that, on an average, about 80 per cent of the source documents were being retrieved. It could be said that this figure did not have particular significance, since it is obviously possible to obtain 100 per cent recall by looking at every document in the collection. Quite apart from going to this extreme, it would have been possible to improve the figure of 80 per cent by 'broadening' the search programme or, as we should say, by making the search programme less specific and/or less exhaustive. The only control on this figure of 80 per cent was that a limit was put on the level of exhaustivity of the search programme. (See Cleverdon,[2] page 14), but this was rather crude, and (as discussed in chapter 6 of the same reference), an attempt was made to assess the relevance ratio. This proved to be exceedingly difficult, but it was obvious that it was an essential part of performance measurement, and, in the test of the WRU metallurgical literature[3] the work was done more thoroughly, as is discussed later in this report. The result of a complete analysis of recall and relevance means that it is possible to plot a series of points, depending, for instance, on the search programme, and produce a performance curve as shown in Fig. 1a.

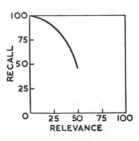

FIGURE 1a

ASSUMPTION FOR FUTURE WORK

A basic premise of the following arguments is that, for a given set of documents and a given set of questions, there will be a maximum retrieval performance; whatever type of index language is used, the performance curves will not be materially altered, and, in fact, the only reason for any major variation from this curve will be inadequacies of the intellectual performance in decisions concerning subject concepts, either in indexing or in searching. For sets of documents in different subject fields, the resulting performance curves would probably differ, and if the same set of documents were used in two separate situations, since there could be two different sets of questions, this in turn could result in different performance figures. Tests at Cranfield have been concerned mainly with the subject fields of science, engineering, and metallurgy, and with these types of document sets and question sets, it appears that the maximum retrieval performance would be as in Fig. 1a. If the subject matter of the collection were organic chemistry, the resulting performance curve might be as Fig. 1b; for sociology it might be as Fig. 1c.

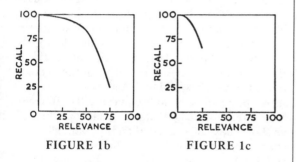

FIGURE 1b   FIGURE 1c

It has to be assumed in this discussion that we are considering idealized conditions, and do not have to take into account losses due to human error. This has been investigated in the first project, and the general allowance to be made for this is known or, alternatively, can easily be ascertained in any given situation, by using the Cranfield test procedure. We have postulated that there is a fixed maximum performance curve for any given set of documents and questions, and have suggested that, with the type of document and question sets tested at Cranfield, this might range from 100 per cent recall at less than 1 per cent relevance to 50 per cent recall at 30 per cent relevance. The important problem to investigate is how an index can be operated most efficiently at any particular point or within any particular range. As an example, it might be a requirement of an index that it should have a recall level of not less than 95 per cent. Alternatively, the requirement may be that the index should normally operate at a level of 25 per cent relevance ratio, but that it should, when required, be capable of giving a recall figure of 90 per cent.

In such an investigation, there are a number of factors to be considered, and of major importance is the concept indexing. Some groups working in this area seem to place more emphasis on search analysis, in finding how variations in search programmes will affect the efficiency, but this seems to be rather a cart-before-the-horse approach. It is at the stage of concept indexing that the future potential performance of the resulting indexes is determined; if a concept is not included, it will not be possible to recall the particular document by that concept, and vice versa. Concept indexing is, it must be emphasized, an intellectual process that cannot be avoided. Current literature sometimes implies that keyword-in-context title indexing, for instance, is automatic indexing. It is automatic in its preparation of the physical index, but the intellectual stage of concept indexing is still there; the only difference is that in this case the concept indexer is the person who wrote the title.

It is the decisions of concept indexing which result in the level of exhaustivity achieved. The extremes of exhaustivity range from where the whole text is included to where only a single concept is indexed for each document. The effect of high or low exhaustivity on the basic performance curve can be readily shown. 100 per cent recall can always be obtained by doing no indexing but by having available for searching the text of every document in the collection. On the other hand, if only a single concept from each document is included in an index, then it is apparent that there will be a considerable drop in recall. We can, therefore, say that, if all other factors are held constant, the effect of lowering the level of exhaustivity will be to drop the recall figure. This will in turn result in an improved relevance figure, and briefly it can be said that

a high level of exhaustivity of indexing results in high recall and low relevance;

a low level of exhaustivity of indexing results in low recall and high relevance.

Little work has been done on the effect of exhaustivity of indexing, and practice varies widely (see chapter 7 of reference 4) without the appearance of any positive reasoning behind the decisions. Inevitably a high level of exhaustive indexing results in higher input costs, and this could be a determining factor with certain physical forms of index. In the Western Reserve University test an attempt was made to ascertain the effect of varying the exhaustivity with the facet index that was prepared at Cranfield. In this index the average number of entries originally included for each document was 12½, and the effect of reducing this by stages to an average of three entries per document was investigated. Table 1 shows the effect that this had on recall and relevance of the documents.

The level of specificity which can be given to the indexing is obviously very different in each of these three index languages; the result is that in a search where the requirements are for A_1, B_1, C_1, although index language III will retrieve all the relevant documents that are retrieved by index

TABLE 1

Recall and Relevance Ratio in Facet Catalogue of WRU Test at Varying Index Entries

NO. OF ENTRIES	NO. OF DOCUMENTS RETRIEVED	RELEVANCE 2		RELEVANCE 2 AND 3	
		RECALL RATIO %	RELEVANCE RATIO %	RECALL RATIO %	RELEVANCE RATIO %
12½	891	83	16.3	64.1	34.6
8	824	80.6	17.1	60.6	35.5
5	643	73.1	19.9	50.7	38
3	491	64.6	23	42.1	41.3

This effect will operate irrespective of which index language is used, and, in passing, it should be noted that the same situation prevails in reverse with the decisions concerning concepts to be used in the search programme. However, before going into the matter of search programmes, we will consider the translation of the concept indexing into the index language.

The aspect of the input stage which is concerned with index languages is specificity, and we suggest that, in so far as their operating performance is concerned, a fundamental difference—and probably the most important difference—between index languages is their hospitality for specificity; this we now consider in its simpler form and show its direct relationship to the index language. It is assumed that an index language includes, as a minimum, all the categories of the subject field, whether given in detail or not, of the documents being indexed.

The first stage, i.e. concept indexing, with its decision concerning the level of exhaustivity of indexing, is assumed to have been completed for a given document and we have concepts A_1, B_1, C_1, D_1, E_1 and F_1. The next stage is translating these into the index language. Assume three hypothetical index languages, I, II, and III containing respectively, 10,000, 1,000 and 100 index terms. In index language I, there is a straight translation of the concepts into $A_1(I), B_1(I), C_1(I), D_1(I), E_1(I),$ $F_1(I)$. Index language II translates into A(II), B(II), C(II), D(II), E(II), F(II) (where A is the containing head for A_1, A_2, A_3 and B the containing head for B_1, B_2, etc.). Descriptor language III translates into ABC(III) and DEF(III) (where ABC is the containing head for A, B, C, A_1, A_2, etc.).

language I, it will also bring out, for example, documents coded A_2, B_2, C_2, resulting in a larger number of irrelevant documents and therefore a lower relevance ratio. In reverse, though the relevance ratio of a search in index language I will be relatively high, it is likely to miss some of the relevant references which would be found by the same search programme by index language III. It might, therefore, be the case that the normal operating level of index languages I, II and III, with all other conditions fixed, would be as shown by points 1, 2 and 3 in Fig. 2. Again, one notes that a lowering

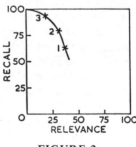

FIGURE 2

of relevance results in higher recall, and of specificity it can be said that

> a high level of specificity in the index language results in high relevance and low recall;
>
> a low level of specificity in the index language results in low relevance and high recall.

Considering again the basic performance curve (Fig. 3), we have shown that the maximum recall figure which can be obtained is limited by the level

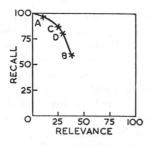

FIGURE 3

of exhaustive indexing; the maximum relevance figure is limited by the specificity possible in the index language. Therefore, a system which combines a high level of exhaustive indexing with the use of a highly specific index language would have the potentiality, dependent upon the search programme, of operating over the wide range of the curve between points A and B. However, a system which combines a low level of exhaustivity and a less specific index language might not be able to operate beyond the narrower limits shown by points C and D, whatever type of search programme was used. However, if this limited range gives a satisfactory performance figure, then it will be obviously more economical to operate.

It is now possible to consider the effects of exhaustivity and specificity in the search programme. Assume that the concept programme of a question requires that a search should be made for A_1, B_1, C_1 and D_1. If it is decided to 'broaden' the search, then this can be done in two ways. On the one hand, it is possible to drop one of the concepts, so that the search is now for A_1, B_1 and C_1. This we would describe as making the search less exhaustive. Alternatively, it is possible to make the search less specific, by substituting A for A_1 or B for B_1 (where A is taken to be an inclusive term covering A_1, A_2, A_3, etc.). It is obvious that by broadening the search in either of these ways, the recall ratio will be improved. In particular, however, we should consider the matter of specificity in indexing and specificity in the search programme. To return to the index languages considered earlier, if one has coded according to index language III, then it is useless to attempt a programme that has a high level of specificity. In fact, it is impossible to do this, since the index language does not include index terms of the required specificity. However, with index language I, it is possible to have a highly specific search programme, which would give a high relevance ratio but a low recall ratio (i.e. point 1 in Fig. 2). If it

is desired to improve the recall ratio, then the search programme can be made less specific, until it reaches a level of specificity of the term codes of index language III. By this time it can be assumed that the recall ratio will have risen to the same level as with index language III (i.e. point 3 in Fig. 2). It is, therefore, shown that, as far as operating efficiency is concerned, there will be for every index language—depending upon its hospitality for specific indexing—a maximum relevance ratio which cannot be exceeded. It will, however, always be possible (by varying the search programme) to improve the recall ratio along the fixed performance curve up to its maximum level, this being dependent on the exhaustivity of the indexing.

AIDS TO EFFICIENCY

If, as is not wholly unreasonable, we consider as a median in the range of indexing languages, one which consists of nothing except an uncontrolled vocabulary of sought terms, then many of the indexing devices mentioned in an earlier section of this paper can be seen to be working in opposing directions. Any device which reduces the number of index terms is working towards improved recall, with the inevitable result that there will be a fall in relevance. Other devices, such as role indicators, are, in effect, increasing the number of index terms and are thereby improving relevance but decreasing recall. These devices have been discussed in an earlier section and the part they will play in the further work will be considered later, but we would now consider the effect of one type of device which is found in many operating index languages.

In the introduction, we said that much of the present theoretical work being done on index languages was trivial. This comment is based on what appear to be logical deductions from the experimental work undertaken at Cranfield. The theoretical work which we have in mind is all concerned with what might be described as the grouping of the terms in the index language. This work is proceeding in many directions; facet classification, clumps, logical associations, word pairs, etc. To describe all this work as trivial shows that we have moved away from a main stream of development in information retrieval, and it may appear difficult to justify the statement. We would first make the point that we say that this work is trivial and do not say that it is useless. This could be translated into more precise figures by suggesting the following. Assume an imperfect index language, covering the field of engineering and metallurgy, which consisted only of an alphabetical list of index terms, and with a normal operating efficiency of 75 per cent recall and 20 per cent relevance. If one gave to this index language the additional device of a grouping of the terms, then we suggest that the recall ratio of 75 per cent might be achieved with a relevance of 21 per cent or, alternatively, that with a relevance of 20 per cent one might have a recall ratio of 78 per cent.

The purpose of any grouping of terms is to lead the searcher to related terms which might have been used by the indexer for relevant information. It is logical to assume that this is a worthy objective and it has been a common assumption that it is also a vitally important objective. Why is it, in fact, of such little importance? The reason is because it is incorrect to assume that the comparison is between an index language without a grouping of terms and an index language with a grouping of terms. The comparison is, in actual fact, between an index language with a pre-arranged grouping of terms and an index language with a grouping of terms that is special and personal each time it is used. In other words, a searcher, whether a librarian or a subject specialist, is capable, to a greater extent than has been generally appreciated, of making a grouping of related terms at the time of the search and in relation to the particular subject of the search. The problem is that a single classification schedule, a single set of cross-references, a single set of thesauri-type headings, or a single set of any other form of grouping, however logically or abstrusely derived, is most unlikely to be of equal value to all the different types of user of an information retrieval system. With a metallurgist, a chemist, a mineralogist, a mining engineer or a design engineer, a single term might well have five different sets of associations, and the individual concerned will be able to decide for himself, at the time of the search, the set of related terms that would be an improvement on a set of pre-arranged groupings. It would, therefore, appear logical that the best method would be to devise a separate set of groupings for each type of user, so as to maximize the chances of improving recall with a minimum drop in relevance. It should be noted that such groupings can be devised independently of the index language, and can therefore be used with any index language.

It is, however, necessary to qualify the above comments, and also to return to the point, raised earlier, concerning the presumed difference in the shape of the performance curve for subject indexes in different subject fields. If we consider pure data retrieval, of the type where it is required to know, for instance, the names of all persons in an organization who joined more than ten years ago, who are graduates and whose salary is less than £1,800 a year, it might be expected that all the relevant information and only relevant information would be retrieved. As one passes from the field of data retrieval to the field of information retrieval, the terminology becomes less precise in its meaning, there is an increasing number of errors due to confusion and the performance of the subject index becomes progressively worse. We have suggested that chemistry, being more precise in its terminology, would permit the compilation of a subject index having an improved performance curve in comparison with an index in the field of engineering and metallurgy of the type tested at Cranfield. On the other hand, many areas in the social sciences have a vague terminology. For example, in the opening pages of this paper, it was considered necessary to give the definitions of many terms that have been used, and it would take little effort to find examples of the same term being used with other meanings, or other terms being used for the same meaning. In such circumstances, it is hardly surprising that retrieval performance is hampered, and it is reasonable to suggest that there would be an increased requirement for a grouping of the index terms. Workers in the field of engineering and metallurgy appear to be sufficiently well acquainted with the terminology of the subject field to make their own grouping of terms, with the result that an index language which lacks a pre-arranged grouping of terms is only marginally inferior to an index language which has such a grouping of terms. We can, therefore, assume that any subject field that has a more precise terminology than engineering will have even less need for a grouping of the index terms.

THE FUTURE WORK OF THE CRANFIELD PROJECT

It might be said of Cranfield I that its main endeavour was that it tried to measure the operating efficiency of complete indexing languages in a simulated real life situation, and also that it used, as its major measure of performance, a relatively crude gauge of relevance based on the retrieval or non-retrieval of a single source document. Cranfield II will differ in both major respects; firstly, it will try to measure the impact on recall and relevance of particular indexing devices—the elements which go to make up a complete index language; and secondly, it will try to use decidedly more precise measures of relevance.

The devices that have been identified are listed earlier, but some further observations on them seem to be called for:

i. Their significance is that they provide different ways of defining classes, i.e. different ways of indicating relations between the concepts which are the subject of a document. Consequently, they differ in the degree to which they produce broader or narrower classes, and thereby assist or hinder specificity and exhaustivity.

ii. The function of class definition in indexing is that the assignment of a document to a particular class or classes (x, say) may allow us to ignore other classes (not-x), on the assumption that the kind of document we seek, if it is not in class x, cannot be in class not-x. Classes are established which will predictably include certain documents, and as predictably exclude others. This assumption can never be realized fully in practice, for classes in documentary classification can never be quite mutually exclusive. A documentary subject description ABCDE is never more than a statement of what the document is *mainly* about. ABCDE does not necessarily exclude FG; these may feature in it in some minor way. A report on 'Laminar boundary layer flow' will reveal, in a single casual aside, half-way through the text, that 'Three-dimensional boundary layer' is assumed. If this concept (three-dimensional) is not indexed, it does not mean that the concept really is banished from the subject content of the article. It is this awkward indeterminacy of the literature to be indexed which we seek to circumvent by exhaustive indexing.

iii. Different class definitions have different focusing or resolving power. If we take the simple correlation of keywords in the title and abstract of a document as a relatively crude device for establishing classes, then other devices, if added to these, either enlarge the scope of the classes or constrain them further. For example, to confound verbal forms, so that the class designations 'Heat,' 'Heated,' 'Heating,' 'Hot,' are extended to designate a single class covering all these different concepts, would clearly broaden the description. This would inevitably increase recall and reduce relevance—but by how much? Or, if we now introduce role indicators into our index language, so that a class designation 'Zinc' becomes several different classes according to the role played by Zinc in the particular subject description, e.g. Zinc (starting material), or Zinc (product), or Zinc (agent), then these classes are clearly narrower, and recall will now decrease and relevance increase. But again, by how much?

iv. Certain of the devices, such as generic and specific terms linked hierarchically, might appear to perform a function different from that of mere class definition. The difference between the operation of *arrangement* in an index, which is designed to display relations between ostensibly separate classes (the chief function normally associated with classification), and the operation of class definition, is often overlooked. In traditional classification, different principles of division might be applied to produce different classes, and then these classes are arranged, usually in some systematic order. But the two operations, of division to produce classes, and the arrangement of those classes, are quite distinct.

The functions of arrangement are well known. It may show clearly various connections between classes (and this function is itself a looser form of class definition); it may help the programming of searches, by suggesting other approaches; it may be economically efficient in the performance of these functions by reason of physical juxtaposition of entries or documents. Cranfield I appeared to indicate that the differences in the arrangement of classes (full classification, A/Z direct, A/Z indirect—i.e. alphabetico-classed) are only of marginal importance in retrieval. But we need to remember context here; the context for which the findings seemed to be valid was that of indexing, not the physical arrangement of documents (which rules out the entire field of shelf display); of a special field, rather than a general collection, where interconnections between classes are more difficult to display thoroughly and far more difficult for a librarian to carry around in his head; of indexing by experienced and skilled indexers, with equally intelligent searchers.

Is arrangement, then, a device to be tested here? Hierarchical linking is certainly to be tested, but how it is implemented—whether by a classified arrangement in the index itself, or by a thesaurus, or by systematic connectives in an alphabetical catalogue—is probably outside the field of our inquiry just now. But independently of the convenience of different methods of performing the function of hierarchical linkage, the extension of the field of likely search which this device implies may be regarded as a form of class definition, whereby membership of a given class carries with it an explicit or implicit indication of the existence of a wider class containing it. Much the same may be said of semantic factoring; for example, to index 'Tempering' as a kind of process, acting on a metal, making use of heat . . . is another device for extending the field of likely search, of broadening the effective class definition.

v. It might be argued that an index language is more than the sum of its parts, and that evaluation of the contribution to recall and relevance of isolated devices will not help to evaluate the complete index languages which are the practical concern of workers in information retrieval. But the evaluation of complete languages is clearly incomplete so long as we do not know which features of these languages are making them work as they do. For example, it could be argued that the good performance of the Universal Decimal Classification in Cranfield I owed much to the unusually thorough A/Z index made for it. It has already been observed that a complete language will invariably contain an assortment of different indexing devices, and the investigation should give some definite measure of the separate contributions these devices make to recall and to relevance.

METHOD OF INVESTIGATION

To obtain reliable measurements of the impact on recall and relevance of the different devices requires careful precautions for their isolation. This will be done by operating in the laboratory conditions which are provided by a set of questions and a strictly limited number of documents providing the answers to be retrieved, so that there can be a 'closed' collection, in which the relevance to each question of each document in the collection is known. The questions and documents are being assembled as follows.

The assumption is that a research paper is written as the result of an investigation which has been undertaken to provide the answer to a question or questions in the mind of its author; also,

that if an author cites references these must have something to do with the subject of the paper. In the field of high speed aerodynamics there are generally from five to ten references attached to each research paper. We are writing to four hundred or more authors of research papers (both theoretical and experimental) in this field. Each author is asked to state, as nearly as possible in the form of a search question, the basic problem which was the reason for the investigation. Also, if there were any subsidiary questions which arose in the course of the work, he is requested to enter up to three of these (see Fig. 4, sheet 1). He is then asked to indicate the relevance of the references to each question in the following scale of 1 to 5:

1. References which are a complete answer to the question. Presumably this would only apply for supplementary questions, i.e. (B), (C) or (D) since if they applied to the main question there would have been no necessity for the research to be done.
2. References of a high degree of relevance, the lack of which either would have made the research impracticable or would have resulted in a considerable amount of extra work.
3. References which were useful, either as general background to the work or as suggesting methods of tackling certain aspects of the work.
4. References of minimum interest, for example those that have been included from a historical viewpoint.
5. References of no interest.

The references will now constitute the basic indexing collection. The original papers which cited the references will be discarded, since the correlation between them and the questions they were designed to answer might be undesirably high. Ultimately, it is intended to obtain a collection of some 1,500 documents and some 400 questions, and for each question there will be some documents with a certain stated degree of relevance to them.

However, it is possible, even probable, that for each question some of the other documents in the collection (i.e. those not quoted as references by the author of the original paper) are also relevant in some degree. The only way to establish this reliably is to examine the whole collection in respect of each single question. This will be done by a number of post-graduate students working in the subject field. Any further documents which they think might be relevant to the question will be

ASLIB CRANFIELD INVESTIGATION INTO

PERFORMANCE OF INDEX LANGUAGES

Please complete and return to:

C. W. Cleverdon,
The College of Aeronautics,
Cranfield, Bletchley,
Bucks., England.

AUTHOR   J. F. Clarke

TITLE   Reaction-resisted Shock Fronts.

REFERENCE   College of Aeronautics Report No. 150, May 1961.

BASIC QUESTION

(A) Has anyone investigated the role of chemical reactions in determining shock wave structure?

(B) Papers on acoustic wave propagation in reacting gases.

(C) Have other types of 'non-viscous' compression waves been investigated analytically or observed experimentally

(D) Is there any simple, but realistic, "model" gas which can be used to expedite analysis?

FIGURE 4 (SHEET 1)

sent to the author of the original paper, who will assign relevance values to them as he did to the references in his paper.

What will emerge will be a closed system in which we have a set of documents (about 1,500) and a set of questions (about 400), and in which every document has been checked against every question. Therefore we know, for every question, exactly which documents in the collection are relevant, and to what degree. It might work out, say, that for a given question there will be two documents that are really important, four of which are useful, three which are marginal in relevance, with all the rest irrelevant.

· LIST OF REFERENCES

Ref. No.		ASSESSMENT Question			
		A	B	C	D
1.	Clarke, J.F. Flow of chemically reacting gas mixtures. College of Aeronautics Report 117.	5	1	5	3
2.	Clarke, J.F. Linearized flow of a dissociating gas. Jnl. Fluid Mech., 7, 1960, pp 577-595.	5	1	5	5
3.	Griffith, W.C. and Kenny, A. Jnl. Fluid Mech. 3, 1957, p.268.	5	5	1	5
4.	Lighthill, M.J. Survey in Mechanics, Ed. by G.K. Batchelor and R.M. Davies, Cambridge University Press, 1956.	2-3	3	1	5
5.	Lighthill, M.J. Dynamics of a dissociating gas. Jnl. Fluid Mech., 2, 1957, pp 1-32.	5	5	5	1

FIGURE 4 (SHEET 2)

Perhaps the most difficult problem in the above procedure is that of giving a measure of the relevance to a question of a particular document. It is probable that a serious element of subjectivity is likely to remain in any measure attempted. Certainly, to attempt too much refinement here is to risk deceiving ourselves; so we are attempting only the few broad distinctions listed above.

Promise of a more objective measurement of relevance may lie in the degree to which a question description matches a document description, and this is being explored. The distinction between 'relevance' and 'pertinence' drawn in some recent papers is certainly a real one. A document may match a question exactly in the matter of conceptual content (which is what we describe in indexing) and yet be of no use (not pertinent) to the requester because it is in a foreign tongue, is too mathematical in treatment, or has been superseded by another paper. Some of these factors can be handled in the index by means of further description, such as the well-known 'form' divisions of book classification and cataloguing. Others are not measurable in any laboratory investigation (e.g. 'I've read this already').

INDEXING

All index languages consist in the first place of a substantial reduction of the language of the original collection of documents themselves to a relatively small and limited index language. This is true even of automatic retrieval systems in which the whole file is scanned, for the machine has built into it a programme which has already rejected much of the language of the text being scanned, for example its articles, conjunctions, etc.

The indexing devices to be measured may be regarded as refinements, of one sort or another, to be imposed on the crude index language (not just vocabulary, but essential relations also) which is obtained by selecting the significant words in the title, summary and text of the document indexed. So our first task is to establish this crude language for each document, and thus for the whole collection. This must provide the raw material, the basic information regarding the document's subject content, to allow us to index the document subsequently with maximum exhaustivity and specificity.

These terms, exhaustivity and specificity, have already been defined, but further explanation of their practical implications seems desirable. Both for indexing and for searching programmes, we regard the limits of broadness and narrowness to be contained within a framework determined by the specificity and exhaustivity of the descriptions used. In indexing, the specificity of a term refers to the degree to which it reflects the precise generic level of the concept it stands for; for instance, to index a 'slender delta wing' specifically is to index it as just this, and nothing less. To index it as a 'delta wing' is to describe a genus to which it belongs, not the particular species itself—and such indexing is not specific. It might be called less specific or more generic—the terms are purely relative.

This is, of course, nothing more than the traditional genus/species relation, which is sometimes thought to be the only acceptable relation in strict classification. Its significance in indexing is that it refers to an inclusion relation which is permanent in character; slender delta wing, for example, is always a kind of delta wing, being included in it, and a document on the one will always be of some relevance to a document on the other.

Exhaustivity in indexing refers to the degree to which we recognize (i.e. include in our subject descriptions) the different concepts in a subject which are *not* in a genus/species relation—which, in other words, come from different categories or facets. For example, a paper on the 'calculation of the laminar boundary layer on a slender delta wing' is exhaustively indexed only if all three categories present are recognized, i.e. the kind of aircraft structure, the kind of aerodynamic flow, and the kind of activity directed at the subject (calculation as distinct from experimentation, say). It might be said that exhaustivity covers also the recognition of the different elements in a hierarchy—e.g. of 'slender' as well as of 'delta.' But the idea of specificity takes care of this; a specific indexing description automatically recognizes those links in a chain which constitute sought terms in the indexing sense, as this example demonstrates.

Exhaustivity does cover, however, recognition of different co-ordinate terms from one hierarchy; e.g. exhaustive indexing of a document on the conductivity of metals a, b, c, d and e would require the separate indexing of each metal.

Except for the Whole/Part relation, these non-hierarchical relations are not inclusion relations, and the connections between members of different categories are not so permanent or so predictable as the connections between members of the same hierarchy, e.g. whereas a search for information on 'Slender, delta wings' would automatically find relevant a document on 'Delta wings,' it would not necessarily find a document on 'Boundary layer' to be so.

Earlier on, we have stated that greater exhaustivity in indexing makes for higher recall and lower relevance, whilst greater specificity makes for lower recall and greater relevance. This may puzzle some readers when they consider the effect on a single subject description of these factors. For example, to index a report as being about '*slender* delta wings' rather than just 'delta wings' narrows the class definition and so reduces the number of documents in the class—i.e. it improves relevance, but reduces recall. If we index a report as being about '*experiments* on the boundary layer of a delta wing,' rather than just 'boundary layer of a delta wing,' we again narrow the class definition (this time by correlation), and so reduce the number of documents in the class; again, we improve relevance, but reduce recall.

It is clear from this that we must distinguish between exhaustive indexing in the sense of making a single subject description truly exhaustive of the subject of the document, and exhaustive indexing in the sense of providing the maximum number of retrieval handles or access points necessary to full retrieval. An indexing system could recognize all the three categories in the above subject by means of separate entries, one for the kind of wing, one for the kind of flow, and one for the kind of intellectual operation. At no point would any one subject description be completely precise, i.e. exhaustive of the categories in the complete subject. But they will collectively exhaust it and provide all the required access points. It is this second sense of the term 'exhaustivity' which we use here. Indeed, it is open to argument whether the first meaning is a practical possibility in indexing. A single subject description of a complete report, to be truly exhaustive, would need to be, at the very least, of the dimensions of a full WRU type abstract. If, however, we recognize that in practice, thorough indexing partitions a document into its 'information items' (or 'themes' as we tend to call them), then exhaustive indexing, in the sense of a single subject description of a theme being a precise and exhaustive description of that theme, may well be an objective.

SPECIFICITY AND EXHAUSTIVITY IN INDEXING AND SEARCHING

Below are two grids, showing the degrees of exhaustivity and specificity possible in the indexing of a document and in the framing or programming of a search question (which is really a form of indexing of the subject implied by the question) to which that document is relevant. The document and question are taken, with slight simplifications, from reference 2, [footnote 2] page 223.

DOCUMENT

'An approximate method of calculating the laminar boundary layer on a delta wing.'
A linear statement of the precise subject omitting implicit terms would be

Slender delta wings—Laminar boundary layer—
                              Calculation

Varying the specificity of indexing—this implies indexing the terms within one or more categories at levels above that constituting 'specific' indexing, e.g. varying the level in the structures category (by omitting the specification 'Slender') would give

Delta wings—Laminar boundary layer—Calculation

or varying the level in the Aerodynamic Entities category would give

Slender delta wings—Laminar flow—Calculation

It should be noted that part of the hierarchy of both 'Structures' and of 'Flow' could be varied in their order of subordination; i.e. they could be altered to: Wings—Slender—Delta, and to Flow—Boundary layer—Laminar. This possibility might add a complication to a pre-co-ordinate system.

Varying the exhaustivity of indexing—this implies the non-recognition of one or more of the categories, e.g. omission in the indexing of the Operations category would give

Slender delta wings—laminar boundary layer

Omission of the Structures category would give

Laminar boundary layer—Calculation

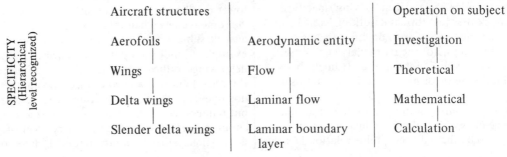

EXHAUSTIVITY (number of categories recognized)		
Aircraft structures		Operation on subject
Aerofoils	Aerodynamic entity	Investigation
Wings	Flow	Theoretical
Delta wings	Laminar flow	Mathematical
Slender delta wings	Laminar boundary layer	Calculation

SPECIFICITY (Hierarchical level recognized)

QUESTION

Three-dimensional boundary layer on slender wings

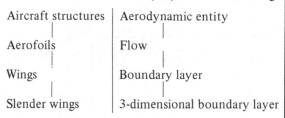

Aircraft structures	Aerodynamic entity
Aerofoils	Flow
Wings	Boundary layer
Slender wings	3-dimensional boundary layer

A linear statement would be

Slender wings—3-dimensional boundary layer

Varying the specificity in searching is exactly analogous to varying the specificity of indexing, e.g. varying the specificity in the Aerodynamic Entity category would mean a search for the broader subject

Slender wings—Boundary layer

Varying the exhaustivity in searching is exactly analogous to varying the exhaustivity of indexing, e.g. the omission of the Structures category would mean a search for the broader subject

Three-dimensional boundary layer

The hierarchical relations shown above are incomplete in two ways.

1. *Multiple generic links* are not shown. For example, a slender wing, from another viewpoint, could be characterized as a low drag wing factor. Theoretically any one term may be considered as a species in a number of different hierarchies, and the grid above could be enlarged within each category to show this:

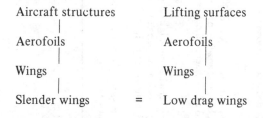

Aircraft structures	Lifting surfaces
Aerofoils	Aerofoils
Wings	Wings
Slender wings =	Low drag wings

2. *Co-ordinate relations* are not shown, although theoretically these may include potentially useful connections, as *Turbulent* boundary layer on slender delta wing.

In the first place, both the indexing and searching will be exhaustive and specific within the capabilities of a given index language; for instance, our first test might be of a language consisting simply of the correlation of uncontrolled 'uniterms.' In the example above, this would mean a search for the description 'Three-dimensional boundary layer on a slender wing' in a file in which the document is indexed as 'Calculation of laminar boundary layer on a slender delta wing.' We will then vary one element at a time, e.g. we will assume a degree of indexing which is less specific, first within one category, then within two categories, and so on, whilst holding the question exhaustive and specific. At each stage, figures for recall and relevance will be noted. Next, the exhaustivity of indexing is varied, then the specificity of the question, and so on.

After completing this stage, a particular indexing device is introduced which has been absent so far; for example, to the simple correlation of uncontrolled 'uniterms' we may introduce the confounding of verbal forms and note its impact on recall and relevance, again testing within a range of variables of specificity and exhaustivity of indexing and searching.

The number of different permutations of variables implied in the above programme is obviously vast and will constitute one of the major problems. We anticipate, however, that many of the theoretically possible combinations of factors will rule themselves out as having no retrieval or search significance; reducing the specificity of the Structure category to 'Wing,' say, and reducing exhaustivity by omitting the Flow category would give us a description 'Wings—Calculation,' which is obviously worthless.

PROBLEMS OF BASIC INDEXING

To provide the raw indexing material for subsequent processing we begin by recording the product of the 'concept indexing.' This means that we enter on a master sheet (see Fig. 5) a statement of what we consider to be all the significant terms, indicating as far as is necessary the relations between them. This is being entered at four levels of description, namely:

i. Abstract
ii. Themes
iii. Concepts
iv. Terms

The abstract provides a brief but general statement of the subject content of the complete document. The themes are required to show the relationship of the concepts, and will be used in connection with such indexing devices as partitioning, interlocking and interfixing. With the concepts, it

B 1069	AUTHOR G. E. Kaattari	Indexer	Date
	TITLE Predicted shock envelopes about two types of vehicles at large angles of attack.	FWL	4/2/63
Base Document A32	REFERENCE NASA Tech. Note D-860		

ABSTRACT   Presents methods for predicting detached shock envelopes of two atmosphere entry vehicles, one a high-drag capsule shape, the other a slender triangular wing (conical vehicle). Predicted and measured shock envelopes were compared for Mach range of 3 to 15 for vehicles at high angle of attack.

THEMES	CONCEPTS & WEIGHTS		TERMS & WEIGHTS		TERMS & WEIGHTS	
Atmosphere entry vehicle—at high angle of attack—in hypersonic flow (Mach 3 to 15)—detached shock envelope of—theory.	Atmosphere entry vehicle	8	Atmosphere	8	Slender	8
	High angle of attack	9	Entry	8	Triangular	8
High-drag capsule entry vehicle—at high angle of attack—in hypersonic flow (Mach 3 to 15)—detached shock envelope of—prediction.	Hypersonic flow	7	Vehicle	8	Wing	8
	Mach 3 to 15	6	High	9	Conical	8
	Detached shock envelope	10	Angle of attack	9	Standoff	6
Slender triangular wing (conical) entry vehicle—at high angle of attack—in hypersonic flow (Mach 3 to 15)—detached shock envelope of—prediction.	Theory	10	Hypersonic	7	Angle	6
	High-drag capsule	8	Flow	7	Continuity	7
	Slender triangular wings	8	Mach 3 to 15	6	Mass	7
Conical entry vehicles—at high angle of attack—in hypersonic flow (Mach 3 to 15)—shock standoff angles—prediction of.	Conical vehicle	8	Detached	10	Wave	10
	Shock standoff angle	6	Shock	10	Surface	5
Continuity of mass flow between shock wave and entry vehicle surface.	Mass flow continuity	7	Envelope	10	High	8
	Entry vehicle surface	5	Theory	6	Shock	6
			Drag	8	Entry	5
			Capsule	8	Vehicle	5

FIGURE 5

will be noted that the same concept may occur in different themes, and similarly the same term may appear in two or more concepts. It should be emphasized that we have no particular system in mind when doing this initial indexing; it is completely neutral.

An additional type of statement that we provide is the weighting of the different concepts, and thus the terms. This is a relatively untried device that appears to have the possibility of being a particularly powerful tool in improving the relevance ratio. If one is doing intellectual indexing, it seems reasonable to suggest that the weighted indexing should also be a subjective assessment. If the indexing is to be done by using statistical techniques, then obviously the assignment of weights is a ready by-product.

If the impact on recall and relevance of the various devices is to be isolated, we cannot afford to have variations in other factors introducing uncontrolled influences. We cannot afford a situation, for example, where the figures for the effect of a particular device are criticized as unreliable because the indexer had omitted some vital term or relation. In particular, we want to be sure that all the relevant documents can be retrieved when indexing is exhaustive and specific, i.e. all the facilities indexwise must be available for complete retrieval from the index language (remembering that complete retrieval is always available to any librarian if he is prepared to abandon his index language and search the whole collection). This will be ensured by checking the indexing of a document against the questions to which it is known to be relevant and making quite sure that the raw indexing material does have this necessary data.

It is an implicit assumption of the provisions we intend to make for indexing that the ability of any index language to describe a subject closely or precisely is crucial if a high relevance ratio is required. If the index language (its vocabulary and its syntax) does not allow precise description, then the most exhaustive and specific searching will not improve matters in this respect. It is interesting to note that the age-old arguments about whether a classification should be detailed or not now has the basic issue determined with reasonable precision. While a detailed classification will provide precision for those who need it, but can be used broadly by those who do not, a broad classification provides facilities only for the second eventuality. At the same time, it is possible that the surprising degree of correspondence in the recall performance of the four different systems in Cranfield I can be attributed largely to the care with which the vocabulary was established in each case, even though the syntax of the schemes varied considerably. It should be noted, however, that the presence or absence of provision for the display of relations will, in certain circumstances, have the same effect on recall and relevance as the presence or absence of provision for vocabulary terms, e.g. a search for *x as an agent* will not be retrieved independently of *x as a patient* unless the index language allows the difference in role to be indicated.

Earlier in this paper, we suggested that the subject area covered by an indexing system might prove to be the most potent factor of all in determining a performance curve. We hope to be able to shed some light on this by testing an index in the field of the social sciences, where we may find that the potency of particular devices will vary significantly from their potency in a relatively unambiguous area like high speed aerodynamics.

FOOTNOTES

*In recent papers we have been using the term 'descriptor language' following on the usage of Mr B. C. Vickery. However, Mr Calvin Mooers has pointed out that the word 'descriptor,' although now somewhat debased in common usage, originally had a precise meaning. We have agreed to restrict our use of the word to this precise meaning and have therefore decided upon the term 'index language.'

*It is, of course, true that the compilation and maintenance of the index language can fairly be said to be an intellectual task. Its use, however, within the context of an indexing operation is a separate matter which requires only clerical operations.

1. VICKERY, B. C. On retrieval system theory. London, Butterworths, 1961.

2. CLEVERDON, C. W. Report on the testing and analysis of an investigation into the comparative efficiency of indexing systems. Cranfield, [College of Aeronautics], October 1962. (Aslib Cranfield Research Project.)

3. AITCHISON, JEAN, *and* CLEVERDON, CYRIL. Report of a test on the index of metallurgical literature of Western Reserve University. [To be published.]

4. CLEVERDON, C. W. Report on the first stage of an investigation into the comparative efficiency of indexing systems. Cranfield, College of Aeronautics, September 1960. (Aslib Cranfield Research Project.)

Evaluation of the MEDLARS Demand Search Service

by F. W. Lancaster

MEDLARS: GENERAL BACKGROUND

The Medical Literature Analysis and Retrieval System has been discussed in detail elsewhere. Only the most salient characteristics will be described here.

MEDLARS is a multipurpose system, a prime purpose being the production of *Index Medicus* and other recurring bibliographies. However, the present study has concentrated on the evaluation of the *demand search* function (i.e., the conduct of retrospective literature searches in response to specific demands). The base of the retrospective search module consists of more than half a million citations to journal articles, in the biomedical field, input to the January 1964 and subsequent issues of the monthly *Index Medicus*. This data base is presently growing at the approximate rate of 200,000 citations annually. Journal articles, of which roughly 45% are in languages other than English, are indexed at an average level of 6.7 terms per item, using a controlled vocabulary of *Medical Subject Headings (MeSH)*. Over three thousand demand searches are processed annually at the National Library of Medicine, additional searches being handled at regional MEDLARS centers in the United States, in the United Kingdom and in Sweden.

Approximately 2400 scientific journals are indexed regularly. About one third of these are indexed *exhaustively* ("depth journals") at an average of 10 terms per article, and the remainder are indexed less exhaustively ("non-depth journals") at an average of slightly under four terms per article.

MeSH consists of about 7000 fairly conventional pre-coordinate type subject headings in thirteen broad subject categories. A hierarchical classification ("tree structure") of these terms is also available to the indexers and the search analysts. In January 1966, subheadings were introduced into the system. Subheadings, of which 53 were in use in 1966, are general concept terms (e.g., BIOSYNTHESIS, COMPLICATIONS) which can be affixed to main subject headings, thus effecting greater specificity through additional pre-coordination. Each subheading can only be used with main subject headings from specified *MeSH* categories. For example, the subheading ABNORMALITIES can only be used with Category A (anatomical) terms, while CONGENITAL is only applicable to Category C (disease) terms. These and other indexing conventions are spelled out in detail in a *MEDLARS Indexing Manual* revised annually.

A demand search is presently conducted, on a Honeywell 800 computer, by serial search of the index term profiles of the 700,000 citations on magnetic tape. This search is essentially a matching process: the index term profiles of journal articles are matched against a *search formulation*, which is a translation of a subject request into the controlled vocabulary of the system. Requests for demand searches are mostly received by mail at NLM, either embodied in a letter or on a "demand search request form"; a higher proportion of the requests processed by regional MEDLARS centers are made by personal vists to the center. The search formulations are prepared, by search analysts, in the form of Boolean combinations (logical sums, logical products, and negations) of main subject headings and subheadings. A generic search (known at NLM as an "explosion") can be conducted by means of the tree structure. An "explosion on A9.44.44" means that a search is conducted on the generic term RETINA (identified as A9.44.44 in the tree structure) and all the terms subordinate to it in the tree structure, namely FUNDUS OCULI, MACULA LUTEA, and RODS AND CONES.

A search formulation may be constructed as a three-level strategy, which will result in a three-section printout (sections 4, 5 and 6) on the high-speed printer. Level 4 represents the broadest strategy employed by the search analyst. Level 5 introduces an additional restriction to this strategy, and produces a subset of the citations retrieved by the broader strategy. Level 6 introduces a further restriction and produces a subset of the citations

SOURCE: Reprinted from a publication issued by the National Library of Medicine, based on research done under GER 12760 (Rome Air Development Center).

retrieved by Level 5. For example, suppose the broadest strategy (Level 4) demands the retrieval of citations whose index term profiles match the following Boolean statement:

TERM A   TERM L
  or   and   or
TERM B   TERM M

Level 5 might ask for the separation, *from the citations retrieved by the strategy above*, of those that had been indexed under TERM B *and* under TERM M (i.e., a subset of 4 is produced). Level 6 is more specific still, and requests that, of the citations matching the requirements of 5, any indexed under the term X are to be sorted out and printed separately. Note that it is possible to employ, for sorting purposes, in Level 5 and Level 6, an index term not forming part of the original (Level 4) searching strategy.

In the printout of the *demand search bibliography*, which is the normal product of a MEDLARS search, the citations are printed in the order: Section 6 (i.e., citations matching the requirements of Level 6), Section 5 (those citations match matching the requirements of Level 5 that were not already printed in Section 6), Section 4 (those citations matching the general strategy that were not already printed in Section 5 or Section 6). This can be clarified by returning to the sample formulation mentioned above. Suppose that 205 citations satisfy the requirements of the general strategy

TERM A   TERM L
  or   and   or
TERM B   TERM M

The profiles of 80 of these citations match the more stringent requirement of 5 (i.e., each citation is indexed under the term B and also under the term M). Of these 80 citations, ten have been indexed under the term X, and thus satisfy the most specific search requirement (Level 6). When the search is printed, these ten citations ("section 6" of the bibliography) appear first, followed by the 70 citations of section 5 (the 80 satisfying the Level 5 search requirement less the ten already printed in section 6), and finally the residue of retrieved citations is printed in section 4 (125 citations).

This three-level search capability is used in two ways within MEDLARS:

1. To produce a search of varying specificity in relation to the request. For example, assuming

a request for literature on drug X used to treat disease Y, particularly where this is shown to lead to side-effect Z, section 6 of the search printout may be designated to include citations relating specifically to the side-effect, while sections 5 and 4 relate more generally to the effects of drug X on disease Y.

2. Merely as a sorting device. For example, consider a request for toxins A, B, C, D, E and F. For convenience to the user, the searcher specifies that citations relating to toxin F be printed in section 6, citations to toxin E in section 5, and section 4 will cover "all other toxins," namely A, B, C, and D. Obviously, in this case the citations in section 6 are not more specific in relation to the request than those in section 5 or section 4.[1]

This 6-5-4 breakdown has been discussed in some detail because

a. it is somewhat peculiar to MEDLARS,
b. it tends to be confusing to people outside of NLM, and
c. an understanding of it is a prerequisite to the comprehension of certain of the results presented in Part 2* of this report.

The final product of a MEDLARS search is a computer-printed *demand search bibliography*, in up to three sections as discussed above, the citations usually appearing in alphabetical order by author within each section. Accompanying each bibliographic citation is a complete set of tracings (i.e., a record of all the index terms assigned to the article).

The MEDLARS evaluation, discussed in this report, was a complete system evaluation inasmuch as it studied all components affecting the performance of the system as measured by the satisfaction of MEDLARS users. The benefit of this type of evaluation program lies not in detecting specific failures, but in identifying kinds of failures that are prone to occur, and indicating in which areas corrective action is most urgently needed.

Overall MEDLARS Performance

The test results have shown that the system is operating, on the average, at about 58% recall and 50% precision. On the average, it retrieves about

---

*Part 2 of the report has *not* been included. It will be found in the original and complete report by Lancaster.

65% of the *major value* literature in its base at 50% precision. However, as previously noted, averages are somewhat misleading in this context. Few of the individual search results fall in the area bounded by the average ratios ± 5%. In fact, the results are widely scattered. Some of the searches appear to have performed very well, with high recall accompanied by high precision. Other searches achieved completely unsatisfactory recall results. The most important factors governing the success or failure of a MEDLARS search were discussed in some detail in Part 2 of this report.

The MEDLARS average performance ratios may seem low when compared with certain figures (e.g., 90% recall at 90% precision) quoted in the documentation literature. Unfortunately, the great majority of the quoted figures are completely without foundation. There is no other fully operational retrieval system, of any significant size, that has exposed itself to the rigours of an evaluation program such as the one here reported. The author considers it extremely unlikely that any other large mechanized retrieval system, if it were evaluated in the way that MEDLARS has been evaluated, would be found to be operating at a higher average performance level.

It should be borne in mind, in considering the MEDLARS figures, that the present evaluation has been conducted as stringently as possible. The author has assumed the role of an impartial (but hopefully constructive) critic of MEDLARS. Whenever a decision had to be made, it was made against the system. An article judged "of value" by the requester was accepted as being "relevant" even though it was found to contain very slight reference to the subject of the request. Known relevant articles that were not retrieved were counted against the system, even in cases in which the requester, in agreeing to the exclusion of certain terms, was himself largely responsible for the misses.

It must also be remembered that "relevant," within the context of this program, has been defined as "of value to the requester in relation to the information need prompting his request to the system." Relevance to an information need is very different from relevance to a stated request. In fact, had we evaluated MEDLARS on the basis of the latter criterion, both recall ratio and precision ratio would have been approximately 10% higher, because we would not have counted against the system the 25% of the recall failures and 17% of the precision failures presently attributed to inadequate user-system interaction.

To counterbalance the stringency of the evalua-

tion, we have to recognize the fact that the analysts preparing search formulations for the various test requests were aware that these searches were subsequently to be evaluated. Almost certainly there was some "spotlight" effect. We can therefore say that the present evaluation has studied the performance of MEDLARS with one component of the system (namely search formulation) behaving optimally. There could also have been some "spotlighting" in the area of user-system interaction. However, as we know, this might have degraded performance rather than improved it.

Figure 7 and Figure 15 [not included] present performance curves for the MEDLARS test searches, the former based on performance points for the various centers, the latter on performance points for the 6-5-4 subsets in 118 searches. By extrapolation, we can hypothesize a generalized MEDLARS performance curve looking something like that of Figure 17.

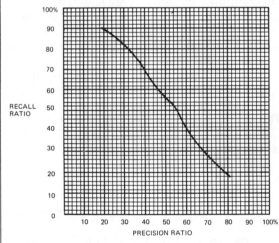

FIGURE 17. Generalized MEDLARS performance curve

From results of other investigations, largely on experimental or prototype systems, using Cranfield-type methodology, we expected (before the study was conducted) that MEDLARS would be performing rather differently than it was actually found to be. In fact, the author expected that the system would function in a high recall, low precision mode in the region, say, of 75-90% recall at 10-20% precision. The results actually achieved over 300 test searches do not indicate a performance *worse* than expected, but they do indicate a performance *different* from that expected.

The fact that, on the average, MEDLARS is operating at 58% recall and 50% precision, indicates that, consciously or unconsciously, the MEDLARS searchers choose to operate in this general area. It would be possible for MEDLARS to operate at a different performance point on the recall/precision curve of Figure 17. By broadening of search strategies one could obtain a much higher average recall ratio, but this could only be obtained at a lower average precision ratio. However, the indications are that MEDLARS could operate in a high recall mode (say 80-90%) at a much higher precision ratio than we could have expected on the basis of other evaluations conducted by means of Cranfield-type methodology.

Obviously, it is always possible to achieve 100% recall for any request by retrieving the entire data base. This is nonsense in that, under these conditions, the filtering capacity of the system is not being brought into play at all. With sufficient broadening of each search strategy, however, it would be possible for MEDLARS to achieve very close to 100% recall for any request without retrieving the entire collection. However, in some searches 100% recall (or close to 100%) can be achieved at a tolerable precision ratio, while in other searches we cannot approach 100% recall and still obtain acceptable precision.

Consider once more the search on nutritional aspects of chromium, and the search* on premature rupture of the fetal membranes. If we conducted the former search on the single-term strategy CHROMIUM or CHROMATES we would obtain 95% recall (we fall short of 100% because of indexer omissions) and retrieve in the neighborhood of 180 citations, of which about one third are relevant. In this case, we can assure the requester of almost maximum recall and still operate at a tolerable precision ration. It does not seem too unreasonable to expect the requester to examine 180 citations in order to find 50-60 of some value to him.

On the other hand, because of indexing omissions and inadequacies of the index language, we could only approach 100% recall in the search on rupture of the membranes by searching on FETAL MEMBRANES and also on all terms relating to pregnancy complications, labor complications, and newborn infant disease. This would retrieve several thousand citations of which only about 30-35 would be in any way relevant. Almost certainly we could not expect the requester to examine several thousand citations in order to find 30-35 pertinent ones (especially since we know,

from the analysis of output screening, that the requester is unlikely to be able to recognize all the relevant items anyway.)

The conduct of a machine search is essentially a compromise between recall and precision. In attempting to obtain a satisfactory recall at an acceptable precision, the MEDLARS searchers are operating the system almost at the 50-50 point, although, as we have noted, there are policy differences between the centers, Colorado choosing to operate in a high precision mode, while UCLA appears to favor higher recall.

We can choose to operate MEDLARS, as it presently exists, at any performance point on or near the recall/precision plot of Figure 17. The crucial question is where should it operate? Intuitively one feels that MEDLARS should be operating at a higher average recall ratio, and should sacrifice some precision in order to attain an improved recall performance. However, MEDLARS is now retrieving an average of 175 citations per search in operating at 58% recall and 50% precision. To operate at an average recall of 85-90%, and an average precision ratio in the neighborhood of 20-25%, implies that MEDLARS would need to retrieve an average of 500-600 citations per search.[2] Are requesters willing to scan this many citations (75% of which will be completely irrelevant) in order to obtain a much higher level of recall?

In actual fact, we know very little about the recall and precision requirements and tolerances of MEDLARS users. This has been a much neglected factor in the design of all information retrieval systems. We have said previously that recall needs, and precision tolerance, will vary considerably from requester to requester, depending upon the purpose of the search. Out of curiosity, the author wrote to ten scientists participating in the evaluation, with a view to determining their actual recall needs and precision tolerances. In each case, through search analysis, we knew roughly how each search had performed and had also made some hypotheses on how many citations would need to be retrieved in order to approach 100% recall. In each case, the requester was asked to indicate whether he was satisfied with the level of performance achieved or whether he would have tolerated a much lower precision in order to get somewhere near to 100% recall. A specimen letter is included as Figure 18, and the answers of the eight respondents are tabulated below:

---

1. Retrieval of 33% of the relevant literature. Total of 25 citations retrieved. About 30% irrelevant.[3] *YES*

DEPARTMENT OF HEALTH, EDUCATION, AND WELFARE
PUBLIC HEALTH SERVICE
8600 WISCONSIN AVENUE
BETHESDA, MD   20014

NATIONAL LIBRARY OF MEDICINE

REFER TO: NLM - R & D

October 30, 1967

Department of Anesthesia
U. S. Naval Hospital
National Naval Medical Center
Bethesda, Maryland 20014

Dear

You will remember that recently we conducted a search for you on the
subject of repair of amputed finger tips, and that you very kindly
assisted us in evaluating the results of this search. There is one
more thing that you could help us with if you would be so good.

We need to know something of the requirements and tolerances of
MEDLARS users. From my evaluation, I believe that the MEDLARS search
retrieved only about 33% of the relevant articles on the precise
topic of your interest. However, to retrieve anything approaching
100% of the relevant literature I believe that we would have needed
to retrieve many more citations in total - possibly about 100, of
which only about 25% would be directly relevant.

The question is: Would you have preferred to look through the
additional irrelevant citations in order to approach 100% retrieval
of the relevant literature?

If you could please return this letter, marked with your answer, I
should indeed be most grateful.

Would prefer (delete whichever inapplicable):

1.   Retrieval of 33% of the relevant literature. Total of 25 citations
     retrieved. About 30% irrelevant.

2.   Retrieval of close to 100% of the relevant literature.

Sincerely,

F. Wilfrid Lancaster
Information Systems Specialist
Research and Development
National Library of Medicine

FIGURE 18

Retrieval of close to 100% of the relevant literature. Total of about 100 citations retrieved.
About 75% irrelevant. *NO*

2. Retrieval of 77% of the relevant literature.
Total of 233 citations retrieved. About 80%
irrelevant. *NO*

Retrieval of close to 100% of the relevant literature. Total of about 400 citations retrieved.
About 90% irrelevant. *YES*

3. Retrieval of 40% of the relevant literature.
Total of 15 citations retrieved. About 10% irrelevant. *NO*

Retrieval of close to 100% of the relevant literature. Total of about 100 citations retrieved.
About 50% irrelevant. *YES*

4. Retrieval of 60% of the relevant literature.
Total of around 100 citations retrieved. About
95% irrelevant. *YES*

Retrieval of close to 100% of the relevant literature. Total of around 250 citations retrieved. About 95% irrelevant. *NO*

5. Retrieval of 75% of the relevant literature.
Total of 333 citations retrieved. About 40%
irrelevant. *YES*

Retrieval of close to 100% of the relevant literature. Total of about 500 citations retrieved.
About 50% irrelevant. *NO*

6. Retrieval of 66% of the relevant literature.
Total of around 400 citations retrieved. About
60% irrelevant. *YES*

Retrieval of close to 100% of the relevant literature. Total of at least 700 citations retrieved. About 70% irrelevant. *NO*

7. Retrieval of 66% of the relevant literature.
Total of 190 citations retrieved. About 50%
irrelevant. *YES*

Retrieval of close to 100% of the relevant literature. Total of about 300 citations retrieved.
About 60% irrelevant. *NO*

8. Retrieval of 36% of the relevant literature.
Total of 10 citations retrieved. About 60%
irrelevant. *NO*

Retrieval of close to 100% of the relevant literature. Total of about 60 citations retrieved.
About 80% irrelevant. *YES*

One cannot draw firm conclusions on the basis
of eight responses of this kind. Nevertheless, the
results are very interesting. It appears that we are
wrong in assuming that most requesters want maximum recall. Five of these eight respondents have
indicated satisfaction with the less-than-maximum
results. At least, they indicate unwillingness to
examine additional irrelevant citations in order to
approach 100% recall. In relation to these responses, the general performance level at which
MEDLARS has chosen to operate would appear
to be a reasonable compromise between recall and
precision. However, no clear picture emerges from
the responses. In # 1 the requester is satisfied
with 33% recall and would not care to examine
100 citations, at 25% precision, in order to substantially improve on this recall figure. On the
other hand, in # 2 the requester is prepared to
examine 400 citations, 90% of which are irrelevant,
in order to approach 100% recall.

Clearly, each individual has his own requirements
in relation to the tradeoff between recall and precision, and we cannot generalize on this subject.
It is important, therefore, that the MEDLARS demand search request form be so designed that it
establishes *for each request* the recall requirements
and precision tolerances of the requester, thus allowing the searcher to prepare a strategy geared as
required to high recall, high precision, or some
compromise point in between. The search request
form will be mentioned again later.

Upgrading the performance of MEDLARS

So far we have considered how MEDLARS is
operating. We have also indicated that the present
system could choose to operate at some different
average performance point on the recall/precision

plot of Figure 17. However, this evaluation program has not been conducted primarily to determine the present performance level. Rather, it was conducted to discover what needs to be done to upgrade the performance of the present system, i.e., what can be done to move the generalized performance curve of Figure 17 further to the right in order to achieve a higher average performance capability (e.g., 58% recall *at 70% precision*, 80% recall at 50% precision, 90% recall at 40% precision). The remainder of this report will be concerned with conclusions and recommendations relating to the various components of the MEDLARS demand search system.

In considering these recommendations, it must be recognized that, although we can do certain things to a system ostensibly to improve recall (e.g., indexing more exhaustively) and other things ostensibly to improve precision (e.g., increasing the specificity of the index language or introducing relational indicators), the present study has shown that there is no clear cut distinction between improving recall capabilities and improving precision capabilities. Recall and precision are strongly interconnected in an inverse relationship, and searching involves a compromise between the two. Therefore, inadequate precision devices can affect recall just as much as they affect precision. As an example, consider search # 93, relating to hypophosphatasia. HYPOPHOSPHATASIA is a fairly recent provisional heading, so the search had to be conducted at a more general level for the earlier material. To avoid an unacceptably low precision ratio, the searcher was cautious in the formulation, using only

METABOLISM,
INBORN ERRORS

and

BLOOD ALKALINE PHOSPHATASE
ALKALINE PHOSPHATASE.

This strategy retrieved only six citations, all relevant, but we estimate that this is but a very small fraction of the total relevant literature. It would be necessary to generalize much more to BLOOD ALKALINE PHOSPHATASE alone (with over 800 postings) in order to obtain high recall. This, then, is clearly a situation in which lack of specificity in the vocabulary has led to recall failures rather than precision failures, and we can expect that recall would have reached an acceptable level had the specific term HYPOPHOSPHATASIA always been available.

Similarly, in search # 181 it was not possible to express *asymptomatic* proteinurias because no specific term exists for this notion. The searcher

attempted to keep irrelevancy within bounds by negating kidney disease terms. Unfortunately, this screened out some of the relevant items also, and achieved 60% recall and 17.4% precision. Again, we would expect both better recall and better precision if an appropriate specific term were available in the vocabulary.

Like situations result from other compromise strategies designed to avoid false coordinations and incorrect term relationships, and we can thus safely say that, in the long run, a system change that adds greater precision capabilities will also tend to allow improved recall performance.

Regarding these conclusions and recommendations, the author has considered it his function to expose system weaknesses and point to work that needs to be done and decisions that need to be taken. He has *not* considered it his present responsibility to carry these recommendations to the point of, for example, designing finished forms or proposing new specific subject headings.

It must also be borne in mind that changes made in the area of searching, or the area of user-system interaction can have immediate effect on the system. On the other hand, it will be some years before changes in indexing and index language can have a substantial effect on the complete data base.

User-system interaction

The greatest potential for improvement in MEDLARS exists at the interface between user and system. A significant improvement in the statement of requests can raise both the recall and the precision performance of the system: 25% of the MEDLARS recall failures and 16.6% of the precision failures are attributed, at least in part, to defective interaction.

We recommend that the *search request form* be completely redesigned along the lines proposed in Figure 11. It is obviously crucial to the success of a MEDLARS search that a request should accurately reflect the actual information need of the requester. For this reason, it is worth investing substantial amount of time and effort in the design of a new request form. In particular, the questionnaires relating to search limitations and to the recall/precision tradeoff (parts 5 and 6 of the proposed form) will require very careful presentation and wording. The search request form will require testing in draft (possibly several drafts) before it is finally accepted and put into use.

We recommend that all requesters be required to complete this form personally, even in situations in which the requester makes a personal visit to a MEDLARS center or to his local library. In personal confrontation between requester and search analyst, the function of the latter should be to clarify the request statement, where necessary, but not to influence it. In particular, a request should not be discussed with a requester in terms of *Medical Subject Headings*, or at least not until the requester's own statement of need has been captured on the search request form.

The MEDLARS index language

We recommend a thorough re-appraisal of methods presently used to update *Medical Subject Headings*. In particular, we feel that the future success of the retrospective search function demands a shift in emphasis away from the external advisory committee on terminology and towards the continued analysis of the terminological requirements of MEDLARS users *as reflected in the demands placed upon the system*. As part of quality control procedures, the *MeSH* group, in cooperation with the Search Section, should undertake the continuous analysis of MEDLARS search requests with a view to identifying areas of weakness in *MeSH* and legitimate requirements that cannot presently be satisfied because of inadequate terminology.

We recommend that the MEDLARS entry vocabulary be regarded as an integral part of the index language of the system of no less importance than *MeSH* itself. The entry vocabulary, which should be the joint responsibility of the *MeSH* group and the Index Section, will require considerable improvement if it is to function adequately. Any significant topic, encountered by an indexer, for which there exists no specific *MeSH* term, is a candidate for inclusion in the entry vocabulary. However, we cannot expect NLM indexers, who are required to adhere to a tight production quota, to maintain an adequate entry vocabulary. It should be the function of the indexers to "flag" topics that require a new *MeSH* term, provisional heading, or entry vocabulary term, for subsequent analysis and action in the *MeSH* group.

The present format of the entry vocabulary, as it exists in the shape of an Authority File on $3 \times 5''$ cards, should be replaced by an alternative amenable to (1) machine manipulation and updating and (2) rapid accessing by indexers and searchers. Every indexer and every searcher, including those at the centers, should be able to consult the entry vocabulary as easily as they can consult *MeSH* itself. This implies, at the present time, an entry vocabulary in book form. Consultation of a continuously updated entry vocabulary in an on-line browsing mode should be within the capabilities of the next generation system.

The introduction of subheadings, in 1966, appears to have been a most valuable improvement to the retrospective search function of MEDLARS as well as to the printed bibliographies. Subheadings afford an economical way of greatly increasing the specificity of the vocabulary. The use of subheadings can obviate the vast majority of the precision failures presently attributed to false coordinations and incorrect term relationships. However, subheadings, in allowing much greater specificity and the expression of complex relationships between terms, present problems in consistency of application. It is important that all subheadings be carefully defined, and that strict rules govern the conditions of their use. One great advantage of subheadings is that the searcher has the option of using them or not using them as the recall and precision requirements of a particular search dictate.

We recommend an expansion in the use of subheadings within MEDLARS, and support the present trend away from pre-coordinated terms (e.g., BLOOD PRESERVATION, LUNG TRANSPLANTATION) in *Medical Subject Headings* to the more flexible approach of optional pre-coordination, at the time of indexing, by means of subheadings. There is need for additional subheadings in the system. In fact, any fairly general notion, applicable to a large number of *MeSH* terms, is a good candidate for use as a subheading (e.g., PRESERVATION, which is potentially applicable to all tissue terms, and such terms as ACUTE and CHRONIC, which are potentially applicable to most disease terms). The author has not considered it his function to produce a list of new subheadings, although in Part 2 of this report he did recommend certain types (e.g., those relating to various characteristics of pathological conditions) that search analysis showed to be of great potential value to the system.

It is the joint responsibility of searchers and the *Medical Subject Headings* group to determine what new subheadings could usefully be incorporated into the system. This can only be done, as it has been in this evaluation, by careful analysis of the types of requests put to the system (their specificity and the conceptual relationships involved), and of search failures occurring through lack of specificity, false coordinations, and incorrect term relationships. We see no need for the introduction of additional syntactical devices (e.g., links and roles) into the MEDLARS index language.

Finally, the search analyses have revealed the need for improved checktags to describe *types* of articles. In particular, it is necessary that, in searching, we should have a simple and foolproof way of distinguishing experimental articles from clinical articles. We should also be able to distinguish single case studies from "large case series." Some requesters are willing to accept the latter, but not the former. Similarly, it would be very useful if articles could be identified by *level of treatment*: we should avoid supplying the researcher on a particular topic with a large number of fairly superficial articles written for the general practitioner.

The MEDLARS searching strategies

A significant number of recall failures have been attributed to the searcher failing to exhaust all reasonable approaches to retrieval. In the next generation system, careful consideration should be given to additional term displays that can be generated to assist the searching function. These displays would differ from the present tree structures in cutting across conventional genus-species hierarchies. They would resemble the *ad hoc* agglomerations of terms ("hedges") that at present tend to be collected by individual searchers for their own personal use. These are really pre-established searching strategies. They are most useful in covering "aspects" or "points of view" in relation to a main search topic (e.g., "nutritional aspects," "genetic aspects," "epidemiology"). Although such pre-established strategies may not be 100% transferable from search to search, they should nevertheless have fairly general applicability. For example, the terms coordinated with SPINA BIFIDA to express epidemiology of this anomaly should surely be the same as the terms coordinated with MONGOLISM to express epidemiology of this syndrome. Once agreement has been reached on a pre-established strategy for a particular generally-applicable concept, this strategy can be stored in machinable form and merely referred to, in a search formulation, by a unique identifying number (in the same way that one can presently request an explosion on a particular tree structure). The repeated reconstruction, and copying down, of strategies for notions that tend to recur frequently in MEDLARS searches is considered to be most uneconomical.

The author is concerned about the increasing complexity of searching within MEDLARS. Each additional vocabulary change makes the searcher's task more difficult. In the design and planning of the next-generation system, it is recommended that a study be conducted on the feasibility of "automatic term replacement" to compensate for vocabulary changes. For example, HALLERVORDEN-SPATZ SYNDROME became a provisional heading on 2/13/65. It is necessary to search on various other term combinations (e.g., BRAIN DISEASES *and* GLOBUS PALLIDUS *and* SUBSTANTIA NIGRA) to retrieve the earlier material. However, searchers should not be repeatedly burdened with the task of determining what term combinations have to be used to retrieve articles predating the specific term. This should be done, once and for all, at the time the new term is introduced into the vocabulary. Thereafter, the searcher should need to use only the most recent, specific term in the search formulation. A computer program should be written to automatically add the terms or term combinations, with appropriate date restrictions, necessary to retrieve the earlier material.

Vocabulary changes add to the complexity of searching, but some of the complexity appears to be self-inflicted. We have already demonstrated that wide variations in complexity of strategies exist between the various MEDLARS centers. It is difficult to generalize on this point but, on strictly economic grounds, a simple-minded approach to searching is recommended in cases in which high recall can be obtained with a tolerable precision ratio. For example, the search on toxicity and nutritional aspects of chromium (# 194), if conducted on the single terms CHROMIUM *or* CHROMATES, could have achieved close to 100% recall (at least 95%), at a tolerable precision ratio of at least 33%, while retrieving only about 180 citations. It seems uneconomical to coordinate several hundred terms with CHROMIUM *or* CHROMATES, in an attempt to cover only the aspects mentioned in the request, and thereby achieve 60% precision in a total retrieval of 94. Presumably, the more complex the search formulation the more time it takes to prepare and the more likely it is to contain logical errors or inappropriate term combinations.

A searcher has the capability, by varying the specificity and/or exhaustivity of the formulation, to construct a strategy designed to achieve high recall (that we would expect to be accompanied by low precision) or one which is more a compromise strategy, sacrificing some recall to an improved precision ratio. At the present time the individual searcher makes a fairly arbitrary decision as to what type of strategy to adopt. Consequently, much time may be spent in constructing a comprehensive strategy in cases in which the requester would be satisfied with much less than 100% recall. If, as suggested, we can use the search request form to capture the recall/precision requirements and tolerances of users, the searcher should in future be able to prepare a formulation matched to these requirements and tolerances.

A substantial number of precision failures were attributed to lack of specificity in searching. It is recognized, however, that search generalization is often necessary in order to obtain satisfactory recall in a search. In a special analysis, we examined this question of search generalization: when it is justified, when not justified, and how it may best be accomplished. We also examined the use of weighted searching (on *Index Medicus* terms) as a useful means of compromising between recall and precision. The results of these analyses, which give general pointers rather than standard rules, are presented in Part 2 of this report.

It has been shown that a search analyst, working from a citation printout, cannot make relevance predictions that will closely replicate the value judgements of the requester himself on seeing the actual articles. Consequently, we suggest that the detailed citation-by-citation examination of a search printout, by a search analyst, is not a particularly valuable expenditure of effort. It would seem more worthwhile to have each search (including printout, formulation and request statement) examined more generally *by a second searcher* with a view to identifying the gross errors that can occur (e.g., use of inappropriate term or term combination, the missing of a complete aspect of the request, or the use of faulty search logic).

The amount of search reformulation (approximately 24% in the present evaluation) that appears to take place at NLM is surprising. Presumably much of this reformulation is done after having seen the search printout. Yet we know that relevance predictions do not closely coincide with the value judgements of requesters. This casts serious doubt on the need for, and value of, such a high level of reformulation. We know of at least one search (# 44) in which the reformulation substantially degraded performance: it retrieved none of the nine known relevant articles, whereas the original would have retrieved 7/9. In other cases (e.g., search # 302, which was eventually conducted on the single term SYRINGOMYELIA), it is hard to understand why a straightforward search would require a second attempt at formulation, with an attendant delay of two months for the requester.

The most legitimate reason for reformulation would be a search spoiled by logical error or by the accidental use of an inappropriate term or term combination. More effort should be made to identify this type of error, which is an offspring of complex formulations, at an earlier stage in the searching process. A reformulation rate of 24% must represent a substantial investment in search analyst time.

Somewhat related to the matter of reformulation is the use of the 500 printout "ceiling" at NLM. As previously discussed, if a search is cut off after printing 500 citations (as it was in the case of 13 of the test searches), this indicates either (a) a substantial volume of literature on the subject of the request, in which case the requester may have legitimate need for a complete printout, or (b) a poor search formulation, in which case there may be a legitimate need to reformulate. We recommend a reappraisal of NLM policy with regard to both reformulation and the use of the search cutoff.

The MEDLARS indexing

The most difficult problem relating to indexing policy, in any system, is the decision as to what level of exhaustivity to adopt. That is, how many terms, on the average, should we assign to a document? In Part 2 we presented many data relating to this question. These now require pulling together in an effort to arrive at some conclusions.

Approximately 20% of the MEDLARS recall failures are attributed to indexing that is insufficiently exhaustive, whereas only 11.5% of the precision failures were attributed to exhaustive indexing. On the surface, then, one would recommend increasing the exhaustivity of the indexing, to improve the recall potential of the system, rather than reducing exhaustivity. It is better to err on the side of additional terms. Without a fairly high level of exhaustivity, it is impossible to achieve a high average recall performance at a tolerable precision level. On the other hand, we can usually improve the precision of a search by employing more specific and/or exhaustive search formulations.

However, from the re-indexing experiments reported in Part 2, we have reason to suppose that:

1. Only a very much higher level of exhaustivity of indexing would allow the retrieval of a significant number of the relevant "depth" articles that are missed because they are not indexed with sufficient terms. Thirteen of these articles (originally indexed at an average of 7.2 terms) were re-indexed (at an average of 9.1 terms), but only two (15.4%) would have been retrieved on the re-indexing. In the other articles,

the "relevant" section is very minor and would probably only be covered if the average term assignment was raised dramatically (say to 25-30 terms).

2. On the other hand, approximately 30-40% of all the relevant "non-depth" articles that are presently missed by MEDLARS searches would be likely to be retrieved if these articles were indexed with an average number of terms comparable to the "depth" average.

We also have reason to believe that, all other things being equal, the MEDLARS recall ratio for depth articles is 70% whereas the recall ratio is only 54% for non-depth.

Moreover, as previously noted in Part 2 of this report:

1. The division by journal into "depth" and "non-depth" creates indexing anomalies. Some of the "non-depth" articles are clearly under-indexed while some of the "depth" articles are clearly over-indexed.

2. Because of term limitations, some of the non-depth articles are indexed in such general terms that it is difficult to visualize a single search in which they would be retrieved and judged of value. In other words, these citations are merely occupying space on the citation file.

To recapitulate, we can say: a substantial number of recall failures occur due to lack of exhaustivity of indexing; a marginal increase in the average number of terms assigned to "depth" articles is unlikely to result in any significant recall improvement while a major increase is unjustified on economic grounds; raising the present "non-depth" level to the present "depth" level is likely to result in a 30-40% improvement in retrieval of relevant articles from non-depth journals; the present division of journals into "depth" and "non-depth" has led to indexing anomalies and to the situation in which non-depth articles occupy 45% of the file but account for only 25% of the retrievals; some of the non-depth articles are never likely to be retrieved and judged of value because they are indexed much too generally.

On the basis of the above, we recommend that the present distinction between "depth" journals and "non-depth" journals be abandoned. This does not mean that all articles from the present non-depth journals should be assigned an average of ten index terms. Rather, it means that each article should be treated on its own merit and sufficient terms should be assigned to index the extension and intension of its content. We see no justification for an overall increase in indexing exhaustivity at the present time.

Although few indexing errors (in the sense of incorrect term assignment) were discovered in the evaluation, a significant number of indexer omissions were encountered. Indexer omissions accounted for approximately 10% of all the recall failures. However, some of these indexer omissions appear to be largely due to lack of specific terms in the vocabulary. If no specific term is available for a concept, either in *MeSH* or in the entry vocabulary, an indexer is quite likely to omit it entirely (rather than trying to cover the topic in a more general way). We believe that indexer omissions will be substantially reduced as the entry vocabulary is improved.

Moreover, a very small spot-check (reported earlier) suggests that perhaps 25% of the failures attributed to indexer omission might not be the fault of the indexers, but might be due to the deletion of a term after the indexer has assigned it. This is further discussed below.

Computer processing

Computer processing was not a major culprit in causing retrieval failures in this study. However, one situation remains to be explained. As described in Part 2, it was possible to check back to the indexer data forms and flexowriter hard copy for four 1966 articles that were unretrieved, although relevant to various test requests, because of "indexer omissions." In the case of three of these articles, examination of the data form confirmed that an important term had not in fact been used by the indexer. However, in the fourth case, the term which the indexer had been accused of omitting (PARATHYROID GLANDS) did in fact appear on the data sheet; it also appeared on the flexowriter hard copy. The term was used twice in indexing, once with the subheading DRUG EFFECTS and once with the subheading CYTOLOGY. This citation was printed in the December 1966 *Index Medicus*, and again in the *Cumulated Index Medicus*, under both main heading/subheading combinations. However, a computer printout of the tracings for this citation now reveals that the term PARATHYROID GLANDS has since been completely deleted.

This deletion probably occurred during some file maintenance procedure. The important question is how did it occur and, more importantly, how often does inadvertent term deletion take place during file maintenance procedures? Unfortunately we have no idea of the possible magnitude of this problem at the present time. This could be the only citation in which this inadvertent deletion has occurred. On the other hand, it could be one of 1000 or even 10,000 cases. We recommend that a separate investigation be made to determine the effect of file maintenance procedures on file integrity in order that the cause and magnitude of this problem can be determined.

The relationship between indexing, searching and MeSH

The tendency towards compartmentalization of indexing, searching and *MeSH* has been noted. This is evident in the following: request analysis and search failure analysis have not been major inputs to MEDLARS vocabulary control; the entry vocabulary, which should be an integral part of the MEDLARS index language, and an essential tool of both indexers and searchers, has been neglected; searchers are not completely aware of indexing policies and conventions; the average indexer has little idea, as far as the demand search function is concerned, of what he is indexing for (i.e., the types of requests that are made of the system).

We recommend that the Library take steps necessary to achieve a close integration between the functions of indexing, searching and vocabulary control. (The writer has not considered it within his present frame of reference to recommend specific organizational changes, nor to study methods whereby such integration can be effected most efficiently and economically.) Although consistency problems may result at first, the present trend towards combining, at MEDLARS centers, the indexing and the searching functions, is considered to be a valuable move in the right direction.

Use of foreign language material in MEDLARS

The comparatively small use made of foreign language material, by demand search requesters, was observed in Part 2. While foreign language articles consume approximately 45% of MEDLARS input costs, we estimate that they contribute no more than 16% of the total demand search usage (i.e., no more than 16% of the articles retrieved and judged of value are in languages other than English).

It is difficult to make specific recommendations on this subject, apart from urging that NLM re-evaluate in general its policies relating to foreign literature. Many requesters complained that translation services are not available to them or that translation is too costly. If NLM continues to devote 45% of its input effort to the foreign material, it might consider adopting a more active role in the translations area (perhaps by acting as a clearinghouse for translations in biomedicine).

The search printout as a content indicator

In the study of output screening, it was noted that titles and tracings are frequently inadequate in indicating the content of articles in the MEDLARS data base. The implication is that, although 58% of all the articles retrieved by MEDLARS are judged "of value" by requesters, by no means all of these articles are recognized as being potentially valuable when they appear as citations in demand search bibliographies. In the light of this, the requirement for including abstracts in the next-generation MEDLARS (as recognized in the *Functional System Specifications for the National Library of Medicine*, July 1, 1967) appears well-justified. In connection with this, we estimate that about 90% of input articles contain a usable content indicator in the form of abstract, summary or conclusions, although not all of these are in English.

Continuous quality control of the MEDLARS operation

A large-scale evaluation, of the type that has been undertaken, is useful in exposing the general weaknesses of the system. Such a study will also bring to light specific indexing failures, specific searching failures, and specific inadequacies of the index language. However, these specific failures must be regarded merely as symptomatic of kinds of failures that occur. A single evaluation study, however comprehensive, cannot be expected to discover more than a very small fraction of the specific inadequacies of the system. For example, we know that it is very difficult, if not impossible, to conduct a successful search on premature rupture of the fetal membranes, or one on gallbladder perforation. However, there are undoubtedly many other legitimate topics upon which MEDLARS cannot conduct a successful search, even though relevant literature exists in the system. Such specific inadequacies can only be discovered through continous monitoring of the MEDLARS operation.

We recommend that the Library, having concluded a large-scale study of the MEDLARS performance, should now investigate the feasibility of implementing procedures for the "continuous quality control" of MEDLARS operations. We recognize that continuous quality control is likely to be much more difficult to implement than a one-time evaluation. Nevertheless we feel that continuous system monitoring is ultimately essential to the success of any large retrieval system.

We visualize that "continuous quality control" would embrace at least the following functions:

1. Recognizing a request, within the scope of the system, that cannot adequately be conducted because of present indexing policies or vocabulary indequacies. Any such requirements that are legitimate, and likely to be recurrent, indicate the need for changes in vocabulary or indexing policy.
2. Recognizing searches that have failed through defective interaction with the requester, poor searching strategies, vocabulary inadequacies, or indexing policies. Recall failures must be recognized by members of the MEDLARS staff, using similar methods to those employed in the present investigation (a heavy reliance would probably be put on the requester's own "known relevant" articles for this purpose). Precision failures must be identified primarily on the basis of feedback from the requester himself, and the present MEDLARS search appraisal form should be redesigned for this purpose.

    Searches known to have performed badly, either in recall or precision, will require analysis to determine cause of failure. Such search analyses will be essential inputs to vocabulary control procedures, to decisions relating to indexing policy, and to search training functions.
3. Recognizing, in the indexing operation, items of subject matter that cannot be specifically expressed by present MeSH terms, and for which no terms exist in the entry vocabulary. The

articles thus affected will require "flagging" by the indexer concerned, and subsequent action by the MeSH group. This action will involve the creation of a new MeSH term, a new provisional heading, or a new reference in the entry vocabulary.

Future use of the MEDLARS test corpus

During the conduct of this evaluation we have accumulated a corpus (of articles, indexing records, requests, searching strategies, and relevance assessments) that can be used for further analysis and experimentation. This corpus is already being drawn upon for a number of purposes, including the conduct of "search workshops" and the comparison of searching strategies prepared by various MEDLARS centers.

We recommend that this corpus should be the basis of further experimentation within MEDLARS. It would, for example, be a most valuable corpus upon which to conduct experiments on automatic indexing. In fact, a small part of it (18 searches and 276 documents) is already being used by Salton, at Cornell University, in the further testing of the SMART system. Natural language, free-text searching of abstracts would be another area of study, well worth investigating, for which the test corpus would be admirably suited (we have real requests and real relevance assessments). Finally, we recommend that the corpus be used for further studies on possible alternative modes of searching the MEDLARS data base. In particular, because many requesters can cite relevant articles at the time they request a MEDLARS search, we suggest that NLM investigate the feasibility of deriving searching strategies automatically, by computer, on the basis of index terms assigned to articles known to be relevant to MEDLARS requests.

FOOTNOTES

[1] It is estimated that a little more than half the searches using the three-level sorting mechanism are of the first type.
[2] Although this sounds like a poor performance, it requires a powerful filtering capacity to reduce 700,000 potentially relevant citations to 600 potentially relevant, without losing a significant amount of the relevant literature.
[3] In each case, the first alternative posed represents the performance actually estimated for the system.

Selected Results from an Inquiry into Testing of Information Retrieval Systems

by Tefko Saracevic

A variety of aspects related to testing of retrieval systems were examined. A model of a retrieval system, together with a set of measures and a methodology for performance testing were developed. In the main experiment the effect on performance of the following variables was tested: sources of indexing, indexing languages, coding schemes, question analyses, search strategies and formats of output. In addition, a series of separate experiments was carried out to investigate the problems of controls in experimentation with IR systems. The main conclusions: it seems that testing of total IR systems controlling and monitroing all factors (environmental and systems-related) is not possible at present; the human factor appears to be the main variable in all components of an IR system; length of indexes affects performance considerably more than indexing languages; question analyses and search strategies affect performance to a great extent—as much, if not more than indexing. Retrieval systems seems to be able to perform at present only on a general level failing to be at the same time comprehensive and specific.

On Testing

In the world of technology, engineering and physical sciences, testing of physical systems is a time-honored and studied tradition—an activity quite formalized with well-structured measures, instrumentation and methodology. Unfortunately, testing of social systems such as retrieval systems, libraries or educational institutions, is neither a time-honored nor a well-structured activity. Because of complexity, competition, cost, and importance to society, the need to test social systems is as real as the need to test physical systems. However, the problems encountered in testing social systems as compared with testing physical systems are staggeringly different in nature. In addition, the hope for exactness in quantification is much smaller, the conduct of tests much more difficult, the complexity of testing much greater and the limitations imposed on generalizing results much more stringent.

Given that we understand the notion of testing in a quantitative sense (where the performance of a system is related to its purpose and the variables affecting the performance are monitored) the following conclusion about testing information retrieval (IR) systems is drawn from this Inquiry:

At present, real and productive testing of *total* retrieval systems, taking into account and controlling all inside and environmental factors is neither feasible nor possible. Furthermore, it appears that generalizable, formal, quantified results of high validity and reliability on all, or even on a majority, of factors affecting the performance of retrieval systems cannot be attained at present.

The reasons seem fairly evident. First, no theory exists which takes into account all, or even a majority, of the factors operating within and upon retrieval systems. Today we have only an intuitive understanding of the objectives and role of retrieval systems within the total context of the communication processes of its users. Thus, it is difficult to construct measures fully reflective of the systems objectives. Second, no adequate knowledge exists of processes involved within or contingent to retrieval systems; without a thorough understanding of these processes, comprehensive testing is not possible. Third, no standardized methodologies exist for experimentation involving retrieval systems. This condition further complicates any testing activity because testing implies comparable standards. Fourth, no adequate understanding of appropriate experimental controls exists; controls are essential in monitoring

SOURCE: An original manuscript (dated May, 1970) submitted by the author.

processes and in sorting out factors contributing to system performance. Fifth, no sustained effort to cumulate and the synthesize existing knowledge in relation to retrieval systems has begun.

Despite these substantive obstacles, progress in evaluating retrieval systems has been made. Realization of all these obstacles involved is progress. Definition of problems is the most important aspect in their solution. The definition of problems associated with retrieval systems, in turn, is the major accomplishment of test activity, such as that conducted by Cleverdon (1) Salton (2) Lancaster (3) and reported in this Inquiry. Thus, although not achieving all of its intended goals, testing activity in the field of information retrieval can claim several specific achievements:

a) developing knowledge on the gross performance effects of a limited number of system's factors,
b) delineating the main relationships between these factors,
c) observing and better understanding of the overall operations of retrieval systems,
d) introducing experimentation into the field,
e) eliminating dogmatic conclusions based upon anecdotal evidence, and
f) uncovering infinitely more problems than it solved—problems that have motivated researchers to higher levels of achievement and greater rigor in their work.

This Inquiry is not exempt from the general deficiencies encountered in testing, and the results do not go beyond the limited achievements enumerated above. Although every attempt was made to achieve rigorous and objective controls, human subjectivity was always encountered, and plays a major role in all results. As in all other tests, the specific numerical results of this Inquiry should be interpreted with a considerable grain of salt; however, it is believed that the general conclusions can help in providing some answers to the perennial question of information retrieval: how can we optimize the communication contact between the available literature (or information in general) and its users while minimizing the interference introduced by necessity by a system.

Aims and Approach

The results reported here are derived from a project entitled Comparative Systems Laboratory (CSL) conducted at the Center for Documentation and Communication Research, School of Library Science, Case Western Reserve University during a four-year period (1963-1968) and supported by a grant from the U. S. Public Health Service. The general aim of CSL was to conduct a comprehensive inquiry into testing of information retrieval systems. Specifically, the aims of CSL were to:

1. define the essential components of an information retrieval system and to construct a system model,
2. identify the variables affecting the performance of the system,
3. design a methodology for experiments which would provide quantitative information concerning variation in system performance,
4. conduct experiments applying this methodology in relation to a limited, specified number of variables, and
5. gain a further understanding of variables and processes operating within retrieval systems and of methodologies needed for experimentation with such systems.

The general approach involved a conscious effort to delineate and to distinguish various test-related activities and to conduct these activities in a prescribed, interdependent order.

Test-related activities in CLS may be divided into four distinct areas:

Theory and General Methodology

A general methodology for testing retrieval systems was developed, including a theoretical framework, a model of an IR system, measures for evaluation of an IR system, and a general method of analysis. This methodology was fully specified by Goffman and Newill. (4)

Experimental Design and Operations

On the basis of the general methodology, experiments were designed and a selection made of components to be varied and to be held constant; operational definitions and procedures were specified in relation to (a) development of components, and (b) comparative testing of components; actual operations followed.

Controls

Controls, including efforts to limit deviation and bias, were attempted at every stage. Independent experiments were conducted in order to investigate the meaning of controls in information retrieval experimentation.

Analysis and Evaluation

Analysis of quantitative results enabled the evaluation of the performance of systems factors under experimentation.

A series of CSL technical reports, issued by Case Western Reserve University, presented various aspects of the Inquiry. Two reports are of particular interest to a full understanding of the experiments: one presents the operational manuals used for constructing and operating various experimental components of an IR system (5), and the other is the Final Report, which comprehensively presents the Inquiry with considerable attention paid to the control-related experiments conducted within CSL (6).

General Model, Measures, and Methodology

Development of the testing methodology involved (a) definition of the system's components in a manner that would permit their assembly into an IR system, i.e., development of a model; (b) construction of measures for performance evaluation of an IR system; and (c) development of a generalized experimental method on the basis of which the measures could be utilized in comparative testing of IR systems.

Model

It was considered essential that the system's purpose and function be specified in the model of an IR system. This is an essential step since performance can be meaningfully evaluated only as a function of the system's inputs and outputs in relation to a given purpose. The basic purpose of a retrieval system was considered to be provision of relevant information to user groups. This purpose was to be accomplished by presenting the users with a set of documents containing relevant information in response to their queries. The eleven major components included in the model of this experimental IR system related either to purpose or to function. The *purpose components* (i.e., goals) included:

1. *the discipline*
2. *the class of users*
3. *the size of the file.*

The *function components* (i.e., components required in processing a query) included:

1. *Acquisition*: Policy determining the content of the file.
2. *Source of input*: Format of the document (e.g.,

title, abstract, full text) used for selecting index terms. (*Index term* is defined as a word or string of words connoting a concept and denoting a class).
3. *Indexing language*: A set of index terms together with a set of rules; the set of index terms is the vocabulary of the indexing language, and is referred to as a *terminology*.
4. *Coding*: Symbolic representation of index terms.
5. *Organization of the file*: Order of the file contents.
6. *Question analysis*: Translation of query concepts into indexing language.
7. *Searching strategy*: Procedure used to search the file.
8. *Format of output*: Physical representation of documents provided to user (e.g., title, abstract, full text) as an answer to a query.

Measures

In order to construct measures appropriate to the evaluation of a system's performance, a distinction was made between (a) the system's assignment of relevance, i.e., documents included in the system's answer, and (b) the user's assignment of relevance, i.e., user's evaluation of the system's answer. These connote relevance at the source and relevance at the destination within a communication process.

An IR system's performance may be evaluated in terms of the degree of agreement between these two assignments of relevance, where the user's assignment is the standard against which a system's assignment is compared. Specifically, the performance of a retrieval system was quantitatively indicated by the measures of Sensitivity (*Se*), Specificity (*Sp*) and Effectiveness (*Es*). *Sensitivity* measures the system's ability to provide a user with relevant members of the file. *Specificity* measures the system's ability not to provide a user with nonrelevant members. *Effectiveness* is an additive combination of *Se* and *Sp*.

Se and *Sp* can be expressed as conditional probabilities:

$$Se = P_R(A)$$
$$Sp = P_R{'}(A')$$
$$Es = Se + Sp - 1$$

i.e., Sensitivity is the probability that given a document is relevant (R) it will be retrieved as an answer (A); Specificity is the probability that given a document is not relevant (R') it will not be retrieved as an answer (A'); Effectiveness is as indicated. These measures may be approximated as follows:

$$Se = \frac{\text{number of relevant documents retrieved}}{\text{total number of relevant documents in the file}}$$

$$Sp = \frac{\text{number of nonrelevant documents not retrieved}}{\text{total number of nonrelevant documents in the file}}$$

As approximated above Sensitivity is equivalent to the measure of Recall, but Specificity is not the same as Precision, since Precision is:

$$Pr = \frac{\text{number of relevant documents retrieved}}{\text{total number of documents retrieved}}$$

General Methodology

The general methodology was concerned with accomplishing a comparative evaluation of a variety of system's components by measuring the variability in the system's performance resulting from alterations in the components. We based this approach on the proposition that although a direct comparison of the performance of systems having different purposes and functions was meaningless, it was meaningful to evaluate the performance of a variety of system's components, given some purpose and function.

A critical problem in implementing the methodology was the establishment of user-relevant sets of documents to serve as comparison standards. One way to establish user-relevant sets would be to provide users with the whole file and ask them to select document sets relevant to their queries. This alternative was rejected as impractical. Instead, user-relevant sets for each query were established by presenting users with universal sets of retrieved answers from which they selected answers relevant to their queries. A *universal set* is defined as follows: given a number of files which indexed the same documents in different ways and/or upon which a number of different search procedures have been applied, the universal set for a given query is a *union of outputs* obtained from searching all the different files with all search procedures. A user-relevant set obtained in this manner permits a comparison of the performance of different files and different search procedures.

It should be realized that when measures such as

Se, *Sp* and *Es* are based upon universal sets defined in this manner, they indicate a comparative and not an absolute performance. For example, if a user-relevant document did not exist within the universal set, because it was not retrieved, all files and search procedures would be penalized equivalently for not retrieving that document as an answer. Thus, the comparative performance holds not only within the framework of a universal set, but also with respect to the compared files or search procedures.

Experimental Design

The experimental design was completely governed by two factors:
(a) The general model, measures, and methodology synthesized above, and
(b) expediency, that is, availability of users, materials, operational facilities and personnel. The design was primarily concerned with operationally defining components (discussed in this section) and with prescribing experimental operations (discussed in Section 5).

I. **Purpose Components.** These components were held constant.
   1. *Discipline*: Tropical diseases, specifically, vector-borne diseases.
   2. *Class of users*: Research investigators throughout the U.S., in the above discipline.
   3. *Size of the file*: 600 documents.

II. **Function Components.** Two of the eight components were held constant; the remainder were varied.
   1. *Acquisition* (constant): Random selection of documents from a year's volume of *Tropical Diseases Bulletin* (TDB), London.
   2. *Source of input* (varied):
      (a) Titles
      (b) abstracts, drawn from *TDB*
      (c) full texts
   3. *Indexing language* (varied):
      (a) *Telegraphic abstract*. A set of index terms, assigned without constraints, by indexers together with a syntactic relationship indicated by the role indicators (roles) and a grouping of terms into levels (links); indexed from all three sources.
      (b) *Keywords selected by indexes*. Index terms contained in a given document; indexed from all three sources.

(c) *Keywords selected by computer.* Index terms selected on the basis of computer program instructions; indexed from titles only.

(d) *Metalanguage.* An experimental indexing language with two sets of index terms: meta (general) terms that describe or indicate the action of the object (specific) terms; indexed from titles only.

(e) *Tropical Diseases Bulletin (TDB) Index.* A set of subject headings and index terms as prepared for the Annual Index of the *TDB.* (The closest comparative sources are titles and abstracts).

4. *Code* (varied): All index terms are represented in:

(a) *English.* English terms without terminology and relationship control.

(b) *Medical Coding Scheme (MCS).* A faceted-type thesaurus in symbolic language which arranges the index terms by employing individual classification for seven classes of terms: geographic and personal names; medical terms—anatomy; medical terms—diseases; organisms; chemicals; chemical and medical processes, techniques and operations; and general terms.

5. *File organization* (constant): A sequential order of all index files handled by a set of computer programs.

6. *Question analysis* (varied): Five types of question analysis, gradually increasing the searching scope; searches were performed separately for each type:

Type A: Enumeration of unit concepts (i.e., principal, searchable English terms describing the subject of a question) selected from the user-submitted question.

Type B: Each of the Type A terms was expanded by locating generically, specifically, synonymously, and collaterally related terms through the MCS thesaurus only (i.e., Type A plus thesaurus).

Type C: Type A terms expanded through any other tool—reference works, dictionaries, personal knowledge—except the MCS thesaurus (i.e., Type A plus English).

Type D: Type C terms expanded further through using the MCS thesaurus (i.e., Type C plus thesaurus).

Type E: Type D terms verified through consultation with the user; if necessary, subsequent revisions—additions or deletions—were incorporated (Type D plus user).

7. *Searching strategy* (varied):

(a) *Question level (or narrow) search statement* is the statement that as completely and accurately as possible reflects the stated question for purposes of searching; that is, it incorporates *all* searchable terms (unit concepts) from the question regardless of their comparative importance; the search statements resulting from Question Analyses Type A to Type E are searched as narrow searches;

(b) *Broad search statement* is the statement that represents the question by only one general subject aspect (not necessarily one term) and all its expansions.

8. *Format of output* (varied):

(a) Bibliographic citation (including title)

(b) Abstract (drawn form *TDB*)

(c) Full text

On the basis of these definitions, a simple null-type hypothesis was formulated:

Variations in the sources on input, the indexing language, methods of coding, question analysis, search strategies and/or formats of output do not significantly affect the performance of an information retrieval system in terms of sensitivity, specificity and effectiveness.

Experimental Operations

Acquisitions and Indexing

Six hundred documents, randomly selected from the 1960 volume of *TDB*, were indexed in five indexing languages. It is of interest to note that 600 documents represent nearly half the world's annual output in open periodical literature on tropical diseases as abstracted by *TDB*, thus for this field it is a significant number of documents. For two indexing languages each document was indexed from three sources of input, yielding a total of nine index files:

Index File	Indexing Language	Source of Input
A	Telegraphic Abstract	Title
B	Telegraphic Abstract	Abstract
C	Telegraphic Abstract	Full Text
D	Keywords by Indexers	Title
E	Keywords by Indexers	Abstract

F	Keywords by Indexers	Full Text
G	Keywords by Computer	Titles
H	Metalanguage	Titles
K	*TDB* Index Entries	Titles/Abstracts

Each index file may be described in terms of two variables: the indexing language and the source of input employed.

Each source of input produced indexes of different lengths, thus actually differences in index length (i.e. number of index terms per document) became the variable in relation to source of input. The title-based files had indexes of approximately 5 to 8 index terms; abstract-based files 23 to 30 index terms; and full text-based files 36 to 40 index terms. The *TDB* Index yielded approximately 11 index terms; thus, it is not directly comparable to abstract- or title-based files.

Operations manuals for indexing in each indexing languages were developed. Seven indexers were utilized: three in Telegraphic Abstracts, three in Keywords, and one in Metalanguage. An eighth indexer prepared the *Tropical Diseases Bulletin* original index slips for computer searching. Indexers were selected on the bases of their biomedical education and previous indexing experience. A three-week training period was introduced in an effort to standardize approach and indexing skills. No indexer indexed more than one indexing language. Separate control experiments indicated that the indexing was of high quality and relatively high consistency. The average intra-indexing consistency was .71 and the inter-indexing consistency was .62. It was found that the highest inconsistency was in indexing general terms. Some 25% of index terms were found to be general terms, while only some 10% of question terms were in that category. It is worth while to note that quality and consistency of indexing are not necessarily related.

Encoding and Thesaurus Construction

Every term in each indexing language was treated as an independent term (i.e., no relations with other terms were specified) and also as a coded entry in a faceted-type thesaurus (i.e., certain relations between index terms were specified). The thesaurus consisted only of terms identified in indexing the documents. The relative performance of these two coding approaches was tested as part of the question analysis procedure by expanding the question with and without use of the thesaurus.

A manual was developed for constructing the thesaurus. Three coders were utilized: one for medical terms; one for chemical terms; and one for general terms. Coders were selected on the basis of their educational background in the appropriate subject areas (MD; PhD in chemistry; BS in biology) and their experience in creating similar thesauri. Coders were reviewed in encoding procedures, and tested for consistency in a separate, control experiment. The classifying (intracoder) consistency of the medical-terms coder was .36, for the chemical-terms coder .86, and for the general-terms coder .93. Other coding tests indicated that the intra- and inter-consistency for classifying medical terms is usually as low as found here; no adequate reasons were found.

A master thesaurus was created containing all unique terms in all nine index files; in addition, for each file a thesaurus was created containing terms unique to that file. The thesaurus from title-based files contained approximately 1700 unique index terms; from abstract-based files approximately 5500 index terms; and from full text-based files approximately 5600 index terms. The master thesaurus contained some 11,000 terms. Since keywords were involved, many terms were grammatical variants of other terms or compounds of simple terms, thus the large volume of the master thesaurus. Despite these factors, there were considerable symmetric differences between thesauri from different files. It is of interest to note that *thesauri* of abstract and full text-based files were of similar length although their *indexes* were not.

Users and Question Asking

Twenty-five user volunteers were recruited with the help of an Advisory Committee from the Communicable Disease Center in Atlanta, Georgia. Each user was a specialist in the field of tropical diseases, and a senior worker in the institution of his primary affiliation. Users came from 13 different institutions. Nineteen users had earned a Ph.D., five an M.D. and one a B.S. Eighteen users were engaged primarily in research, six in teaching and one in treatment. The specific subject interests most frequently cited were entomology, mycology, parasitology, microbiology, toxicology, bacteriology, and serology. The users' role was to submit questions appropriate for searching; to discuss the question with the systems analyst, when necessary; to assess the relevance of the universal set to the query; and to provide information about themselves and their activities related to the experiment. In order to assist users in performing their question formulating task and to impose some control and standardization on this task, a manual and forms for question-formulation were developed. Users were instructed to provide questions related to their current research interest and to describe their work. Questions were compared with work descriptions to ascertain if a relation existed; it did for all queries. The text of queries is presented in Part III of the CSL Final Report. (6) The users submitted 141 queries, of which 136 were searched, and 124 included in the final analysis.[1]

Question Analysis and Searching

Each question analysis type was applied to every query, resulting in the successive enlargement of the query's scope. Terms were expanded within the restriction that all terms achieved through expansion had to be connected to each other and to the original term by a logical "or."

The result of each question analysis was a set of terms. These terms were then combined into a search statement. The search statements resulting from question analysis Types A through E were on the narrow level (i.e., reflecting the question). The broad level strategy was established on the basis of the primary subject concept requested in the query. Each query was searched over all index files, in all question analysis types, and on both search strategy levels, yielding a possible maximum of 54 searches per query; however, since in some cases some different types of question analyses for a given query were equivalent it was possible to run a lesser number of searches per query and superimpose the results.

A manual for question analysis and another for construction of search statements were developed together with appropriate forms. Question analyses and searching were performed by four systems analysts, selected on the basis of subject education and experience in information retrieval. One systems analyst held a Ph.D. in chemistry and information science; one a M.D.; one a B.S. in biology with an M.S. in library science; and one a B.S. in biology and chemistry.

In order to allow comparability of output over question analyses and search levels, it was paramount that all question analyses and searches for a given question be consistent. To ensure the maximum consistency, elaborate computer-aided and manual control examinations were initiated.

Every search for every question was checked for consistency in scope and exhaustivity against other searches for that question, as well as for a similarity in the analysis approach with other questions. Errors were eventually corrected and, where necessary, new searches initiated. It was surprising to find that despite every attempt to insure consistency, a large number of inconsistencies were found. Initially, there were 4,091 search statements written for the 124 questions. After these search statements were checked, 2,590 had to be corrected and re-run, and 356 new search statements were added. Thus, a total of 2,947 additional searches were run; 4,448 searches were included in the final analysis. This output control examination demonstrated that question analysis and construction of search strategies is subject to great human inconsistency.

Relevance Judgements

For each question the output (answers) from all searches were merged, and a union of unique answer documents (universal set) was formed for submission to the user. Answers were presented to the user in three formats: titles, abstracts and full texts. In the rating instructions, the user was to evaluate titles first, then abstracts and then full texts. Relevance judgements of each document representation vis-à-vis query was made on a three-point scale: Relevant (R), Partially Relevant (P) and Nonrelevant (N). The following definitions were provided:

"A *relevant document* is any document which on the basis of the information it conveys, is considered to be related to your (user's) question even if the information is outdated or familiar to you.

A *partially relevant document* is any document which on the basis of the information it conveys is considered only somewhat or in some part related to your question or to any part of your question.

A *nonrelevant document* is any document which, on the basis of the information it conveys, is not at all related to your question."

The user recorded his judgment on a listing of document accession numbers and returned this to CSL. These relevance judgements established the user-relevant set for each query, and became the standard for comparing the performance of variables and for analysis or results. However, some unexpected restrictions on relevance judgements, as explained below, were found to exist.

Although the experimental design called for all relevance judgements to be performed by users, certain operational deficiencies prevented this. At the time users' questions were submitted, only three index files (A, B and C) were fully completed. The other six files were at various stages of completion due to operational problems. Under these circumstances it was decided not to wait for completion of these six files, but to search comprehensively the available three files, and to submit the answer-documents retrieved from those files to users for evaluation. It was assumed (a) that there would be an insignificant number of additional (and therefore nonuser evaluated) documents retrieved from the other six files, and (b) that whatever was later retrieved from these files would not be relevant. The first assumption proved to be false but the second assumption was correct. This was the situation:

1. In answer to *124 questions* posed by *24 users*, index files A, B, and C retrieved *1518 answers*; these were evaluated by the users as to relevance to their queries.
2. The other six index files yielded an additional *1108 answers*; these answers were not evaluated by the users.
3. The total output at the source was *2626 answers* of which *58% was evaluated* by the users.

The 1108 nonevaluated documents were assigned relevance ratings by two independent methods. In one method an expert in biomedical communication (MS biology, MSLS, 10 years experience) extended (interpolated) the users' relevance judgements to the nonevaluated answers. Working with the query and the user's evaluation of answer documents to that query, he evaluated the additional documents. A second method involved textual similarities between the evaluated and nonevaluated answers for each query. Relevance ratings were made on the basis of textual similarities. This method is described by Gifford and Baumanis. (7) On the basis of both methods 6 Relevant documents and 7 Partially Relevant documents were found amongst the 1108 nonevaluated answers, all others were Not Relevant. We were satisfied that we received an excellent approximation of user judgements through these methods.

It is interesting that the addition of different index files produced a considerable magnitude of additional retrievals almost all of which were non-

relevant. This finding is taken to demonstrate that the files responded equally well in retrieving relevant answers, but that there were large, symmetric differences in the retrieval of nonrelevant answers. These differences, by and large, may be ascribed to indexer decisions regarding peripheral terms.

Another operational problem associated with relevance judgements resulted when three users indicated a willingness to devote only a limited amount of time to evaluating relevance. These users evaluated only the full texts. Since the final analysis involved relevance judgements on the full-text, this limitation had no effect on any variable except "formation of output." Thus, data from 99 questions were used for analysis of the results of the variable "format of output," and data from 124 questions were used for all other variables.

Answers

Altogether 2,626 answer documents were retrieved for all 124 queries. Of these, based on *full text* judgements, there were:

$$249 \text{ Relevant } (R)$$
$$139 \text{ Partially Relevant } (P)$$
$$2238 \text{ Nonrelevant } (N)$$

This is the standard against which the performance of all variables, except "format of output" was measured.

Of the 600 documents in the files, 540 documents (90%) were retrieved as answers. The 388 relevant and partially relevant answers were produced by 209 documents (30% of the file). Thus, the answers were not associated with a small portion of the file showing that questions and documents were diversified.

The distribution of the *total* $(R + P + N)$ number of answers retrieved in relation to questions, was as follows:

31 questions had between 1 to 5 answers
23 questions had between 6 to 10 answers
34 questions had between 11 to 20 answers
18 questions had between 21 to 40 answers
12 questions had between 41 to 80 answers
 6 questions had between 81 to 160 answers

The distribution of the number of answers judged *Relevant* (R) in relation to questions was as follows:

61 questions had no R answers
51 questions had between 1 to 5 R answers
 8 questions had between 6 to 10 R answers

3 questions had between 11 to 20 R answers
1 questions had between 21 to 40 R answers

Since almost one-half of the queries found no relevant answers in the searches, it may be concluded that the system variables performed "badly" for these queries—a fact shown in the analyses of results. Eight percent of the remaining queries found 1-5 relevant answers. This indicates stringent relevance standards by users.

Control-Related Experiments

A series of control-related experiments and studies were carried out in order to recognize source factors that substantially contribute to variations of results, and in order to learn more about the interaction among factors. For reasons of brevity, these control-related experiments and studies are only enumerated here, although some of their results have been incorporated into the description of CSL, e.g., indexers' and coders' consistency. A full description of control-related experiments can be found in (6). Section 7, General Conclusion, does take these results into account. The control experiments and studies included: a study of indexers and indexing consistency; an analysis of variations in the length of indexes and thesauri; a study of coders and coding consistency; a study of characteristics of the *TDB* index and of the relation between indexes constructed for manual and machine searching; an analysis of the consistency of question analysis and of searching; a study of the reliability of relevance extension (interpolation) from users' judgements to a judgement by an expert; an analysis of sources of differences in results between index files; an analysis of index term frequencies; a study on the validation of a thesaurus; a study on the relation between text of questions and text of relevant and nonrelevant documents; an exploration of procedures for optimization of search strategies; and a study of the nature of questions obtained in relation to the nature of the file.

Results

Method of Analysis

The method of analysis was quite simple and followed the notion that comparative results were to be obtained. No statistical tests were employed because it was felt that the data did not satisfy the basic assumptions under which these tests should

be employed—most notably, independence of data could not be assumed.

The method of analysis for *one* given question consisted of comparing the number of $R, P,$ and N answers obtained from each variable (e.g., index file, search strategy level, question analysis) to the universal set for that question. In addition, outputs for some variables were combined in unions and compared to other unions of variables or to the universal set. For example, the union of output for all title-based files was compared to the union of output for abstract-based files and full-text based files; the union of output for all three Telegraphic Abstract Files was compared to the union of output for all three Keyword files; the union of output for all question analysis types was compared to the output for broad search, etc.

The method of analysis for *all* questions consisted of summing the output (i.e. number of $R, P,$ N answers) for individual variables, or their combinations, and comparing that sum to the total output for 124 questions was 2626 answers: 249 R, 139 P and 2238 N answers—this was the standard for comparison. The measures (Se, Sp, Es) were calculated after the sums for each variable were obtained. Thus, the measures do not indicate means but proportions of total output. In order to simplify here the presentation of measures, partially relevant answers are treated as non-relevant answers. The standard for calculation of comparative measures then becomes:

249 Relevant answers, and
2377 Partially relevant and
      non-relevant answers $(P + N)$

Since these judgments were made on full texts, all the analyses are based on full-text judgements.

It should be noted that the total number of answers is also a measure—it is an extremely powerful indicator of the magnitude of retrievals generated by a variable. In the design of systems the magnitude of expected retrieval may be an extremely important criterion affecting design decisions. The total size of expected output is also an important consideration for users. This simple measure is a powerful objective indication of quantitative performance and thus it is discussed at some length in the presentation of results.

Sources of Input

Table 1 compares results obtained from title-, abstract-, and full text-based index files. In order to concentrate only on variations due to source of

TABLE 1: COMPARATIVE PERFORMANCE OF TITLE-, ABSTRACT-, AND FULL TEXT-BASED FILES

Union of index files based on:	NARROW SEARCHES			BROAD SEARCHES		
	Total	R,P,N,	Se,Sp,Es	Total	R,P,N,	Se,Sp,Es
TITLES	113	51	.20	533	91	.37
		11	.97		28	.81
		51	.17		414	.17
ABSTRACTS	503	147	.59	1666	199	.80
		56	.85		98	.38
		300	.44		1366	.18
FULL TEXTS	754	181	.73	2322	238	.96
		70	.76		125	.12
		503	.48		1959	.07
ALL 9 FILES	871	197	.79	2626	249	1.00
		83	.72		139	0.00
		591	.50		2238	0.00

Legend:

   Narrow searches: union of all question analysis types.

   Total: total number of answers retrieved.

   R,P,N: respective numbers of relevant, partially relevant and non relevant answers retrieved.

   Se,Sp,Es: respective measures of Sensitivity, Specificity, and Effectiveness.

inputs, results from files based on identical sources were combined. Thus, results for titles are from the union of outputs of the four title-based index files (A, D, G, H); for abstracts, from the union of files for the three abstract-based index files (B, E, K); and for full texts from the union of files for the two full text-based index files (C, F). Results are shown for narrow searches and for broad searches. The last row indicates results from the union of output of all nine index files.[2]

   Some interesting observations and relations emerge. The ratio of *index lengths* (number of index terms per document) between titles, abstracts, and full texts was approximately (see section 5.1):

$$1 : 4 : 6.$$

The ratio of the *total outputs* (T) between title-, abstract-, and full text-based files was approxi-

mately:

$$1 : 4 : 7 \text{ for narrow searches}$$
$$1 : 3 : 5 \text{ for broad searches}$$

The ratio of *Relevant + Partially Relevant answers* (R) for the same files was approximately:

$$1 : 3 : 4 \text{ for both broad and}$$
$$\text{narrow searches}$$

And the ratio of *Nonrelevant answers* (N) for the same files was approximately:

$$1 : 6 : 10 \text{ narrow searches}$$
$$1 : 3 : 5 \text{ broad searches}$$

Thus, taking x, the length of indexes, as an independent variable, all three values (T,R,N) behaved in a remarkably linear fashion. T, R and N could be approximated by the simple equation,

$$y = ax + b$$

where a and b are constants, and x is the length of indexes. *Figure 1* graphically represents the linear behavior of total (T), relevant $(R + P)$ and non-relevant number of answers as a function of the length of indexes
In particular:

$$T = a_1 x + b_1$$
$$N = a_2 x + b_2$$
$$R = a_3 x + b_3$$

By using the data from this experiment it can be calculated that the constants, a_1, a_2, a_3, are related approximately as:

$$a_1 \approx 1.5 a_2 \approx 3 a_3$$

or,

$$a_1 \approx 3 a_3$$
$$a_2 \approx 2 a_3$$

In general, it seems that a linear increase in the length of indexes provides a linear increase in the total number of answers, as well as a linear increase in the number of relevant and nonrelevant answers. However, the *coefficient* of increase is largest for the total output, somewhat smaller is largest for the total output, somewhat smaller (approximately $\frac{1}{3}$ smaller) for the nonrelevant answers, and considerably smaller (approximately $\frac{2}{3}$ smaller) for the relevant answers. As indexes increase in length, we may say that n-times longer

Figure 1:   Effect of Length of Indexes on the Total Number, Number of Relevant (R+P) and Number of Non Relevant answers retrieved.

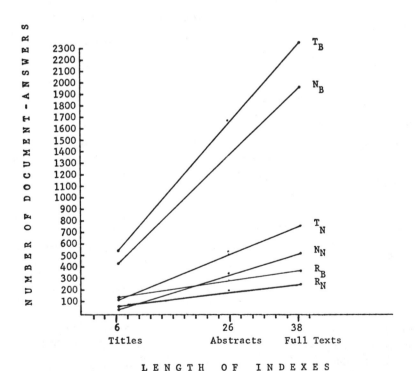

Legend:

T_B, T_N: Total number of answers retrieved by broad and narrow searches respectively.

R_B, R_N: Number of relevant plus partially relevant answers retrieved by broad and narrow searches respectively.

N_B, N_N: Number of nonrelevant answers retrieved by broad and narrow searches respectively.

indexes will probably produce *n*-times larger outputs. Furthermore, the longer the indexes, the more relevant answers will be retrieved, but a far greater number of nonrelevant answers will be retrieved, too.

In relation to measures, it can be seen that *Sensitivity* rises for narrow searches from .20 (title-files) to .59 (abstract-files) to .73 (full text-files) and for the broad searches from .37 to .80 to .96 respectively—a very significant increase throughout. At the same time and for the same files, *Specificity* drops for narrow searches from 197 to .86 to .76 and for broad searches from .81 to .41 to .12—a very significant decrease throughout. Thus, for the respective files Effectiveness increases for narrow searches from .17 to .45 to .48, and for broad searches it goes from .17 to .20 to a very low of .07. Overall then, the abstract-based index files (between 23–30 index terms in length) were most effective.

In any case, it can be seen that the variation in sources of input (i.e., length of indexes) produced a considerable variation in results. With respect to this variable, the null-hypothesis can be rejected.

Indexing Languages

Table 2 compares the results obtained from the four indexing languages in which titles have been indexed; *Table 3* compares the three indexing languages in which abstracts have been indexed; *Table 4* compares the two indexing languages in which full texts have been indexed; *Table 5* compares the union of output from the three files (A, B, C), representing Telegraphic Abstracts as an indexing language, with the union of output from the three files (D, E, F), representing Keywords chosen by indexers. The results are given for narrow as well as broad searches. For comparison between these outputs and the total output from all files refer to the last row of *Table 1*, showing the results obtained from the union of all nine index files.

The results indicate that the four different indexing languages which were applied to titles (Table 2) showed remarkably equivalent performance. It seems that regardless how titles are indexed, the performance is the same. Of the three indexing languages applied to abstracts (Table 3) the first two (TA and KW) showed some slight differences in performance with Keywords performing better, but the third language (TDB Index) was considerably lower. This result can be attributed to index length: while the first two languages had indexes of approximately 23-30 terms, *TDB* Index had only 11-12 terms per index.

TABLE 2: COMPARATIVE PERFORMANCE OF THE FOUR INDEXING LANGUAGES USED IN INDEXING OF TITLES

Indexing Language	NARROW SEARCHES			BROAD SEARCHES		
	Total	R,P,N	Se,Sp,Es	Total	R,P,N	Se,Sp,Es
TELEGRAPHIC ABSTRACTS (File A)	98	46	.18	507	87	.35
		9	.98		26	.82
		43	.16		394	.17
KEYWORDS (File D)	96	42	.17	497	83	.33
		9	.98		24	.83
		45	.14		390	.15
KEYWORDS BY COMPUTER (File G)	92	40	.16	491	78	.31
		10	.98		25	.83
		42	.13		388	.13
META LANGUAGE (File H)	99	45	.18	499	87	.35
		10	.98		25	.83
		44	.15		387	.17

TABLE 3: COMPARATIVE PERFORMANCE OF THE THREE INDEXING LANGUAGES USED IN
INDEXING OF ABSTRACTS

Indexing language	NARROW SEARCHES			BROAD SEARCHES		
	Total	R,P,N,	Se,Sp,Es	Total	R,P,N	Se,Sp,Es
TELEGRAPHIC ABSTRACTS (File B)	340	120 39 181	.48 .91 .38	1274	178 84 1012	.71 .54 .25
KEYWORDS (File E)	419	130 46 243	.52 .88 .40	1464	186 82 1196	.75 .46 .20
TROPICAL DISEASE BULLETIN INDEX (File K)	122	55 11 56	.22 .97 .19	653	101 32 520	.41 .77 .17

The two indexing languages applied to full texts (TA and KW) performed differently, with TA performing better. For the same two languages the differences were much more pronounced for full texts than for abstracts.

The overall performance of Telegraphic Abstracts and Keywords (Table 5) did not differ very much, although Telegraphic Abstracts performed somewhat better. This slightly better performance factor cannot be entirely attributed to the characteristics of the indexing language. Rather it should be seen as a combination of factors. For

example, it has been seen that as the source of input lengthens (title abstract full text) the performance differences between languages increase. As a matter of fact, full texts can be seen to be the source of whatever differences occurred.

A separate analysis of factors contributing to differences in results between full-text files (File C, Telegraphic Abstracts, and File F, Keywords) was undertaken in order to illuminate the problem. Taking symmetric differences, it was found that File C retrieved 45 relevant answers that were not retrieved by File F, and File F retrieved 10 rele-

TABLE 4: COMPARATIVE PERFORMANCE OF THE TWO INDEXING LANGUAGES USED IN
INDEXING OF FULL TEXTS

Indexing language	NARROW SEARCHES			BROAD SEARCHES		
	Total	R,P,N,	Se,Sp,Es	Total	R,P,N,	Se,Sp,Es,
TELEGRAPHIC ABSTRACTS (File C)	547	169 63 315	.68 .84 .51	1863	228 120 1515	.92 .31 .22
KEYWORDS (File F)	536	133 44 359	.53 .83 .36	1750	193 85 1472	.78 .34 .11

TABLE 5: COMPARATIVE PERFORMANCE OF TWO INDEXING LANGUAGES: TELEGRAPHIC ABSTRACTS AND KEYWORDS

Indexing language	NARROW SEARCHES			BROAD SEARCHES		
	Total	R,P,N	Se,Sp,Es	Total	R,P,N	Se,Sp,Es
TELEGRAPHIC ABSTRACTS (Union of files A,B,C	625	187	.74	2080	243	.98
		72	.81		134	.23
		368	.55		1703	.20
KEYWORDS (Union of files D,E,F	673	163	.65	2113	221	.89
		61	.79		104	.20
		449	.43		1788	.09

vant answers that were not retrieved by File C. The causes for File F missing the 45 relevant answers were studied. For each missing answer, the following were examined and compared: the text of the question, both indexes (C and F), all related search statements for both files, and the text of documents. As far as the causes could be distinguished, the best assessment is as follows:

CAUSE OF NON-RETRIEVAL	NUMBER OF INCIDENTS	PROPORTION OF ALL CAUSES
a. Indexer did not index an important term	23	.51
b. Indexer did not index a term but could not have been clearly required to do so	14	.31
c. Question analyst did not search for a near synonym	5	.12
d. Ambiguous code and dictionary error	2	.04
e. Computer error	1	.02
	45	1.00

Thus, the majority (51%) of incidents may be attributed entirely to the decision of the indexer not to index a term. A combination of indexers' decisions and limitations of the indexing language accounts for approximately 31% of the missing documents. Thus, 82% of the misses may be attributed, in one way or another, to indexes. Question analysis accounted for 12% of the misses despite the stringent controls imposed. Thus, 94% of the misses can be attributed to human decision-making, at various stages and in various functions of the system.

A major disappointment was that Telegraphic Abstracts, with its elaborate system of roles and links, did not suppress nonrelevant answers more efficiently. An analysis revealed that the syntax of roles and links was not utilized in searching because it was not applicable to the way the questions were asked. Role indicators were originally used in only 10 of the 124 questions; upon reexamination it was seen that an additional five questions could have incorporated some role indicators. Of these fifteen instances, only five queries produced answers with a significant suppression of nonrelevant documents. It was concluded that role indicators do aid in suppressing nonrelevant answers, but that they can be used only rarely and that they often suppress relevant answers.

The evidence gathered on indexing languages is not conclusive. It may be possible that indexing languages, as defined in CSL, do not affect performance—whatever differences exist seem to be attributable to a complex of factors, most important one being the length of indexes. Thus, in relation to indexing languages the null-hypothesis can neither be clearly accepted or rejected.

Question Analysis and Search Strategy

Table 6 presents the comparative performance of the five question analysis types, considered narrow searches, and the broad search; various question analysis types are denoted by letters, and the union output from all question analysis types is denoted by *U(QA)*.

In itself, there was nothing significant in the particular method for or definition of question

TABLE 6: COMPARATIVE PERFORMANCE OF THE FIVE QUESTION ANALYSIS (QA) TYPES
AS NARROW SEARCHES AND BROAD SEARCHES

	NARROW SEARCHES						BROAD SEARCHES
	QA(A)	QA(B)	QA(C)	QA(D)	QA(E)	U(QA)	
TOTAL	261	369	768	833	755	871	2626
R	106	130	180	192	184	197	249
P	31	42	79	83	73	83	139
N	124	197	509	558	498	591	2238
Se	.43	.52	.72	.77	.74	.79	1.00
Sp	.93	.90	.75	.73	.76	.72	0.00
Es	.35	.42	.47	.50	.49	.50	0.00

Legend:

QA(A): question analysis Type A:
terms from question only

QA(B): QA(A) plus expansion of terms through thesaurus

QA(C): QA(A) plus expansion through any other source but thesaurus

QA(D): QA(C) plus expansion through thesaurus

QA(E): Verification of all analysis by the user

U(QA): Union of output from all QA types

analysis types employed. They were chosen first, as being representative of many types and methods of analyses available, and second, as allowing for an orderly differentiation in results, especially in comparing the utilization of the available thesaurus. However, their great effect on the magnitude of output and on the overall performance was one of the surprising findings in CSL.

For instance, the size of total output rose from $QA(A)$ to $QA(E)$ as 1 : 1.3 : 3 : 3.3 : 3. The rise is impressive: from the lowest, 261 answers for $QA(A)$, to the highest, 833 answers for $QA(D)$. Sensitivity rose and specificity fell in a direct relationship to the size of output. Again, it was observed that an almost linear relationship existed between the total output and the number of relevant and nonrelevant answers. It is interesting to note that when only the question terms were used, $QA(A)$, approximately 35% of all relevant documents were retrieved and approximately every second retrieved document was nonrelevant. By using elaborate analysis procedures, $QA(D)$, we

were able to approximately double the retrieval of relevant documents but now only every fourth document retrieved was relevant. The low performance of $QA(A)$ suggests that questions need elaboration at all times.

The performance of the thesaurus proved to be disappointing. Only when another tool, including personal knowledge, was used in question elaboration was retrieval of relevant documents increased. Thus, it seems that question analysis should not depend only on a thesaurus of the type employed. Either more powerful thesauri are needed or a thesaurus-based analysis should be supplemented by personal knowledge and other tools. In this context two aspects should be mentioned: first, only one function of a thesaurus was tested, namely its use in question analysis, and second, the major single cost in CSL was the construction and maintenance of the thesaurus—an important factor.

The effect of user interviews in question expansion yielded unexpected findings. Strangely, the contact with users, $QA(E)$, evidently led to deletion of some terms from previous analysis types; as a result fewer relevant documents were retrieved. This does not mean that contact with users in general is not beneficial, it does mean that user contact as built into CSL was *not* successful.

Quite a disappointing finding was that no question analysis on the narrow search strategy level came near to generating as many relevant documents as did the broad search strategy level. The increase in relevant documents, of course, was achieved at a considerable price in retrieval of non-relevant documents. As a matter of fact, the price was found to be staggering: the broad searches retrieved approximately four times as many non-relevant documents as the union of all QA types in order to retrieve approximately $\frac{1}{4}$ to $\frac{1}{5}$ more relevant documents. Thus, it appears that as the retrieval of relevant answers works its way asymptotically to its maximum, the retrieval of nonrelevant ones soars almost exponentially. Completeness seems to exact a very high price. The majority of nonrelevant answers in this experiment stemmed from the broad searches.

It is quite evident that the questions analysis and search strategies affect performance to a great extent—thus, the null hypothesis in respect to these variables can be rejected.

Relevance Judgements on Different Formats of Output

As mentioned previously, formats of output were treated separately. Excluded from analysis of this variable were all extension relevance judgements and questions for which relevance judgements were obtained only on full texts. Data came from 99 questions submitted by 22 users yielding a total of 1085 answer documents.[3] The ability of users to recognize relevance in different formats was analyzed, full-text judgements being taken as the standard. It is of interest to specify assumptions underlying the test of this particular variable. The full text provides the maximum length and maximum information available; thus the judgement of the full text was taken as final. If so, then the user's judgement of the shorter representations (titles and abstracts) can be expected to differ occasionally; in a sense, to "err" in two directions: leniency or strictness. Such "errors" appear to indicate an inability on the part of the user to determine final relevance from the shorter representations. This should not, however, be construed as a test of the user, since

he is limited by the degree to which shorter formats accurately represent the content of the full text. Thus we can only be concerned with a user's performance on shorter formats.

The above reasoning rests on three additional assumptions: first, that a user does make the judgement on the text content of a shorter representation and not on other clues, such as author, journal, date; second, that the judgement on each document in the set is entirely independent of judgements on other documents in the set; and third, that judgements on one format were independent of judgements of other formats, i.e., that the users followed the instructions fully.

The judgements were distributed over the three formats as follows:

No. of Answers Judged:

	RELEVANT	PARTIALLY RELEVANT	NOT RELEVANT	TOTAL
Titles	167	157	762	1086
Abstracts	175	169	742	1086
Full Text	207	723	723	1086

This data, of course, does not provide a complete picture of the ability of the users to determine relevance from shorter formats, because it provides only the totals and does not indicate how the actual membership of the set of answers judged relevant varied from format to format. Thus it was necessary to tabulate for each pair of formats the changes of all possible relevance judgements as generally indicated by section A in *Table 7*: the entries in the cells represent the number of answers judged R (or P or N) on the shorter format that were judged R (or P or N) on the full text. For example: entry R-R denotes the number of answers judged relevant on titles (or abstracts) which were also judged relevant on full texts; entry N-N denotes the number of answers judged nonrelevant on titles (or abstracts) which were later judged nonrelevant on full texts. The diagonal cells represent no change, and all other cells represent change of judgement from shorter to longer format. Section B of *Table 7* shows the changes in relevance judgements between titles and full texts, and Section C between abstracts and full texts.

In order to express the data as proportions of full text judgements, we have chosen to express the users' ability to determine relevance or nonrelevance by the same measures as used previously on systems performance:

Sensitivity measures the users' ability to recognize

TABLE 7: CHANGES OF RELEVANCE JUDGMENT: A--SCHEMATIC DIAGRAM OF ALL POSSIBLE
CHANGES BETWEEN A SHORTER FORMAT AND FULL TEXT JUDGMENTS. B--CHANGES
BETWEEN TITLE AND FULL TEXT JUDGMENTS. C--CHANGES BETWEEN ABSTRACT
AND FULL TEXT JUDGMENTS.

A.

		Judgments on Full Texts (Final Judgment)		
		R	P	N
Judgments on Shorter	R	R-R	R-P	R-N
Representation	P	P-R	P-P	P-N
(or 1st Judgments)	N	N-R	N-P	N-N

B.

		Full Text Judgments		
		207 R	156 P	723 N
Title	167 R	131	13	23
Judgments	157 P	33	95	29
	762 N	43	48	671

C.

		Full Text Judgments		
		207 R	156 P	723 N
Abstract	175 R	160	3	12
Judgments	169 P	23	125	21
	742 N	24	28	690

relevant answers by their titles or abstracts in comparison with full texts (ratio of *R-R* and *R* on full text)

Specificity measures the users' ability to recognize nonrelevant answers by their titles or abstracts in comparison with full texts (ratio of *N-N* and *N* on full text)

$$Effectiveness = Se + Sp - 1$$

In order to simplify the calculations, the partially relevant answers were counted together with nonrelevant ones. The results are as follows:

	Se	*Sp*	*Es*
Titles	.63	.96	.59
Abstracts	.77	.98	.75

An overall analysis revealed that of 1,086 document answers 843 (78%) were judged the same way on all three formats; 897 (85%) were judged the same on titles as on full texts; and 975 (90%) were judged the same on abstracts as on full texts. Thus, the answers that had different judgements on different formats constitute 22% or $^1/_5$ of the total.

However, the evaluation measures revealed an interesting picture: agreement on what is relevant was considerably lower than agreement on what is nonrelevant. Hence, the relatively high over-all agreement is more attributable to a high agreement on what is nonrelevant than on what is relevant. The sensitivity measure reveals that users recognized 63% of all relevant answers on the basis of titles and 77% on the basis of abstracts. At the same time they recognized 96% of nonrelevant answers from titles and 98% from abstracts.

Let us now compare user and system relevance assignments on different document formats. This comparison is intriguing because a system cannot be expected to assign relevance any better than a user; it is desirable, however, that a system perform as well as a user. On the basis of this Inquiry, the Sensitivity of users on titles was placed at .63, and the highest sensitivity of title-based index files was .37 (broad search). The sensitivity of users on abstracts was placed at .77, and the highest sensitivity of abstract-based files was .80. Thus, users performed considerably better in recognizing relevant titles than did systems, probably because the users can read "to or from" the titles and accompanying bibliographic citation. Users and systems performed similarly on abstracts. On the other hand, users were considerably better than systems in recognizing nonrelevant answers (specificity): the systems didn't even approach the users' ability to recognize nonrelevance.

Although not directly investigated in this Inquiry, cost ought to be incorporated in assessing this system's performance. It is clear that the cost of supplying titles or abstracts to users is lower than that of supplying full texts. Since losses due to a false user assignment of relevance are really not great (approximately $1/3$ on titles and $1/5$ on abstracts), shorter formats may indeed be the more economic form of output. The cost of throwing away nonrelevant titles or abstracts is much less than that of throwing away full texts.

In conclusion, it seems evident that different formats significantly affect users' relevance judgements, thus the null hypothesis in relation to this variable can be rejected.

General Conclusions

The summary below incorporates conclusions drawn from selected results reported in this paper, as well as from other results presented in the Final Report of the Comparative Systems Laboratory.

1. The human factor, i.e., variations introduced by human decision-making, seems to be the major factor affecting the performance of every and all components of an information retrieval system.

2. The output components—handling of questions, method of question analysis, and construction of logical statements for searching—seem as important in their effect on system performance, as input components. On the basis of this Inquiry, the output components can be considered the major components of an IR system.

3. The length of indexes (i.e., variation in number of index terms per document) seems to affect system performance considerably more than does the particular indexing language used; given the same index length various indexing languages tend to perform similarly. Although files based on titles perform worse than files based on abstracts or full text, they appear to give the user an adequate base for making relevance judgements.

4. The syntactic features of indexing languages (roles, links) do not reduce the overall retrieval of nonrelevant answers; in rare instances they may do so. The actual and transformational syntax of questions and the simplified syntax as specified by roles and links do not coincide to any great extent.

5. It seems that no expansion of question terms (i.e., question analysis types) can insure retrieval of all relevant answers in the file.

6. It seems that all relevant answers in the file can be retrieved only through broad searches; however, the price in retrieval of nonrelevant answers in that case is considerable.

7. User questions cannot be searched as stated; as a rule expansion of question terms is necessary. Expansion based upon a thesaurus (as that used in CSL) does not add sufficient, related terms. It appears that expansion is best achieved when every available tool (including personal knowledge) is used. Construction of a thesaurus was the single most costly aspect of CSL.

8. The contact with users (as conducted in CSL in order to validate and expand on question terms, did not improve the system performance; as a matter of fact, and quite surprisingly, it slightly decreased the performance.

9. A relatively close phraseological connection was found to exist between the texts of questions and the texts of documents judged relevant by users, a connection not found between questions and documents judged nonrelevant by users.

10. The format of output seems to influence significantly the users' relevance judgements.

Users can make a more accurate estimate of relevance from titles than systems. In any format users are much better on judging non-relevance than systems are.

11. It seems that the performance of retrieval systems could be optimized through judicious and complex work on search statements; however, and unfortunately, the method for optimization cannot be stated in general terms, but only described from question to question. An optimization seems to be possible, but a useful generalization as to what that optimization involves is elusive.

12. The handling of questions, i.e., elaboration of all related terms by which a concept could be expressed, and the construction of an adequate search statement, are costly, time-consuming, elaborate, tedious, error-prone but unmistakably necessary jobs. Without doubt retrieval system needs to have designed into its operations elaborate procedures and adequate capacity in terms of people, cost, time, etc. for the handling of questions.

13. At present it seems that retrieval systems, regardless of their design, analysts' claims and available technology are able to perform only on a general level. As a rule they produce a tremendous amount of extraneous or non-relevant material; their effectiveness is low. This is a fact of life that researchers, designers, operators, users and funders must learn to live with, at least in the forseeable future. The reasons for low effectiveness are not simple—they need thorough investigation. However, not all of the reasons are related to the system itself.

ACKNOWLEDGEMENTS

George Baumanis, Marilyn Bobka, Elaine Brown, Carolyn Gifford, Irene Hazelton, Leslie Rothenberg and J. B. Subramaniam were the technical staff of the Comparative System Laboratory. They carried the burden of work. Without their dedicated and enthusiastic effort the project and this paper would not have been possible. William Goffman was in many senses the "Father" of the experiments. Thanks to Dr. Kenneth Warren as a pilot user and to the 24 other users for their time and effort. Alvin J. Goldwyn guided the project and grant over the years to its completion. Most helpful suggestions were received from the students of the School of Library Science, Case Western Reserve University—the project served also as a most successful educational laboratory.

REFERENCES

1. Cleverdon, C., The Cranfield Tests of Indexing Language Devices, *ASLIB Proceedings*, 19 (No. 6):173–194 (1967).

2. Salton, G. and M. E. Lesk, Computer Evaluation of Indexing and Text Processing, *Journal of the Association for Computing Machinery*, 15 (No. 1):8–36 (1968).

3. Lancaster, F. W. Medlars: Report on the Evaluation of its Operating Efficiency, *American Documentation*, 20 (No. 2): 119–142 (1969).

4. Goffman, W. and V. A. Newill, Methodology for Test and Evaluation of Information Retrieval Systems, *Information Storage and Retrieval*, 3 (No. 1):19–25 (1966).

5. Saracevic, T. and L. Rothenberg, Procedure *Manuals for the Comparative Systems Laboratory Experiments*, CSL:TR-8, Center for Documentation and Communication Research, School of Library Science, Case Western Reserve University, Cleveland, O. 199 p. 1967.

6. Saracevic, T. et al., *An Inquiry into Testing of Information Retrieval Systems*, CSL:Final Report, 3 Parts, Center for Documentation and Communication Research, School of Library Science, Case Western Reserve University, Cleveland, O. 611 p. 1968.

7. Gifford, C. and G. J. Baumanis, On Understanding User Choices: Textual Correlates of Relevance Judgments; *American Documentation*, 20 (No. 1):21–26, (1969).

FOOTNOTES

[1] Of the 17 queries not included in the final analysis, 5 queries were rejected as being outside of the file; 7 queries generated no output, and the universal sets for 5 queries were not evaluated by the users. One user failed to return any evaluation of answers. For the 24 users and 124 questions included in the final analysis, the range of the number of questions submitted by users was between two and ten, and the mean number of questions per user was five. The questions were fairly evenly distributed across the total group of users

[2] In reading the table note that the values for effectiveness were calculated from values of sensitivity and specificity *prior* to rounding them to the second decimal point; thus, on occasion the Es values may display a discrepancy from values which would have been obtained if Es were calculated from the rounded Se and Sp values.

[3]Titles were submitted together with bibliographic citations; titles contained on the average some 5 to 9 words. Abstracts included titles and bibliographic citations; abstracts were photocopies from *Tropical Disease Bulletin* and averaged 250 to 400 words. Full texts were photocopies of original journal articles and averaged 2000 to 4000 words.

Additional Readings

I THE CHALLENGE

Bolt, Beranek and Newman, Inc. *Toward the Library of the 21st Century. A report . . . sponsored by the Council on Library Resources.* 1964.

Gerard, R. W., editor. *Computers and Education.* 1967. See especially the essay by Robert M. Hayes, p. 111-150.

Hammer, Donald. "Automated Operations in a University Library" (*College and Research Libraries,* 26: 19-29. January, 1965).

King, Gilbert W. *Automation and the Library of Congress.* 1963.

Knight, Douglas M., editor. *Libraries at Large.* 1969. See especially p. 319-329.

Licklider, J. C. R., *Libraries of the Future.* 1963.

II VARIETIES OF RESPONSE

Automation in Libraries. Papers Presented at the Canadian Association of College and University Libraries Workshop on Library Automation . . . 1967.

Byrn, James H. "Automation in University Libraries—the State of the Art" (*Library Resources and Technical Services,* 13: 520-530, 1969)

International Business Machines. *Library Mechanization Symposium.*

Library Technology Reports. *Circulation Systems.* 1965.

Salmon, Stephen R., editor. *Library Automation . . .* 1969.

III THE THEORY OF MANAGEMENT

Fasana, Paul J., editor. *Automation in Large Libraries. Implications for the Administrator and the Manager.* 1968. See especially the essays by Lipetz and Rosenthal.

Veaner, Allen B. *Major Decision Points in Library Automation.* Preprint. Prepared for the Association of Research Libraries Automation Committee. 1970.

IV NEW SERVICES

Bregzis, Ritvars, "Library Networks for the Future" (*Drexel Library Quarterly,* 4: 261-270. October, 1968).

Connor, Judith H. "S.D.I." (*Library Quarterly,* 37: 373-391. October, 1967)

Intrex. Report of a Planning Conference, ed. by Carl F.J. Overhage. 1965.

Kent, Alan. *Specialized Information Centers.* 1965.

V CATALOGS AND THE COMPUTER

Hayes, Robert M., "Economics of Book Catalog Production" (*Library Resources and Technical Services,* 10: 57-90, 1966)

Kieffer, Paula. "Baltimore County Public Library Book Catalog" (*Library Resources and Technical Services,* 10: 133-141, 1966).

VI COPYRIGHT

Clapp, Verner W., "Copyright Dilemma, " (*Library Quarterly,* 38: 352-387. October, 1968)

Heilprin, Laurence B., "Technology and the Future of the Copyright Principle" (*American Documentation,* 19: 6-11. January, 1968).

VII INFORMATION RETRIEVAL TESTING

Lancaster, F. W., *Information Retrieval Systems.* 1968.
Salton, Gerard. *Automatic Information Organization and Retrieval.* 1968.